A YEAR WITHOUT FEAR

A Daily Devotional

BY DON NICELY

TATE PUBLISHING, LLC

Published in the United States of America
By TATE PUBLISHING, LLC

All rights reserved.
Do not duplicate without permission.

All Scripture references are King James Version,
unless otherwise indicated.

Book Design by TATE PUBLISHING, LLC.

Printed in the United States of America by
TATE PUBLISHING, LLC
127 East Trade Center Terrace
Mustang, OK 73064
(888) 361-9473

Publisher's Cataloging in Publication

Nicely, Don

    A Year Without Fear/Don Nicely

    Originally published in Mustang,OK:TATE PUBLISHING:2004

    1. Christianity 2. Devotional

    ISBN 0-9753933-4-0 $19.95

Copyright 2004

First Printing: August 2004

DEDICATION

I'd like to dedicate this book to the four most important people that God has allowed to grace my life. Each of these people greatly contributed to my spiritual development in making me who I am today. Without them, my life would have had no purpose; I would have wandered aimlessly from place to place finding no rest for my feet. All I can do today is thank you for contributing to me.

First, I'd like to thank my Master, the Lord Jesus Christ, for dying on a cross for my sins. Without His ever continuing patience for me I don't know what I'd do. He loved me when I wasn't the least bit concerned about the awesome sacrifice He made for me. And for that, Jesus, I can hardly wait to see you face to face, but for now - thank you.

Next I'd like to thank my spiritual father, Bro. Leon Ross who has since gone home to be with the Lord. He used to encourage me by telling me of the "city whose builder and maker was God." Leon loved the unlovable, which, I'm sad to say, I was a part of at one time. Even when I was looking for excuses to blame Christians for, he remained blameless in my eyes. Once, as a young lost teenager, Leon noticed that I was doing without the basic necessities, but I had a dream as most young people do; so he reached into his pocket, and fished out a one hundred dollar bill to aid me in my need. He never knew it in this life, but that one hundred dollar bill bought my soul that day. His generosity will never by forgotten. Boy, what a cheap price for a soul; thank you Leon for leading me to the Lord Jesus.

Then I'd like to thank my mentor, Rev. Glen Shugars, who took me under his wing and fashioned me with patience and perseverance. Pastor Shugars is the most patient man I know, serving the same church for over thirty years. He took a green, very impatient young man and molded him into Christ's image. Thank you, Pastor Shugars for being my first and only pastor.

And finally, but certainly not least, I'd like to thank my motivation, who is my lovely wife, Susie. It's because of her patience, kindness and love for me that I've been able to dream and follow God's plan for my life. The day I met her was certainly the greatest day of my existence. At times I've wondered what my life would've been like if I never would have met Susie, and I must admit I believe it would've been most miserable. She certainly is the best helpmeet any man could ask for. Thank you, honey, for being my one and only wife, and my constant source of motivation.

    ~ Don

INTRODUCTION

About three years ago, I was watching a news report on the television about the overall physical health of Americans. In the report I noticed one staggering fact that, up until that time, I had never considered before. The leading cause of death between men and women these days is heart failure. Instantly, the Holy Spirit took my mind to the Scriptures located in Luke 21:26–28. It deals mainly with the happenings that will take place in the last days, prior to the return of the Lord Jesus Christ. It reads as follows: "And there shall be signs in the sun, and in the moon, and in the stars; and upon the earth distress of nations, with perplexity; the sea and the waves roaring; men's hearts failing them for fear, and for looking after those things which are coming on the earth; . . . and then shall they see the son of man in a cloud with power and great glory."

Suddenly, God began to deal with me about addressing the subject of fear more than just from my pulpit. Yes, I could preach to my group, which is only a handful compared to the body of Christ that are suffering from unnecessary fears. So I searched in local bookstores and through major catalogs and libraries looking for a book that addresses the subject of fear conclusively. I was very discouraged about what I found. Then one day I was reading one of the books on fear that I'd picked up over the years and noticed that the author had said that God, in His Word had placed 365 verses in the Word of God that deal with no fear or "fear not." One for everyday of the year. Instantly the thought came to my mind; "What would it be like to live an entire year without fear?" Thus the name for this devotional was born; A YEAR WITHOUT FEAR."

Today you are about to embark on a journey through an incredible year. It doesn't matter where you start in the book, just as long as you finish. Each day, except for the first and the last are written to sustain themselves. God is not concerned with how we start the race only how we finish. I pray that your race, known as the Christian life, will be deeply enriched through the lessons in the book. Some are from personal experience, and I was deeply emotional as I wrote them. In fact, one of the days I had to stop after I'd written the page, and take a break to get the tears out of my eyes, just to rejoice at how far God has brought me through the years. Other lessons are from experiences from people just like you and me who faced great odds, but overcame them to become free of their fears. And, of course, there are the ever popular Bible illustrations that the greatest author of all time included in His best selling work known as the Holy Bible. To get the most from this devotional let it inside you by studying the verses that are included in the daily verses and hiding them in your heart to help you overcome any fears that you may be experiencing. Today I pray that this be the first day that you live "A YEAR WITHOUT FEAR!"

Living fearlessly in Christ,

D. L. Nicely

UNDERSTANDING GOD-GIVEN FEAR

Fear is a God-given emotion that every person on earth experiences from time to time. It's an uneasy feeling in us that is aroused when we feel our lives are threatened or in danger.

We can fear in many different areas on our lives; the social realm, the spiritual realm, the emotional realm and the physical realm. In order to determine whether our fear is justifiable or not we must ask ourselves two important questions.

1) Is there a real threat or danger?

2) Is my fear in balance with the threat or danger?

When there is a real threat or danger, fear is a positive response that will get you to take action. For instance let's say the community you live is under a tornado warning, and suddenly the neighbor across the street calls you and tells you he sees a tornado hovering over your house.

Fear will cause you to head for the basement of the house for safety, and not the refrigerator for a glass of milk. Fear is good in this context, but the problem lies in the fact that most fears are not based on real dangers. Most are based on feelings that turn into phobias (which are things you dread) such as crowds, bridges, darkness, etc. These are the fears we will discuss in this book.

These fears are what rob us of our God-given peace and the abundance with which God so richly wants to bless us. Most of these unrealistic fears are caused by a "spirit of fear," which can completely immobilize us from progressing in our spiritual walk with God. Always remember God has not given us a spirit of fear.

Daily Verse: "For God has not given us the spirit of fear; but of power, and of love and of a sound mind."

11 Timothy 1:7

FEAR OF ADVERSITY

It is the fifteenth century, and only one man has the unshakable conviction that the world is round and not flat like so many brilliant minds believe. History tells us that Christopher Columbus stood alone in his belief. He wanted to prove his conviction by sailing west in search of the east. Did Columbus find support for his belief? The royal court accused him of being pompous and arrogant.

The church accused him of being a heretic and the rest of

Europe considered him to be a fool. So what enabled Columbus to over-come all the adversity and discouragement of his critics? Evidence sug-gests that he believed he had a God given dream and that God was able to get him through all the adversity. When the choir of voices in oppo-sition sang loud against his dream, he only listened to the still small voice of the master calling him to the open seas. As the years passed he finally obtained a commission from Queen Isabella, and sailed west. What's the rest of the story? No other man affected the western culture like Christopher Columbus. Just as Columbus drew his strength against adversity, by believing God had a specific purpose for his life. So can we obtain that strength also?

Each of us has been uniquely equipped to contribute something to history, by an all knowing, all powerful God. Our task is to discover our God-given destiny and accomplish it for him. Unless we understand our destiny, most of our time will be spent on performing menial tasks. So remember that God has a specific purpose and task for each of us to accomplish no matter how much adversity or pointless alternatives comes our way.

Daily Verse: For I know the thoughts that I think toward you, saith the Lord, thoughts of peace, and not of evil, to give you an expected end."

Jeremiah 29:11

FEAR OF TERRORISM

While the threat of terrorism is very real today, especially for Americans since the September 11 attacks on New York Cities World Trade Centers; we must find comfort in what the Holy Bible has to say about the subject. Amazingly, secured in the writings of the Chronicles is a story, very much in line with a terrorist attack. So open the Bible to 11 Chronicles, Chapter 20, blow the dust off the pages and read on.

It's the story of a good king, one of the few good kings of Judah. His name was Jehoshaphat. One day he was just having a good day rul-ing his kingdom like every other day, when he got word from his spies that three enemies of Judah were planning an attack. Normally this wouldn't have alarmed him but the reason for the attack was because his armies were off fighting a battle elsewhere, and by the time he got the message it was too late to recall them. These three adversaries had scaled mountain cliffs to sort of sneak in the back way unnoticed. Doesn't that sound like a sneaky terrorist? By the time he found out where they were, they were in his backyard. The Scriptures say that

Jehoshaphat feared. Thank God, he's a human, that's a very real response to a very real threat. So what did the king do? Did he hide in the palace? Did he hurry down to the local grocery store to secure bread, milk, and cheese for his family? Did he quit his job so he wouldn't have to go outdoors? No! Verse 3 gives us the answer, " . . . he turned his attention to seek the Lord."

God is so well pleased when we come to Him in our times of need. In fact, sometimes those needs are even created by Him, to draw us closer to Him. In Jehoshaphat's case when he prayed that day he prayed a real prayer. It was a prayer of power and authority. Verse 7 says, "Didst thou not, O our God, drive out all the inhabitants of this land before thy people Israel, and give it to the descendants of Abraham Thy friend forever?" Or, "God didn't you give us this land to be ours forever?"

God was moved that day, He spoke through a prophet to say "Don't worry, do not fear, you won't even have to fight these guys, I'll do it for you, just go out and watch me fight for you! (my Paraphrase). All of Israel got a good night's sleep that night and in the morning Jehoshphat sent out his choir to sing praises to their God. Meanwhile, as the three enemies ate breakfast, they got mad at each other over something and destroyed each other. Doesn't that sound like a terrorist? Fear knocked at the door, faith answered and no one was there.

Daily Verse: "Be strong and of a good courage, fear not, nor be afraid them; For the Lord thy God, he it is that doth go with thee, he will not fail thee, nor forsake thee."

Deuteronomy 31:6

FEAR OF TIME

Albert Einstein once said "Everyone who is seriously involved in the pursuit of science becomes convinced that a spirit is manifest in the laws of the universe-a spirit vastly superior to that of man, and one in the face of which we with our modest powers must feel humble." Even Einstein in all brilliance had to conclude that God is in complete control of our lives. Whether we fear our time is slipping away from us or we are not making the best use of what we have been allotted, God is still in control. Scripture says, "The steps of a good man are ordered by the Lord." He is in complete control of our time. Only God is unchangeable and eternal. This is what the German born physicist Einstein meant when he ventured to say "all time is relative," or the faster one travels the slower time is.

In practical terms let's suggest that you would enter a spaceship bound for the center of our Milky way Galaxy. The distance to be traveled is a mere 176,340,000,000,000,000 miles. Let's also suggest that you will travel at the speed of light, which is 186,000 miles per second. From the start to finish the journey would take approximately twenty-one years. However on the earth where time is slower, 30,000 years would have passed before you reached your destination. So time is not eternal. Only the Eternal God of all that exists is unchangeable. Time is God's creation, - He uses it, He owns it, and it is under His complete control. In His remarkable generosity He has shared a small portion of it with each of us. Therefore our task is to discover what He wants us to do, and do it for Him.

Daily Verse: "Redeeming the time, because the days are evil."
Ephesians 5:16

FEAR OF GOD'S WILL

"Arise, go to Nineveh, the great city, and cry against it, for their wickedness has come up before me," cried a compassionate God. So what did Jonah do? Scripture states "He rose up and fled to Tarshish from the presence of the Lord." You see disobedience, to God's will always, always, always remove you from His presence. But did he get away? Hardly. David wrote in the Psalms "Where can I go to get away from your presence? If I make my bed in hell thou art there." Jonah was commissioned because he was a prophet. He knew the character of his God. He knew his God was forgiving and takes no delight in the death of the wicked. He knew if he walked the lonely dark streets of Nineveh preaching repentance and they repented, God would forgive them.

Jonah's problem was his patriotism. Nineveh was the wicked city of the Assyrians. They were known for their cruel torture of their enemies. Jonah knew that if he spared the Assyrians, they would come back and punish Israel. He simply believed they were not worthy of salvation. Many people are like Jonah today, they have the mistaken idea that they must choose between doing God's will and being miserable, and doing what they want to do and being happy. Nothing could be further from the truth. God knows the big picture and He has a way of developing it in our minds.

Jonah made three wrong decisions and all three led him in a downward path. He went down to Tarshish; he went down into the bottom of the ship; and he went down into the bottom of the sea. All this led him down into the belly of a fish! After three days in the belly of a fish, the Lord spoke again, "Arise, go to Nineveh, that great city and proclaim to it the word I am going to tell you." Did Jonah go this time? You better believe he did. His three day class in "whale university" taught him that God knows best. Did the great city of Nineveh repent? Yep, and they went on hundreds of more years until God finally judged them in the book of Nahum. Always remember that God has the big picture, and if we allow Him to develop it in our minds, we will always do His will.

Daily Verse: "For it is God which worketh in you both to will and to do of His good pleasure".

Philippians 2:13

FEAR OF THE DEVIL

Let us dispel a lie of the enemy right from the start; you are not alone in your struggle against the devil. "Struggle" is a good word to use, because that is exactly what it is: a struggle of the mind, and struggle of the will. Sometimes it can seem like an all-out combat against just living a mundane and menial existence. Today I want to stress that we have a very real enemy, known as the devil, but in doing so I don't want to over-emphasize his power over our lives.

Today let's pull the blinders from our eyes so we can get a good look at just who or what the devil is. First of all, he's a sinner. "He who sins is of the devil, for the devil has sinned from the beginning."(1John3:8). Then he's a thief. "The thief does not come but to steal, and to kill, and to destroy" (John 10:10). Next he's a trapper. "And that they may come to their senses and escape the snare of the devil, having been taken captive by him to do his will" (2 Tim. 2:26). Finally he's a deceiver. "Lest Satan should take advantage of us; for we are not ignorant of his devices" (2 Cor. 2:11). There are many more negative characteristics we could expose about the devil but this is enough for now.

The important thing to realize is that we are in an invisible war, between two worlds; the physical world where we can touch, feel, hear, see, and taste with our natural bodies, and the spiritual world where we cannot see, but must use our faith to operate in exclusively. Satan works diligently to keep us ignorant of the real battle going on around us. He tries hard to keep us in the dark about his working in our lives. He feels if we think that things happen as a result of just happenstance, he can better operate against us. Some people ignorantly believe the battle is against God and the devil. God is in no battle. He has no enemies. After all who could stand against the creator of all things? Instead the real battle is against God's children and the children of the devil. Who are the children of the devil? They are simply those who have not asked Christ for a pardon for their sins. They foolishly believe they can stand neutral on the subject not joining any sides. Jesus put it this way, "He who is not with me is against me" (Luke 11:23). So why not join the winning side and watch your fears of darkness melt away as you turn on the light inside.

Daily Verse: "Ye are of God, little children, and have overcome them; because greater is he that is in you, than he that is in the world."

1 John 4:4

FEAR OF MARRIAGE

Many people have a drastically wrong idea of what marriage really is. In God's mind marriage is a covenant agreement between two people for life, so should we not be cautious of whom we choose to spend all our days with? I'm reminded of the story of the business man who, while traveling one day on an airplane, sat next to a man dressed in a very expensive suit. Everything about the man looked dashing except the man had his wedding band on the index finger of his right hand. Carefully the man stated, "Hey buddy, you have your wedding band on the wrong finger." Sadly the man looked at his hand and whimpered "That's OK, I married the wrong woman." Let this not be our condition some day.

Today we live in a sad state regarding the sanctity of marriage. Presently the divorce rate is keeping up with the holy matrimony, mainly because most people are choosing to just live together rather than to "tie the knot." In some situations even our government is advising that people divorce each other and live together to improve their economic status.

Sometimes I'm surprised by the immaturity of some young people who come to me for marriage counseling before taking the plunge. This one young couple in particular comes to my mind. She was already pregnant, and they were already living together (as most are) and she was only sixteen years of age. I require a parent to be present in these circumstances. Usually when I'm finished with my sessions I always ask both parties if there is something about the other they don't like. Now is the time to discuss it, not three months down the road, where it will lead to some big fight. Immediately the young lady went on the defensive "Oh no, nothing," she said, "he's perfect." I could see that statement put him in the silence mode. He wanted to say something, but what do you say after someone says your perfect? Finally after some coaching on my part I got him to open up. "Well, there is one thing," he said. Suddenly she sat up from her slumped position to hear what her honey "didn't like" about her. "I wish she would at least pick up the house a little bit, it looks like a pig sty." Then he immediately added " . . . but, I know she'll change after we get married." I thought her mother was going to go into cardiac arrest, when she blurted out, "Son you're in for a surprise, because what you see is what you're going to get!" Truer words were never spoken.

Marriage for some reason doesn't bring out the best in us but the worst. And yes, it is possible to marry the wrong person. However, if you will treat that wrong person like the right person soon they will become the right person, it is primarily up to you.

Daily Verse: "Rejoice with the wife of thy youth"

Proverbs 5:18

COMMON CAUSES OF FEAR

Most fear fits into the category of unrealistic fear. Basically we can call it by this simple little acrostic, F.E.A.R., False Evidence Appears Real. They are not based on a real danger, but are way out of proportion to the danger involved. But keep in mind, your spiritual status in life can often determine what is realistic and what is not realistic. For instance it would be realistic for a non-Christian to fear death, while such a fear is unrealistic to a Christian. A non-Christian may fear God as a harsh, judgmental, being ready to smack them on the head with a club if they do wrong. While the Christian knows that although God does judge sin, he is also a loving, forgiving, compassionate, being ready to forgive if we are ready to receive. Now let's take a look at the four major causes of fear, keep in mind that there could be more than four, but we will only use four for this study.

1) Parental Influence: A major portions of our fears are passed down to us from our parents. Let's say a mother who is afraid of thunder storms always works the children into a frenzy when a storm approaches. Although her actions are not intentional, the children learn to fear. Parents who tell their children that the boogie man will get them at night, teach their kids to fear the dark.

2) Guilty Conscience: Proverbs 28:1 states, "The wicked flee,

when no one pursues them." A guilty conscience can produce all kinds of fears in our lives.

3) Seeking Attention: Some people exaggerate their fears in order to get special attention. For instance some people may say, "I'm afraid of mice, or spiders or snakes." And before they know it they have developed the fear. Fear is a horrible thing; it is nothing more than negative faith. Knowing this should teach us to watch what comes out of our mouth.

4) Past Experiences: Say you have had a bad experience riding a horse, suddenly without knowing it you have a memory of being afraid of horses. These type of fears must be worked through slowly and carefully.

Daily Verse: "There is no fear in love; but perfect love casteth out fear:"

1 John 4:18a

FEAR OF GOSSIP

The story is told about the devout church going woman who heard a juicy story about her pastor. Soon she was on the phone discussing the matter with all her friends. After a period of time she found out that the information she had received was false. Suddenly conviction settled in her heart, for thinking such things about her pastor. So being the Christian woman she was, she called her pastor on the phone and pleaded with him for his forgiveness. Being a man of God he readily forgave her, but he asked one request.

"Anything pastor," the woman pleaded.

"Today is a particularly windy day; would you meet me at the corner square at around noon?"

When noon came she found the pastor standing on the corner with a feather pillow in his hands. "What's with the pillow?" the woman asked.

"Here, take this pillow, and scatter all these feathers in the wind," requested the pastor.

The woman did as the pastor asked. As she shook the feathers into the wind and watched them blowing away to the four winds, the pastor explained, "I forgave you for the gossip about me, but the damage you have done is like trying to pick up these feathers all one at a time. You have ruined my good reputation by spreading lies."

Proverbs 18:21 says that the power of life and death are in the tongue. The Psalmist prayed, "Set a watch, Oh Lord, before my mouth, keep the door of my lips." Gossip can be a very destructive force, destroying all good reputations in its path. Anyone who willingly participates in it is soon to find the pain it leaves behind. Only by God's help are we able to refrain from allowing our tongues to wag there raging fire. Remember the tongue is in a slippery place, and has no brakes to stop it. Only your decision not to participate will help. He that gossips to you will gossip about you.

Daily Verse: "Death and life are in the power of the tongue; and they that love it shall eat the fruit thereof." Proverbs 18:21

FEAR OF GAINING WEIGHT

Sadly to say this is a major problem today. Millions of people are slaves to their own appetites, allowing their lives to be run by a fork. It has been said that most people dig their own grave with a spoon. I think the story of fourteenth-century Duke by the name of Raynald III illustrates it best. Many of his followers called him by a Latin nickname, Crassus, which means "fat." He was grossly overweight, and always in a dispute with his younger brother Edward. Finally, one day Edward won out over Raynald and imprisoned him in his own castle. He had a room built around him complete with windows and doors. He promised Raynald he could have his title back anytime he wanted it; all he had to do was leave the room. This was an unbelievably easy task for most people, since no door was locked and the windows were open. The problem was that Raynald would have to lose some weight to fit through, and Edward made sure that wouldn't happen by keeping his brother supplied with all the delicious foods he liked. So instead of dieting to get out, Raynald gained more weight and stayed imprisoned. For more then a decade Raynald was trapped in that room by his weight. Finally Edward passed away, and Raynald was released from the room by tearing out a wall, but by this time his health was so bad, he died less than a year after his release. Here's a man who lived more than a decade a prisoner to his own appetite.

God promises in his word, that his people do not have to live in bondage to anything or anyone. The answer is quite simple. It's the same answer Jesus found when he walked the earth. It can be found hanging on the walls in most churches. Some women wear them around their necks or in their ears. The answer is the cross. Jesus was the example for us when he chose to allow himself to be crucified on a rugged wooden cross. Scripture puts it this way, "Crucify the flesh, and don't fulfill the lust thereof." Crucifixion is not easy, it wasn't for Christ. But it truly is the only answer out of bondage. Maybe you'll have to respond the way I have so many times - by holding my arms stretched wide and asking the Holy Spirit to drive the nails for me, for I wasn't able to do it.

Daily Verse: "And put a knife to thy throat, if thou be given to appetite."

Proverbs 23:2

FEAR OF FAILURE

Did you know that Thomas Edison failed at producing the light bulb over ten thousand times? With everyone ready to give up, he confidently claimed, "This is not failure, this is good science, we now know ten thousand ways it won't work."

The story is told of an eastern gentleman who went west in pursuit of gold. He secured the dream of many people in that time. Go west and strike it rich, hit the mother lode, its there for the taking. So he bought the equipment, moved west, and purchased a used gold mine. Weeks turned into months and no gold to be found. After selling off his remaining worldly possessions, just to dig a few more feet, he finally had to admit failure. He threw the equipment down, and sold the mine for a train ticket back east. The new owners, took the equipment and dug eighteen more inches in a hole of the previous owner, and struck one of the biggest mother lodes of the west,

There once was a cattle rancher in East Texas who had dreams of drilling for oil. His cattle business wasn't doing so well, since his stock watering tanks kept getting this film on them, which was making his animals sick. So instead of raising sick livestock, he found someone to purchase his ranch as is, so he could go off in search of oil drilling dreams. Shortly after the rancher left on his quest for oil, the new owners had the water in the stock tanks checked to see what the cause of the film on top could be. They had hopes that they could find something to put in the water to make it drinkable for the cattle. Instead they discovered that the film was a type of wax that only appears on top of large oil deposits. So they drilled for oil, and struck one of the largest oil deposits in Texas at the time.

There are countless of stories of men and women who "couldn't see the forest for the trees." Remember failure is not failure until you give up. Defeat does not come to a man, until that man admits it. Failure is always the path of least resistance and that path is paved with all kinds of good intentions. Don't be afraid to fail, Babe Ruth failed 1,330 times at the plate. But he is only remembered for his 714 successes, although his failure record still hasn't been topped by anyone in baseball.

Daily Verse: "Pride goeth before destruction and a haughty spirit before a fall."

Proverbs 16:18

FEAR OF RISK TAKING

In a survey of people dying of terminally ill diseases, number two on the list of things they would do differently in their life if they could was "take more risks in life." The pursuit of false security has caused many people to give up on their hopes and dreams for a better life. They have settled for the grasshopper complex that many in the children of Israel caught after spying out the Promised Land for forty days. They confidently spoke, "Yes the land does flow with milk and honey as the Lord has promised, but we look like grasshoppers in their eyes." Now, how would they know what they would look like to them unless they asked them? Can you see the absurdity of this scenario, walking up to a giant, and saying, "Oh, by the way, I was just wondering, how do we look to you?" Joshua and Caleb were the only two in all those people who were willing to take the risk. They had been delivered from the land of failure (Egypt) and they wanted the land of promise, (Canaan). Well, the tens out numbered the twos that day, and Joshua and Caleb had to wait forty years on their Promised Land parcel. But listen to the words of Rahab the harlot, forty years later, as she talks about the incident forty years prior. "And she said to the men, I know that the Lord hath given you the land, and that your terror has fallen on us, and all the inhabitants of the land faint because of you. For we have heard how the Lord dried up the water of the Red Sea. . . . . . and as soon as we heard these things our hearts did melt, neither did there remain anymore courage in any man" (Joshua 2:9–11). They were afraid forty years ago! Just as God had promised, if only they would have taken the risk and crossed into the Promised Land. Don't miss God's best, by settling for what is good.

Daily Verse: "His lord said unto him, well done, good and faithful servant; thou hast been faithful over a few things I will make thee ruler over many things; enter thou into the joy of the Lord."

Mathew 25:23

FEAR OF MAKING BAD CHOICES

On March 3rd, 1995 a thirty-eight year old man decided to cross the Illinois eight-lane Tri-State Toll way. After successfully crossing the four northbound lanes, he rose up his head and accidentally allowed the wind to blow his hat from his head. Immediately without thinking, he began to chase his hat, and was struck by a northbound semi-trailer trucker and killed. How many people have lost everything, while chasing after nothing? It has been rightly said that your decisions determine your destiny. So make your decisions wisely, for you must either live with them or die with them. We cannot afford one day of indecision. The minute we become indecisive, and fail to choose, is the time when someone steps up and chooses for us. Some people choose to put their life in the hands of circumstance. This is a sure fire way to live in constant discouragement.

One of the best ways to make good choices, is to include God in the decision making process. "If any of you lack wisdom, let him ask of God, who gives to all men generously, and without reproach, and it will be given to him" (James 1:7).

Sometimes God may direct us to do nothing. But remember, you can't make a career of doing nothing. There once was a man who weighed every decision too carefully. He would say to himself, "On the one hand . . . but on the other hand." His opposing thoughts weighed so heavily on him that he always chose to do nothing. When he finally died they carved a big "zero" on his tombstone. In life you must choose to shoot or carry the bullets, fish or cut bait, but one thing for sure, if you don't do something, there's not going to be any dinner for you tonight.

Daily Verse: If any of you lack wisdom, let him ask of God.. . ."
James 1:7

FEAR OF PAIN

Pain is the motivator for change that pleasure never will be. We, being the humans that we are, never understand God's divine plan. Sometimes we are confused as to why he would allow suffering in our lives. This little illustration from the animal kingdom teaches us human beings, the value of pain in our lives. When a mother giraffe gives birth to its baby it drops the infant calf from about five feet off the ground. The calf a little shaken up from the fall quickly spins and puts its legs under its body. The mother quickly positions her body over the calf and then does an unspeakable thing to her infant. She lowers her head and swings her long outstretched leg backwards and kicks her infant head over heels. If the baby fails to get up she then goes over and repeats to process until the calf finally arises to its feet. When the calf finally gets up she does another despicable deed to her child. She goes over and knocks it off its feet. Why would a mother giraffe do this to her child? In the wilds of Africa, home to most giraffes, a baby giraffe has many natural enemies. Leopards, hyenas and, of course, lions - all enjoy feasting on young giraffes if they can. In fact these predators are all attracted to the smell of the afterbirth. The mother knows if she doesn't get her calf up and running soon after birth it will surely be eaten.

With all this in mind, you can see how God has used painful experiences in your past to protect you in your future. When life throws a blow at you and knocks you down, get up and keep going. It is God who is helping you get up, so you can use this experience to better serve him. Remember if the pain isn't real, the ability to help others through their problems will not be possible.

Daily Verse: "He healeth the broken in heart, and bindeth up their wounds."

Psalms 147:3

FEAR OF PANIC ATTACKS

Part One:

In 2002 after finishing a seven year term as pastor of a church in a small town in Ohio, God revealed to us it was time to move on. Our ministry could better serve his plans for us if we would move to a location which was two hours from our current location. The church we had been serving in was a small church unable to pay a full salary to its pastor. I worked full time in a Fortune 500 company the entire seven year pastorate. My company had a branch company near our new residence, so I transferred by inter-departmental transfer to keep my almost eight years seniority. That was the beginning of my nightmare.

The previous owners of the house we bought wouldn't move out of our new house, so we spent two weeks living half-way between our new address and old one, in a one room motel. When we finally did get to move all our stuff was in storage buildings. The van we paid one thousand dollars for to move with broke down on the first load and had to be towed. I stepped on a nail, and had to stop moving to go get a tetanus shot. My back felt like it was going to give out emptying those buildings. My new job put me on the graveyard shift and reduced my salary by $8.00 an hour. Our new home came with new expenses. Our utilities went up about 150 %, our insurance was raised several hundred dollars; to make it short, everything was more expensive at our new address. And that's tough with a cut in pay of about 30%. The new job wasn't working out, and the new ministry brought its own frustrations. Our new house demanded, much needed immediate attention. All these things placed me in a position I've never experienced before - a position of absolute panic. Before work every night, I would feel a very real pain in my chest. The pain was extreme pressure that made my heart feel like it was going to explode. My breathing would get fast, my mouth would get so dry, and my mind would get this deep sense of dread. My wife who is a nurse, would say, "Don, you're having panic attacks."

"No way," was my response, "I'm not afraid of anything."

Finally, one night, while I was at work, I leaned over my workstation in despair, and asked God. "What am I going to do now?" Instantly He broke in, and spoke to my heart one phrase that changed the whole course of my personal storm. "Be still and know that I am God." Almost immediately all my panic left, and my whole attitude changed with the situation. Just knowing that God is in charge of your life can remove all fear, and panic.

Daily Verse: "Be still and know that I am God;"

Psalms 46:10a

FEAR OF PANIC ATTACKS

Part Two:

What is a panic attack? I think it's easier to tell what something is, by defining what something is not. A panic attack is not a bad day. It is not a feeling of being depressed. It is not a bad mental attitude that can be changed by confessing or reading. It is a very real, dark, horrible fear. The best way I can describe it, is to have pure, unadulterated terror about the life. You don't exactly know what you're afraid of, or what is happening to you. All you know is that you're terrified.

Symptoms of a panic attack include a dryness of mouth, heart palpitations, increase in heart rate, nausea, diarrhea, chills, hot flashes, trembling, etc. Most of these symptoms by themselves are nothing, but when they are connected to panic, you think you are dying. Confusion sets into your thoughts, and you begin to have difficulty controlling them. You begin to anticipate every moment of your day with harsh feelings and dread. So how do you get out of the panic trap? First begin to breathe deeply when you feel the attack coming on. Slowly breathe in the power of the Holy Spirit, and breath out the problems and worry. Try to control your thoughts by lying still and relaxing your body. You may need to take medication according to your doctor's prescription to accomplish this task. Try to control your thoughts by focusing on the Lord. Begin to think thoughts like everything is going to be ok. Everything is going to be fine. Everything is going to be alright. Try to forget about your problems, and cast your cares on him.

   Daily Verse: "Casting your cares upon him; for he careth for you."

I Peter 5:7

FEAR OF GUILT

   Your mind is like a television set on a certain channel. You are watching the channel of faith, belief, and repentance when Satan stops by just to change the channel on you. "Don't watch that channel." Satan says. "Watch this one right here; it promotes lack, unbelief, and doubt." What is the channel? It's the channel of the past. It's the channel where Satan keeps playing reruns in your mind. All your short comings, failures, and disappointments are played over and over again. Soon you feel guilty, and condemned. Neurologists tell us that the brain controls the central nervous system. If you have an anxious thought, immediately you feel your heart beating faster and faster. Adrenalin begins to pour into your body, increasing your endurance and muscular strength. God put adrenalin in each of us to help us face adversity. You've probably heard of mothers lifting cars off their children trapped underneath, or farmers lifting tractors off farm hands that were caught beneath. Ordinary people doing superhuman, impossible feats done in the face of danger. The problem with adrenalin is that when guilt and condemnation pound at you day in and day out, it's like pouring a bucket of adrenalin into your body. If this is repeated frequently enough, your nervous system gets all messed up. Soon you feel as though you are so low you will have to look up to a snake's belly. Soon you begin to believe you are worthless, and of no use to anyone. You receive a constant high, and let down until even performing normal functions in life are difficult. This is why it is so important to search your heart every night before going to sleep. Allow the Holy Spirit to tell you if there is something you need to repent of, before the devil tries to beat you down with it. If you need to repent, just repent, get cleansed and move on. It's time to walk free of guilt and condemnation in the name of Jesus!

Daily Verse: "There is therefore now no condemnation to them which are in Christ Jesus, who walk not after the flesh, but after the spirit."

Romans 8:1

FEAR OF STRIFE AND UNFORGIVENESS

Part One:

In front of every house there are two doors. One door says unforgiveness, and the other says strife. Satan uses both these welcome mats as a license to steal, kill, and destroy our lives. In this hour we need to close every door and remove these welcome mats from our lives once and for all. First we will discuss strife and tomorrow we will cover unforgiveness. What is strife? It is a seed Satan tries to sow into our lives to confuse us and get us into contention. Strife is the cause of most divorces, and relationship breakups today. When you become quarrelsome you will always look for reasons to disagree about something. If someone rebukes you, instantly you become defensive, and hateful. The problem with strife is that once you are trapped by it, you don't even know it. You are constantly discussing the situations of other people's lives that don't concern you. Proverbs 27:17 puts it this way, "He that passeth by, and meddleth with strife belonging not to him, is like one that taketh a dog by the ears." If these symptoms belong to you, you need to do something quick! God's Word declares " . . . and a servant of the Lord must not strive; (II Tim. 2:24).

The first thing you should do is begin to take charge of your words. Don't let them run freely from your lips. David asked that God would put a watch over his tongue to avoid the problem of strife. You must also learn to agree with people. Agreement is the greatest enemy Satan has ever faced. Agreement is the greatest success law on earth. The bible says "Two are better than one; because they have a good reward for their labour. If they fall, the one will lift up his fellow" (Ecc. 4:9–10). We really do need each other.

Daily Verse: "For where envying and strife is, there is confusion and very evil work."

James 3: 16

FEAR OF STRIFE AND UNFORGIVENESS

Part Two:

Unforgiveness is a disease that eats at our very core of existence. It's no wonder when Jesus concluded his itemized teaching on the Lord's Prayer in Mathew 6:14, he goes right into a teaching about forgiveness. Forgiveness is the root of Christianity. We can be forgiven of our sins by the righteous acts of the son of God.

One of the best illustrations of forgiveness appeared in the Chicago Tribune back in the nineties. According to the article, a London, England couple was having some problems with their marriage. One day a fierce argument found its way to the driveway of their house. The wife then got into the car, and ran over her husband with it. The wife was immediately jailed, and the forty-five year old husband was hospitalized. Five months later the husband was released from the hospital with forty-five leg fractures, and a skull fracture. Then the husband did a remarkable feat of human kindness. He petitioned the court for his wife's release; for he claimed that he couldn't live without her. The man now was wheel-chair bound never to walk again, yet his love for his wife was unshakable. With all charges dropped, the Newcastle court could do nothing but suspend the wife's sentence and release her. When asked a few months later by the local paper how things are going, the husband replied, "We are back together and happy, but my wife sure is argumentative." Unforgiveness is best dealt with head on, turning everything over to God, for his handling.

Daily Verse: "And be kind one to another, tenderhearted, forgiving one another, even as God for Christ's sake hath forgiven you."

Ephesians 4:32

FEAR OF DEPRESSION

Depression is an emotional expression that can come on any of us. In fact according to one survey done by the National Institute of Mental Health, at any one given time one-third of the American population can be suffering from depression. History records great men such as Abraham Lincoln and Winston Churchill, suffered great periods of depression. Even the bible gives us a glimpse of notable characters that suffered from this deadly foe. Micah lost confidence in people altogether: "Trust not in a friend." Elijah the man who outran horses, killed hundreds of false prophets in one event and called fire down from heaven to consume his enemies laid under a Juniper tree and asked God to take his life. Solomon the richest man who ever lived got to the point where he hated life. And, of course, David, his father got to the place in his life where he lost faith in God, and said, "I will surely die at the hands of Saul." Depression is a powerful emotion that can catch the best of us. So what is a person to do when depression knocks on our minds door?

First, recognize that depression is not some stage you are going through. Don't treat it too lightly; it's responsible for countless of broken homes, physical breakdowns, and suicides each year. Next, search for a cause. Ask yourself, "Why am I feeling so depressed? Do I have some unconfessed sin? Have I been greedy for gain? Do I have unrealistic expectations about my life? Have I taken some criticism by my piers too personally? Am I being too impatient? Do I have an unforgiving attitude toward someone? Or am I just too tired from working so hard?" All these reasons plus, of course, a medical imbalance could be the cause for your depression.

Whatever you do take immediate action, and plan for a personal victory. Always remember that you can begin to step out of depression now, and enter into a life filled with joy and peace.

Daily Verse: "Pleasant words are as an honeycomb, sweet to the soul, and health to the bones."

Proverbs 16:24

FEAR OF PLANNING

Our world is filled with many failures. One of the major causes of failure today is the failure to plan our lives. Most trust something as important as their life to just chance. I believe this is crazy, but millions do it daily. Some people even excuse their laziness because they claim planning is against God's will, citing scriptures such as Mathew 6:25, "Therefore take no thought for your life," or James 4:15, "For they ought to say if the Lord will, we shall live and do this and that."

However, neither of these passages condemns a person for setting God-given goals for their life. A life lived without a plan is a life lived in disorder. The old adage, "if you fail to plan, you plan to fail," still rings true today. God is a God of planning. He has intricately designed a universe in His plan. Think of how much planning has gone into designing the human body. One of the best bible references to God being a planner, and His will, is that we plan our own lives as found in

Luke 14:28–30. "For which of you, intending to build a tower, sitteth not down first, and counteth the cost, whether he has sufficient to finish it? Lest haply, after he hath laid the foundation, and is not able to finish it, all behold it begin to mock him, saying this man began to build, and was not able to finish."

You can see that God expects us to set specific goals and make plans to reach them instead of just hoping things will work out for the best.

Daily Verse: "A man's heart deviseth his way; but the Lord directeth his steps."

Proverbs 16:9

FEAR OF BITTERNESS

One the most effective tools against sincere Christian believers today, is the tool of bitterness. Bitterness has the power to make you into its slave. It can kill your spirit and wipe all smiles from your heart. As God tries to pour blessings into our lives, bitterness can dam up the river to your soul.

The story is told by Charles Bracelen, the author of Lee: The Last Years, of a time when Robert E Lee visited a Kentucky lady after the Civil War. The woman stood in front of her house and stared bitterly at the remains of a tree she was fond of while growing up. Federal artillery fire had left not much more than a few limbs, and a charred trunk. The woman wept as she looked up into the eyes of the confederate general, expecting to hear words of condemnation about the northern troops. Instead Lee said, "Cut it down, my dear madam, and forget it." Lee understood it was better to forgive the injustices of the past, than to let bitterness take root in our lives and poison every part of our existence. Bitterness must be mastered or it will master you.

The first step toward rooting out bitterness is admission. Admit it is a sin. Admit it's wrong and damaging. Admit that you need to let go and let God. When bitterness tries to flood your life, soak your mind in the Psalms of David as he cried out to the Lord. Allow his words to displace or choke out any form of bitterness that seeks to take root. Never allow a day's worth of bitterness to rob you of the success, and joy that God has prepared for you.

Daily Verse: "Looking diligently lest any man fail of the grace of God; Lest any root of bitterness springing up trouble you, and thereby may be defiled."

Hebrews 12:1

FEAR OF DYING

Many people in our fast paced society have this almost incurable fear; the fear of not knowing the dreaded day. The day that has been predetermined by God when we should depart this natural life and enter into eternity. This fear is not only horrible, but has the power to take the life away from those who suffer from it. This little true story that happened several years ago best illustrates this fact:

Back in the railroads "hay-day" people were hired to go along at night and chase out freeloaders and squatters who were looking for a free place to sleep. One of the men was doing his job, when he noticed someone had left the door on a refrigerator car wide open. He thought, "I wonder if someone is trying to steal something, I better check it out." As he got to the back of the car, he heard a horrifying noise out front. Someone had slammed the door on the car with him trapped inside. Immediately he began to yell and pound on the door. All to no avail. Whoever locked the car was already out of hearing range. "Oh, No, what am I going to do now? I can't survive the night in a refrigerator car," he thought. He knew the constant cold would lower his body temperature until he would freeze to death slowly. Minutes seemed like hours while trapped in the well insulated coffin. Thoughts like I'm getting so cold entered his mind. Finally realizing he was not going to make it, he decided to record his final thoughts, by drawing on the dust on the floor. Slowly he wrote with his finger as he got colder and colder. His last thought to be recorded was, "I am so sleepy, and I must go to sleep." This was not unusual, for anyone who freezes to death has a sudden urge to go to sleep.

The next morning a railroad mechanic opened the refrigerator car and was horrified by what he found. Here was a normal healthy man sitting against the door frozen to death. An autopsy was performed to determine the cause of death. The autopsy results proved that the man had indeed frozen to death. So what's so unusual about this story? What the man trapped in the freezer didn't know, was the refrigeration unit in the car was broken, and the temperature in the car that night never got below 55 degrees. He may have needed a sweater, but it was hardly cold enough for him to have frozen to death. He froze to death in his mind. Always remember, no matter what you fear, it has the power to take your life.

Daily Verse: "Precious in the sight of the Lord is the death of His saints."

Psalms 116: 15

FEAR OF WORRY

Worry - the leading producer of our gray hairs. Some people have such a problem with worry, that they worry they won't have anything to worry about! How should we handle worry? Try to handle it the way this little British grandmother did during World War II.

At the height of the London bombing blitz, no matter how much the lady's son would plead with her, she wouldn't leave her flat in the city. She felt a duty to help the wounded, and the helpless. Her duty was more important than her safety. Week after week her son would visit her in the city and try to get his mom to move to the suburbs with him to be safe from the bombing. Each time she would simply point to a small sign on the wall which read, "Don't Worry! It May Never Happen." Then, one day it did happen. Her apartment complex was bombed. Two- thirds of the building was completely destroyed. As soon as the son heard the news, without regard for his own safety, he frantically rushed to his mom's flat. When he arrived, he found his mom sitting in her favorite rocker, singing her favorite hymn. In exasperation, her son shouted at her, "Do you still trust your stupid little sign now?"

"Oh my goodness," cried the grandmother as she rushed to turn the sign around. When she turned the sign around it read, "Don't Worry You Can Take It." It is a documented fact that ninety-nine percent of what people worry about will never happen to them.

Daily Verse: "Now the just shall live by faith;"

Hebrew 10:38a

THE FACTS AND EFFECTS OF FEAR

There was a time in every one's life when they did not have unrealistic fear. But I'm sorry to say that type of fear plagues many lives today. For most, some traumatic experience happened in their life and a fear developed. Then the fear is carried from the past into the present. Here are a few of the facts and effects of these types of fears:

First of all, all fear is real, even if it is not realistic. Just because something is not realistic, (or shows immediate danger) does not mean it won't seem real. Usually, our minds will feed our fears with the "what ifs." What if I would have done it this way, or what if they show up, etc?

The focus becomes shifted to the fear if you allow this to happen. It will soon begin to grow in your mind, until your mind becomes completely preoccupied with the fear itself.

Finally, the power of God, and the truth about the situation are not as meaningful as the fear. If this behavior is allowed to persist, it will affect your entire life, until it seems as though you are living in torment. I John 4:18 puts it this way, "There is no love in fear, but perfect love casteth out fear; because fear hath torment." When we become preoccupied with our problem, it causes us to be tense and irritable. The torment of fear can even affect our physical well being through headaches, high blood pressure, ulcers, increased heart rate, etc. Even our social relationships can be drastically affected by our fear. We could tend to be reclusive, or maybe unresponsive to other peoples actions toward us. Some people may even label us as a "little weird."

The wealthiest man of the early twentieth century, Howard Hughes, died alone in his massive penthouse apartment because he was afraid of catching some disease and dying. He wore plastic gloves all the time. He ate with sterilized silverware, and walked on newspapers to avoid sickness. The irony of the situation is he died from a disease.

Daily Verse: "For the thing that I greatly feared is come upon me, and that which I was afraid of is come upon me."

Job 3:25

FEAR OF SUFFERING

The story is told of a British minister named, W. E. Sangster, who one day noticed a soreness in his throat and a numbing feeling in his leg. When he finally took the time to go to the doctor, he was diagnosed with an incurable disease that caused progressive muscular atrophy. The doctor told him that his muscles would waste away, and his throat would become so weak that he wouldn't be able to swallow. Even his precious voice would soon fail and disappear. What would you do in this situation if you got that scenario from your doctor?

Sangster threw himself into his work with abandonment. Realizing that every day was precious, he came to the conclusion that this illness was a gift from God. He concluded that he would have more time for prayer, and he would be able to write like never before. So one day in a moment of prayer, he pleaded, "Let me stay in the struggle Lord, I don't need to be a General, just give me a regiment to lead."

Soon his legs gave out completely, and his voice faded in the distance, but God answered his prayer. He wrote countless articles and books, and helped England organize her first prayer cells. When people were tempted to pity him, he would simply say, "I'm only in the Kindergarten of suffering compared to my Lord Jesus."

Why are many of us so tempted to expect nothing more than a pie in the sky existence? Did not our Lord learn obedience by the things he suffered? Did not the apostle Paul, on the night of his call to ministry learn the things he must suffer? Why then do we find it so hard to accept the fact that this suffering we may be experiencing could be the will of God for our life? Should not our prayer be in times of trouble, "God give me more grace to endure?"

Daily Verse: "But the God of all grace, who hath called us unto his eternal glory by Christ Jesus, after that ye have suffered a while, make you perfect, stablish, strengthen, settle you."

I Peter 5:10

FEAR OF IGNORANCE

Today we live in a society that, for the most part, knows nothing about God. The church is no longer the center of social activity as it was in yesteryear. Instead it has become an event to add to an already crowded schedule, perhaps once or twice a year, for most Americans. Instead of living our lives for the one true God, Jehovah, the creator of the universe, many are slumbered in pure ignorance. A spiritual slumber if I may.

One day a woman went shopping for her daughter. She thought she'd get her a nice piece of jewelry, at the jewelry store in the mall. The thought of getting her a nice cross necklace entered her mind. She walked into the jewelry store and approached a store clerk who stood behind a showcase. "I'm looking for a necklace with a gold cross," said the lady. The store clerk was pleased to assist her, so he quickly looked over the display case and said, "Do you want a plain one, or one with the little man on it?"

Today Jesus is not the central focus of most lives. As some children grow up, the name of Jesus is just another swear word their parents use when they get mad or upset with someone. I myself, being raised in the house of an atheist father, never heard of the person of Jesus Christ, or the work that he did on the cross for my sins. Finally after I was grown, and living on my own, I wandered into a church one day at the invitation of a friend. I can remember how confused I was to find out Jesus was a person who loved me enough to die for me.

Contrary to popular belief, ignorance is not bliss in spiritual matters. It's what you don't know that could be killing you.

Daily Verse:" Having the understanding darkened, being alienated from the life of God through ignorance that is in them, because of the blindness of their heart."

Ephesians 4: 18

FEAR OF CHANGE

Year after year the southern Alabama farmers were accustomed to planting only one crop. And the one crop was, of course, cotton. They were cotton farmers and that's what they intended to be; at least that's what they thought. Then one year the dreaded boll weevil moved in and devastated their cotton crop. So the next year most of the farmers mortgaged their homes and planted their one crop again. Hopes were high for a bumper crop harvest this year. But, the insect came back and destroyed the entire crop, wiping out most of the farmers completely. Only a few farmers survived the devastating two years with the boll weevil foe. So, in the third year the farmers that remained thought they would try to rescue their farms by experimenting with a new crop; a crop they had never considered planting before. After all why would a cotton farmer plant peanuts? But, peanuts are what they planted and they couldn't believe what happened next! The peanuts thrived in their soil, and there was such a demand for peanuts that one peanut harvest paid off all the accumulated debt for the two years loss. They even had money left over for a profit. From that day forward they became peanut farmers, and became very wealthy from the change. Some of the farmers even got together, and had a monument erected on the town square to the boll weevil. Saying "If it had not been for the boll weevil we would have never discovered peanuts."

Why is it we are so hard to get out of our comfort zone and embrace change? I believe if we would accept change in our lives more readily, we too would find out what the cotton farmer of southern Alabama found out all those years ago. "There's gold in that there 'adversity.'"

Daily Verse: "Behold I show you a mystery; we shall not all sleep, but we shall all be changed."

I Corinthians 15:51

FEAR OF BEING ALONE (LONELINESS)

Ever since Adam's relationship with God was disrupted by sin, man has suffered the pain of loneliness. We live in such a self-centered world, with no concern for one another. Loneliness is a sad feeling of being left out, unwanted, or even rejected. It cares not what your social status of life is. It plays no favorites. It can strike rich or poor, young or old, men or women, healthy or unhealthy, even the godly or the ungodly. It is estimated that more than seventy-five percent of all Americans suffer from chronic loneliness. Lonely people tend to vacation on what I call P.L.O.M. trips. Poor little old me. This kind of attitude buries its' captives in a world of self-pity, feeling that nobody really cares or understands. Some lonely people try to fight their loneliness by escaping to a world of drugs, alcohol, and other mood altering diversions. Even our Lord and savior Jesus Christ was not immune from the effects of loneliness, when he cried from the cross, "My God, My God, why have you forsaken me?" (Mathew 27:46).

So what is a person to do to combat the feeling of being alone? First we have to go to the root of this destructive force. Ask God to cleanse you of any combative tendencies, which may be driving people out of your life. Then, you should decide to challenge the sin of self-pity, and correct the feelings of worthlessness you may have about yourself. Realize that Christ died to give you worth and abundance in this life. Finally, challenge the fears that have brought you low by reaching out to others, and taking the time to develop new relationships. One of the most important keys to defeating loneliness is initiative. There are countless of people out there in the same ship of despair that you are in. They are in need of a friend to enter their life and help them defeat the beast of loneliness.

Daily Verse: "A man that hath friends must show himself friendly; and there is a friend that sticketh closer than a brother."

Proverbs 18:24

FEAR OF CRITICISM

I think the best illustration of someone criticizing someone else's work; can be found in the story of Nehemiah. Be sure there are plenty of people out there who don't want to do the work, but sit and wait for someone to step up who will, just so they can criticize them.

Listen to these words recorded in Nehemiah 4:3 concerning the quality of the walls being rebuilt in Jerusalem: "Now Tobiah, the Amorite, was by him, and he said, "Even that which they build, if a fox go up, he shall even break down their wall." Wow! What striking words of encouragement. Go ahead Nehemiah, build your wall, but it won't even stand the weight of a fox. Does this not sound like so many people in our society today? They have no solutions to the woes of our land, but they are quick to criticize someone who tries. So what was Nehemiah's response to these words of criticism? First, he prayed a quick fifty-four word prayer - asking God to take care of these enemies of his will. Then in verse 6 it says, "So built we the wall; and all the wall was joined together unto the half thereof; for the people had a mind to work." Nehemiah asked God to come on board and watch his back, while the people who had a mind to work finished the project.

Never give up your dreams and accomplishments in life, because of someone else too narrow minded to dream. I'm reminded of the words of the famous Finish composer Jean Sibelis, as she consoled a young musician who had just been cut to pieces by critics after a performance, "Remember, son, there is no city in the world where they have erected a statue to a critic."

Daily Verse: "Speak not evil one to another, brethren;"
James 4:11

FEAR OF THE PAST

"Bury your past or your past will bury you." These words are as true for all of us, as they were for a famous lady evangelist by the name of Kathryn Kuhlman. She had enjoyed an anointed ministry of teaching, and preaching, until she met a man named Winthrop. He was another evangelist traveling with his wife and children. In the course of time she fell in love with Winthrop, and asked him to leave his wife, and children for her. His feelings for her were the same, so he did as she had asked. This was the beginning of the end. No matter how much we think, and reason things out in our mind, wrong is still wrong in God's book. Her ministry got put on hold, and she sat on the platform, and did nothing while her husband ministered. Neither of their ministries had the flowing anointing they had once had. Sometimes you can do the right thing wrong. It's kind of like taking a shower without removing your clothes first. It's the right thing to do, but the wrong way to do it. One day she found herself in a debate with God over her husband. God drew a line in the sand, and said it was either Him, or Winthrop. She willingly chose God, and soon departed on her way from her husband. After days of repenting and confessing, she found herself standing on a road with a dead end sign. Thoughts of her past mistakes flooded her mind, and filled her with condemnation. Suddenly, God broke into her thoughts with what seemed like a clanging gong. "Kathryn, what mistakes?" asked God? She proceeded to remind him of her sin with Winthrop. All God could do is ask her "What sin, Kathryn?" You see, when God forgives us of our wrongs, and failures, He doesn't remember them. They never existed according to his book. They are completely wiped away from the slate. Someone has said, he tosses them into the sea of forgetfulness, and puts up a sign that reads "no fishing allowed." As for Kathryn and her ministry; it became world famous until people were coming from all over the world to be in her meetings.

Daily Verse: "For by grace are ye saved through faith; and not of yourselves; it is a gift of God:"

Ephesians 2:8

FEAR OF TEMPTATION

Every born again Christian soon realizes that although he has been adopted into God's eternal family, and has been forgiven of all his sins, they still must face temptation. This world we are living in is hostile toward God, and is ruled by the prince of the power of the air. Every temptation comes in many different forms, and we must be quick to recognize them, if we are to achieve our victory over them. The big question, or fear for some, is this, "Is it a sin to be tempted?" The answer is an astounding, "NO!" The bible claims that Jesus, the son of God, was tempted in all as we are. Yet we know that he lived without sin. Someone has said, "You can't stop ideas from coming into your mind, but you don't have to invite them in for a cup of coffee."

Contrary to popular belief, not all temptation is a direct attack of Satan. The fall of Adam and Eve resulted in all of mankind receiving a sin nature. So it is this fallen nature, so filled with its lusts and evil desires that causes most of the temptations in our life. According to I John 2:16, all temptation falls into three different areas. Each has the power to bring us into sin, and its bondage: the lust of the flesh, the lust of the eyes, and the pride of life. We can see the effectiveness of these three areas so vividly in the attack of Eve in the garden.

First, the bible says that the serpent beguiled Eve, that's how he works, in deceit. He noticed that she thought the fruit looked good, (lust of the eyes), then she desired the fruit, (lust of the flesh), and desired to be as a God knowing good from evil, (pride of life). So he quickly began to place doubts into her mind about God's concern for her and her husbands well being. This all led to her being tricked to sinning against God's word. Today temptation is the same, and James gives us the prescription for staying clean in temptation. "Submit yourselves therefore to God, resist the devil and he will flee from you" (James 4:7).

Daily Verse: "My brethern, count it all joy, when you fall into divers temptations."

James 1:2

FEAR OF THE FUTURE

Uncertainty, about the future, is for some the pain of the present. This uncertainty, has spawned a crop of would be phychics, and fortune tellers. Some people today never fail to consult their astrological chart, before making any decisions. Others go from palm readers to tarot card forecasters, just to get a glimpse of tomorrow. Even in the bible days this was a problem. The problem became so bad, that God proclaimed, no witch would be allowed to live in the land of Israel. So he required that Saul his chosen king, carry out this task for him. Saul's campaign, for the Lord, was to either run them from the land, or put them to death. Either way, there was no fortune telling going on legally in Israel. Saul did a great job, until one day God rejected him, for his disobedience with handling the Amalikites. The bible says that God stopped talking to him, by dreams, visions, or the prophets. In other words, Saul had placed a wall of disobedience between him and God. What do you think Saul did? I Samuel 28:7 says, "Then said Saul unto his servants, seek me out a woman that hath a familiar spirit, that I may go to her, and inquire of her." Even Saul, the witch hater of the Old Testament, was willing to compromise his own conviction, to seek information about his future.

Uncertainty about your future can lead you to take drastic measures. The society we live in today is so hungry for the supernatural that they chase after soothsayers as much as they do physicians. They have become the prescription for everyday health. The problem is, God has not changed his view on them. He still calls them an abomination to have in the land. He still forbids his people from having any contact with them. God requires his people to be a people of faith, and trust. Our faith should not be in what is going to happen, but in trusting God to be with us no matter what happens. Does not the bible still say of Jesus, "I will never leave you or forsake you?"

Daily Verse: "Take therefore no thought for the morrow; for the morrow shall take thought for the things of itself. Sufficient unto the day is the evil thereof."

Matthew 6:34

FEAR OF THE DARK

Living in darkness, is a terrible experience. Researchers living in the different sections of the world that experience prolonged darkness, say that after a short period of time, they become depressed. They begin to dread each passing day. This little story tells us how important just one light can be to our existence.

Years before president Borja of Ecuador, was elected to the office, he was imprisoned in his own country. It was a struggle for democracy in Ecuador, and the military cracked down. He was soon arrested, and thrown into a cold dungeon without trial. The prison had no windows, and no doors. It was so bad that three days seemed like three years. He endured the solitude and darkness until he felt like he was going to go crazy. Just when it seemed unbearable, the huge steel door opened, and someone stepped through the darkness without saying a word. He knew someone was in the room with him, for he could hear a clanking noise, like someone was trying to fix something. Quietly he waited in the darkness, until the huge steel door slammed, and things got quiet again. A few minutes later a light in the corner blazed brightly, and he finally figured out what the quiet person was doing. Someone had perhaps risked their life to connect the electricity back to Borja's cell room. From that moment on he realized the importance of light, which made his imprisonment at least bearable. Even more so, are we not the light in this dark world? Scripture states; that evil men love darkness because their deeds are evil, but Jesus said; we (his people) are the light of the world shining the glorious light of the gospel into the darkness of sin. So let's re-connect our electricity back to the source by prayer, and shine brightly so we can lead many out of darkness and into God's light.

Daily Verse: "And art confident that thou thyself art a guide of the blind, a light of them which are in darkness."

Romans 2:19

FEAR OF SUBMISSION

The bible commands Christians to; be subject to one another, (Ephesians 5:21). It is a reasonable command to let others have the right-a-way in life, to avoid head on collisions.

A short while after the Civil War was ended; Sherman was scheduled to march in a triumphal parade down the streets of a large U. S. city. The night before the parade he called General Howard to his room for a conference. "General Howard," said Sherman, "you were with me at the head of one of my divisions that marched through Georgia. You should rightfully ride at the head of your division tomorrow, but I've been asked to let the General who proceeded you have that honor. I really don't know what to do."

General Howard replied, "I think I'm entitled to represent the division, since I led them to victory."

"Yes I agree," Said Sherman, " . . . but I believe you are a Christian, and I was wondering if Christian consideration might lead you to yield your rights, for the sake of peace?"

"Oh, yes," said Howard, "in that case, of course I will yield."

"Good," Sherman said, "I'll arrange it, and by the way, you report directly to me at nine o'clock in the morning - you will be riding beside me at the head of the army."

God's word declares that if we'll make room for God to work, He'll be faithful in our life. When we submit our rights over to him, it gives him the opportunity to exalt us to higher places of honor. Why would you settle for just having the honor that you deserve, when the God who created all things wishes to give you his favor? One day of favor with God is worth decade of labor without him.

Daily Verse: "Submitting yourselves one to another in the fear of God."

Ephesians 5:21

FEAR OF SELF-PITY

"Now the word of the Lord came unto Jonah, the son of Amitta, saying, arise, go to Nineveh, that great city, and cry against it, for their wickedness is come up before me. But Jonah rose up to flee to Tarshish from the presence of the Lord" (Jonah 1:1–3).

What! He's going to run from the presence of the Lord, in the opposite direction of his assignment. Why, in world would he do that?

What could possibly be going through his mind to invoke action such as this? The answer is quite simple, even though it may not be obvious to the casual reader.

Jonah is a patriot, and he wants to rescue Israel from coming calamity. You see Jonah was also a prophet, and prophets of the Old Testament, could foresee judgments coming to their nations. Jonah knew that Nineveh had no preacher, and without a preacher telling them to repent, there would be no repentance. Jonah reasoned that he could spare his beloved Israel impending judgment from God. The only thing this self-imposed savior didn't count on was the 'Whale Seminary' that God had prepared for him. So after spending three days in a whale's belly he decided to obey God, and preach repentance to Nineveh. Do you know what happened to Jonah? After preaching repentance to the whole city, he went to the edge of the city, and sat down to see what would happen. The city repented in sackcloth and ashes. This invoked Jonah to anger. He got upset with everyone, even God Himself!

This is the greatest illustration of self-pity in the whole bible: "Therefore now, oh Lord, take, I beseech thee, my life from me; for it is better for me to die than to live." (Jonah 4:3). What a pathetic excuse for a preacher. God in his endless compassion prepared a gourd plant to shade Jonah from the blazing hot son. Jonah got exceedingly glad over the gourd. Then the next day God sent a worm to destroy the plant. The plant shriveled up and died and Jonah got mad again. God was trying to teach Jonah about the uncertainty of life. How he should be more concerned for the welfare of others rather than his own selfish ambitions.

That's what self-pity does; it keeps you focused on the wrongs of your own life. Instead God wants us to be our brother's keeper.

Daily Verse: ".He that hath pity upon the poor lendeth to the Lord; and that which he hath given he will repay again."

Proverbs 19:17

THE FEAR OF THE LORD

"Be thou in the fear of the Lord all the day" (Proverbs 23:17). Some people do not understand the difference between the fear of the Lord, and the fright of the Lord. If you have bowed before God and accepted his gift of love and mercy, through the Lord Jesus, you have no cause for fright. The fear of the Lord to you is a godly thing, a wonderful, beautiful thing to be experienced. No matter how extensive we discus the subject, it would be impossible to thoroughly cover it. So this day we will just discus the fine points.

The fear of the Lord includes, but is not limited to, respecting, or reverencing Him. Although the bible tells us to tremble at his presence. The man who fears the Lord gives Him His place of glory, honor, reverence, praise, thanksgiving, and sovereignty He deserves. The person who fears the Lord, allows him to hold a special preeminent position in their heart, which allows His desire over theirs, His will over their own, and hates what He hates and loves what He loves. If you fear God, you will serve him. Solomon, in all his wisdom, after amassing great wealth beyond others before him, and doing everything that would make his life more pleasure, came to one final conclusion; "Let us hear the conclusion of the whole matter; fear God, and keep His commandments, for this is man's all" (Ecc. 12:13). He even goes as far as to state that any life, lived apart from the fear of God is lived in vanity. God's Word promises many blessings to those who fear him, and these are just a few.

Prayers answered (Hebrews 5:7)
Angelic protection (Psalms 34:7)
God's attention (Psalms 33:18)
His provision (Psalms: 34:9)
Great mercy (Psalms 103:11)
Assurance of food (Psalms 111)
Wisdom, understanding, and time management
(Proverbs 9:10–11)
Peace of mind (Proverbs 15:16)
Riches, honor, and life (Proverbs 22:4)
Complete satisfaction in life (Proverbs 19:23)

Daily Verse: "The fear of the Lord is the beginning of wisdom."
Proverbs 9:10

FEAR OF UNHAPPINESS

Have you ever heard someone say; "If I only had a million dollars, I'd be happy." Well social scientists are finding out that money doesn't make you happy. In fact, researchers are finding out that in most cases, the more money people make, the more they want, so happiness keeps escaping their grasp. In fact, increasing wealth more often produces unhappiness. Today's average life span is 25,550 days; can you afford to spend just one of them being unhappy? Most of the time unhappiness is just the fruit of something much deeper. It is a root that goes down deep in the soul and touches where you live. Today's pursuit of materialism, has misdirected us from what is really important. Have you ever asked the question, "What on earth am I here for?" When you finally answer that question, you are on the pathway toward your own personal happiness. John Chalmers quoted it this way; "The grand essentials for happiness are: something to do, someone to love, and something to hope for."

An elderly woman once felt a bitter sense of unhappiness, and loneliness. She had lost her husband a couple years prior, and her life had become meaningless, without purpose. She approached her young pastor, and asked for his wise council. After, listening intently to the woman's pleas, the pastor said; "Sister, you need to bake some cookies, package them in sandwich bags, and look for some children in need to give them to." Immediately the woman took offense, "Bake some cookies!" she exclaimed, as she stormed out of the church. Days went by, until she decided not to return to the church anymore. As the weeks passed, she wouldn't return the pastors phone calls, nor would she answer the door to anyone. That's what Satan likes to do; he likes to get you into isolation, so he can begin to feed you on a diet of lies. One day the woman was washing dishes and looking out the window at some children playing basketball, at the nearby park. The thought of cookies entered her mind. "Ah, what the heck? I don't have anything else to do," she said to herself. So she baked some cookies, packaged them in bags, and out the door she went to the park to deliver cookies. The children were so happy to get the cookies that they asked for more. Quickly, she baked more cookies, and soon had all the kids in the neighborhood calling her the "Grandma Cookie Lady." She went back to her church, and apologized to her pastor as she thanked him for showing her a new found happiness.

Remember, what Benjamin Franklin said; "The U.S. Constitution doesn't guarantee happiness, only the pursuit of it, you have to catch up to it yourself."

Daily Verse: "A merry heart doeth good like a medicine: But a broken spirit drieth the bones."

Proverbs 17:2

FEAR OF ABUSE

When you've been exposed to cruel and abusive behavior it's hard to once again trust people. People wear masks most of the time, until it's difficult to know who the genuine article is. I remember reading the sad story of a woman who was abused as a child. She tells her story:

"My sister, and brother, and I were all abused as children. The truth is, my parents appeared very Christ like in church. When people from the church just dropped in unexpectedly, my mother would hide her cigarettes, and smut magazines under the couch. Dad would beat our mother until she would scream and yell for him to stop. She would hide her pain by drinking and sleeping a lot. Many times while mom was either asleep or passed out, my Dad would come and get either my sister or me to use sexually. My Mom never knew this was happening. One time my sister told our Sunday school teacher what Dad was doing. They came to our house for a visit, but Dad was so sweet, and kind - nobody believed her. In fact, Dad just shrugged it off as a big miss-understanding about my sister beginning to develop physically, and being uncomfortable giving hugs. He even made my sister apologize to the men for telling stories. When the men left my dad took off his belt and beat my sister over and over again. Then he knocked her down, and kicked her in the stomach. When I grew up all I wanted to do was get even."

This woman's story is all too common. So just how do you get even for such abuse, and mistreatment? The answer is quite simple, yet seemingly impossible. You don't get even. There's no such thing as getting even when it comes to relationships. Sure it's tough, but resentment is a two-edged sword. It can cut both ways with bitterness, and hatred. Unfortunately, you may have to live with some of the pain, and memory for the rest of your life. But Christians are tough people, aren't they? In fact, they're the toughest people on planet earth. We serve a tough God, a God who is able to blot out all transgressions against Him. A God who practices what he preaches. He tells us to bless those who hate us, and he does that everyday. He says, we should love those who are our enemies and pray for those who mistreat us, and while Jesus was dying on a cross, he looked to the heavens, and pleaded with His father to forgive them for what they were doing to him. Of course it won't be easy, but when we decide to become a transitional person, we soak up all the pain, and put an end to the abuse forever. We put a stop to it once and for all.

Daily Verse: "Bless them that curse you, and pray for them which despitefully use you."

Luke 6:28

FEAR OF INTIMACY

Some people are afraid to get personal or intimate with others, for fear that they will get hurt. The fact is that only through intimacy, can there be any reproduction. You show me a person who doesn't allow himself to open up to others, and I'll show you an unfruitful soul. The word intimate means to be very close, or familiar with someone. The problem is, this leads to vulnerability, and it is possible you could be taken advantage of. This is the risk of being intimate with someone, but the very root of Christian salvation is deeply imbedded in intimacy.

Jesus prayed in the garden in John 17:3, "And this is life eternal, that they might know you the only true god, and Jesus Christ, whom thou hast sent." Once we get intimate with God, we never know loneliness again. We can continually pour our hearts out to him, and never worry about being perceived as overly emotional, or pitiful. A person, who is intimate with God, has a calm, strong, sense of control about his life. There is evidence of an unseen control, holding their hand in times of adversity.

True friendship on earth is very rare. In fact it's almost non-existent. It means that you totally identify with someone in thought, soul, and spirit. God allows us to have personal relationships, to enable us to learn how to become intimate with him. Many good Christians know the blessings of his word, but do they really know him? Only by looking at a life, can we tell if someone knows their God. The Bible declares that fruit bearing is always the result of intimacy with God.

One last note about intimacy: The root word in intimacy, is intimidate, which means "to make afraid by threats." The devil knows all about you, he has made a career out of getting to know you on a personal level. He knows all your shortcomings, and failures, and he's quick to remind you of them in a moment of weakness. Anyone that you have become intimate with knows which buttons to push to set you off. This is one of the cautions of becoming intimate with others. Trust me, it's worth the risk. A friend has been so appropriately described as someone who knows you, and still wants to be your friend.

Daily Verse: "Jesus said to him, have I been with you so long, and yet you have not known Me, Philip?"

John 14:9

FEAR OF CONFLICT

Conflict is a part of every human being's life today. It means, to be antagonistic, incompatible, or at war with someone. Today, in our pressure cooker world, conflict comes in many forms. Husbands and wives, children and parents, even countries are in constant conflict with one another. Even our spirit is in conflict with our flesh as we speak. Everyday, when we wake up in the morning, we can expect to experience some form of conflict. The trick is to be an over comer in the battle of conflict. If the truth is to be known, we are a Dr. Jekyll, trying to hold back a Mr. Hyde personality from escaping, and asserting himself in malice or violence.

The first man to discover the explosive power of conflict was Cain, the first recorded birth in the Bible. He allowed his jealousy against his brother's worship to release Mr. Hyde, and soon he was a murderer, marked by God to wander his remaining days in hopelessness. It would be fair to say the first conflict on earth was a Holy War against the proper worship procedures of God.

The same today, everyone knows what's right, and no one wants to give in to the other's feelings. If you are trapped in a conflict, and you want to resolve it, I'm going to give you a win/win situation. Be understanding before seeking to be understood. You must seek to understand the other person's point of view, before you can ever hope to make them understand you. Start a line of communication that is not defensive: maybe say, "I heard you say . . . , is this what you meant?" Or, "Am I understanding you correctly, that you are saying . . . ?" I want to understand you correctly . . ."

Finally, to make your conflict strategy work, you must practice the "give in" principle. That principle says, "I don't always have to have my own way. Let's compromise so both of us can win." I personally think one of the most Christ-like, and courageous things a person can do in conflict is to give in to someone else. It's often the most loving thing you can do for someone else.

Don't get me wrong, there are some subjects in which two people will never agree on. For instance, my wife is always cold, and I am always hot. Believe it or not, many times this difference causes conflicts when traveling in an automobile together, especially in the winter time. She wants the heater on high, and the windows rolled up in the winter. This type of situation, almost suffocates me in the car, so my wife has come to a compromise, she let's me roll the window down some, and I let her turn the heat on high. We have learned to agree to disagree. Remember the words of John Drakeford, "By people we are broken, and by people we are put together again."

Daily Verse: "All things are of God, who hath reconciled us to himself by Jesus Christ, and hath given us the ministry of reconciliation."

II Corinthians 5:18

FEAR OF TEENAGE PREGNANCY

Think for a moment about the scrutiny Mary the mother of our Savior, must have gone through just to bring Him into this world. Aren't you glad, Mary was Pro-Life, and not pro- Choice? No matter what the situation in which our Lord was born, it brought hardship to His mother. Don't get me wrong, every Jewish girl wanted to be the one to birth the promised enmity seed who would defeat the devil. In fact, if a Jewish girl didn't birth a man-child she was considered to be "cursed by God." She would never have the opportunity to be the "one." Although, this teenage birth was in the will of God, there are many such pregnancies that people question. I know teenage pregnancies are on an epidemic climb today, some one million a year, and rising. So what should we do when we face such a trying situation, as an unexpected birth? Everyone who faces this situation will have to come to their own conclusions. But let me give you God's perspective on the situation. "Children are a heritage from the Lord, the fruit of the womb is a reward" (Psalm 127:3). Children are referred to as a reward from God. A reward is something given in return for something done. Believe me after having six of my own; there were times when it seemed more like a punishment than a reward. But, as I watch them grow, and develop there own families, I see them practicing the same principles we did. This alone gives me a reward. The world promotes a different attitude toward children. Many view them as burdens, rather than blessings. Many have chosen, for the sake of convenience, to abort the unwanted child of a teenager. I feel this is a tragic mistake, and should be avoided at all costs.

The Creator's words to his newly formed family was, "Be fruitful and multiply." God is still the creator of all life and we have no right to terminate any life, under any circumstances. Many so-called "unwanted pregnancies" have gone on to do great things for God's kingdom.

The Apostle Paul put it this way in Eph. 2:10, "We are His workmanship, created in Christ Jesus for good works." The word "workmanship" means, to be a "manufactured product, a specific design produced by a skilled artisan." So remember, all children, no matter what the condition of their birth, are a work of a master designer.

Daily Verse: "Thine eyes did see my substance, yet being imperfect; and in thy book all my members were written, which in continuance were fashioned, when as yet there was none of them."

Psalms 139:1

FEAR OF DISCOURAGEMENT

Discouragement means "to be without courage." This is the condition some people get into when all hope seems to be gone. A heaviness of spirit puts the soul in a dis-array. A story is written that describes how Satan uses discouragement to defeat us:

One day the devil was having a 'going out of business sale.' He put all of his useful tools up for the bidding for whoever would purchase them. He made beautiful signs to display his sale items; Malice, Envy, Deceit, Hatred, Jealousy, Adultery, Temptation were among the products. Each item had its own price. Under the table was a well worn tool, slightly wedge-shaped and harmless looking? One of the would-be customers asked the devil the price of the tool under the table. "Oh, that tool isn't for sale."

"Why?" asked the customer.

"Because that is my most valuable tool." Replied the devil. I use it more than any other tool. When nothing else will work, this tool will.

"What is the tool?" asked the customer.

It's "discouragement," the devil proudly said. "I can use it to pry open and get inside any man's mind, when I can't get in with anything else."

Satan is the master of using the circumstances of life to discourage us any chance he gets to. Nobody is immune from his dart of discouragement. David and his mighty men were away from there homes on a raid, when the Amalekites invaded and captured all the women and children. His men were so distraught; they were planning on stoning David for his weak leadership.

David could have collapsed under the weight of his load of discouragement, but instead he worked on solving his problem. This passage of Gods Word gives us the best method of overcoming this weapon of the enemy. "But, David strengthened himself in the Lord his God" (I Sam. 30:6). Next, he asked God for direction in what to do. God told him to get his men together, and attack, and he would give him a great deliverance. What was the result of David's obedience? "They recovered all!" David's victory came when he refused to accept defeat in his spirit. So instead of asking God "why?" we should be asking Him "how?"

> *Daily Verse: "Why art thou cast down, O my soul? And why art thou disquieted within me? Hope in God."*
>
> *Psalms 43:5a*

FEAR OF THE OPINION OF OTHERS

The society we live in often imposes certain values, and standards on us that can force us to feel inferior, second-rate, and even somewhat abnormal. Many people today feel as though they don't matter to anyone. Also many are trapped in a web, of what other people think of them.

There is also a constant scrutiny between self as to how others perceive them. When a person is rejected they are quick to build up walls of defense to ward out unwanted opinions. The problem lies in the fact that the same walls that were built for defense also serve as a prison to hold them captive. They live in a constant state of dismay, saying to themselves, "I wonder what I did wrong to them," or "What do they think of me now?" Sometimes people are snared by their particular ethnic race; they feel like because they were born to this race, or ethnic group, they have been robbed of their human dignity. Others have had so many failures and setbacks in life, they can hardly look someone else in the face without feeling inadequate or unworthy. So how do we deal with such feelings as we are all prone to them?

First and foremost, realize that there is only one opinion that matters. When the rubber meets the road, only what God thinks about your life is the opinion that counts. Once when umpire Babe Pinelli called Babe Ruth out on strikes, the 'Babe' was furious. He yelled at Pinelli, "There are 40,000 people in these stands who know that last pitch was a ball, you tomato head"

Pineli looked at the 'Babe' and calmly replied, "Maybe so, but mine is the only opinion that counts." So remember, that no matter how many times you are squeezed by the press of what someone may or may not think of you, remember that only the opinion of the Celestial Umpire is the one that counts.

Daily Verse: " . . . and bringing into captivity every thought to the obedience of Christ"

                                                    II Corinthians 10:5b

FEAR OF TRIALS

One day a young boy was playing in his back yard. He was like every other ten year old; he liked to collect things from nature. He would gather pretty colored leaves in the fall, unusual rocks, and of course a critter or two every now and then when mom wasn't watching. One day he found a very unusual find, a cocoon that held a living moth. Quickly, but carefully he snatched up the limb it was fastened to and carried it into the house and up to his bedroom. Day after day he watched the silk wrapped ball waiting in anticipation as to what would emerge. Finally, after what seemed like forever, the little ball began to squirm. This was it, he thought, "I wonder what will come out." Minutes seemed like hours as he watched the little bug wrestle with its silk prison. Then suddenly a hole poked through the silk. Out popped the head and shoulders of what looked like a very large moth perhaps the great emperor moth. He watched intently for several hours, until it seemed as though the moth was stuck. He decided that something must be wrong, so he went and got a pair of his mother's sewing scissors, and snipped the opening large enough for the remaining moth to pop out. To the boys amazement out popped a moth that had a large swollen body, and small shriveled wings. He expected the moth's wings to stretch out and grow beautiful but instead they shriveled up more until all the moth could do was waddle around, and eventually die without ever flying. What the boy didn't know was that the constricting cocoon was necessary to force the body fluid out of the body, and into the wings. God has made the struggle a necessity for beauty. The merciful snip from the boy, in reality was cruel, as it doomed the creature of its God given struggle.

In the same tone, the book of James puts it this way; "My brethren, count it all joy, when ye fall into divers (many) temptations; knowing this that the trying of your faith worketh patience. But let patience have her perfect work, that ye may be perfect and entire, wanting nothing" (James 1:2–4). Is it possible that the struggle we face, or the trials of the life we live, could be God-ordained? The answer is an astounding "Yes!" God does use trials to shape us into the servant he wants us to be. The struggle is God's way of working patience in us that will complete us in our walk with him.

Daily Verse: "Beloved, think it not a strange concerning the fiery trial which is to try you, as though some strange thing happens to you."

I Peter 4:1

FEAR OF WARFARE

If you were to select one word that would describe your daily life, what word would you select? Stressful, Intense, Hurried, Boring, Routine, Exciting. For many people the word would be warfare, or struggle. Often our daily life seems to be a constant battle to defeat discouragement, depression, and just plain old mundane. We wrestle against a maze of circumstances, that can leave us somewhat paralyzed as to our next move. Everyday people battle broken homes, poor health, fractured relationships, and or course our ever diminishing finances. All these adverse conditions can lead someone into frenzy about their life. If you are feeling like this describes your life, get your chin up, because you are not alone. In fact, the Apostle Paul often described life as combat, conflict, and continual wrestling to get ahead.

In fact, no other subject in scripture gets more controversy than the subject of warfare. Either people will avoid the subject altogether with a kind of ostrich, hide my head in the sand mentality, or they see demons in everything, from trees, rocks jewelry, even wastebaskets.

Make no mistake about it, we have a very real enemy, and his name is Satan. He has put together quite an army of demons in the last six thousand years, and he is very organized. In fact he is much more organize that most or us. He is quite capable or setting a course of events in your life to rob you of the faith you have in God if you allow him to.

The first thing you must do is open your spiritual eyes and realize that you live in two worlds at the same time. You live in a physical world of sight, touch, taste, and you live in a spiritual world, that operates completely by faith. Remember that Jesus told us in the gospels that the natural world governs the spiritual world; "Whatever you bind on earth shall be bound in heaven, and whatever you loose on earth shall be loosed in heaven;" Understand that there is an invisible war taking place right now for your soul. It's a battle to the death, and only the victor gets to live.

Scripture tells that most people alive are completely blind to this fact; "But the natural man does not receive the things of the Spirit of

God, for they are foolishness to him; nor can he know them, because they are spiritually discerned:" (I Cor. 2:14).

With this in mind know that the real battles you face in life are not against people, but against demonic spirits that are bent on robbing you of your faith. You cannot live on neutral ground; there is no safe haven to hide, other than in Jesus. So when the struggles of life come against you - do what the Psalmist David did. He ran to his hiding place, his strong tower, his rock, which was his God.

Daily Verse: "For we do not wrestle against flesh and blood, but against principalities, against powers, against the rulers of the darkness of this age, against spiritual hosts of wickedness in the heavenly places."

Ephesians 6:12

FEAR OF DISTRACTION

Distraction has been called one of the devils four deadly 'D's: Delay, Deceit, Depression, and Distraction. Distraction is simply having your focus from God's perfect plan broken. Broken focus is the leading cause of energy waste and time loss today. God had so graciously given each of us the same amount of time each day to accomplish his purposes. Rich or poor, old or young; it makes no difference - we all get twenty-four hours a day and that's it. With this in mind, you can't afford to waste anytime on unproductive friendships, and unworthy causes. Although Satan will try to bring rabbits into your life to chase, don't follow them, they lead nowhere.

It has been said that distraction is a criminal's greatest strategy. They enter a store as a group, and then they split up in groups of two. One group will go to one end of the store, and begin to make noise, while the other group fills their pockets. Everyone's attention is looking at the noise, or the distraction, while the shoplifters are robbing them blind. This is how the thief of our soul works. He brings some worthy cause or some promotion to our flesh into our life to get our attention. Once our attention is off our mission, then he has us right where he wants us. The whole purpose of distraction is to get us to miss the mark God wants us to hit.

In the book of Exodus God had purposed his people would spend about forty days in the wilderness, while they spied out the land of promise. Instead, they got distracted by the giants they saw, and the cities were walled and fortified, so they reasoned within there hearts that there was no way a group of ex-slaves could defeat them. The result

- they missed God's mark for their lives and spent a year in the wilderness for everyday of unbelief they lived. Can you afford a single day of distraction? Although life is filled with many surprises, always remember that paths without obstacles, don't lead anywhere. If the mark God has selected for your life is of any significance you can be assured that Satan has distractions lined up to lead you astray.

You cannot save time, bank it, or collect it. You can only do as Jesus did, spend it wisely. Organize a daily agenda, and keep it. Invest your time wisely, and don't allow the crisis of the moment to distract you from your list of priorities.

Daily Verse: "Turn not to the right hand nor to the left: remove thy foot from evil."

Proverbs 4:27

FEAR OF HURTING INSIDE

"Why died I not from the womb? Why did I not give up the ghost when I came out of the belly? Why did the knees prevent me? Or why the breasts that I should suck?" Does this sound like a man whose hurting inside? Of all Bible characters, Job is surely the most shining example of a man of suffering. He lost his family, career, finances, home, retirement, investments, friends, and his health - all in a matter of a few months. He went from an important official sitting at the city gates to a loner sitting in the ash heaps of where his house once stood, before it was destroyed by a whirlwind. We see him taking pottery remains, and scraping his ulcerous sores that cover his body from the top of his head to the soles of his feet. Job is an example to all of us that God is still with us even in extreme suffering. Even when we hurt down deep into the very soul of our being God is still with us.

So what is the source of suffering, sorrow, and pain? Why it's sin of course, when sin entered the world, so did pain, and suffering. God never created sin, but man was created with a free will, and sin is simply disobedience to God's will. So along came the tempter who tempted man to disobey. Man did so and there you have it . . . sin. Since Satan created his own sin, his best way to get back at God, was to cause his crowning creation, (man) to create his own sin.

Now as for Job, his suffering was not a result of his sin. In fact, Job was considered "a perfect and upright man who feared God, and eschewed or avoided evil." His suffering was a result of his righteousness. Since he was so righteous he was a prime target for an enemy attack.

Whatever the causes of the pain you feel inside remember you are not alone, God can always be found standing near making sure the attack doesn't go too far. "And the Lord said unto Satan, Behold, he is in thine hand; BUT save his life" (Job 2:6).

The real test of spirituality is how we respond to distress. Be careful not to make too much out of the minor difficulties of life. Learn to develop positive attitudes toward people and God when times get hard. It may seem too difficult at first but be assured, it is vitally important to relieving you of your adversity.

As for Job, the Bible declares that God visited the captivity of Job and gave him twice as much as he lost, even a longer life.

Daily Verse: "If thou faint in the day of adversity, thy strength is small."

Proverbs 24:10

FEAR OF THE UNKNOWN

A mother and father wanting to do something exciting for summer vacation, decided to take their two children to Carlsbad Caverns, in New Mexico. When they reached the deepest part of the tour, in order to dramatize the complete darkness and solitude of the cavern, the guide reached over and switched off the light. Instantly darkness enveloped the rock-laden room. The little girl quickly began to cry from the utter darkness. Soon to follow was the reassuring words of her older brother, "Don't cry, somebody around here knows how to turn on the light."

When I think of that story, I am utterly staggered at the thought of what Abraham must have thought, when God spoke to him, and asked him to pack up and leave his home. Think about it wife, what would you do if your husband woke you up one morning, and said; "Honey, pack what you can carry - were leaving this land."

"Where are we going?" you would say.

"I don't know," would be his reply.

"Why are we leaving?" you would say.

He would calmly answer, "Because, last night God woke me up in a dream and told to move."

Did not their actions take a giant step of faith, considering how they were not worshipers of Jehovah, at the time? In fact, all the people were idol worshipers, until God spoke to Abraham's father, Terea. You see Terea began the journey into the unknown, until he got to Haran. At Haran, he got comfortable, and died there. Haran was halfway between Ur and Canaan. Please don't get stuck halfway from fulfilling your dreams for fear of the unknown. Just take the step of faith as God directs, and depend on him to turn on the light.

Daily Verse: "A man's heart deviseth his way: but the Lord directed his steps."

Proverbs 16:9

FEAR OF MAN

"When I consider thy heavens, the work of thy fingers, the moon and the stars, which thou hast ordained; what is man, that thou are mindful of him?" (Psalms 8:3–4). Although David penned this psalm, could this be the response of an angel at creation? He sees this awesome, mighty, God who just finished creating a universe, take interest in something as insignificant as a lump of clay, called man. The Bible declares that the fear of man is a snare. Being afraid of what man can do to you will trap you in its clutches.

Rosa Parks the black woman, who became the mother of the civil rights movement, was arrested in 1955 for not giving up her bus seat to a white man. Soon, thousands of protesters boycotted and marched. Finally, the Supreme Court ruled that racial segregation was unconstitutional for all men were created equal. Later, when asked of the ordeal, she said; "When I sat on the bus that day, I was only thinking of getting home. But I made up my mind, after so many years of being miss-treated; I was not giving up my seat. I did not feel any fear sitting there. I felt the Lord give me strength to endure whatever I had to face."

When you know what you're doing is right, just settle it in your mind and you will find courage in your heart. Jesus put it this way in Luke 12:5; "But I forewarn you whom ye shall fear; Fear him which after he hath killed, hath power to cast into hell, yea, I say unto you fear him."

Daily Verse: "The fear of man bringeth a snare: but whoso putteth his trust in the Lord shall be safe."

Proverbs 29:25

FEAR OF INTIMIDATION

In 1979, the greatest illustration of the power of intimidation, took place in a bank robbery, in Dallas, Texas. A man walked into a Dallas bank and told the teller not to sound the alarm. Then he gave her instructions to put all the money from her drawer into his briefcase, which he politely handed her.

She was terrified and quickly she emptied her drawer containing over $40,000.00. The man quietly shut the briefcase and walked out without saying a word. After the man left the building, she quickly sounded the alarm. In just a matter of moments the man was apprehended, just slowly walking down the street.

Normally bank robbers go straight to jail. But the problem with this case is when they picked up this guy, he had no weapon. He also didn't use a weapon to rob the bank. Nor did he threaten anyone at anytime. He simply just walked into the bank, in a non-threatening manner, and asked the woman to put all the money from her drawer into it. According to the law, since there was no weapon, or any threat of violence, then there really wasn't any bank robbery. Actually, the man did nothing illegal. The teller didn't have to do what the man said, since he didn't force her or threaten her life with a weapon - the man walked away with $ 40,000.

This teller is like so many Christians today. They are always being intimidated by something. Most of the so-called dangers we face in our lives, are nothing more than the devil, trying to intimidate us into a corner. Remember, the devil is a big talker, but you and I don't have to be listeners that just sit back and listen to his lies.

Daily Verse: "What shall we then say to these things? If God Be for us, who can be against us?"

Romans 8:31

FEAR OF AGING

Once a retired lawyer from Arles, France, decided to make what was considered by many a very reasonable business decision. For five-hundred dollars a month, he bought the rights to take over an Arles, France apartment. The only catch was, he couldn't move in until the current resident, a 90 year old woman named Jeanne Calment passed away. Well, taking all things into consideration, he weighed the odds, and went ahead with the purchase.

Some thirty years later, and $180,000 dollars poorer, he had still not moved into his apartment. On February 21, 1995, Jeanne celebrated her 120th birthday by sending the lawyer a card which jokingly states; "Sorry I'm still alive." She was verified as the oldest living person on earth. Medical scientists have researched her life, to discover the secret to her longevity. She ate two pounds of chocolate a week for years, smoked until she was 117, and rode a bicycle until she was 110.

Someone once asked her what kind of future she expected, and she jokingly said; "I expect a short one. The only thing I regret in life is that it took me 110 years to become famous."

As the psalmist penned, "Teach us to number our days." We also must make the best of our lives, as we live them now.

An older gentleman once told me that God grants each of us seventy years, and by grace eighty, and the rest of the years are borrowed time. Make sure you use all your days wisely. I've heard it said that no man on his death bed wishes he could spend one more hour at the office.

Daily Verse: "So teach me us to number our days that we may apply our hearts to wisdom."

Psalms 90:12

FEAR OF INFERIORITY

Webster defines inferior as "being poor in quality." Is it any wonder the devil tries to dump inferiority complexes on us to bring us down low? It's a cancerous condition which corrupts our emotions, actions, thoughts, attitudes, and values. If left unchecked, it will produce a deep sense of unwanted, unneeded, feelings that can cause us to withdraw, and even isolate ourselves. In Bible days there was a man who experienced this feeling. Listen to his words as he spoke to King David about his life. Then he bowed himself, and said, "What is your servant that you should look upon such a dead dog as I?" (II Sam. 9:8). The dog was considered the vilest creature in those days, and here he is calling himself a dead dog. Wow! That's an inferiority complex. Who was this overly depressed man? Would you believe he was in the lineage to be a king? He was King Saul's grandson, Mephibosheth. What happened in this man's life to cause him to have such an inferiority complex? When it was time for God to appoint another king, David was his chosen servant. David's army was raiding Jerusalem, and Mephibosheth's nanny grabbed him, and began to run in fear for his life. He was just a small child, and she accidentally dropped him, and broke both his legs, damaging them beyond repair. From that day forward he was lame in his feet. Then she moved him to the middle of nowhere, way off the beaten path, to a town called LoDebar.

All his growing years, she warned the young man, "You need to hide from David, or he will kill you." When, in reality, David was looking for someone of the house of Saul that he could bless. He wanted to honor his covenant he had with his friend Jonathon. Who happened to be Mephiboseth's father by the way. Instead he is living in a place called LoDebar, which means; a place with no pasture - a cursed land that can't sustain life. Why is he living in such a dreadful place? Because the land was so wasted, no one else would want the land. It would be like living in Death Valley. So what does David do? He finds Mephiboseth - lifts him up, gives him a place to eat at his own table, and gives him back everything his grandfather King Saul possessed.

So don't let inferiority keep you from possessing what is rightfully yours in Christ. Come out of LoDebar at once.

Daily Verse: "For we are his workmanship, created in Christ Jesus unto good works."

Ephesians 2:10a

FEAR OF NOT BELONGING

Have you ever felt like the black sheep of the family? Good! You're in good company. That means you're a candidate to be called "a man after God's own heart." Before David was anointed to be king, he was just a teenage boy doing what his father expected him to do. He was a sheepherder tending a few sheep. At the same time God was speaking to the prophet Samuel, to go to the house of Jesse, and anoint one of his sons to be the next king. So after some assurance from God, he went to the house of Jesse and called for him to bring all his sons before him. So Jesse calls for all his sons except for David; after all David is just a ruddy, young boy. Samuel was so impressed by all the big strong boys Jesse had. Every time one passed by, God said, "This is not the one I have chosen."

"Is this all the sons you have," Samuel asks?

"Well there's David, but he's in the field with the sheep," Jesse answered.

"Go bring him to me," Samuel said, "I shall not sit down until I see him."

When David walked in, the Lord said, "Anoint him, this is the one I have chosen."

Immediately Samuel did as the Lord commanded. I imagine David felt periods of loneliness and 'not belonging' to the family after this.

It seems as though David was in his own little world doing what was expected of him. But he did have one thing going for him. God sees everything going on. You may feel like you don't belong anywhere, that's okay - Moses, Ezekiel, Joshua, Jeremiah, Elijah, Elisha, Daniel, and many more great men and women in the Bible didn't fit into the cookie cutter mold either. So, as I said before, remember you're in good company.

Daily Verse: "And I will be a father unto you, and ye shall be my sons and daughters, saith the Lord Almighty."

II Corinthians 6:18

FEAR OF SICKNESS

Today we live in the age old debate as to the cause of sickness. Does God make people sick to achieve his purposes? Or, is the devil the cause of all sickness? Well, since sickness is a curse, it would tend to reason that sickness was caused by the fall of man in the garden. In any case, read this true story about the power of conversion:

One of the finest brain surgeons in the nation was diagnosed with cancer. He was suffering from severe abdominal pain so he underwent an examination. In the mean time, he began attending a small church in Burnet, Texas. A spiritual awakening came into his life, and he found himself committing his life to Christ. On a return visit, to his doctors for treatment, they were amazed that his cancer was totally gone. When asked about his miracle he said, "Before my conversion, I was a good surgeon, but I was harsh with my patients, and couldn't shed a tear." Now he admits that he talks to them about Christ. He also sends them notes of encouragement, using scriptures to comfort them. He said he genuinely cares for them. Did he receive his miracle healing from God, or did the doctors incorrectly diagnose his cancer? Who cares? I think the real miracle in this story, is that God can take a heart of stone, and replace it with a heart of flesh. Does God use sickness to get his will accomplished? You judge for yourself.

Daily Verse: " . . . for I am the Lord that healeth thee."

Exodus 15: 26

FEAR OF THE LACK OF APPRECIATION

Our lives are not measured by their duration, but by their donation. The problem lies in the fact that we live in such a selfish world. Children are growing up today, with the thought that the world owes them a living. Christmas presents are unwrapped, and when it's all said and done, the kids look at the parents, and say "is that all there is?" Then they begin to fight with the other siblings over what they didn't receive. Where did they learn such atrocious behavior? You guessed it; Mom and Dad taught it to them, because "more is caught than taught."

Jesus experienced this ingrate attitude one day as he was walking through the city. "Afar off stood a group of lepers, ten in number, crying with a loud voice 'UNCLEAN.' "Jesus called out and they responded, "We wish to be healed," was the plea.

"Go show yourselves to the priest, as Moses commanded," was the Master's answer, not wanting to break the law. Suddenly, as they went their way, they were all completely healed. However, only one returned to give God the glory, and Jesus asked him "Where are the other nine?"

He's still asking "where are the nine?" Are we so wrapped up in our own life that we fail to appreciate what God has already done for us?

It has been appropriately stated, that nobody cares how much you know, until they know how much you care. God has made our life much like a tennis match. Those who don't serve well usually lose the game. Serving others out of appreciation, is not entirely unselfish, for God in sovereignty, has promised that the giver always receives. And whatever you make happen for someone else, God will make happen for you. So the next time you sit down to a meal, please don't forget to look up first.

Daily Verse: "Knowing that whatsoever good thing any man doeth the same shall he receive of the Lord."

Ephesians 6:8

FEAR OF DEMON POSSESSION

Contrary to some liberal theologies, demon possession today is very real, and, yes, people still are possessed today. How do I know? I've experienced this fact first hand. I remember back in my younger years when I began my ministry; I was working with teenagers at a particular church in Ohio. This young girl, probably about sixteen, started to attend. She would sit as I preached with her arms crossed, and stare at me with this blank look as I delivered the Word to the best of my ability. Her stares were such a distraction to me I had to refrain from looking at her. Finally at the end of my message, I gave the invitation for those who wanted to make a commitment to Christ this night. I asked all to come forward, and demonstrate to God their sincerity. I bowed my head as I made the appeal, and to my amazement, when I opened my eyes this girl was in the group. Quickly, I made my way to this girl, and asked what she wanted God to do for her this night. "Leave me alone," was her reply, in a very deep, and non-human voice. I slowly backed away from her to ask the Lord, what to do since I had never had such an encounter before. The Lord prompted me to have her say; "Jesus is Lord." So I asked her to say this very simple phrase. Unfortunately she was unable to do so, no matter how hard she tried. I calmly, under my breath, looked into the girl's eyes, and said in a whisper, "I command you in Jesus' name to leave this girl." Almost instantly I saw her eyes lighten up as something was apparently leaving her. Her words to me in a whisper as she was becoming so overwhelmed she could hardly stand was, "I felt him leave."

Demon possession is very real in this world we live in. Further research revealed that the young girl in the above story was an avid Ougi board user, and loved to play role playing games that involve calling on spirits for assistance.

Today with the reality of television what it is kids' think of these things as harmless little games, but instead they are very real deceitful tactics the enemy can use to enter our lives. If you want to avoid the opportunity of allowing these things in your life, then stop playing in the devils playground. Quit reading your horoscope, stop calling psychics, quit watching fortune tellers and necromancers on television. And by all means check out what your kids are involved in.

Daily Verse: "Wherefore come out from among them, and be ye separate, saith the Lord, and touch not the unclean thing; and I will receive you."

II Corinthians 6: 17

FEAR OF LOSS

Life is filled with ups and downs. One moment we are flying on cloud nine, and everything is going fine. Then in an instant, without warning, you're plunged into a pit of despair. Parents may lose a child to an expected circumstance, or sickness. Johnny may lose the championship baseball game and think it's the end of the world. Little Tammy may fall down during her cheerleading tryout and not get picked for the team. What I'm trying to say is, loss is a fact of life, and if you're going to continue living, you're going to have to learn how to cope with it. Loss can be very painful at times. Pain is something we may feel on the outside, but really it effects us deep in our hearts. Listen to how Olympic speed skater Dan Jansen learned how to keep loss in proper perspective, and not cave in and give up on life.

When he was only nine years old Dan was competing in his home state of Minnesota for a youth national championship. He was doing a great job, and sure to place high in the scoring, that is until he tripped over a hose, that had been set up for a lane marker. When it was all said and done, that one trip cost him the one point he needed to win. So that day he went home a loser. He was grief-stricken the entire ride home, which was six hours in length. He only raised his head up to wipe away the tears that filled his eyes when suddenly his father broke the silence of the ride home with this statement. "You know, Dan, there's more to life than skating around in a circle." That one statement helped Dan go to the 1984, 1988, and 1992 Olympics in hopes of a gold medal. Was he successful? The answer is, yes and no. Did he win a gold medal? No, but in all attempts he took home something more valuable than Olympic gold. He took home his pride that he could get back up and stand for victory even in the face of loss.

When life throws a loss at you, stand tall and get up and try again.

Daily Verse: "For I know that my redeemer liveth, and that he shall stand at the latter day upon the earth."

Job 19:25

FEAR OF BROKEN PROMISES

Remember the days where your handshake was your word. Contracts involving great sums of money were settled on nothing more than a shake, and a promise. Today things are much different. I think the root cause of the constant deception today, is the fact that people don't understand the power of "covenant." A covenant is simply a contract between two parties. Most older covenants were sealed with blood, thus the cutting of hands, and the shaking, or mixing of blood by striking hands together. This meant that as long as one family member from either family was alive there was a lasting, bonding contract between the two families. Whatever the agreement - it must be kept for generations to come.

Is this not what God has done for us? Has He not made a covenant with us, and sealed it with his Son's blood. When Jesus was dying on the cross He was sealing God's covenant with man. Anyone who was involved with the covenant would have the scars from the covenant on their body. Jesus so appropriately bears the scares of God's covenant with us. Look at his nail- pierced side where blood and water flowed, when He was pierced through with the soldiers spear. Take a look at His hands, feet, and forehead where nails and thorns ran Him through. Yes, He bears the marks of the covenant, which was sealed with His own blood.

Whenever I am tempted to be disappointed over someone letting me down, I remember the broken promises I have made to Jesus, for which he has so graciously forgiven me. You may trust the Lord too little, but you will never be guilty of trusting him too much.

Daily Verse: "And he said, the things which are impossible with men are possible with God."

Luke 18:27

FEAR OF BEING BARREN

"Give me children, or else I die." This was the cry of a barren woman as she watched her sister give their husband child after child. "And she vowed a vow, and said, O Lord of hosts, if thou will indeed look on the affliction of thine handmaid, and remember me and not forget thine handmaid, but will give unto thine handmaid a man child, then I will give him unto the Lord all the days of his life" (I Samuel 1:11). That's the pleading of a barren woman. In Bible times being barren was considered being 'cursed' by God.

Even in these modern days, many women feel the stigma of not being able to conceive a child and fulfill her role as a mother. First, and foremost let me reassure you that you are not cursed by God if you cannot conceive. Although, all children come from the father of all life, only He can see the big picture for everyone.

In my travels as a pastor, I've come across several women with this problem, and none of them bring more joy to my heart, than the one I'll call Teresa (not her real name.) She found out that it would be physically impossible for her, and her husband Tom, (not his real name) to conceive a child together. She and Tom, with unwavering faith, began seeking God for a miracle. They knew they would be good parents for they had a lot of love to offer some wonderful child. After much prayer, God assured them that they would be parents. Then He gave them a desire to adopt deprived children from underdeveloped nations. At the time of this writing, they have just received their second child, and who knows where it will end? Although we are not their pastors anymore, they send us email updates on what God is doing in their lives.

Now, you can choose to be upset with your current status of parenthood, or you can do what Teresa and her husband Tom did, and make a difference in the life of someone else. God specializes in the physically impossible, and He can work a miracle out for you.

Daily Verse: "He maketh the barren woman to keep house, and to be a joyful mother of children . . ."

Psalms 113:9

FEAR OF DISCOMFORT

Many people in our land today live lives that are given to recreation. There is nothing wrong with recreation in itself. But some people go too far with recreation. Some people get so involved with recreational activities, that they don't have any time for important things. All they want to do is put in their work week, and head for the hills, or lake, or amusement part, or whatever. They don't want to be a part of anything that could bring discomfort in their life. Discomfort, is described as "anything that removes comfort, or having uneasiness about life." And we run from these things like the plague. For some reason we think everything in life has to work out just right. Anytime we see some resistance to something we're a part of, we instantly feel it's not God. God can't be leading me into something that could cause me pain. Dear friend, listen to me, comfort is not a part of this world. This life is not supposed to be comfortable. If this life was completely comfortable there would be no longing to go to heaven!

Scripture states; that in this life we shall suffer persecution. But in the next life, God will wipe away all tears, and offer us a life of joy, happiness, and, yes, complete comfort. So when a season of pain is attacking you, just remember that's exactly what it is, only a season. Seasons come and seasons go, but one thing is for sure - they are always changing. Sooner or later the season of peace and comfort will be back around in your life.

God could have kept Paul and Silas out of prison, he could have kept Daniel out of the lions den, he could have stopped Job's children from all being killed by the whirlwind, but instead He has promised to go with us in every hard time, and bring us through victoriously.

Daily Verse: "Let your conversations be without covetousness; and be content with such things as you have: for he hath said, I will never leave thee, or forsake the."

Hebrews 13:5

FEAR OF FIRE

Many people today carry around the marks on their body from this very forcible foe. Fire is extremely dangerous, reaching temperatures over 400 degrees in most fires. Without throwing caution to the wind, let's look at how fire has been used in the past to improve our quality of life.

In the 1960s, a group of people decided to use fire as a source of regeneration. So the prairie restoration movement, as they were so appropriately called, began setting regular fires to the prairie. This burn would remove all the unwanted dead grass, and allow for the re-growth of new grass. The results were beautifully, blossoming prairies. One man stated; "As the thick black smoke roared across the dead prairie grass, it was like experiencing the raw power of nature."

What emerges from the charred remains is brand new life - life that is full of nutrients from the old plants of before. In the same way God uses his consuming fire to remove any unwanted fields from our old lives. The Holy Spirit is often described in Scripture as a fire burning brightly in the hearts of His followers. He heats up our lives with adversities to bring any unwanted dross to the surface, and then as the refining fire is burning hotter and hotter, He skims away the unwanted, useless things that keep us from drawing closer to Him. Many people are quick to complain as these fires burn in their lives. Some unknowingly suppose the devil to be the source of their problems, when all the time God is standing in the shadows watching to see our reactions to the "Refiners fire." So, before you jump out the window in the midst of your fire, always remember that God is able to sustain you the way He did for the three Hebrew children:

The king decreed that when the music was played, all would bow to his image. The boys said we will only bow to one King in worship, and his name is Jehovah. The king became angry at this response and demanded the furnace be heated up seven times hotter. Then as the Hebrew boys were bound and thrown into the fire, the fire was so intense that the guards that threw them in caught on fire and were completely consumed. But, as for the boys, the only thing that burned on them was the ropes they were tied up with. The king was amazed as he looked in the furnace, because he saw not only the three boys he threw into the furnace, but also a fourth man, that looked like the Son of God. So he demanded that the boys come out, and as they came out the fourth man stayed in the fire. And guess what? He's still in the fire waiting for you.

Daily Verse: "For our God is a consuming fire."

Hebrews 12:29

FEAR OF BLASPHEMING THE HOLY SPIRIT

The Holy Spirit is the spirit of love, peace, grace, mercy, comfort, and, of course, joy. He is a person, not an it. In fact, He is the third person of the Godhead, which makes Him, God. Since He is a person, He has a personality, which means He can be ignored, offended, quenched, rebelled against, and of course, vexed. Of all the negative actions against the Holy Spirit - vexing him can be the most dangerous. Isaiah 63:10 puts it this way; "But they rebelled and vexed His Holy Spirit; therefore He was turned to be their enemy, and He fought against them."

Wow! I don't want God to fight against me, do you? So what is it we can accidentally do, that would cause God to be our enemy, and fight against us? Nothing! The key word is accidentally. There is absolutely nothing you can accidentally do that would cause God to fight against you.

In the New Testament, Jesus performed a wonderful miracle - healing a crippled man's hand. The next thing you know, the Pharisees are mad and accusing him of healing by the power of the devil. They were upset because he did it on the Sabbath day. Jesus immediately begins teaching about the order of the kingdom, and how the enemy must be bound before His kingdom can be spoiled. He went on to say that all blasphemy can be forgiven, except blasphemy against the Holy Spirit. So, just what is this "unpardonable sin?" Well, it's not something you can accidentally do that would offend Him into punishing you eternally. God is not that fragile. Some people live in a constant fear that they have offended the Spirit to the point of rejection. If this is you, just go ahead right now and smile, because you are not guilty of this offence. Those who have blasphemed the Holy Spirit, don't worry about it, they just go ahead and live unconcerned lives.

Blaspheming the Holy Spirit has its roots in rebellion. If you refuse to commit your life to Christ in this life, and don't find a pardon for your sins before you leave this world, you will blaspheme the Spirit of God, and never find forgiveness. One must completely rebel against

His convicting power and completely refuse and reject His prompting toward salvation before you can be guilty of the "unpardonable sin."

 Daily verse: "If we confess our sins, he is faithful and just to forgive our sins, and to cleanse us of all unrighteousness."

I John 1:9

FEAR OF THE LOSS OF A CHILD

  Most parents will agree that they, without hesitation, would take the suffering and even death away from their children if they are able. There was a small boy riding in the car with his father one day. Everything was going just fine, until suddenly a large bumble bee, flew in the window of the car. Immediately the boy began to panic for he was deathly allergic to bee stings of any kind. In a matter of moments, after a sting he would swell up and not be able to breath. Quickly, his father reached his hand out and swatted at the bee. Unfortunately the bee landed or the little boy's lap which made him petrified. So without thinking his dad quickly snatched the bee from his lap and squeezed it real hard. After a couple of minutes, he opened his hand, and released the bee. Once again the bee flew around the young boy's head, and caused him to panic. When the father, saw the fear in his son's face, he held out his hand palm up. The little boy looked at the palm of his father's hand to see the stinger of the bee lodged in the callused palm. His dad replied, "Son don't worry about the bee, I've taken the sting out of it for you."

  Our Father God has removed the sting of death from our lives, by sending his only begotten Son into this world to die on an old rugged cross. Deaths stinger has been removed. If you've lost a young child, although the pain is great, take comfort in knowing that God in his infinite mercy, has taken the sting out of their death, and has received them with open arms.

 Daily Verse: "O death where is thy sting? O grave where is thy victory?"

I Corinthians 15:55

FEAR OF THE LAW

  Contrary to what some people believe, laws were made to protect you, and not restrict you. In fact, Romans 13 informs us that God is the source of law, and lawgivers; "Let every soul be subject unto the higher powers. For there is no power but of God: the powers that be are ordained by God. Scripture goes on to tell us that if we resist these authorities we are actually resisting against God. And if we are a good law abiding citizens then we have nothing to worry about. (For the rulers is not a terror to good works, but to evil. Will thou then be afraid of the power, and do that which is good and thou shall have praise of the same" (Romans 13:3).

God has been creating laws, and enforcing them since time began. Let's for the sake of illustration, say you're a skydiver, and one day you are at 10,000 feet and you decide that your going to jump without a parachute today. You want to feel the complete freedom of the wind without the restraining feeling of a parachute strapped to your back. Although, the jump may feel exhilarating, there's a very serious problem awaiting you in a few minutes. One of God's natural laws is going to try, convict, and judge you all at once. Gravity is going to cause you to hit the ground at several hundred miles an hour and leave nothing more than a lump of clothes.

God's moral laws are much the same as His natural laws. Yes, they are restricting at times, but the good from them far out weighs the restriction. God wants His people to be a people of distinction. A people that others, who are outside of His will, can look at and identify as His living epistles. For some people, you may be the only Bible they will ever read. You may be the only law they will obey, so does this not give us a commitment to be more like Christ in these matters? Christ never broke a human law, while he lived His life; in fact He even paid a tax that He didn't owe just to keep peace. Let's, let Him be our example.

Daily Verse: "For Christ is the end of the law for righteousness to everyone that believeth."

Romans 10:4

FEAR OF INADEQUACY

So you think you are unable to do the task, someone has asked you to do. You feel a deep since of lack in the area of ability. You can't understand why you have to be the one asked to do it. In fact, maybe when you were younger you would have been better qualified to do the task, but now you are tired, and you feel like you are too old to start now. Well, if these seem like your excuses, then you fit right along with the only person in the Word of God to get the privilege of sitting down and talking to God face to face.

This man was raised in a time when slavery was prevailing and his family was slaves. In fact the master was so strict that to avoid over-population of the slaves he instructed all the midwives to kill all the male babies, by tossing them into the river. They just couldn't do it to this one little male baby; after all he was so beautiful. So they gave him to his mother to hide. She hid him for as long as she could until his cries could be heard outside of their home. Then for fear of what the king would do to them if the child was discovered, she prepared an ark, and placed him in it, and placed him in the river. His little boat drifted into a princess' swimming hole, and by God's awesome providence He gave the baby favor with the princess. She raised him until he was over forty years old. In a moment of anger he struck down an Egyptian that was persecuting one of his fellow brethren. When his unrighteous act was found out, he had to flee to the middle of nowhere just to escape a certain death sentence from the king. And that leads us to the point of the story. Forty more years go by, and all he's done for those years is tending someone else's sheep. Then one day he notices a very unusual sight. It's a bush that is on fire, but it isn't being consumed. As he approached the bush, he began to hear a voice, which told him to remove his shoes, for the place he was standing was holy ground. He removed his shoes, and slowly approached the bush. Then the voice commanded; "Come now therefore, and I will send thee unto Pharaoh, that thou mayest bring forth my people the children of Israel out of Egypt" (Exodus 3:10). Listen to the response of the old man who was given such a calling at over 80 years of age. "Who am I that I should go? But behold they will not believe me, or harken unto me. . . . . . I am not eloquent in speech. . . . . . and I am slow of speech and of slow tongue . . ." Three times he gave excuses for his inadequacy, and three times God responded with, "I will go with thee." Should not we also remember that God has made the same promise to us? We can live in the faith that He is with us. Oh, by the way, do you know who I'm talking about? That's right. Moses was his name.

Daily Verse: "And He said, certainly I will be with thee."

Exodus 3:12

FEAR OF STORMS

One day the disciples, most of which were fisherman, were sailing on the sea when suddenly a storm came upon them; a storm that was unlike any they had ever experienced before. It was sending huge, boisterous waves well over the bow of the tiny boat, and onto the deck. The disciples in all their efforts couldn't bail the water fast enough. They frantically looked at the back of the boat to see Jesus' response to this impending danger. They were completely amazed by what they saw. Jesus was asleep in the back of the boat. He had no idea that a storm was threatening to sink the boat. So what did Jesus do, after He wiped the sleep from His eyes? He rebuked the storm by saying "Peace be still!" Suddenly, all is calm - the storm vanished as fast as it came. Then He turns and shows us a side of Him we only see a few times in Scripture. "Why, were you afraid, oh ye of little faith?" God is deeply hurt when we allow the circumstances of our life to overwhelm us. When we allow our fears of the unknown to captivate our thoughts, God is upset, since He doesn't like you to share your thoughts with anybody or anything else.

Many kinds of storms arise in life. Suffering is sometimes in Scripture compared to a natural storm. When we experience some type of inner disturbance, it has a way of affecting us physically, mentally, emotionally, and of course, spiritually. In a storm that originates from Satan, he will try to hinder you from fulfilling God's purpose for your life. This type of storm is neither necessary, nor in God's will according to Scripture. In these storms we must learn to exercise our God-given authority to remove them from our lives. In storms that are created because of our disobedience, like Jonah's, we must learn to quickly allow God to work in our life by getting us back on track. Quickly ask Him for forgiveness and seek His mercy immediately.

Whether you face storms in or out of God's will let it be known that you are going to experience storms in this life. Matthew 7:24–27, informs us that storms will come to those who build their lives upon God's Word also. If you've built your house on the proper foundation of obedience to his commands, your house will stand.

Daily Verse: "Yea, and all that will live godly in Christ Jesus shall suffer persecution."

II Timothy 3:12

FEAR OF NIGHTMARES

Much debate has been given in recent years as to whether God still uses dreams or nightmares to speak to us. In several bible instances he has spoken his will to people while they were asleep, and when they woke they did as he demanded. In one particular case God needed to raise a prisoner from one of the deepest dungeons in Egypt. So one night when the Pharaoh, went to sleep, God broke into his dream world long enough to give him a nightmare about his kingdom. Pharaoh dreamed that seven fat cows came out of the river, and then behind them came seven skinny, and malnutrition cows. Suddenly the malnutrition cows ate all of the fat cows, and were just as skinny as before. Pharaoh awoke. Finally, after putting his thoughts to rest, that it was only a dream, he was able to go back to sleep. Then he dreamed another dream. Seven fat ears of corn popped up in the field, and behind them came seven very skinny, windblown ears from the same field. Quickly, the skinny ears ate up the fat ears, and were just as skinny as before, and then Pharaoh awoke again. This time his nightmares so stirred him in his spirit, he couldn't rest until he found out the meaning of his dreams. He called on the assistance of all his magicians, and astrologers, but none could give him the meaning for his dreams. Finally, the butler remembered this guy in prison who could interpret dreams. So he went to Pharaoh and told that two years ago when he was in prison for wrong doing, a prisoner interpreted his dream for him correctly. Without hesitation Pharaoh called for Joseph to be brought to him. Joseph interpreted the dream for Pharaoh and so impressed him that he made him second in command over the most powerful nation of the world, at that time.

God is able to get you where he wants you to be in a hurry if you will just be faithful with the gifts he gives you no matter what your situation. As for dreams or nightmares, of course some of them you might experience are late night pizza oriented. Some may even have there origin from the demonic, but it's been my experience that these type of dreams won't stick with you like a God-Dream.

Daily Verse: " . . . and your young men shall visions, and your old men shall dream dreams."

Acts 2:17b

FEAR OF CORRECTION

Every good father knows the benefit of correcting his children. Children just left to making their own decisions always are quick to get into mischief. Now, to the one being corrected, although deep down inside they may know it to be necessary, they don't like it. The bible puts the subject of chastisement this way; Now no chastening for the present seemeth to be joyous, but grievous: nevertheless afterward it yieldeth the peaceable fruit of righteousness unto them which are exercised thereby. (Heb. 12:11) But did you know whom the Lord loves he corrects: For whom the Lord loveth he chasteneth, and scourgeth every son whom he receiveth. (Heb. 12:6)

With this is mind isn't God's correction necessary for our spiritual development. God is not satisfied with good he wants us to have his best. Most of our stunted spiritual grow stems from not letting God make our decisions for us. We are like the self-wise child who thinks he knows what's best to choose for dinner, so he chooses ice cream and chocolate cake every day. Soon to find out that what may taste the best is not always the best thing for you.

In scripture we have a story of a man who made an unwise choice with the advice of his wife. They had decided to help God out in fulfilling his promise to them. After all they had been patiently waiting on God for twenty-five years, surely he must have forgotten. So they reasoned in their hearts that God must want us to have children through our servants. So Sarah gave her Egyptian maid to her husband to get pregnant, and he did. Then a son was born to them, and they were so happy, until God revisited them and told them he was ready now to give them a child with each other. They laughed in God's face, and he replied, "Is anything too hard for the Lord?" Sarah had a child, and now Abraham had a problem. The Egyptian woman got jealous of the attention given to Sarah's child. Sarah noticed it and immediately informed her husband that something had to be done with that woman and her child.

Now is where we see the chastening of the Lord. He told Abraham to send her away and he would not see her or his son anymore. So Abraham gave her a bottle of water and sent them on their way into the desert. Can you imagine the pain of doing something like that to your teenage son? Let us not make unwise decisions that result in the chastening of the Lord.

Daily Verse: If you endure chastening God dealeth with you as sons; for what son is he whom the father chasteneth not?
Hebrews 12:7

FEAR OF A NEW JOB

Does your present job delight your morning, or does it feel like drudgery into an endless day? Being in the proper job, or career, is one of the most important keys to finding happiness in life. God has placed a command in his word that man should enjoy his work; "To rejoice in his labour; this is a gift of God" (Ecc.5: 19). The prophet Isaiah put it this way; "Mine elect shall enjoy the work of their hands." Do you enjoy your job, or are you unhappy with it? Many things can contribute to you not enjoying your job, from an overbearing boss, to conflicts with other employees. Maybe your job is just unrewarding, and you need a change. Whatever the cause for your unhappiness, you need to ask yourself a few questions.

Am I using my God-given abilities and talents in my present job? Is this current job just a "Training ground" for eventual promotion to where God really wants me? Does my current job provide me a sense of accomplishment when I go home at the end of the day? Do I need more income to better provide for my family? Do I have hidden skills that I could use to earn extra income with? If you answered yes to more than two of these questions, then you may be working the wrong job. Before changing careers though you should also ask yourself with an honest heart, have I really given this job my best? Remember, that no matter which job you're currently involved in, God is your boss. You are to give your work your best, and perform your duties as unto the Lord. After all, God created work way back in the garden, when he gave Adam and Eve the responsibility of dressing the garden, and keeping it.

So if you decide to make the change, keep these few keys in mind to help you unlock the happiness, and satisfaction you're looking for.

Find employment that allows you to use your gifts,
   talents, and abilities to there fullest.
Project the nature of Jesus in your new work with Joy and Enthusiasm.
Learn everything you need to know about your new job, so you can do your best.
Quickly admit any mistakes you may make, and seek to correct them.
Don't be afraid to ask for help if you don't know how to perform the task at hand.
Give your new boss an honest day's work, for an honest days pay.
Do more than is expected of you, be a second mile employee.
Remember, That God is your Employer

Daily Verse: "With good will doing service, as to the Lord, and not to men."

Ephesians 6:7

FEAR OF PUBLIC SPEAKING

Rated high on the list of top ten fears, is speaking in front of other people. In fact in some surveys it's in the top three, right along with flying, and snakes. The fact of the matter is, very few people will ever have to make a career from public speaking. But everyone will be called upon from time to time to make a stand and speak while others watch. So for you that may be a little fearful about speaking in front of others, read this fantastic story about a public speaker who can't talk:

His name is Charlie Wedemeyer and he led the Los Gatos, California High school football team to their only state championship. That doesn't sound too impressive, unless you consider the fact that he is wheel-chair bound, and the only parts of his body he can move is his eyes, and mouth. Charlie has Lou Gehrig's disease. The disease has so affected him that speech doesn't even come from his lips. His faithful wife, Lucy, does his interpretation for him. Although, traveling is very difficult for Charlie, he and his wife Lucy are regular speakers at churches, prisons, schools, and company gatherings. They bring a powerful message of love, hope, and never give-up attitude, to wherever they are called upon to speak. Charlie's spirit proves that, the way of a winner is on the inside and not on the outside. Physical limitations do not have to decide whether you are on top or not. It's our attitude that makes us a winner or not. Charlie speaks and Lucy so vividly interprets and the world is little better, because it has heard from the only public speaker in the world who is unable to talk.

Daily Verse: "Now therefore go, and I will be with thy mouth, and teach thee what thou shall say."

Exodus 4:12

FEAR OF MENTAL BATTLES

It is my conviction that Satan is planning an all out attack against the minds of God's people as never before. He knows that all battles are won in the arena of the mind. He knows that if he can capture our minds, he can defeat us, and spoil our lives. But the good news is Satan does not have enough darkness to extinguish our light. Our light comes from the light of the world Jesus Christ. We must learn to live one day at a time.

Satan's greatest mental attacks come when he bombards your mind with negative thoughts; put downs, questions of God's intentions for your future, anxious thoughts, and just a flood of worries. When these attacks persist longer than a day, you need to know what God says about the mind. God promises in his word soundness of mind. (For God has not given us a spirit of fear; but of power, and love, and a sound mind. (II Timothy 1:7) When the devil begins to raise questions about potential problems or hurtful situations that may arise, you need to combat these thoughts with a renewing of the mind. Everyday feed your mind from God's word. Meditate on the scriptures, and memorize (hide them in your heart) them so that you won't sin against God.

You must learn to act, and not react to mental battles. David learned that he could run to his strong tower in times of trouble, which was God's Word. Whatever attacks you face you must find a scripture to counter attack. For instance if, your having financial attacks, meditate on scriptures that promise God's financial prosperity to his people. These scriptures will give you a base to stand on, so you won't fold under his constant pressure.

God has made you the custodian of your mind, and commanded you to take control of those two gates on both sides of your head known as ears. Get rid of anxious thoughts in a hurry, before they take root and begin to affect you.

Daily Verse: For God has not given us a spirit of fear, but of power, and love, and a sound mind.

II Timothy 1:7

FEAR OF STRESS

Stress is one of the most prevailing plagues of the twenty-first century. Our lives are so fast-paced it's like we live in a pressure cooker. Just living with the complexities of modern life can cause stress to reach epidemic proportions. Stress simply creates a physical, mental, and emotional strain. Stress is a factor that can affect the unbeliever, and believer alike. The Apostle Paul put it this way, "We were PRESSED out of measure." If left unchecked, stress can lead to several destructive symptoms such as stomach problems, heart problems, ulcers, migraines, hypertension, insomnia, high blood pressure, drug dependency, just to name a few.

So what is the cause of this deadly destroyer? Many things can cause stress, but the leading cause is simply meeting the demands of life and not getting enough rest and relaxation. When stress accumulates over a period of time, it can lead to the burn-out syndrome.

So what can we do to lighten the stress in our life? First look at the situations and circumstances that happen in your life from a Godly perspective. Is this problem too hard for God to help me with? I'm sure after you see things as God sees them you will put them in his hands. Then you must learn to pace yourself. Get out of the rush hour of life.

Too many times we are forced to sprint past God's beauty with a get it done yesterday mentality. Slow down or you will suffer the consequences of stress. Try to organize your daily schedule better. This will remove the clutter of trying to do too much. Also you will learn to not waste valuable time on low priority items. Some Christians believe that rest is a dirty word. Don't embrace the burn out for Jesus mentality; even Jesus knew the value of taking a break. Sometimes the most spiritual thing you can do in your life is take a nap. Then get back to fellowshipping with him in his word, and in prayer. Soon you will feel a release in your spirit as God's spirit floods your life with his peace, and stillness. Quality time spent with him is never time wasted. When Martha was getting all stressed out because her sister Mary was not helping her in the kitchen, do you remember what Jesus told her? "Martha, Martha, Mary has chosen the better thing," which was sitting at Jesus' feet and listening to every word he spoke.

Daily Verse: "Be anxious for nothing, but in everything by prayer and supplication, with thanksgiving, let your requests be known to God."

Philippians 4:6

FEAR OF RESPONSIBILITY

Today deadbeat dads have children all over town, with out the slightest concern for there welfare. Mothers, sad to say are leaving them, on door steps or in front of public assistance buildings. And yes there is an ever increasing population of people who don't want to work. What is the cause of this epidemic? Some people fear of taking responsibility for their actions. The Bible is very clear about responsibility, it says, if any man shall not work, neither shall he eat. That one thought alone leads me to a story of a man who has shirked responsibility; to the some of costing New York tax payers over a quarter of a million dollars and climbing.

This certain man goes into the finest restaurants in New York, He admits he likes to live good, then he orders a meal, and eats , then drinks a bottle of the finest wine, then when the check arrives, he just shrugs his shoulders, and tells them he doesn't have any money. So he patiently waits for the police to come and arrest him. Off to the slammer he goes where he can get a shower, a warm bed, and three squares a day. More than thirty-one times he has pled guilty to the charge of robbing a meal from some of the finest eateries. On one charge he spent over three months in the slammer. A good trade as far as he is concerned. Instead of sending him to jail maybe the judge should offer him a job, and really punish him. What has caused such a person, to not be willing to live a responsible life? Well I don't know if there is an answer to that question. In my experience of dealing with people, there just seem to be some people in this world who think the world owes them a living. They are totally dependent on the good will of other people for even the basic of necessities.

Maybe what Will Rogers the famous actor of yesteryear said is the culprit to our modern day dilemma, "There are two eras in American History; the passing of the buffalo, and the passing of the buck."

Daily Verse: "Let him that stole steal no more; but rather let him labour, working with his hands the things which is good, that he may have to give to him that needeth."

Ephesians 4:28

FEAR OF COMMITMENT

Commitment means to keep your word, no matter what. I'm sad to say that finding people who live committed lives is getting harder and harder. Today it is very easy to say one thing and do another. That doesn't mean its right; it just means it's too easy to get out of commitments. Today people stand before a holy God and make commitments to each other for better or worst, and within thirty days they are nullifying their commitments. People will promise you the world, just to get you to buy there product, only to be disappointed again with the terrible service, and quality. No so in Daniels day. This was a man who understood the power of commitment.

Daniel and his three friends were taken captive to Babylon while they were still in there teenage years. When asked to be promoted to the kings' service they were delighted, until they saw what was on the menu. If they were to serve the king, they were going to have to eat things that were unlawful for them to eat being Jews. So they prayed and talked to there keeper about not eating these abominable meats and they promised they wouldn't shirk there duties for lack of strength. Well God gave them favor, and the king liked the boys, so they grew up as some of his highest officials. Then one day when Daniel was an old man some of his competition decided they needed to get rid of him. They noticed that Daniel was committed to his prayer life, in fact three times a day he went to the window and prayed to his God. So they tricked the king into signing a decree that would punish anyone found praying to any other God, besides the king for thirty days. What did Daniel do? He went to his window three times a day and prayed to his God. You see we are to obey mans laws unless they conflict with God's laws. They had Daniel arrested for breaking the law. The punishment for such an offense was to be thrown into a den of hungry lions. Now instead of eating Daniel the lions kept him warm that night, until breakfast, but remember Daniel didn't know God would shut the mouth of the lions before he kept his commitments to Him. It's just who Daniel was.

You see when you begin to live a committed life it's who you become. Commitment becomes as natural as breathing. You don't think twice about doing the right thing because that's who you are. God has caused us to be human beings, not human doings.

Daily Verse: "Commit thy way unto the Lord; trust also in him; and he shall bring it to pass."

Psalm 37:5

FEAR OF BLINDNESS

Helen Keller once said," What's worse than being blind, is having eyes to see, but having no vision." So why do many of us wander through life completely unaware of the woes that go on around us? I myself found this startling reality out a few years back when my wife and I went on an anniversary cruise. It had been the first time we had really got away without the kids for ten years. We were very excited as we boarded the cruise ship. Things went alone fine until nightfall. Then the people on board the ship began to get intoxicated, after all without my knowing it I had booked us on a" party ship," that was nothing more than casinos and lounges. Oh well, we still had a good time just being with each other. But I believe God had ordered my steps with this divine appointment, so I could see how the hurting of this world were still trying to drown out there sorrows with another beer. I watched people intently try to "strike it rich" with one armed bandits only to leave with disappointment again. This woke me up to the mission field that God has placed around us.

The same thing happened to a man more than 137 years ago. Late one night while his wife rested for an early morning bible study, in which she was to be the teacher. He walked the streets of London. His journey took him down into the slums, where he noticed that about every fifth building was a pub. Most didn't care how old you were, if you had the money you could buy a bottle of gin. He saw little children climb the steps up into the pub and make there purchases. His heart began to break. Quickly, he ran home to wake up his wife and tell her he had found God's destiny for their lives. So in 1865 they opened, what they called at the time "Christian Mission" In the slums of London. Its soul purpose was to minister to the down and outers of society. His mission was to the people that everyone else would just ignore and walk by on any typical day. The hopeless ones that no one else wanted to be around. The founders of this great vision, were of course William, and Catherine Booth, who later renamed their project "The Salvation Army," Which now has members in the millions, and can be found in more than ninety- one countries worldwide. Wow! What a vision!

    Daily Verse: "Job said, I was eyes to the blind, and feet to the lame."

Job 29:15

FEAR OF CRISIS

    One day a pastor was called upon to comfort the bereaving widow of a close friend of his. As she sat in tears staring into the open with a blank stare, he persisted in giving her the textbook answers for why God would let such things happen to such a good man. She quickly rebuked him with this statement; "I don't need that kind of God, I don't need to understand all this, I need a God who is bigger than my mind." She is exactly right, in the midst of crisis, we don't need a friend. We need a God. So much endorsement today is put on "What a friend we have in Jesus," we have somewhat brought God down to the human level. Don't get me wrong, I know Jesus is my best friend, a friend, who sticks closer than a brother, according to the scriptures, but when I go to a doctor and they tell my I have a cancerous tumor, I don't want a friend who can only comfort me. I want a God who is able to reach down and touch my body in its point of need if he sees fit. Today many of us are like the plastic surgeon, who accidentally received a jolt, while trying to fix an examining room lamp. The shock of electricity sent his heart into erratic palpitations of over 160 beats a minute. He quickly, diagnosed himself as a potentially life threatening condition, and immediately prepared the defibrillator to shock his heart back into rhythm. He dragged himself on the table, and wiped petroleum jelly all over his chest, then gave himself two separate shocks of 100 watts. The feat was so powerful. It knocked him off the table unto the floor. Although, his heart began to beat regular again, an investigator for the case said he would have been much better off if he would have called 911 and asked for help. She went on to say, " . . . if he would have passed out after the first shock, he could have easily died."

Like this doctor, as soon as we enter into a crisis, we want to rely on ourselves, rather than call for help. Life can be extremely risky if you only depend on yourself for assistance. In a moment of crisis, we should immediately know that as the scripture says; "my help comes from the Lord."

Daily Verse: "He that trusteth in his own heart is a fool: but whosoever walketh wisely, he shall be delivered."

Proverbs 28:26

FEAR OF ACCUSATION

God's word pulls off the veil and allows us to see into the spirit realm on a few occasions. Look at what Satan said about Job who was one of God's most faithful followers.

"Doth Job fear God for nothing? Hast not thou made a hedge about him, and about his house, and about all that he hath on every side? Thou hast blessed the work of his hands, and his substance is increased in the land. But put forth thine hand now, and touch all that he hath, and he will curse thee to thy face." Again listen to what Zechariah the prophet saw in Zechariah 3:1; " . . . and he shewed me Joshua the high priest standing before the angel of the Lord, and Satan standing at his right hand to accuse him." Do you see a pattern here? Satan is always trying to get into God's presence to accuse you. Listen to what the second half of Revelation 12:10 has to say about Satan; " . . . for the accuser of our brethren is cast down, which accused them before our God day and night." Last night when you went to sleep to get some much needed rest, Satan didn't, he went to accuse you. Today when you woke up to start your day, Satan has already been at work looking for something to accuse you about. He is a persistent fellow isn't he?

Today he is the cause of so much malicious gossip, that people find it hard to trust one another. Even church people lived fractured lives because of the adversaries work. Relationships have been severed through criticism, and backbiting. And an all out spirit of mistrust is prevailing. So how is a man or woman to survive these attacks? How are you supposed to find a balance between surviving and pleasing God?

You must come to the realization that the battle will never be over until you learn to die to what people say about you. That may not be the answer you wanted to here, but it's the truth anyway. Learn to rely on the shelter of God's cross the way Jesus did. People were accusing him of all kinds of things as he hung on the cross, but he just hung there and, got along with them. In fact he prayed for them, because he understood that they were blind to the truth, else they wouldn't have done such an awful thing to an innocent man. The moment someone accuses you just remember the source, pick up the cross, and enjoy the immunity.

Daily Verse: "Blessed are they which are persecuted for right-eousness sake for theirs is the kingdom of heaven."

Matthew 5:10

FEAR OF PROVISION

Many people today believe prosperity and poverty are both matters of who you are born to, or if you are lucky enough to live in the right family. They falsely believe that some people were meant to be born poor, and some were meant to born rich. God shows us in the book of Exodus that he is able to provide for us, even in the middle of nowhere. Everyday when the children of Israel woke up there was fresh manna on the ground. All they had to do was gather it, grind it, and make bread. Can you imagine everyday for forty years, fresh manna on the ground? Where did it come from? They didn't know, they didn't even know what it was. The word manna means, "What is it?" All they knew was that it had the power to sustain them. It caused their shoes to grow with their feet; it was some pretty amazing stuff. Just as God could provide for them, he can provide for us the same.

You may be living in poverty or need right now. You may be in a financial wilderness as you read this and your heart could be troubled at the thought that it is not God's will for you to be there. If poverty were God's will for his children, He would not bring any of them out of their circumstances if it was godly to be poor. God would not have made all his former patriarchs very wealthy. If you don't have enough money to meet all your needs then by all means follow God's principles for his provision. God is able to change your poverty into prosperity in a matter of moments. He is able to take a few crumbs and turn them into a whole loaf.

In my own life, I can tell you of a time when God had someone pick us up at our house, and drive us to a small car lot, hand us the keys to an $11,000 mini van which someone, not involved with a church, bought for us. They paid tax, title, and even bought the license plate for us. Why did this happen? We learned God's principles for provision early in our Christian experience. We tithe 10 percent, give to needs, and sow into fertile soil. When you sow seeds, and expect a harvest to come from it, God will never let you down. Good sowing!

Daily Verse: "The liberal soul shall be made fat: and he that watereth shall be watered also himself."

Proverbs 11:25

FEAR OF EMERGENCY

Quick, call the fire department. Have you called 911 yet? What did the doctor say about that lump you found the other day? These are common phrases and questions asked by many people today. Our world we live in is a world that is filled with emergencies. It is a fast-paced world where we are all subject to the urgency of the moment. One moment you can be sitting at home watching television, and the next moment you could be standing outside watching your house burn to the ground, while your waiting on the fire department to arrive. In the same way we should be as urgent to discern the times we are living in today. Today, as we go through our busy days God's Word is being fulfilled before our very eyes. Reading the newspaper can be like reading the Bible. The first order of business to the busy twenty-first century dweller has to be to prioritize their life. Don't get caught up in all the stress of the times. Most of our time is spent dealing with the pressures and forces that work against us to prevent us from having productive, joyful lives. In all truthfulness, most of what we read about in the newspaper, or watch on television, are really battles over priorities. Satanic influence seeks to bog us down with unnecessary stress over what is going on all around us. This can lead us into reacting to the urgency, rather than the proper behavior which is to respond to felt needs.

God desires his people to live in this world for a period of years in hopes that they will leave a mark on it when they're gone. That's His ultimate will for your life. Leave the world a little better than you found it

Daily Verse: "No man that warreth entangleth himself with the affairs of this life; that he may please him who hath chosen him to be a soldier."

II Timothy 2:4

FEAR OF POWERLESSNESS

Money, fame, and power are the three most common goals for most people's lives. They think if they can just make enough money, they'll be happy the rest of their natural lives. That's what Charles Schwab thought, the president of one of the largest independent steel companies of the twenties. He died penniless. Jesse Livermore, the greatest 'bear' Wall Street ever saw, committed suicide. Leon Fraser, also committed suicide even though he was president of the Bank of International Settlement. Head of the world's greatest monopoly, Ivan Krueger, also took his own life unrepentantly. So if money isn't the answer, what about fame? Surely the famous are happy with their lives. I don't know about that either. An untold number of famous singers have gone through history as being either drug addicts, or alcohol abusers. Some famous singers in history have been so depressed that they even ending their lives. So being a movie star must be the answer. How many unhappy broken marriages and families do you have to have before we realize that fame isn't the answer either?

Power must be the key to happiness then. Well your idea of power, and the true, real power might be quite different. Alexander the Great, one of the world's most powerful men of his time, drank himself to death as a young man because he had no more places to conquer. He felt his life was over while he was in his thirties.

I think the best illustration of real power can be seen in New York City. Go to Fifth Avenue, stand in front of the RCA building. There you'll see a statue of Atlas, the Greek god. He is known as the most powerful man in the entire world. In the statue he is holding the world on his shoulders, and I might add he is straining under its weight. That's the way a lot of us live our lives thinking we have to do every-thing ourselves. Sometimes the weight of the world makes us feel like collapsing under the pressure. If this is you, then go across the street from the RCA building into St. Patrick's Cathedral. Go behind the great big high altar, where you'll find a statue of the boy Jesus, probably about eight years old. He also is holding up the world, but he is using only one hand, and I might add it is of no effort to him at all. The real key to our living a happy life in this world is to depend on Jesus for everything. Admit that you are totally powerless in yourself and in need of his constant attention. He is never too busy to help us hold up our part of the world.

Daily Verse: "If ye abide in me, and my words abide in you, ye shall ask what ye will, and it shall be done unto you."

John 15:7

FEAR OF HOPELESSNESS

It has been said that you can live your life without faith. Life will even go on without happiness, but as soon as hope is gone, your life is over. This is an appropriate statement.

One day a young man in his mid twenties sat with a gun in his lap. It was a small caliber 22, which he often used in his hunting escapades. He was contemplating ending his short, but discouraging life. He was the product of a broken home. His mother had moved to California, while he was in his mid-teens, and his dad had left him all alone to fend for himself. Soon he found he was homeless, left to the mercy of the elements. It was really hard at first, for it was Christmas time, and all were celebrating with their families while he was left to live under a bridge, just so he would have shelter. On particularly cold nights he would seek refuge in the back seat of some car which had been carelessly left unlocked - all alone in this world, just him, and his tattered blanket. As time passed and he grew, he was determined to make something of himself. He finished high school as a graduate. He went on to start his own business which was beginning to take off. He met a woman and had a child with her. Marriage was not a priority, being raised in the house of an atheist father. He commonly heard the phrase, "It's nothing more than a piece of paper," so he chose not to marry her. Now, here we are, back in the living room, with the pistol lying on his lap. His little girl has been snatched from his life as her mother moved on to another part of the country. After all, they didn't have that piece of paper between them. He is slumping to an all-time low. There is no hope for a better life. Everyone will always leave me, is the thought that runs through his mind. He goes as far as to pick up the pistol and spin the chamber looking at the bullets as they rotated by. Suddenly, the phone rings, should I answer it, is the quick thought that runs through his mind? So he gets up, and answers the phone. It's a young man, which he is fond of. This young man also lost his father to sickness when he was quite young. The young man asks, "What are you up to, are you busy?

"Ah, I'm not doing anything," was his reply.

"I have something for you, I built you a TV in electronics class, and I'm going to bring it up so we can watch this special show tonight."

The boy and the young man had shared an interest in science fiction programs, and there was a new show coming out, and the boy wanted to make sure the young man could watch it. As he hung up the phone, the thought went through his mind, somebody does care about me, so he put the gun away and waited for the arrival of the boy, which by the way ended up staying with the man for almost a week, because he sensed a unusual amount of pain in the mans life.

Who was the young man? It's the author of this book, and even now as I type these words tears are welling up in my eyes, remembering how that boy, Francis W. Burkhart saved my life. That was more than twenty years ago and next to God, and my lovely wife, Susie, he's still my best friend in this world.

Daily Verse: "Which hope we have as an anchor of the soul, both sure, and stedfast . . ."

Hebrews 6:19a

FEAR OF DISORDER

Order means the "accurate arrangement of things." You would not sleep in your garage, or think of parking your car in your bedroom. You don't mow your grass with a pair of scissors, or cut your hair with a lawnmower because of order. Order is doing the right thing, at the right time, in the right place. So, disorder means to break the proper flow of how things are supposed to work. Every one of us should fight to bring order into our lives every day. The enemy's process will be to disrupt the flow of order in your life. Order can be disrupted with the simple act of throwing your coat over a chair, or laying your dress on the bed, instead of hanging it up. How many of you have spent hours trying to find your car keys or cell phone. If you would simply have a place for them, and build a routine out of putting them there, you would find order. I am not a particularly neat person, but when my office gets cluttered I feel this agitation begin to erupt deep in my spirit. Then I must get up and take action to clean it. I know people who constantly search for bills, and then when they find them, they are late, so they begin to get a sour attitude with everyone around them. All this aggravation could have been avoided with a little order.

Someone has said you can tell how a persons mind is arranged by taking a look at their garage. Are the things just thrown in there, or are they neatly stacked and separated in there proper place. Many of us have been raised with busy, nonstop, disorganized lifestyles. We might have to use a little creativity to finding the proper order for our lives.

Some people will justifiably say I'm going to take my whole weeks vacation and get things in order around the house. This might be a commendable practice, but I promise you one week will not put your life in order. If you think that, you're better off spending your vacation with your family at the beach or something else just as relaxing. I suggest that you begin with small things like putting your clothes away after you wear them. Why not take your dishes to the dishwasher when you're done? How about opening the mail beside a wastebasket, and properly disposing of the junk mail and flyers before you even open it? Famous wealthy millionaires have learned the secret of simple order.

Donald Trump, one of the most successful men of our modern day once said, "I hired one woman whose entire job is to keep my life in order." Should we do any less if need be. Just how important is your life to you?

Daily Verse: "Seest thou a man diligent in his business? He shall stand before kings; he shall not stand before mean men."
Proverbs 22:29

FEAR OF FINISHING

It has been appropriately stated; there are many who start life enthusiastically, but few who finish with there head up. Quite frankly starting a project is the easy part. There's always lot's of vision at the beginning of a race, but usually about half through, reality sets in that there can be only one winner ,so many start to slow down and fade into the sunset. God is not pleased with starters. He is only pleased with those who have the tenacity to finish the course they began with him.

In 1883 John Roebling and his son, Washington, began an unthinkable feat. It was a seemingly impossible task to build a bridge that would connect the city of Brooklyn to Manhattan Island. Bridge experts at the time said it was impossible. John always one who loved a challenge decided to hire a crew and go to work with his son on the project.

After only a few strenuous months, an on site accident took the life John, and mortally wounded his son Washington. The accident left Washington unable to talk or walk. "That's it, the projects over, we knew it couldn't be built," said some of the engineers proudly. But what they didn't know was that Washington Roebling was no quitter. He lay in his hospital bed and developed a code by tapping on his wife's arm what he wanted to say. Soon they were back in full production with Washington just tapping away how he wanted it done, and his wife interpreting his instructions. Washington tapped out instructions for more than 13 years, until the bridge was finished, and received its final christening. Finishers get the job done no matter what the obstacles or how long it takes. Jesus was a finisher, and he taught that sometimes the road God selects for us is not always paved with roses and comfort, but if we will finish our course we will find satisfaction in him.

   Daily Verse: "I have fought the good fight, I have finished my course, I have kept the faith."

II Timothy 4:7

FEAR OF SURRENDER

Have you ever tried to rescue a drowning man? Any good life-guard worth their salt knows that when a person is drowning they are dangerous. If you approach them in their state of panic, they are quite capable of dragging you to the bottom with them. They don't care how well you can swim, or how much you know about swimming, all they care about is being saved from drowning.

Any experienced lifeguard will wait until the person is done thrashing, sometimes only an arm's length away. Then when they are finished, and they realize they can't help them self, the lifeguard reaches out, and pulls them to safety. In the same way God totally waits, sometimes only an arm's length away, until we are done making a mess of our existence. Then he steps in and grabs us sometimes from the muck and mire of sin, and completely cleans us off, as he sets us on solid ground. Some people have such a fear, in surrendering their complete lives to the master. They don't trust him to keep them completely safe. They fear he will take things away from them that they like. For the most part some of these fears are true. He will take away your desire for illicit behavior. He also removes the desire to want to self-destruct your life with drugs, alcohol, and all the host of other bondages.

If you are truly surrendered to God, you will never be aware of your own effort to remain surrendered. Your entire life will be completely consumed with the One in whom you are surrendered to. You are only totally surrendered to God, when you give yourself to him as much as he gave himself to you. John 3:16 says that God so loved the world that he gave his only begotten son, that whoever believes in him will not perish but have eternal life.

God's surrender to us is shown in His allowing His Only Son to be put to death on a cruel cross so that we could once again have fellowship with Him. Do you know of a greater surrender? If Jesus was willing to die for us, should we not be willing to live for Him?

Daily Verse: "Peter began to say to Him, See, we have left all and followed You."

Mark 10:28

FEAR OF ECONOMIC COLLAPSE

It's so amazing how quickly time passes, just a few short years ago the whole world was in such a stir about what was called the Y2K. Scriptures were being poured out like water; People were capitalizing from the impending possible doom of a full scale computer crash. The effect of which could send the United States into third world country status overnight, according to some reports. People were buying up gold, and other precious metals in hopes of having trading clout, when the paper money system was sure to fail. Stockpiles of food, water, and other emergency supplies were hoarded up, should the stores be force to close. Was I worried? Well maybe a little, not to point of stockpiling a years worth of supplies. We bought a kerosene heater for a heat source. Stored about ten gallons of water, and some extra camping gear to cook, and see with. Oh yes, we put away a few can goods, like we always do. What can keep you from going into a panic of the future of our economy? You must know who your source is. When the economy fell in the Old Testament, God sent a raven to feed His man of God - maybe from the kings table, who knows. When a famine threatened to wipe out the existence of God's people in Genesis, He always sent them to Egypt for supplies. Egypt has always been a type of the world. Scripture does say, "The world or (sinner) will gather wealth to give to God's people. But to the sinner he giveth travail, to gather and to heap up, that he may give to Him that is good before God" (Ecc. 2:26b).

With this in mind why would you fear what is going to happen in our economy? If you are faithful to God's economy then what or who shall you fear? So what, the stock market isn't earning money, God's stocks have never went down. You say that real estate prices are plummeting, so what scripture states that God owns the whole earth and he sure isn't worried about what one little plot of land is worth. Don't get me wrong, I'm not advocating that we abandon all caution about our finances, what I am saying is whether there is a financial ruin or not, God is, and always will be in complete control. He knows how to get resources to his people in need. Maybe we will have to tighten our belts, and loose a little weight, but most of us could stand a little bit of that anyhow.

> *Daily Verse: "A good man leaveth an inheritance to his children's children: and the wealth of the sinner is laid up for the just."*
>
> *Proverbs 13:22*

FEAR OF VIOLATION (RAPE)

What a terrible tragedy to be violated by someone else. To have someone put you in the place of an animal, as they force themselves upon you. Today rape is in record proportions. It is especially popular among our teen age society. Is it no wonder, a recent Roper poll revealed that seventy-two percent of all teenagers that admitted to having sexual intercourse, did it in the homes of their parents or partners. Sixty percent said their parents knew it was going on, and said nothing. The rapid increase of pornography in magazines, and on the internet has lead to a creation of sexual monsters, barely out of puberty. Even scripture is not silent about this terrible feat of violation.

It records that one of David's sons named Amnon had a crush on his half sister named Tamar. He secretly plotted a way to fake a sickness to get out of his daily responsibilities. Then he requested that his sister Tamar come to his house, and fix him something to eat. She gladly obliged since she was a pretty innocent teenager. After she prepared her step brother something to eat, she politely called for him to come and eat. He cunningly called for her to feed him in bed, pretending to be too sick to get out of bed. Quickly, he demanded that all the servants leave as Tamar fed him. They left, and when she came to the bedside, he grabbed her and forced himself upon her. She pleaded with him not to do this wickedness, but he ignored her cries for mercy, trying to fulfill the lust that was burning so hot within him. As soon as he was finished with her, his passion turned from lust to hatred. He couldn't stand to look at her, anymore, so he demanded she get out of his presence immediately. In those days if a woman was violated in this manner, and the man wouldn't marry her, she was considered an outcast, and could not marry afterward. She was forced to live out her life at her brother Absalom's house, and not take a husband. What happened to the young man Amnon? Absolutely nothing, until about two years later when all of David's children were at a feast, and Absalom had his servant take Amnon's life while he was getting merry on wine.

Today, very liberal laws and the promiscuous lifestyles so many people live, make it is almost impossible to prove this offence in a court of law. If you have been victim to such an atrocity, as rape, or fear that you will be, my heart goes out to you. There is no justice; you could punish someone with that could make up for your pain. Take comfort in the words of the Apostle Paul as he wrote to the Romans. He certainly was no stranger to suffering. For I reckon that the sufferings of this present time are not worthy to be compared with the glory which shall be revealed in us. Because the creature (us) itself also shall be delivered from the bondage of corruption into the glorious liberty of the children on God (Romans 8:18, 21).

Daily Verse: "For this is the will of God, even your sanctification that you should abstain for fornication."

I Thessalonians 4:3

FEAR OF THE SECOND COMING

One day there was a man, who was a good man; he just didn't want anything to do with church, God, or anything spiritual. He faithfully brought his wife, who was a devoted Christian lady to church every week. They lived a reasonably far distance from the church, so he chose to sit in the car and read the Sunday paper, while she did what he considered her weekly duty. On one particular Sunday, something happened. Instead of the usual noise, as he called it, usually coming from the church, he heard dead silence. He waited for about thirty minutes past the usual time, and then he slowly meandered up to the building to put his ear as close to the stained glass window as he could. He heard nothing, there was complete silence. He could have heard a pin drop that is if somebody was in there to drop one. He wondered where everyone went, as he went back to the car. He waited another thirty minutes, looking at his watch every two seconds. Finally, the suspense was killing him. "Oh, no, that rapture thing must have happened that Betty is always talking about and I've been left behind. Oh my!" he said as he burst through the church doors and into the sanctuary. To his amazement, everyone was still there. They were all on their knees praying that God would touch his heart, and lead him to salvation. A quiet hush settled on the congregation that lasted more than an hour. The man was in such a state of panic, he didn't even stop at the door, he boldly walked down the aisle of the little church and found a place at the altar beside his wife, as he asked her how to give his life over to Christ. The man was gloriously saved that day.

Do you fear you will be left behind at the return of Christ? You don't have to fear. Jesus tells us in the gospels, that those who are His will go with Him when He returns for His church. Today there is much debate, as to whether you will go in the rapture, before, during, or after, the tribulation. This should not be near as much concern for Christians as it is. What you should be concerned about is whether you're going or not. Not when it is. Are you ready should the trumpet of Gabriel blow today? If your answer is 'no,' then make yourself ready by confessing your sins right now to God, and putting on the robe of righteousness so you will have something to wear in the next life. Good flying.

Daily Verse: "Watch therefore, and pray always, that ye may be accounted worthy to escape all these things that shall come to pass, and to stand before the son of man."

Luke 21:36

FEAR OF BEING UNSATISFIED

For many decades God's people have felt that they should have just enough food to eat, and the simplest clothes to wear. There was a misconception that if they barely made it, they would be considered holy. Somehow poverty became the measuring stick for spirituality. It was a sign that you were dead to this world, and had a REAL love for God. I'm writing today, to tell you nothing could be farther from the truth. In fact, you're going to have to search another Bible, other than the one I read to find one of God's people in the Old Testament that wasn't well off.

Instead, we have sat back, and allowed immoral rock singers, and others like to control all the wealth. As they write songs about how they get no satisfaction. It's no wonder they can't find satisfaction. It's not in money, jewelry, gold, mansions, fancy cars or stuffed bank accounts. Satisfaction is found only in the person of Jesus Christ. Many people fear they will miss the world and the things of the world if they turn their lives over to God. They fear he will leave them empty and in need. Listen to me dear one, God is able to meet every need. Do you need a friend? He's the only true one. Do you need him to help you with your finances? He owns the cattle on a thousand hills and shares them liberally with his children. Do you need the proper spouse? He is able to lead you right in the path of the perfect person, after all He knows everyone, and knows who will be just right for you. In my own life, I had this huge empty void, not being able to find the right mate, and I was almost thirty years old. I gave my heart to Christ, and fell so in love with Him, that He filled that empty void. He decided to share my heart with someone else, so he put my lovely wife Susie right in the front pew of our church, we were both attending at the time. I think he wanted to make sure I didn't miss her, because He sat her right in front of me every week. Soon we were in love and starting a new family. Since then I've found satisfaction.

When God is the satisfaction of your heart, then He will share His other wealth with it. God doesn't care how much stuff you have, He just doesn't want the stuff to have you. When He tests you and can find out that you can be trusted with things, then they will materialize in your life. God is a good father, and knows just when your ready for the right thing. So let Him lead you into maturity, and enjoy Him.

Daily Verse: "Surely goodness and mercy shall follow me all the days of my life: and I will dwell in the house of the Lord forever."

Psalm 23:6

FEAR OF CIRCUMSTANCES

One day I asked a parishioner, "How are you doing John (not his real name)?"

He snapped back "I'm doing pretty good I guess, under the circumstances."

I quickly replied, "What are you doing under there?"

The unnecessary fact of society is most people are living under their circumstances. Even Christian people, have a gloomy look on there face, more than they should. Have you ever noticed that life is lot like baking a cake, not that I'm any expert in cake baking, since I personally have never baked one. But, I know you have many ingredients; flour, shortening, eggs, sugar, baking powder, vanilla, and any other flavoring you might want to add. It doesn't matter how much quality you have for each ingredient it you try to eat them alone they taste terrible. But, you put them all together and mix them just right, place them in an oven, for just the right time, and out comes a delicious treat.

Just as in most of our lives, much of what we call natural life is tasteless. Some of it may even taste rather horrible. But if you trust God with your life, He is able to take all the ingredients of your life, (your circumstances) and mix them together just right to make a banquet out them, fit for a king.

Settle it in your heart today, that for you the word happenstance doesn't exist. You have been carefully selected by the Master to endure, whatever life throws at you. Trust that you are carefully being baked in the "refiners' fire," so that what will come out is a finished product, that any person would be proud to be. You are not alone in the midst of your heartache. God's compassionate heart aches too.

When Jesus called Paul, who was Saul at the time, into the ministry, here were his words, found in Acts 9:4: "Saul, Saul, Why persecutest thou me?" What was Saul doing at the time that could actually be considered persecution to Almighty God? He was taking a stand against Christians. In fact, he was having them arrested and some even put to death in the name of God. He stood and held the coats of those who previously stoned Stephen to death in Acts 8. And this was to be no exception, he was on his way to Damascus to bring persecution against the church there when Jesus knocked him off his feet, and blinded him in this natural world. In that blinded state he learned to depend on Jesus for his every move. In fact, his next words, after he found out who was responsible, were, "What will thou have me to do, Lord?" These should be our words also when life throws a curve ball at us trying to strike us out.

Daily Verse: *"Thou wilt keep him in perfect peace, whose mind is stayed on thee: because he trusteth in thee."*

Isaiah 26:3

FEAR OF SIN

St. Augustine has appropriately stated, "The punishment of sin is sin." Sin is simply any disobedience against God's word. We are all born into a contaminated state known as a sinner. This is the reason for the necessity of the new birth. This puts us in another position with God. We are removed from our slave (to sin) status; to a child of God, received by an adoption, into his family. That one act, removes the power of sin (death) from your life.

Although, rebirth removes the power on sin, it doesn't remove the deceptiveness of sin. When I think of how deceptive sin is, I think of a plant known as the Venus Fly Trap. This flower admits a sweet odor that any unwary fly can't resist. Its beautiful crimson-tipped leaves spread open real wide to make the treat more inviting. Suddenly an unsuspecting fly crawls inside looking for a delicious morsel of nectar, only to find itself trapped by the hair like sticky substance. Finally the pedals close, and it's all over for the unsuspecting victim. A couple hours later the pedals will open up again, ready for another prey, with only the husk left of the last meal.

That's much the way sin is; it invites us in, promising us the world, with all of its glamour and show, only to leave a husk of what was our former life we had. Sin always promises more than it gives. Of course, the Bible even states that there is "pleasure in sin for a season." But when that season is over, you will be awfully disappointed.

Are you afraid of sin? If Christ does not reside in your heart, you should be. It still has dominion over you, to get you to act in its 'beck and call.' Then with the power it has over your life, it can drag your soul to hell, when your days on this earth are finished. But if Christ resides in your heart, sin has no more power over you. You have the authority to resist any sin that can come against you.

Even your flesh (human nature) has to obey what you tell it to do. When you are submitted to God, you can resist the devil, and he must leave you alone, for a season anyway.

Daily Verse: The soul that sinneth, it shall die."

Ezekiel 18:20a

FEAR OF DEBT

Debt is a spirit. A spirit that is very able to put you in a feeling of hopelessness. You feel as if you are aimlessly drifting in a river that has no end, and you have no paddle to fight the current with. In the Old Testament, debt was the only reason to be put in prison, according to God's law. In fact, in the book of Second Kings we have the story of an old prophet's wife, who was about ready to lose everything she had, including her sons to debtors' prison. Here we have a faithful widow, who has accumulated so much debt, for whatever reason, she is about to lose her only means of support, her two sons. Along comes the prophet Elisha, and he wastes no time in asking her, "What do you want me to do for you? And what do you have in your house?"

She starts to think in terms of a natural sense and answers, "Nothing," then she adds, " . . . except a pot of oil."

"That's enough," the prophet says. When you have the Holy Spirit (represented by the oil) you have all you need to conquer any spirit. Remember I told you that debt was a spirit in the beginning.

The prophet gave her specific instructions on how to borrow, which was something she had the ability to pay back (vessels). Then, she shut the door on doubt, and she and sons began to poor the oil into the vessels. Notice that the oil flowed as long as she had vessels to fill. The lesson being that God has more than enough resources to get you out of debt, if you have the sense enough to stay out of it, afterwards.

She paid all of her debts with the oil, and had enough left over to live on.

How about you? Is the joy gone from your life because of debt? Wake up child of God; you know deep down in your spirit that God wants more for you than to barely exist from payday to payday.

Make no mistake about it your deliverance will be a progressive walk with him. You must retrain your mind into thinking, without using credit for every situation. Once a drastic change takes place in your thinking, then you can begin the simple steps to payoff the debt that exists. Search the scriptures for in them are answers to amazing debt cancellation principles. According to scriptures the only debt God wants you to have is the debt of love.

Daily Verse: "Owe no man anything, but to love one another; for he that loveth another hath fulfilled the law."

Romans 13:8

FEAR OF DOCTORS

Since the time of the middle ages man has feared the practice of medicine. Maybe even before that, who knows for sure? But the startling truth is God is behind the great advancement physicians have taken in recent years. Some would disagree that God has the power to heal as he chooses, and has no need for medical science. I wholeheartedly agree that God has the power to perform miracles even in this day. Although, I also know that God is Sovereign, and he still has the final say so over my health, no matter how much I claim healing, in my body.

God is not threatened by the practice of medicine in the slightest, in fact on several occasions; he prescribed medicine as the cure for sickness. One of such occasions is neatly tucked away in the book of Second Kings chapter twenty. Hezekiah, one of Judah's few good kings, had a sickness. The prophet Isaiah was given a word from the Lord to deliver to the king personally. He walked into the king's court and said these words, "Set thine house in order; for thou shall die, and not live." After delivering the message of impending doom, he turned and without any further instructions. Hezekiah was deeply hurt by the prophet's words of discouragement. So with tears in his eyes, he turned his face to the wall and prayed a thirty-five word prayer, which so touched the Lord's heart, that before Isaiah got out of the palace he was sending him back with another message. Isaiah returned and told the king that God had heard him, and decided he was going to give him fourteen more years of life, then he gave these instructions. In verse 7 he says, "Take a lump of figs, and place it on the boil." When they did as instructed, Hezekiah was later totally healed from the practice of medicine.

When I think about doctors I'm reminded of the story of the little boy who was playing in a woodpile, and got a splinter in his finger. Quickly, he ran to his mother to show her his problem. She went to get her needle from the sewing box that she had used of several occasions to remove splinters. When he saw the needle he yelled, "No, I want God to take the splinter out, and I want him to do it all by Himself." You see he knew if mom did it, it would hurt coming out; experience had taught him this. Mom waited, and waited maybe a couple hours or more. The little finger began to get red, and sore, and then she proceeded to take the needle and remove the little distraction. While removing the splinter she taught the little boy this lesson. Sometimes God uses others to perform his work, and sometimes it hurts a little. Don't fear spending time with one of God's servants, should the need arise.

Daily Verse: "But unto you that fear my name shall the Sun of righteousness arise with healing in his wings; and ye shall go forth."

Malachi 4:2

FEAR OF WEAKNESS

Fighting spiritual battles can be quite taxing. If fact they can leave you feeling drained, and empty on the inside, desperately needing a refill. Some people fear that if they let their weakness show they will be taken advantage of, whether it is spiritual or natural. Scripture claims that even young people would grow weary of life, and fall by the wayside. So what is our main problem that keeps us drained? Pride is the culprit my dear one. When you don't admit your weakness, you open a path of problems that the enemy just loves to block. Pride is what kept a naive school teacher from checking with the Better Business Bureau first, before investing her life savings in a scam investment with a swindler. Later, after all her investment was gone, and the agent couldn't be found, she approached the Bureau. They asked if she had ever heard of the Bureau before. She replied that she had known all about it, all along. They politely asked why in the world didn't you come to us first to find out if the business was legit. Her answer was "I was too afraid, I thought maybe you would tell me not to do it."

Is this not how many treat God's Word, they don't read it for fear of what it may tell them to do.

God's Word claims that weakness is not to be feared, but instead to be admired. Paul the apostle, in the book of II Corinthians chapter twelve tells of an incident in his own life that became quite distressing to him. He states that because of the abundance of revelation God has shared with him, a messenger of Satan came into his life to buffet him. He tells us of his pleas with God, three as a matter of fact, to remove this thorn in his flesh. Listen to God's response to his cries for help. "My grace is sufficient for thee, for my strength is made perfect in WEAKNESS."

Paul's comment to the Lord's answer is that he would rather glory in his infirmities so that more of God's power would be allowed to enter his life. As with us when we force pride to get off the throne of our lives, and quit trying to always, "figure it out," we give God the permission he's waiting on to take charge. Then we will be able to boldly claim like the apostle Paul, "When I am weak, then I am strong."

Daily Verse: "He giveth power to the faint; and to them that have no might He increaseth strength."

Isaiah 40:29

FEAR OF RECONCILIATION

Reconciliation is a big word that simply means "to settle a fight . . . to put an end to a quarrel." Scripture pulls no punches, when it tells us to do it now. Agree with thy adversary quickly, was the words of our Lord Jesus Christ in the gospel of Matthew. You see we are not afforded the luxury to sit around and stew over conflicts we have with our fellow man. We (Christians) have a job to do on this planet among the human race. It's been given to us as a command from our master. He has in trusted us to be ministers of reconciliation. We are to reconcile lost man back to God, by means of our public witness. Read the words of Paul, "And all things are of God, who hath reconciled us to himself by Jesus Christ, and hath given us the ministry of reconciliation."

We have a special call, all of us, to reconcile this lost humanity back to God.

Now as for us, we walk around, and want to make sure all of our rights are met. This is a natural thing, it's just being human. But reconciliation is not a human thing, it's a God thing. Only God has the ability to change us to the point where we can be effective at this ministry.

In the book of Genesis there's the story of two brothers who were twins. One was a hunter and his daddies pick of the two. The other was a mommy's boy who liked to stay around the tent and cook. Now the older, whose name was Esau, decided to go hunting one day and the venture proved unsuccessful. On his way back from the field he stopped by the tent to see what was cooking, after all he was hungry after a hard days hunt. His brother Jacob was fixing a pot of lentils (beans). Esau quickly asked for a bowl before he starved to death. Jacob demanded that he trade his birthright, as being the firstborn for the bowl. He unthinkingly did, and that launched a string of deceits between these two brothers that would separate them for more than twenty years. After a twenty year stay in a foreign land Jacob tries to return home, but soon learns that his brother and four hundred of his men are coming out to meet him. In fear he sends a generous gift on ahead to meet with his brother, and goes off alone to pray and ask for God's favor. That night he wrestled all night with the Angel of the Lord, and wouldn't let him go until he blessed him. Finally at daybreak the Angel changes his name from Jacob (Deceiver) to Israel (He that rules with God) and gives him the favor he's striving for. He was a changed man; he even walked with a limp afterwards. Then he began doing what God had wanted him to do all alone reconcile the nations. You see God has the time to wait on you.

If you have someone with whom you have anger in your heart toward, confess it quickly and move on into the ministry God has called you to, and do not fear what man can do to you.

Daily Verse: To wit, that God was in Christ, reconciling the world unto himself, not imputing their trespasses unto them, and hath committed unto us the word of reconciliation."

II Corinthians 5:19

FEAR OF EMBARRASSMENT

Have you ever embarrassed yourself to know end. Preachers are notorious for saying some of the silliest things from the pulpit. I'm tempted to tell you of my most funny blunder from the sacred desk, but I've been embarrassed enough by that one already. I'm sure if I were to ask you what you're most embarrassing moment was. Instantly without hesitation it would pop into your mind.

We tend to remember those times, I think in hopes of not repeating them. The problem is that some people use them for excuses of why they can't do this or that. They are too afraid to make a mistake again.

I remember reading about the famous evangelist D. L. Moody,

who taught many a young man how to preach. He would take his young protègès aside just before they took the pulpit. Those watching this gesture of the great mentor would kindly think, "What a responsible man of God to take his young men and pray with them before they delivered the words of the Almighty." In reality what he was doing with them was to make sure that before they stood to preach, they checked there zipper. He would say, "Young man it doesn't matter how anointed you are, or how powerful the words you're speaking are, if your zipper is in the south position you'll lose the audience." It's hard to recover after an embarrassment like that.

Overly shy people tend to shrink within themselves, and just turn red faced when caught in embarrassing situations. They tend to act like the cat that got burned on a hot stove. He will never get burned again, because he won't even approach a cold stove now. If you have been embarrassed in the past and you feel immobilized to do the things you want to do. I always say

"Go ahead take a chance, in a hundred years nobody will remember."

Daily Verse: My flesh and my heart faileth: but God is the strength of my heart, and my portion forever.

Psalm 73:2

FEAR OF UNWORTHINESS

Have you ever felt a deep sense of unworthiness? This is not always a bad thing. In fact repentance is what leads us to unworthiness. Even when John the Baptist the great preacher of repentance was approached by Jesus to be baptized, he quickly blurted out, "I need to be baptized by you, and you come to me." Later when he preached about Jesus' unfailing mission he stated, "There is one among you, whose sandals I am not worthy to untie" A deep sense of unworthiness led him to be known as the greatest prophet who ever lived, according to the words of Jesus. John knew what many of the bible heroes knew, Jesus cannot come into our life and do a work in us a long as we have anything in his way hindering his hand. He desires to do things for us if WE can move. Paul understood this principle of unworthiness to the point where he even stated that his life was not even his own anymore. If fact it wasn't even his faith he was living out. Read the words of Galatians 2:20; "I am crucified with Christ: nevertheless I live; yet not I, but Christ lives in me: and the life which I now live in the flesh I live by the faith of the Son of God, who loved me, and gave himself for me"

Only when you come to the point in your life to absolute unworthiness can you begin to live out the faith of God. After all he is the only one who really knows what your worth anyway.

Whenever I think of understanding value and the true worth of something my mind races back to a story I once read. It's about a man who was a gem dealer. He decided to visit a mineral show one day. As he slowly walked along not really wanting to purchase anything, he noticed a large blue-violet stone about the size an orange. Being an expert, his heart began to race as he saw a fifteen dollar price tag on it. He calmly questioned, "You want fifteen dollars for this stone?" The clerk looked at the rock in its raw state, and noticed it wasn't near as pretty as the other stones in the display case, so he lowered the price to a mere ten dollars. It was quickly purchased, and later certified as a 1,905 carat, natural star sapphire. Its appraisal value was later determined as more than two and a quarter million dollars. Only someone who has a powerful love for gems would have been able to recognize the value of that stone. In the same tune, only a lover of souls knows the true value of people like you and me. He knows that our value is way more than a few million dollars.

Daily Verse: Fear ye not therefore, ye are of more value than many sparrows.

Matthew 10:31

FEAR OF A PHYSICAL HANDICAP

Julie was like any other typical thirteen year old girl. She was a little embarrassed to have her friends around her parents. She made every effort she could to keep them away from her mom, for she was really embarrassed with her mom's appearance. It wasn't that she was ugly, but that she was disfigured to some degree. She had these awful burn scars that covered both arms, and ran up one side of her face. It made her look grotesque in Julie's young mind. And what made Julie really upset, was that her mom never tried to hide the scars at all. One day in a moment of need, Julie finally worked up the courage to ask her mom how she had received those horrible scars. Something she had never been able to ask before. Her mom loving said "Oh, my dear, the scars came at a time when you were just a baby. I was doing the dishes one day, and you were in your playpen, playing with your toys as you normally did when some how you must have knocked your blanket into an electric space heater that was too close to your playpen. I heard you laugh, and came to see what was going on, suddenly I saw you standing in the midst of roaring flames, which soon engulfed your whole body. Without thinking, I threw my body into the flames wrapped a blanket around you, and pulled you back through them. Unfortunately, my clothes caught fire, and my hair burned from one side of my head. The fire badly burned my skin, before I was able to get my clothes off. I spent several months in the hospital receiving skin graphs and having my burns cared for. Honey, I never talked to you about it before, because, I didn't want you to blame yourself for my scars.

When we see people that bare the scars of this unpredictable life we live, we should not shun them or be distracted by their appearance. We should remember that we have a Lord and Savior, who still bares the scars of our sin. Yes, he has braved the fires on hell and the pain of death, so we would not be left marked by our wrong deeds. His body is still marked - his hands, his feet. There still remains a scar in his side where the Roman soldier thrust his spear through. He chose to take these physical handicaps in his body, because of his love for us.

Daily Verse: "For it became him, for whom are all things, and by whom are all things, in bringing many sons unto glory, to make the captain of their salvation perfect through sufferings."

Hebrews 2:1

FEAR OF DISHONOR

It has been stated throughout scripture, by numerous writers that honor is to be treasured. In fact one writer claimed that a good name is worth more than gold. You can buy more gold, but can't buy your good name back. Dishonor is correctly hailed as bringing shame, or disgrace to someone's name.

History records that one day our great president Abraham Lincoln sat down to his desk to write a letter to a woman who had lost five sons to the horrors of the civil war. He consoled her in her loss, and commended all her boys as heroes. When the truth was found out, only two of her sons had actually died in battle. Two were coward deserters, and one was a prisoner of war, who was later returned to his mother. Reporters found out about the letter and criticized Lincoln for his misinformation. Lincoln then commented that he was not misinformed. "Mrs. Bixby did lose all five of her sons to the war. Does it really matter if two deserted and two were killed, and one was captured in defeat? I felt she deserved some token for all the pain she has endured." After all what possible good would it have done for him to smear her son's names?

Don't let the mistakes of the past chain you in a prison of defeat. Take the bible and smash the locks on all the hurts, and disappointments of yesterday. Realize that today, is the first day of the rest of your life. Choose to make a connection with those around you and establish the relationships necessary to heal your pain. Become a friend of God, for he can remove any wrong that we may have committed. Remember God has faith in you, for he has entrusted his reputation to your hands. We have the awesome responsibility of holding his name up before a world that is out of sync with him. Let this be our quest.

Daily Verse: "Remember ye not the former things, neither consider the things of old. Behold I will do a new thing; now it shall spring forth; shall ye not know it?"

Isaiah 43:18

FEAR OF RESTLESSNESS

Thousands maybe millions of people suffer from an uneasiness about life. Unable to relax, they live in a constant state of disturbance. Rarely are they given to being still and quiet. What's the cause for all the disrupted lives? Many things, some people are prone to being overly busy, because of the type of personality they are.

Even Jesus the son of God realized that natural bodies need rest. After a particularly hard days ministry, in Mark 6:31, Jesus says "Come ye yourselves apart into a desert place, and rest awhile."

He and his disciples had been so busy ministering to the needs of others, they couldn't find any time to rest or even eat. Jesus was telling his disciples to come apart, before they come apart. Some people feel they are so important to their job, that they can't even take a vacation. Are you one of these types of people? Do you think you're that important?

Job had this feeling too - questioning why things were happening to him. God sharply rebuked him, and asked him how many stars did he create? He asked Job, where he was when God was setting the boundaries of the oceans, and creating the angels. In short, God wanted to know who was in charge, He or Job. I ask you today, are you so important that you can't take a break? What was God doing before you came along? I promise you he can get along without you for awhile. He is quite capable of holding things together.

I speak from experience; I used to be a workaholic. I would never leave my church for fear that something would happen while I was away. And on some occasions, things did happen while I was away.

But a real reality settled into my life the day I was walking my oldest daughter down the isle, to give her away in marriage. I looked at her as beautiful as she was, all dressed in white, and the thought rushed through my mind, "Well she's gone now, and I never did anything with this child." I left that day unhappy with my past performance as a father. Since that day, although too late for her, I have taken my family on regular yearly vacations every year, building memories that will long outlast their childhood.

Daily Verse: "Come unto me, all ye that labour and are heavy laden, and I will give you rest."

Matthew 11:28

FEAR OF DISAPPOINTMENT

If you journey with God very long, only one thing about the adventure that will be crystal clear. He is faithful to complete the work in you that he started. The first thing we must get straight is, we really don't know ourselves. We are quick to spot envy, greed, laziness, and pride in others, but fail to see the same qualities in our own life. We think we understand the difficulties, and struggles of others, and then God opens our eyes and shows us the same shortcomings in our own life. The truth is, there are vast areas of rebellion, and stubbornness very much alive in each of our lives. God can't teach us anything until he quiets down the raging voice that is always talking in our heart. You must get rid of the idea that you understand yourself. Usually that is the last bit of pride to leave your heart. Intellectual pride is usually the hardest to get rid of.

For this reason, God creates disappointments and difficulties in our lives to remove any conceit that may exist. Sometimes we are slow to allow him to work, so he takes his time, and the struggle could last a considerable while. When God finally manages to get us alone through sufferings, heartbreaks, disappointments, or any such difficulties, then he can begin to speak to us. When we finally have nothing else to say, then God can teach us what he wants to. With this in mind don't be so quick to rebel against his action in your life.

The disciples were very confused at Jesus' teachings. Two of them wanted the two highest seats of honor in his kingdom. One was a thief, stealing from the ministry treasury. And of course Peter was stuffed full of pride. They didn't understand hardly anything about Jesus' real mission until after he resurrected from the dead. The big disappointment of losing him opened their eyes to his real purpose. In much the same way God has set up disappointments for each of us to teach us our real mission in life.

Daily Verse: "We know that all things work together for the good to those who love God, and are called according to his purpose."

Romans 8:28

FEAR OF PUNISHMENT

Why me Lord, why are you punishing me? These are the words of someone who doesn't really understand about the Lord. I was in that position once in my life. The devil kept telling me that God was afflicting me, and punishing me for something I was doing wrong in my life. At times he had me thinking that I was being punished for my thoughts. Then one day it hit me, what would be the purpose in God punishing me for something I never did?

In Bible times many had the same misconceptions about God. As Jesus was walking along one day he noticed a man who was blind. The disciples misinterpreted the cause of the man's blindness. One of them asked, "Who sinned, the man or his parents that caused him to be born blind?"

Jesus responded, "Neither one was the cause of his blindness, but this blindness was so that God's miracle working power could be made manifest." Then he anointed the man's eyes with clay, moistened with his own saliva. He commanded that the man go wash in the pool of Siloam. When the man did so, he was totally healed. Later, he was subjected to an all out interrogation by the Pharisees. He responded by teaching them that Jesus had to be of God in order to do such miracles. This offended the Pharisees, and they left him alone.

Settle it in your heart today that God is not punishing you for your wrongs. Yes, he does punish sin. But that is in the final day. All sin will be judged, and punished with the lake of fire. For now, the ills of life are caused by sin - not our personal sin, but the sin of all humanity, due to the fallen nature of all humanity. Scripture says the whole creation is "groaning" to be delivered from the sin curse. Satan is the author of all disease, sickness, and of course death. I think it's a great injustice of society to call the disasters of our day, "Acts of God." He really has nothing to do with them at all. He is the author of life not death.

Daily Verse: "For the son of God is not come to destroy men's lives, but to save them."

Luke 9:56

FEAR OF SACRIFICE

One of the greatest human sacrifices known in the twentieth century came in a four-foot-six-inch package. Yes, she was known as Mother Teresa. But she was way more than a nun. She started her ministry career with great ambitions of fame, and the like. That is until she was touched by the pain and suffering of India, which became her whole life, and commitment.

In 1994 she was called upon to deliver a speech at the National Prayer Breakfast in Washington D.C. All the usual dignitaries were present. The atmosphere was a casual conversation that is until the eighty-three-year-old Mother Teresa was wheeled into the room in a wheelchair. As she took the podium, a dead hush filled the room. Then she shocked all the leaders present with a speech about how America had become a selfish nation. She strongly spoke against abortion, and the fact that if a mother had the right to take the life of her child, how we could expect others not to do the same. She rebuked our land for losing the real meaning of love, which was as she explained, "giving until it hurts."

She said America was sending out a message that anyone could get what they wanted in life if they used enough force. In closing she made a heart-wrenching appeal to all pregnant women who didn't want their children. "Don't kill your child, but give it to me, I'll care for it." Did Mother Teresa mean what she said? Her actions speak louder than her words, at the time she already placed more than three-thousand children in homes with families. She had completely dedicated her entire life to caring for lepers, and children - the ones that society casts aside.

She not only gave herself to serving humanity, but also to serving her Master. Jesus said the greatest love you can show your friends is to "lay down your life" for them. Jesus was Mother Teresa's example, One by whom she decided to mold her life, who are you molding your life after? Today most of us are strangers to sacrifice. Sacrifice to some is to make it to church on time on Sunday morning, or to give up the daily football game to go back to church on Sunday night. Don't fear what God will do to you, fear what he will do without you.

Daily Verse: "Greater love hath no man than this, that a man lay down his life for his friends."

John 15:13

FEAR OF STARTING OVER

For some reason many people think that you only get one shot at things, and if you mess up, that's it–you're done! Think of what it would be like if your parents maintained that attitude toward you as you were growing up. The moment has arrived; you are probably between the ages of one and two for most. Dad has the camcorder out, but you don't even know what it's for. Mom places you on your feet beside the couch, and then she backs away and says "Come here." You sit down, but that doesn't frustrate mom. She has seen you recently let go while you were standing up. She knows you are ready to take your first step, and she wants to make sure the moment is preserved forever on video tape, thus the reason for the staged act. She quickly, stands you up, and backs away again, and once again holds her hands out and says, "Come to mommy." You decide, "What the heck, I don't have anything else to do, so you give it a try, and with that first step you wobble, and fall flat on your seat. Suddenly, mom's whole mood changes, and you look at dad, and he's packing up the video camera. Then you wish you could try again, but mom picks you up, and puts you in the walker, and forcefully tells you "That's it, you had your chance to walk. I'm not wasting anymore time with you - you're a failure."

Aren't you glad that scene didn't take place in your life? After all you might still be crawling everywhere you go if it had. No, your parents lovingly kept encouraging you, and trying get you to walk until finally you took off, usually without anyone watching I might add. The same is true with our heavenly father, he desires us to be a success in this life he has given us. We just have to learn the power of starting over.

Did you know that the founder of the Kentucky Fried Chicken chain Colonel Sanders, went bankrupt in several business attempts, and finally with his social security checks he started the chicken business, which is still famous long after his death. Honda lost his entire plant to a fire before he started over and built their first car. Thomas Edison was sixty-seven years old when his Menlo Park plant burned completely to the ground without insurance. The next day he received a visit from Henry Ford who wrote him out a check for $750,000 dollars. The check was interest free, and was just a deposit should he need more. Why was

Ford so generous? Because one day after repeated failure in developing the gasoline engine, Ford was ready to give up and Edison encouraged him to press on, which Ford did and the rest is history. He was just repaying Edison just a small portion of what Edison had given him. When your tempted to give up, keep pressing on, that's my encouragement for you today.

Daily Verse: "But exhort one another today, while it is called today."

Hebrews 3:13

FEAR OF UN-CONTENTMENT

Most people today live in a constant state of un-contentment. Even though the message of Paul the apostle was, with food and clothes let us be content. But for some reason we think that the more things we have, the happier we will be. One day there was this very wealthy man walking along the docks. As he strolled along he noticed a fisherman who was very lazily sitting in his boat, drinking a canned beverage. "Is your boat disabled that you can't fish anymore today?" asked the rich man.

"No I've already caught enough fish for the day," was his reply.

"But it's barely past noon, and you're done for the day." the rich man asked.

"Yeah, I don't know what I would do with any more fish if I had them," the fisherman said.

"Why, you could sell them and make more money, then buy, a fleet of boats, and hire employees, make more money, and then you could be wealthy like me."

"Then what would I do?" questioned the fisherman.

"You could sit back, and finally relax." said the rich man.

"If that's the case, I think I'll skip all the work, and just sit back right now, and relax, I must already be rich."

Yes, wealth is determined by different standards.

Some people think that the more things the have, the happier they will be. This just isn't true. Our only contentment in life comes in the person of Jesus Christ. He's the friend to the lonely, the husband to the widow, and the Father to the fatherless. He is our anything, and everything we need. The next time you are tempted to look on the other side of fence to the other guy's yard for happiness, remember he has to mow his grass just like you.

Daily Verse: "But godliness with contentment is great gain."
I Timothy 6:6

FEAR OF BONDAGE (ADDICTION)

Bondage is very well defined as something that enslaves or traps. It's something that can make you into its servant. It's a snare that unless you are set free from it, you will be destroyed by it. They are very deceptive, most unwary people held in there grasp, are completely unaware. Much like the method Eskimos hunt polar bears with. The need for polar bear meat is detrimental to the survival of the tribe. Eskimos will kill a seal and dip their razor-sharp knife blades in its blood. Then they will bury the knife blade up in the ice. Bears have a powerful sence of smell. As they hunt the frozen tundra, they will smell the seals blood on the knife. They furiously begin to lick the blood off the razor sharp knife with their tongue. The knife will split their tongue open, and since their tongue is froze from all the licking they don't realize that blood they are so hungrily consuming is their own. The more they bleed, the more they lick the warm blood until they slowly bleed to death. Along comes the Eskimo hunter, only to find a dead polar bear, a few feet away from the knife.

Strangely enough, the polar bear, and the person trapped in some addiction, have a lot in common. First they are both looking for an easy fix. They want something that doesn't require much labor. It's a fight to be released from bondage; in the same way it's a lot of work to catch a seal under the ice. Drugs and alcohol may taste good at first, but in reality, they are killing you slowly. First you begin to lose your sense of feeling. You act though you need more, and more until soon what you already have is unimportant. The constant thirst for more leads you to indulge in more potent things, until there is no way out. You're trapped; and you see no escape from your cage.

God is your only hope. He is your only way out. If you find yourself caught in some form of bondage from this world, fall on Christ and let him break you to pieces. Only through your desire for freedom, and his power, are you able to be set free.

Daily Verse: "Stand fast therefore in the liberty wherewith Christ hath made us free, and be not entangled again with the yoke of bondage."
Galatians 5:1

FEAR OF THE OCCULT

An unbelievable increase in the worship of the devil has suddenly begun to manifest itself in our land today. Waves of rebellion brought on by rock groups and the like, have stirred the hearts of today's youth. As the nation slips further and further away from God, the forces of darkness have been at work in a widespread attack. It is conservatively estimated that between ten and twenty million people today practice some form of witchcraft. Movie stars are openly displaying their psychic abilities on television. The land is so hungry for the supernatural, that people are eating anything as though it is from God. Necromancers (people who talk to dead people) are getting prime time television spots, and hailed as heroes.

What is the occult? The word occult comes from a Latin word which means secret, hidden, and mysterious. It deals with operating outside the five normal senses. In short the occult is a very real force today that is growing by leaps and bounds.

The occult's main operating force is deception. People are persuaded to experiment with what appears to be a harmless, and before they know it they are trapped in satanic bondage.

Scripture says, "There is a way which seemeth right unto a man, but the ends thereof are the ways of death." (Proverbs 14:12) Demons impersonate loved ones at séances to fool, hurting people into doubting what the word of God says. Unsuspecting people are lured to mediums, searching for what the future holds for them.

So what is a responsible Christian to do? First stay away from all the practice of evil. Shun the Zodiac signs, astrology, card readers, and the host of other things that are set up to trap you. Instead trust God to lead you into the future he wants for you. God promises to direct you, protect you, and supply all your needs. Sometimes we have to learn patience, and allow the Holy Spirit to lead us. He is the only one who knows the real future. He is the only source of real power that exists in this world. If you want to know what your future holds, ask God, and read his word, and he will speak to you. Surrender to his will, and trust him to bring his word to pass.

Daily Verse: "Regard not them that have familiar spirits, neither seek after wizards, to be defiled by them; I am the Lord your God."

Leviticus 19:31

FEAR OF DISHARMONY

Harmony has been defined by Webster as "an agreement in action, ideas, and relations." So disharmony is the breaking of the arrangement of things; to make things out-of-sync. Many people today fear they don't fit in. They fear their presence is unnecessary. They would rather be "left out," than to make others uncomfortable, when in reality they should be celebrating their uniqueness, instead of trying to be in the "cookie-cutter" mold. Many people fret over the harmony of things. Some even believe finding total harmony is an impossibility.

Over four-hundred years ago Charles V was Emperor of Holy Rome, as it was called. He loved to spend his time in his palace in Spain. His favorite pastime was to try to get all six clocks in the palace to chime at exactly the same time. He spent months on the project, but no matter how hard he tried it seemed an utter impossibility to get all six to chime at the same time on the hour. He could get three, four, but not six. Finally, he gave up and wrote in his memoirs that it was as impossible to get six different clocks to chime at the same time - as impossible as getting six different nations to agree on the same things.

Now with modern technology we know how to get six different clocks to chime at the same time on the hour. You have to power them all by the same source, and calibrate them all to the same standard time. In the same way if we all want to be in harmony with each other, then we have to all be connected to the same source, (Jesus Christ), and live by the same standard.

Jesus really only gave one standard to live by in the Holy Scriptures. It was the standard of holiness, not some external look imposed on its followers, but an internal clock that goes off when something you're involved in is wrong. The Holy Spirit, God's barometer for holiness, speaks to us on the inside to correct our behavior, and appearance. This creates a harmony between us and God, which in turn spills over onto others with whom we come in contact. Is holiness important? It is if you plan on seeing God someday.

Daily Verse: "Follow peace with all men, and holiness, without which no man shall see the Lord."

Hebrews 12:14

FEAR OF UNBELIEVING CHILDREN

No good parent wants to see there children lost, and without God. Some unknowing parents have tried to lean on scriptures like Proverb 22:6. "Train up a child in the way he should go: and when he is old, he will not depart from it." What they didn't know was what the Scripture actually means. It does not mean to take your child to church on Christmas, and Easter. It doesn't mean you went to church faithfully, but never allow the church to get in you. You never studied the word at home; you never showed your children what the real Christian experience is all about, which is a relationship with Jesus Christ, the son of God. When you train up a child in the way they should go, that means you show them there is only "one way" to go. It's like a river flowing in a canyon. It can't flow over its banks; it has to flow only down the center of the canyon. That's the only way to go for the river. In the same way your children, though they have strayed, they know that there is only one correct way, and they come back to the right way. The negative side to the promise of Proverb 22: 6 is they may be old before they come back, and you may never see it. Either way if you've showed them the way they should go, they will come back, take comfort in those words.

Studies have shown in England that the crime rate and Sunday school attendance detrimentally affect each other. When Sunday school attendance is high, the crime rate is low, and vice versa. So one good way to train your child in the right way to go is to take, and yes, I said take, them to Sunday school. Show them the value of God's Word, and how important it is to build our lives around its teachings.

Always remember that children spell the four letter word "love" differently. They spell it T-I-M-E. Many people have developed a workaholic lifestyle that is actually lazy. It's easy to get lost in some job. It takes a lot more effort to build a relationship with your kids, when you both are in different generations. As I write this book I have one teenage boy at home left, Jacob. He and I are on two entirely different sides of the spectrum. The thirty years difference in our age has created quite a bridge to be gapped. What he likes, (video games, skate boarding, etc.), I have absolutely no interest in. But I know in order to build a relationship with him I must find some common ground to work in. So since we both like the outdoors, we've began to build some bridges with golfing, (which we both stink at I might add), fishing, and hunting. Find some common ground with your kids and begin to show them the right way to go.

Daily Verse: "And thou shalt teach them diligently unto thy children, and shalt talk of them when thou sittest in thine house, and when thou walkest by the way, and when thou liest down, and when thou risest up."

Deuteronomy 6:7

FEAR OF DISCIPLINE

Many parents in times past have feared to discipline there children. Books were written by permissive parents, some by people that had never reared children at all. These books claimed that studies had shown that disciplining, or correcting a child would damage the child's self-esteem.

Whatever the source of their studies, it certainly wasn't the Word of God. The Scriptures are very clear that proper discipline at the right time molds the child instead of breaks the child.

Proverb 13:24 says, "He that spareth his rod hateth his son: But he that loveth him chasteneth (disciplines) him betimes." Proverbs 22:15; "Foolishness is bound up in the heart of a child; but the rod of correction shall drive it far from him." Proverbs 23:13–14; "Withhold not correction from the child: for if thou beatest him with the rod, he shall not die. Thou shalt beat him with the rod, and shalt deliver his soul from hell." Now the Bible does not give a parent permission to abuse a child, but to discipline the child. It has been appropriately quoted that a pat on a child's back is what develops character, especially if it's done low enough at times. But this is only one form of discipline, listen to how Winter Olympics gold medal winner Tommy Moe's father disciplined him into becoming a winner instead of waste. In 1986 when he was only fifteen years old he was on top of the world, being invited to join the U.S. ski team. The problem was he had a passion for carousing, and a desire to smoke marijuana, and drink beer. His coaches found out that he had sneaked out one night to get high, and kicked him off the team. His dad was furious, and stated that he had just the thing to help the boy. He ordered the boy join him in Alaska to work on the construction site with him. Starting at 4:00 am and working twelve to sixteen hours a day disciplined the boy quite well. In fact his dad purposely worked his son's rear off. After the summer was over Tom Sr. asked his son which he preferred, to ski in Argentina, or work with him on the construction site. He decided to get serious about his skiing career, the rest is history. In 1994 he won the gold medal in the Winter Olympics held in Norway. When asked what he attributed his success to: "It was the mental torture, of the job that humbled me real fast," claimed Tommy in an interview. In the same way we must find what it is that would properly shape our child into responsible men and women of God. That's God's will for our children.

Daily Verse: "He opened also their ear to discipline, and commandeth that they return from iniquity."

Job 36:10

FEAR OF RUIN

Dwight L. Moody once said; "I have never met a man who has given me as much trouble as myself." For some reason we are, our own worst enemy. We refrain from anything that can cause the slightest bit of pain. We seek nothing but comfort and ease. We are afraid to take on any challenge that has the possibility of leaving us in ruin. Consequently, we live our lives wishing we would have tried. Some people live in a constant state of, "what if." Always remember the fear you fear is mostly within yourself and nowhere else. Most problems only exist in your imagination.

Scientist's have learned in recent years that hardship, and change may be good for you. Experiments with large Biospheres (which are controlled environments under glass) have shown that without the elements wearing against the trees they become weak and frail. Inside the self-sustaining community, they have created deserts, oceans, forests, every conceivable type of environment except wind. After two years, the trees within the sphere begin to swell at the bottom and split. They got so weak they couldn't hold up under the pressure, so they simply fell over. The trunks were too weak to stand. In the same way we must remember that God is able to use hardships to bring us to the place of success, he has chosen for us.

In the gospels there is a story about the disciples out on the sea. A storm arose and they feared they were going to drown. They looked out over the sea and saw a Jesus walking on the water. They mistook him for a phantom, and were sure they were going to sink. Custom was at the time if you saw a phantom on the sea; it was a sign your ship was going down. Jesus quickly assures them that they are going to be all right, and that it truly is him. Peter then risks everything and requests that "if it is really you, Jesus, then let me come to you." Jesus response was, "Come." Then the unbelievable happens, Peter risks losing his own life, just to demonstrate his faith to Jesus. He even walked on the water for awhile, until he took his eyes off Jesus and began to look at the storm. How close to Jesus was he when he lost faith, and began to sink? One arms length away. Jesus reached out his arm and pulled him to the surface. We can be that close to God and slip, if we look at the bankruptcy of our own life. Only you can hold yourself back, only you can stand in your own way; and of course only you can be the one to help yourself.

Daily Verse: "So that we may boldly say; the Lord is my helper, and I will not fear what man shall do unto me."

Hebrews 13:6

FEAR OF HARD TIMES

As I am writing this story it is Christmas time and the air is filled with "Christmas cheer." Every store you so graciously visit has the sound of a jingling bell. Outside in the cold is Salvation Army workers ringing the bell of hope for so many. I can hardly pass their red pots of charity for the under-privileged without giving something. But do you know how many waged the war of hard times, just to have the privilege to ring those bells? In 1878 when the Booth's founded the "Christian Mission" as it was called in those days, they were met with anything but holiday cheer. Records state that many of their members attended the meetings carrying dead animals in both hands. Dead rats and house cats were thrown at them as they approached the meeting site and if members didn't catch and carry the putrid cargo along, the attackers would pick them up and throw them again. In 1889 no less then six-hundred of their members were reported to have been insulted in some way. Most of their street preachers had pots of human urine dumped on them as they ministered the gospel. Even their children were not immune from the amazing amount of hard ship they were forced to endure. On several occasions children reported having lime thrown in their face by local hoodlums. Newspapers punished the group and even called Booth, "Field Marshal Von Booth." The police force wouldn't even lend itself to help them when local attackers broke up their meetings and damaged their meeting places by throwing things threw their windows, and destroying the insides while no one was present. What could have possibly caused Booth to hang in there, through such persecution? It was his unfailing love for his purpose. He knew that without a doubt he was on a mission ordained by God. His mission was much the same as Christ's. His followers endured hardships like good soldiers. So the next time you see one of the Salvation Army's soldiers ringing those bells of Christmas Joy, remember the suffering and hardships its ancestors endured to have the privilege.

Must we endure hard times to fulfill God's will for our life? At times maybe, some more than others. Just remember that God has promised to walk us through anything that is in our path of righteousness. He will not leave us comfortless. He will dispense as much grace in our life as we need to make it through the adversity that we face.

Daily Verse: "Thou therefore endure hardness, as a good soldier of Jesus Christ."

II Timothy 2:3

FEAR OF SUPPORTING A FAMILY

Along with the privilege of being a parent also comes the awesome privilege of taking care of the child. The Bible demands that as believers, we not shirk our responsibility by abandoning our families in their time of need. I Timothy 5:8 demands: "But if any provide not for his own, and especially for those of his own house, he hath denied the faith, and is worse than in infidel," (unbeliever). In the times we live in, cost of living is on the rise, and it is sometimes necessary that both husband and wife work to support the family. Fear of not having enough resources to meet the demands of the day has led many to live from "paycheck to paycheck." Someone has said most families are one paycheck away from bankruptcy. So just what is a provider to do against such insurmountable odds?

First, realize that God is able to meet every need. We must use practical common sense in making future purchases not to bombard ourselves with unnecessary debt. If we are careful to avoid making purchases that will put a strain on us, we should have no problems providing for our families. God has promised that he will provide for His families, which are us.

I remember reading a story called Les Miserables, (perhaps you have seen the Broadway production/musical). It is a story of a very poor family who has nothing but bad luck no matter how much good they did. One night in a moment of desperation, the father steals a loaf of fresh baked bread from the window sill. He reasoned that his family was starving to death and it was necessary. He was caught, and later found guilty. The punishment for stealing that one loaf of bread: life imprisonment under severe hard labor in a maximum security prison. His sentence in prison was difficult, under a very harsh warden. The father was continually being punished for things for which he was not guilty. So he cunningly escapes. Now a fugitive, he ends up in the home of a minister as a charity case. The minister begins to trust him with the whole house, then one night the ex-prisoner decides to steal silver candle sticks from the minister and run. But he's not a real experienced thief, so once again he is caught. Fearing he will be turned in and have to go back to the awful prison, he attempts to dash away, when the minister stops him and does the unthinkable. The kind minister begins to load the would-be thief's bag with other items that he could sell for money. He tells the man that everything he had belonged to God and if he could use them to better someone else's life then so be it. The mercy received that day changed one man's life forever. He too became a man of charity, helping everyone with whom he came in contact, and finally raising the daughter of a local prostitute.

This story portrays a truth - that no matter how hard life may be, God is able to get us in the position to help others if we allow him. He will help us provide for those we love if we trust him. Oh, by the way, decades later, he was caught by the warden of the prison where he had once been incarcerated. But the warden realized that the former prisoner was a just man, and decided to serve the man's sentence for him by handcuffing himself, and jumping into the local river.

Daily Verse: "I have been young, and now I am old; yet have I not seen the righteous forsaken, nor his seed begging bread."
Psalm 37:25

FEAR OF PERVERSION

Today's society is so confused. We live in a time when right is portrayed as wrong, and wrong is publicly demonstrated as right. Children grow up with two mommies, one filling the role of the mom and the other acting like the dad. Schools are now teaching the children that there is an alternative lifestyle if they should choose. Churches are overlooking what the Bible forbids as an "abomination to God," and ordain admitted homosexuals as bishops, all in the name of diversity. Perversion is an accepted way of life today. Today pornography is on the rise in various forms. It produces sexual addiction that wars against the soul. It arouses sexual desires without providing godly sexual fulfillment. Lives are overwhelmed with sensual fantasies and desires, leading to all types of unhealthy experimentation.

God has placed certain sexual restrictions upon us to protect us. Sexual gratification outside the boundaries of marriage may be intensely pleasurable at first, but it only leads to emptiness and sorrow. The Bible warns us to recognize that sex can be a powerful weapon the enemy (Satan) can use to undermine our physical, mental, and spiritual well-being. He knows that many are very vulnerable in this area. God also knows what a difficult time we can face, so he has given us several cautions in his Word.

I Corinthians 6:18 says, "Flee fornication. Every sin that a man doeth without the body; but he that committeth fornication sinneth against his own body." Fornication has the power to lead us into dangerous compromises that become disastrous. Those animal impulses and those earthly appetites that lurk deep inside our members must be put to death. Make no provision for the flesh by yielding to the carnal impulses of the old man.

Scriptures exhort us to possess our own vessel (body) in sanctification and honor, not in passion or lust. So what should our response be to these desires within? We should decide to dedicate our lives to the pursuit of holiness, and the advancement of God's kingdom on this earth. Look at sexual gratification in marriage as a beautiful gift from God.

Remember that irregardless of your possible past perversions, God sees the born-again Christian as a virgin. He says, "If any one is in Christ, he is a new creation; old things have passed away; behold all things have become new."

Daily Verse: "For ye are bought with a price: therefore glorify God in your body, and in your spirit, which are God's."

I Corinthians 6:20

FEAR OF JUDGEMENT

Judgment Day - the dreaded day for so many. It's like April 15th to a man who has been evasive in his tax bill. (But much more serious). There will be no excuses that will hold water on that selected day, although I'm sure many will be given. Research has been done to find out the top excuses business executives give for failing to hold up their end in the job. Number one on the list is, "It's not my fault." Kind of sounds like Adam doesn't it? Number two on the list: "It was someone else's fault." Okay, I suppose the devil made you do it, right Eve? You know these excuses didn't hold up for them, and they won't hold up for us either. God will judge as an impartial judge on Judgment Day. On that day "mercy" will shut its mouth. And yes, "grace" will not be a witness at this trial. God will fulfill the role that was taken by a man in a small frontier town several years ago in the old west.

One day a man was riding into town, and he saw a horse get spooked with a wagon attached to it. In the wagon was a small child, screaming for help. The man dashed to the rescue, chasing after the frightened horse. Risking death, the man jumped into the wagon, and stopped the horse, thus saving the young man.

As time passed, the rescued boy grew up and became a criminal. He was finally caught, and forced to appear before a judge to be sentenced for a serious crime. In the final moment he looked up into the face of the judge and recognized him as the man who had stopped the horse all those years ago and saved his life. So on the basis of that experience, he pleaded for mercy from the judge. The answer from the bench soon silenced the young man. "Young man, that day I was your savior, but today I sit in the place of your judge, and in order for justice to be served I must sentence you to death."

Today is the day of grace. And yes these days are long. But someday grace will be put away, and mercy will be silenced. Justice will step forward and demand its rights and the righteous judge, Jesus Christ will take the stand as "His Honor." He will judge mankind for their deeds they performed in their bodies. The Scriptures pronounce that the books will be opened, and every man must give an account of what has been written in the books. With this in mind, what type of people ought we to be? Should the Christian fear the judgment? Absolutely not! They have been judged with Jesus on the cross, and found "not guilty," due to the "lack of evidence."

Daily Verse: "And as it is appointed unto men once to die, but after this the judgment."

Hebrews 9:27

FEAR OF DESPERATION

In moments of desperation some people have resorted to drastic measures. In 1993 Armenia was desperate for fuel resources. For two winters they suffered from a total oil and gas blockade from the neighboring country of Azerbaijan. Trees had become their main source of fuel and they were using over a million of them a year. Not willing to endure another cruel Armenian winter without resources, they were so desperate they considered a very hazardous thing.

Tucked away in their country was a closed Russian nuclear power plant that had been ruled unsafe in 1989 because of rusting containment tanks. Since the plant was built in the 70's, it had no safety containment building for protection against accidental leaks. To make matters even worse, it was constructed on one of the largest known earthquake zones in the country, making it a double death threat. Since the capitol city of Yerevan with hundreds of thousands of people was a mere twenty-five miles away, they deemed it wise to shut the plant down. I'm glad to say the plant remained closed, but just consider how desperate those people were to even consider re-opening it. Moments of desperation often lead people into doing things they wouldn't even consider in ordinary circumstances.

Sometimes people even choose to go back into sin after leaving the sorrow behind. Only to later find they regret the action taken in the moment of desperation. Don't put your hopes in an old rusty power plant that has the potential to destroy you and all others around you. Don't take those you love into a pit of despair because you think God has forsaken you in your time of need. God promises to help us when it looks like we stand alone. The famous poem, "Footprints in the Sand," explains it best, when the man turned and only saw one set of footprints when his life was the most difficult. He questioned,"Why did you leave me Lord, when I needed you the most?

"Oh, my son I never left you - those were the times I carried you," replied the Lord.

Daily Verse: "And having no root in themselves, and so endure but for a time: who, afterward, when affliction or persecution ariseth for the word's sake, immediately they are offended."
Mark 4:17

FEAR OF BEING AVERAGE

Do you know who your greatest enemy is? I can guess what some of you are saying. Some are saying the devil, others who are more spiritual, are saying "the flesh." Still others who are a little bit more carnal than some, are saying, "My mother-in-law," (Just kidding). In reality the greatest, most powerful enemy that every successful person must face is named "average." In fact, a man has written a whole book to defeat, "the enemy called average." "Average" means you are halfway between success and failure. Most Christians have to live an A+ life just to bring some people up to a C in life . . . and C is just to be average.

Stop trying to only live "within your means." Let me explain. If your life is spent just earning a good living, then it won't be long until you will forget how to live. So many people are planning for the rainy day so much that they don't even notice that the sun is shining today. God plans so much more for us than we are willing to except. He wants us to make bigger plans, dream bigger dreams, and just have an all around larger outlook on life. He promised He could do more for us than we can even ask or think. No, I'm not advocating you spend beyond your means, I'm saying; don't live within your means.

Today we live in a world that will make room for a man that has a purpose. If you know where you're going in life, you won't have any problems finding someone to follow you. With Christ we've been given a "conqueror mentality." In fact, Scripture announces we are "more than conquerors in Christ Jesus." Decide today that you will find God's plan for your life and depend on him to bless you in it. All the finances in the world will not guarantee success if you don't have purpose. What most people need in life is a purpose. Purpose will bring the fulfillment for which most people hungrily seek. Billy Sunday, one of the great evangelists of yester-year once stated; "most men don't fail for lack of talent, but for lack of purpose." Do you know where you're going? Average people have no direction; instead they use the" hit or miss," mentality. They end up someplace, but aren't satisfied because they never accomplished anything. They always hit the target because, they shoot the arrow anywhere and then go and draw a bull's-eye around it, claiming to have been aiming there all along. Average people are just happy to hit any target at all. Winning people have a specific purpose that brings them more fulfillment than money. Remember that the only thing people do without a purpose is grow older. If the shoe fits, by all means don't wear it, if you do, you limit yourself to how much you can grow. God has given you more potential than you can use in a lifetime, so don't settle for "average."

Daily Verse: "Now unto him that is able to do exceedingly abundantly above all that we ask or think, according to the power that worketh in us."

Ephesians 3:20

FEAR OF CHILDBIRTH

Marriage is the greatest union this side of heaven. The purpose given by God for marriage is procreation: to repopulate the earth, to fill it with children who will grow, and become responsible citizens. When the big day finally arrives and the wife tells her hubby she's expecting, it is an exciting day. I am speaking from experience on this one. But it is also the beginning of several unknown fears. Will it be normal? Will he have all his fingers and toes? Will she have black hair or blond hair? Many questions will flood your mind before the little one comes along. Listen to this tragic story of two parents who used their faith to carry them through a horrible ordeal.

In the fifth month of pregnancy the doctor requested a special ultrasound. He spent a considerable amount of time performing the ultrasound which alarmed the couple. They were so happy to finally be expecting, but now the alarmed father asked, "Is everything okay?" Their joy would soon turn to sorrow at the answer from their doctor.

"I'm sorry, but we have some problems," replied the discouraged doctor. "The child has a clubbed foot, cleft palate, deformed heart, missing portions of the brain, and possibly has spina bifida. In any case I'm sorry but the probable result will be a spontaneous miscarriage. If not you will have to decide if you want to carry this fetus to full-term. I warn you though, if it is born, it won't live more than a few hours outside the protective womb."

What terrible news for a young, excited couple to receive. In this case we are privileged to see firsthand the awesome power of God, in his remarkable grace. The couple knew what the doctor was asking them to do, but they decided that if the only life their child would know was in the womb, they decided to make the womb the safest place it can be. After all who has the right but God, the creator of life, to say how long a life should be? I pray you are not ever put in the situation of these dear parents, but remember, God gives us more grace to endure in times of need.

Daily Verse: "Thine eyes did see my substance, yet being unperfect; and in thy book all my members were written, which in continuance were fashioned, when as yet there were none of them."

Psalm 139:16

FEAR OF COMPROMISE

Man, in his natural state, fears compromise. He wants to win every battle, argument, and of course never admit that he may be wrong. A story is told of how President Lincoln once felt pressure from a politician about the war. He issued his command to the Secretary of War, which was Edwin Stanton at the time. Stanton read the orders and laughed. He refused the orders abruptly and proclaimed Lincoln to be a fool. The response of Stanton was quickly told to the President, and many watched to see his response, to Stanton's insult. The president calmly replied, "If Stanton thinks I'm a fool then I must be one, for he isn't wrong about very many things."

The President went on to research his previous commands, only to discover that Stanton was indeed correct, and that the previous order would have been a terrible mistake. So without further response, he quickly withdrew his orders. Do you have a teachable, compromising spirit like Abraham Lincoln? Are you able to admit when you're wrong, and accept the consequences for your actions? Wars in families today are increasing because nobody wants to admit that they are wrong.

Instead, year after year goes by: children angry at parents, parents discouraged with how their children have grown up, or they may feel forsaken. Instead if one side would only admit that they were wrong, and ask for forgiveness, God could work out their disagreements, and heal the hurts.

Today God is able to perform amazing deeds in our life if we can only displace the opposition against us. Our human nature demands justice, when we have been wronged by someone. But God's Word commands that we forgive quickly, even if the offence is from an enemy. In fact, it even exhorts us to "pray for those who despitefully use us," and to be like God and forgive without hesitation. Our Father promises that we can have this spirit if we lean on him for every decision.

Daily Verse: "Agree with thine adversary quickly, whiles thou art in the way with him;"

Matthew 5:25a

FEAR OF GHOSTS

Throughout much of human history there has been the legend of ghosts: disembodied spirits of dearly departed loved ones, trapped between the afterlife, and now. These precarious spirits are supposed to inhabit old houses, castles, and even trees. Their main job in the afterlife is to haunt these places as if it were they're solemn duty. This just isn't true. Satan has very carefully developed this theory to attempt to destroy the faith of many. For the most part he is very successful in deceiving unsuspecting people with his lies about the afterlife. So what is the truth about death, and the afterlife? God's Word is a very clear about what happens to people when they leave this plain of existence. The redeemed of the Lord, those who have committed their lives to Christ, will go on to be with him in heaven. No sleeping in the coffin, no wandering the world disembodied, no appearing to loved ones, no inhabiting other bodies, no being reborn as someone else. You simply go to heaven to be with Jesus, waiting on him to bring you back in the millennium. If you die without Christ, you are destined for hell, a place of fire and torment, awaiting the Great White Throne Judgment where you will be judged for the sins you committed in this life.

You may have heard testimonies of people who claim to have seen "ghosts" as they are called, so what gives? The so-called ghosts of today are disembodied spirits, but instead of loved ones - they are demon spirits. For instance the "familiar spirit," as it is called, makes itself familiar with the deceased and then will appear as the person in order to deceive the loved ones. The Bible tells the story of a demon coming out of the ground in what would be considered a séance. He appeared in the form of the prophet Samuel. The demon talks to a witch for King Saul, and completely deceives him as Samuel. In the story Saul never sees the demon, but instead uses a medium from Endor to tell him what the spirit looks like. Because he uses the description of the witch, he determines it must be Samuel talking to him, a tragic mistake, which later cost him and his sons their lives.

Following after demon spirits has led many people into ruin. These "ghosts" as they are called, are very deceptive, getting prime time television spots to propagate their religion. Don't be deceived, and absolutely don't be afraid. The only "Ghost" we should be listening to is the Holy Ghost, and He is God himself.

Daily Verse: "A man also or woman that hath a familiar spirit, or that is a wizard, shall surely be put to death;"

Leviticus 20:27

FEAR OF MEMORY LOSS

Why is it if a young man forgets something, it's completely overlooked, but you let an old man forget the same thing, and people are running around screaming, "Alzheimer's." Memory loss is just as important as meditation. In fact can you imagine what it would be like if you remembered everything you ever heard? God has conveniently given us memory loss to help us cope with the pains of life. Make no mistake about it, I realize that there are very real conditions that cause memory loss and these should be treated. At the same time realize that forgetting some things in your life is a really spiritual thing to do. The Bible informs us that God himself has the greatest case of memory loss. It promises us that if we confess our sins, and forsake our old life, he is faithful enough to forgive us of our sins, and, of course, forgiving means forgetting. The word of God also encourages us by telling us that he throws our sins over his shoulder, into the "sea of forgetfulness." Which, by the way, is the deepest sea known to man.

Have you ever had an experience that was particularly painful, and you wish you could forget about it, but no matter how much you try to forget it, it just keeps replaying over in your mind? Maybe it was some failure in your life, or the loss of a loved one. Rest assured, and take comfort God has promised when we get to heaven he will wipe away all tears, and the pain of past hurts.

No more will we be plagued by the words people have ridiculed us with in school. No more will our shortcomings stand like walls in our path of happiness. But we will spend our days making new memories with God himself, face to face.

Many have wondered; will I know anybody in heaven? The Bible tells us we will "know, as we are known," or yes, we will know our loved ones and friends in heaven. Only the bad things will be wiped away from our memory. I don't know about you, but I can hardly wait.

Daily Verse: "And God shall wipe away all tears from their eyes; and there shall be no more death, neither sorrow, nor crying, neither shall their be any more pain: for the former things are passed away."

Revelation 21:4

FEAR OF INFIDELITY

Nothing in this world feels better than a good marriage. In reverse, nothing in this world can bring as much pain as a bad one. Your home can be like living in heaven, or can be hell on earth. A couple doesn't have to have all the big fancy things in life to be happily married. If they have that special intimacy with each other and a little romance; that can carry them for quite some time. But if the wedge of unfaithfulness is driven between them, it's a hard thing to overcome.

Today marital infidelity is one of the leading causes of marriage breakups. Too many people have fallen for the "Hollywood" mentality of marriage; fall in love, get married, and live happily ever after. It just isn't true, you must work at marriage to make it last. Don't get me wrong, love is the source of power behind every successful marriage. But Hollywood's idea of what love is and what true love really is, are entirely different; what most call love is really lust.

Many times our lives get overextended and this produces a drain of energy. Fatigue sets in and the time to build a good relationship seems impossible. People begin to compare their marriages with others, and they begin to look around, and start having unreal expectations about their marriage. What is happening is they are being set up by the "sex trap." Satan hates a good marriage and he will use every device at his disposal against it.

Soon you begin to justify your unfaithfulness to remove your guilt. Then the person begins to hide their true feelings under a shadow of need for fulfillment. Soon the vows of marital purity get buried under the need for gratification. Your needs are all that matters at this time and you begin to look for someone else to fulfill them. This is the deceit of the enemy. Once you violate your sexual standards to enjoy the pleasures of sin for a season, there's no going back.

So how do we avoid the "sex trap" of the enemy? First, decide to keep Christ at the center of your marriage. Ecclesiastes states that a "three fold cord can hardly be broken," signifying that when God is in the middle it's hard to break the bond. Realize that your marriage has joined you as one flesh, which means you must maintain good communication with your mate. Why not create a little romance now and then to keep the spice in your marriage? Remember what you did to get your mate is the same thing it takes to keep them. And finally of course, keep the sexual intimacy very much alive in the marriage. It is impossible to "know each other," as the Bible puts it, without sexual intimacy. Always remember that instead of maintaining a "what can I get attitude," we need to be concerned about, "What I can give," to the relationship.

Daily Verse: Marriage is honorable in all, and the bed undefiled.

Hebrews 13:4

FEAR OF DISOBEDIENCE

Disobedience killed God's original purpose for Adam and Eve. They chose the pleasures of sin for a season, and thus spent the rest of their days, over nine-hundred years, enduring the punishment for their sin. Moses, one of the greatest Old Testament models of what Jesus would be like, lost his inheritance to the Promised Land, by allowing his temper to get the best of him, and choosing to disobey God's command to speak to the rock. Instead, he did as he had done before and struck the rock with his staff. Forty years of faithful service couldn't make up for that one act of disobedience. Moses wanted a miracle more than he wanted God's favor. He got his miracle because of the grace of

God, but lost the favor of God. Miracles are wonderful, but they aren't worth the price of God's blessing. They are only temporary, while blessings are eternal. It has been said that what many people try to replace with sacrifice could be easily done with obedience. Why would God punish disobedience so strictly? Because disobedience is sin, and sin cannot go unnoticed. God is a just God and must punish all sin, in order to remain so.

Some people ignorantly believe that since God is so good that he won't punish all disobedience with the same measure. This is a false assumption of a fabricated God. This type of God only exists in the mind of the willingly disobedient.

Disobedience has it's origin in the heart of Satan. He chose to attempt to steal God's glory for himself, instead of giving it to whom it was due. He passed this trait on to us through the disobedience of Adam and Eve, and now we must fight the urge to take from God what rightfully belongs to Him. Let us intentionally strive to obey God in everything that we attempt to do in life. This way we are sure to come out a winner, and being a winner is God's perfect plan for his people.

Daily Verse: "For if we sin wilfully after we have received the knowledge of the truth, there remaineth no more sacrifice for sins."

Hebrews 10:26

FEAR OF JEALOUSY

"Now Israel loved Joseph more than all his children, because he was the son of his old age: And he made him a coat of many colors. And when his brethren saw that their father loved him more than all their brethren, they hated him, and could not speak peaceably with him," (Genesis 37:3–4).

Although jealousy is a subtle fear, it has several characteristics that identify it as such. It usually takes place in people closest to you. Sometimes friends, family, and yes, even spouses are not immune from its venomous strike. It slithers in, much like a serpent between you and another chosen for its prey.

What makes this fear so harmful is that it doesn't want to steal your blessing; it wants to hinder you from receiving one altogether. Case in point; we see a father in the above Scripture doing a very dangerous thing for any good father to do. He is playing favorites among his children. Notice that Joseph doesn't have to do anything wrong to get his brothers mad at him. All he did was be the recipient of a beautiful gift from his dad. This alone sparked a fear of jealousy in his brothers, that later turned to hatred. This story allows us to learn a very important fact about jealousy. If it is left to itself, and not dealt with properly, it turns to hatred, which can later even spawn the desire for murder; which is exactly what happened with Joseph. If Jacob would have recognized the jealousy of his sons and quickly responded by having tunics made for all his children, he would have spared himself many years of heartache. You see the brothers interpreted the coat as a sign that Joseph would be receiving all the inheritance when their father passed away. I'm so glad we have a heavenly Father able to pick up the pieces after someone harms us, and turn the situation for our good. God remained with Joseph through the whole ordeal and later fulfilled a vision that He had given him early in his life.

No one is immune from the spirit of jealousy. Beware that you don't harbor a jealous spirit toward anyone else. It will hinder God's plan for your destiny if allowed to work in your life. How do you recognize this fear? Do you try to discourage your friends from accomplishing things for God by talking down their dreams? You almost seem to suppress them by negative remarks. If this is you, then by all means repent, now! Command this jealous fear to leave now, before it's allowed to take root in your heart.

Daily Verse: "For jealousy is the rage of a man, therefore he will not spare in the day of vengeance."

Proverbs 6:34

FEAR OF SPIRITUAL PRIDE

"I will ascend into heaven, I will exalt my throne above the stars of God; I will also sit on the mount of the congregation on the farthest sides of the north; I will ascend above the heights of the clouds, I will be like the most high." These are the words of the creator of all sin, Lucifer as he was called in those days. Lucifer looked at himself and saw a shining coming from the glory of God on his life and decided that it was radiating from him. Thus spiritual pride was conceived in his heart which the Lord tells us corrupted his wisdom, and gave him an "I" problem.

Spiritual pride is perhaps the greatest of all sins. It is the original sin, the beginning of all our independence from God. Spiritual pride always gives us a false sense of self-sufficiency. If you give in to the fear of spiritual pride, it will lower you to the lowest pit in life. Spiritual pride has led successful men and women who once had prominent positions in life to the rat-infested ghettos of our nation. Spiritual pride is what blinded Adam and Eve in the garden into seeking the desire to be as God, knowing good from evil. So what do we do to defeat the fear of spiritual pride? The answer can be simply found in the life of Jesus Christ. Philippians tells us that although Jesus "was in the form of God, he made himself no reputation, and took the form of a servant, and became born in the likeness of a men. Then he humbled himself, and became obedient, even to the death of the cross." Humility is the answer to defeating the pride fear in our life. We must not seek our own agenda, but seek God's. In the garden of Gethsemane, the night before Jesus was arrested, he prayed this prayer, "Not my will, but thine be done." He totally realized that in praying that prayer, he was setting himself up to be crucified on an old rugged cross the next day. The sum of Christ's complete life can be summed up by witnessing His submission to God's will that night in the garden. Through humility Jesus was elevated into God's glory; let us follow him to reach our own destiny.

Jesus exhorted us that when we are faced with the choice between pride and humility, always choose humility.

Daily Verse: "Pride goeth before destruction, and an haughty spirit before a fall."

Proverbs 16:18

FEAR OF LAZINESS

Did you know that God says an ant has more wisdom that a lazy person? He goes on to say that since a lazy person doesn't take the initiative to get busy, they will be forced into labor by others. It will seem like slave-labor to them and they won't find satisfaction. God has called each of us to be co-rulers with him; why would you settle for being a common field hand? This little story explains how God depends on our diligence to get his will accomplished on this earth:

One day Bill decided to visit his friend Tom, to see how he was doing in his new house. When Bill arrived at Tom's he couldn't find his friend, so he decided to go to the back of the house to see if his friend was out there. In the back yard he noticed his buddy on his knees in the garden pruning his flowers. "Wow, you sure are lucky Tom that God has blessed you with such beautiful roses," said Bill.

"Yeah, I guess your right Bill," replied Tom.

Then Bill turned and looked at Tom's backyard and added, "Boy, Tom, God sure has blessed you with a beautiful sculptured lawn."

Tom enjoyed the praise of his friend, but he just had to comment, "You know Bill, God sure has blessed me, but you should have seen this place when He was caring for it all by Himself."

Yes, God does bless us, but it takes our diligence to bring out the full potential in things. In fact, Scripture promises "the hands of the diligent shall be made to rule." You make the decision right now, whether you will be known as a sluggard, or a success.

Daily Verse: "The hand of the diligent shall bear rule; but the slothful shall be under tribute."

Proverbs 12:24

FEAR OF COMMUNICATION

Of all God's wonderful creatures in creation, only man has been gifted with the ability to speak. Speech has allowed us to communicate with one another. However, a sad fact in our society is that some people choose not to communicate with each other. They choose to stay disconnected from the rest of society. They fear that communication in the past has given them pain, so they will refrain from further communication with others to protect themselves. This keeps them in their own little prison, called life; never experiencing God's fullness.

Once there was an elderly woman from a small town in Massachusetts. She was a very unfriendly woman, never communicating with anyone in the neighborhood. She was so cut off from society that when she died, no one even knew about it. In fact, nobody even missed her. This is not an uncommon thing in the separated society in which we live today. But she was dead for over four years before anyone even knew about it. Police could only guess that she must have died of natural causes in her house all alone. She was so removed from her family that her brother didn't even miss her; in fact he thought she had been put in a nursing home. The postal service was holding her mail, and the neighbors were cutting her grass, until someone finally found her dead in the house. Neighbors of the middle class neighborhood felt sick that this had happened but one of them stated that no one was to blame, because for forty-years the old woman lived in the neighborhood and never once talked to anyone. In fact, she never wanted anyone to bother her.

What a sad epitaph to have written about your life. Communication is difficult at times, but we must make the effort to build relationships with others. We must take a chance at being hurt in order to make our lives rich and fulfilling. When you have cultivated a friendship with someone through communication it can be lasting and fruitful. Don't fear what man could do to you; take a chance and start talking to someone you don't know today. Also, in all your communication, don't forget to talk to God everyday through his Word and by prayer.

> *Daily Verse: "But if we walk in the light, as he is in the light, we have fellowship one with another, and the blood of Jesus Christ his Son cleanseth us from all sin."*
>
> I John 1:7

FEAR OF PROGRESS

Progress is the act of moving forward to completion. Many people in the world today completely hate progression. They're always talking about the, "good old days," when they were younger. In my mind the only thing, that could make the old days good, would be a short memory. I feel confident that this is true in most people's lives, if they would only admit it. Today we have such comfortable vehicles to drive, and such convenience in the technological realm; I don't know how the old days could have possibly been better. Jesus demanded that we learn the principle of "forward march," when he quoted this scripture in Luke 9:62, "No man having put his hand to the plow, and looking back, is fit for the kingdom of God." Lot's wife, who longed for the old life she had back in Sodom, turned to look back at God's judgment on the city, and changed into a pillar of salt. I hope you can see that God is very serious about our moving forward with him. He promises us he is faithful to complete the work in us that he began. God is a finisher, and progress is nothing to fear.

The country of Australia has made a decision to be a progressive agent in these days of uncertainty. They chose two unlikely creatures to cover their coat of arms. The emu, a bird that doesn't fly, and a kangaroo, which is a seemingly harmless creature. When asked why they chose these two animals for such an important item, their response was that they are progressive. Further study reveals that these two critters have one common denominator. Neither one has the ability to go backward. The foot of the emu is so arranged that if they attempt to take a step backward, they stumble and fall down. The kangaroo's large tail prohibits them from moving in reverse. Let these two animals be an example to us that we should follow. God is not pleased with anyone who decides to go back after beginning a journey.

Daily Verse: "But we are not of them who draw unto perdition; but of them that believe to the saving or the soul."

Hebrews 10:39

FEAR OF EVIL

Evil is a force that is very much alive today. You don't have to look very far to see its ugly head at work. Just pick up the weekly newspaper or watch a nightly news report on television. A mother murders her children; a father molests his innocent offspring. A world leader executes thousands of his own countrymen. As I write this today, one of the worlds greatest forces of evil, Saddam Hussein, has just been caught and arrested by the United States and will stand trial for his crimes against humanity; which by the way began when he was twelve years old when he used his first gun to commit his first murder. Yes, evil is alive and well. The Apostle Paul warned us that evil would increase to the point where only by God's armor would we be able to stand its powerful force, "Wherefore take unto you the whole armor of God that ye may be able to withstand in the EVIL DAY . . ." (Eph.6:13). What was Paul's answer to taking on evil? Stand your ground dressed in God's full armor. Jesus exhorted us in his famous Lord's Prayer to ask God to "lead us not into temptation, and to deliver us from evil," or the evil one.

No amount of money can protect you for the harmful effects of evil. Evil is like radiation poisoning, it is virtually invisible to the naked eye, it cannot be felt right away, but shortly after involvement, you will be destroyed; poisoned with an incurable sickness that will surely take your life.

Is our response to fear evil? Absolutely not! The psalmist David penned these words in his "Shepherd's Psalm" as it is so commonly called. "Yea, though I walk through the valley of the shadow of death, I will fear no evil; for thou art with me; thy rod and thy staff they comfort me."

David took comfort in the fact that God had promised to be with him no matter what situation he faced, even death. He mentions two instruments God would be using in his life. The rod; which shepherds used for correction. And the staff; which was the tool used for direction. David was stating that though he walked along a path of evil, he was confident that God would take His rod and beat him (or direct him) back to the straight and narrow; or use the crook of the staff to "yank" him back toward the right way. Either way he would walk the right path even if it led to death. We are forced to face evil daily in the times in which we live, however let us not live in fear.

Daily Verse: Abstain from all appearance of evil.

I Thessalonians 5:2

FEAR OF SURGERY

I remember thinking, "Boy that table sure is small, I sure hope I will fit on it." Not only was it small but it was also cold, as my partially nude backside lay against the cold stainless steel. I remember thinking, and praying, "Jesus, I need you now - I can feel the presence of fear in this room." Just moments prior, while holding my compassionate wife Susie's hand in the preparation room, her prayers were warding off this evil entity. But now here I am alone, and a little frightened, and that makes me vulnerable to deceitful attacks. "Oh, Jesus, I need you now," was the last thing I remember saying as the anesthesiologist lowered the mask over my face. This was my first surgery since high school when I had a knee repaired from a football injury. This operation was to remove a cancerous tumor found in my thyroid, by, of all people, my chiropractor. Just the thought of having a doctor cutting around my vocal cords left me a little uneasy. After all, I'm a preacher, and as Paul once said, "Woe unto me if I preach not the gospel." Well the surgery lasted over six hours and all went well; I've been cancer free for a couple of years now, praise the Lord!

Are you facing the knife? Sounds ominous don't it? Draw strength from the promise of our Lord that He will "never leave us or forsake us." He promised to care for us in every situation we would face. I don't know that it's possible to remove all the uneasiness we face when we must put our life in the hands of others.

I do know from experience that He will see you through it. Any time you go through crisis, remember just that, you're going on through, and you're going to come out the other side–"shining as the noon day sun." You can't have a testimony, without the test.

Daily Verse: "Trust in the Lord at all times; ye people; pour out your heart before him: God is a refuge for us."

Psalm 62:8

FEAR OF DECISION-MAKING

Throughout this wonderful life we've been given by God, there are many roads we may choose from. Some are clear, like the yellow brick road in the movie, The Wizard of Oz, and some are not so clear. The road becomes unclear when we are faced with a crossroads and we must make a choice. Some people are completely crippled because of indecision. Listen to this humorous story from our former President, Ronald Reagan that taught him not to live a life of indecision.

One day when he was just a small boy, his aunt took him to a shoe cobbler to have a new pair of shoes made for him. The cobbler asked, "Do you want a round toe or a square toe?" Reagan couldn't make up his mind on such a short notice, so he asked to come back in a day or two after he had thought about it for awhile. The cobbler readily agreed since he was really busy anyway. A couple of days later the shoemaker was walking up the street to the market, and happened to run into the young Reagan. He asked," Have you made up your mind yet young man?"

"No, I still don't know what I want," answered the boy.

"Very well," said the shoemaker.

A few days later young Reagan was called upon to pick up his new shoes and when he received them he couldn't believe his eyes. One shoe had a round toe and the other had a square toe.

"I had to look at those shoes everyday, until I finally grew out of them, and they taught me a very valuable lesson in life. If you don't make your own decisions somebody else will make them for you," said Reagan in his later years.

Although, this story is humorous now, it wasn't to the young Reagan. Indecision can leave us with some very painful memories, to forget. If you are facing major decisions in your life, and you are not quite sure what to do, ask God for His wisdom. He promised to give it to anyone who asks. Seek council from wise counselors like pastors and other leaders; see if they can offer some light on the subject that maybe you haven't considered before. Most important of all, allow God to speak to your heart through prayer and His Word, and when you hear Him, allow the peace of God to rule your decision. If God grants you peace, then go ahead as planned, but if no peace persists, then do nothing.

Daily Verse: "Thy word is a lamp to my feet and a light to my path."

Psalm 119:105

FEAR OF ALIENS

Is there life on other planets outside this small planet we call home? Your guess is as good as mine. The Bible is completely silent on the subject. Although the Bible does tell us that there is a very sophisticated network of fallen angels at work in our heavenlies. These angels are at work as we speak, to deter our prayers from reaching the throne of God. Scripture states that once our prayers reach God's throne they are stored up in vials to be poured out in the end times. Daniel tells us of an angel named Gabriel, who appeared to tell him about a war in the heavenlies over his prayer life. We also know that since the enemy couldn't win the heavenly battle he tried to defeat Daniel in an earthly battle by having him thrown into a den of hungry lions. What was the crime Daniel did to deserve such a cruel sentence? He prayed to his God three times a day. Do you know that Daniel is the only one recorded in the Bible to be persecuted for praying? It seems only fitting that God would use such a shining example of perseverance to share His awesome revelation about the end times.

Many books have been written about the subjects of UFO's. Some claim that most of the sightings are government experiments in electrogravitic propulsion, as opposed to jet propulsion. Others claim some of them are satanic apparitions used to shipwreck the faith of people who believe in them. I don't know about you, but if I was the devil, and I wanted to cause people to lose faith in the coming of the Lord, I would try to plant doubts and fears into their minds, as to the truth, so they were sure to believe my lie. Without question I totally believe that one day after the rapture of the church, people will be running around blaming it on aliens who beamed everyone on board their spacecraft. Hollywood has prepared us to believe in teleportation, warp speed, and light-year travel. Not that I think S. S. (Steven Spielberg) or Lucas are intentionally trying to cause our faith to waver, but Satan, as deceptive as he is, will use these beliefs to propagate his lies in the end times. So what about little green men? Only God knows for sure.

Daily Verse: "And there was war in heaven: Michael and his angels fought against the dragon; and the dragon fought and his angels."

Revelation 12:7

FEAR OF A POOR SELF-IMAGE

Although the prison door has been opened by Jesus Christ our Lord and Savior, many of His dear people are still locked inside the prison of poor self-esteem; held captive by the opinion of others. Many are like Lazarus after Christ called him back from the dead. He came out of the grave but he still was imprisoned by the grave clothes and wasn't totally set free until the words of our Master rang loudly in his ears, "Loose him and let him go!" We have been set free from the power of sin, which is death, but some are still wandering around the tomb wrapped up in death's grave clothes. For you dear ones who are living in this condition, I repeat the words of the Master in the personal tense, "Be loosed and set free!"

So what is poor self-esteem? It's a deep feeling of being weighed down with a sense of inadequacy. You possess no personal sense of self worth. Past experiences and unresolved guilt from past mistakes can cause you to slumber in a state of remorse and self-condemnation over the value of your life. Sometimes social pressures from society work to diminish our image by the way we look or act. If a woman doesn't possess a "Barbie," figure, she feels unattractive. Countless of millions of dollars are poured into promoting fitness equipment that will give us the perfect body, although God's Word claims that bodily exercise only "profits a little."

You may be wondering how to correct the fear that you're not of any value. A few simple steps could boost you up the ladder of self-worth quite quickly if you will only follow them.

First, realize who you are in Christ. You're not a sinner saved by grace, just hoping to make it into heaven some day by the skin of your teeth. You're a child of Almighty God. Scriptures declares that you are "His workmanship created in Christ Jesus for good works." You are a "new creation," and all "old things have passed away." Decide today that you will guard this image of you by arresting any thought that says otherwise. You are the only policeman of your mind, and the only one who can lockup those negative thoughts about you in solitary confinement. Openly accept God's awesome love and forgiveness toward you, confess any wrongs you may do, and believe that He will remove any presence of them from your record. The most important thing you can do for yourself is to forgive yourself, just as Christ has forgiven you - unconditionally.

Daily Verse: "And will be a father unto you, and ye shall be my sons and daughters, saith the Lord Almighty."
II Corinthians 6:18

FEAR OF CARRYING HEAVY BURDENS

We must understand the difference between burdens that God intends for us to carry and burdens which he demands us to "cast onto him." God's first man to serve in the Pastorate had to learn this early on in his ministry. Moses was given the toughest congregation any man has been called to serve; a group of three-million newly redeemed converts, who have not been associated with true religion their whole lives. They were confined to a "slave's mentality," for this was the only life they knew. Then Moses comes along and frees them by mandate from his God; his goal being to mold them into victorious conquerors. Soon the continuous rebellion of the people and the weight of so much responsibility forced Moses to pray this prayer in Numbers 11:14, "I am not able to bear all this people alone, because it is too heavy for me." I believe God was sitting back saying, "Finally, now I can use this guy." What was God's answer to Moses prayer? "Find me seventy men of integrity that you know personally Moses, and I'll spread the burden out among all of you equally."

Just as Moses learned which burdens were his to bear, and which were not; so must we. We should never bear the burden of sin, either our own or our loved ones. Also don't ever bear a burden of doubt. The burden of doubt must be quickly thrown onto God without hesitation. If you allow unnecessary burdens to persist in your life, you too will end up as Moses did; even weary about the very life you live.

Any God-given burden will squeeze the grapes of our lives to produce the new wine of fruitfulness He so desires for us. Burdens not God-breathed only produce a whine in our life and must be dealt with, before they poison the entire vine. God intended that His "joy," be our only "strength," as we need to live in this world of uncertainty. He brings us to the point where we are finally ready to have real fellowship with him, only to hear us complain how others don't have it as hard. In Matthew's gospel Jesus tells us to "take His yoke" upon our shoulders for it is "easy to bear," and "light" to carry. Just what is He asking us to do? He wants us to join ourselves to His team; to climb up beside him, put His yoke around our shoulders and let him help carry the burdens of this world. After all, He carried the weight of all sin on his shoulders once, and He has proven himself to be faithful to the task.

Daily Verse: "Come unto me all ye that labour and are heavy laden, and I will give you rest."

Matthew 11:28

FEAR OF WITNESSING YOUR FAITH

Sharing one's faith is sometimes a lot more than selling religion door to door like some business. Someone has appropriately stated that most "people don't care how much you know, until they know how much you care."

Once an unsaved man went to the doctor and was diagnosed with terminal cancer. He would soon be leaving a lovely wife and daughter behind. He worked for a thoughtless employer who immediately fired him once they found out about his sickness. The sick man's family had to use up all their life savings and insurance policies just to fight the disease. One day after a particularly hard day, he was feeling sorry for himself when he heard a knock at the door. When he answered the door, it was a happy Christian out canvassing the neighborhood to share his faith. Impatiently the sick man looked the Christian in the eye and said, "All you Christians care about are what happens to you after you die. I don't care about what will happen after I die, I have real problems now. I have only a few months left to live, and I'm leaving my wife penniless, and my daughter's college fund has been used up to care for me." He then proceeded to cuss the Christian out, and forced him to leave the premises at once. The Christian, who was a leader in the church, began to think about what the man had said. He then decided to do something about the man's problems.

A couple of weeks passed and the sick man heard another knock at the door. When he opened the door he couldn't believe his eyes; it was the man that he so belligerently ran off a few weeks prior. Immediately, his anger began to flare up again until the Christian man blurted out, "Sir I'm sorry I offended you the last time I was here, but I decided to do something about your problems. I talked to a realtor friend of mine who has agreed to sell your house for your wife, after you're gone, and has offered to give his commission from the sale to her. Some of us at the church have agreed to make the payments for your wife until it is sold. The earnings your wife gets from the house should pay for your daughter's college expenses. Also, I have a friend who owns apartment buildings, and he has agreed to give your wife a unit, with free utilities and a monthly salary if she would manage the rest of the units for him." Suddenly the sick man began to weep, for he had never seen the gospel displayed so personally before. He opened his heart and was gloriously saved that day.

Isn't that the message Jesus preached to the world? The Bible claims that Jesus went everywhere doing good, and healing all who were oppressed of the devil. Shouldn't we preach the same message and put aside our theology books, to allow the Holy Spirit to touch this sin cursed world with his power?

Daily Verse: "Ye are our epistle written in our hearts, known and read of all men."

II Corinthians 3:2

FEAR OF WAITING

Can you imagine being old enough to draw social security for the last two decades, before you decide to start your family. That's how old Abram was when he listened to his wife, who was tired of waiting on God to fulfill His promise to them. After all, doesn't God expect us to do our part in fulfilling His will for our lives? Listen to what the Scripture says about the ordeal; "And Sarai, Abram's wife took Hagar her maid the Egyptian, after Abram had dwelt ten years in the land of Canaan, and gave her to her husband Abram to be his wife. And he went in into Hagar, and she conceived; And Abram was fourscore and six years old, when Hagar bare Ishmael to Abram," (Gen. 16:3, 4, 16).

God had made a promise to Abram and Sarai, and it was taking too long, so they decided to help God out, since they knew best. After twenty years of waiting, they noticed their bodies were giving out. "We must have missed God," they reasoned, "He must want us to do it the way every other barren couple does it." In patriarch times, if the master's wife was barren she would allow her husband to impregnate one of her servants. Then, during the birthing process the servant would lay between the spread legs of the mistress; to symbolize that the child belonged to the mistress. All this was beautiful at the time, but all they managed to do was get in God's way.

It's kind of like the man who was walking down the street one day when he noticed his neighbor struggling to get a dishwasher out through the door of his house. He immediately ran to the door to offer his assistance. After ten minutes of struggling at the door-way, the owner finally said, "I don't think I'm ever going to get this stupid dishwasher in the house."

"Oh, you're trying to take it in the house? I thought you were trying to get it out of the house," said the friendly neighbor. Those who want instant gratification usually find it hard to stay out of God's way. Interference just delays things even longer in most cases.

Lack of patience was one of the main reasons King Saul was rejected as King of Israel. He was ready to go into battle against the Philistines, but they couldn't go until the priest made the sacrifice and blessed the battle with God's favor. So he waited and waited on Samuel to come and do the sacrifice, then after seven days he could wait no longer, so he sacrificed the animal himself, contrary to God's commandment. As soon as he was finished, Samuel arrived. Samuel told Saul that he had overstepped his boundary for the last time. God had rejected him to be King from that day forward all because he couldn't wait.

If we could only see behind the scenes we could see what God has in store for us. Maybe he has to do more to get things ready for us. Don't be afraid to wait on God to fulfill his promise to you. But while you're waiting apply these four pieces of advice from the psalmist, David in Psalm 37.

"Trust in the Lord . . . Delight yourself in the Lord . . . Commit to the Lord, and finally, Rest in the Lord."

Daily Verse; "But they that wait upon the Lord shall renew their strength."

Isaiah 40:31a

FEAR OF BURNOUT

It's the third lap of the Daytona 500 Auto Race. Donny Allison is driving his quarter of a million dollar car around the infield side of the track, when all of a sudden he coasts the car to a complete stop. Immediately, everyone wonders, "Is something the matter with Donny?" No he's getting out of the car. "Did his car blow up?" No there's no smoke. So what would make a racer like him stop in the third lap of the race? Someone forgot to put gas in his car, and he ran out of gas! It's a costly mistake for a race car driver, but it's a deadly mistake for a Christian. It doesn't matter how powerful the car is or how skilled the driver is, if there isn't any gas in the tank, nobody's going anywhere.

Burnout is much the same. A Christian must be refueled, recharged, and replenished on a regular basis or they will burnout. Burnout doesn't happen overnight. It's a slow process of burning the candle at both ends, until finally the wick meets the middle, and there's no more light to shine, no more strength to run on, and no more motivation to keep you going. Soon you can't stand the thought of doing another job, so you resign all your obligations. You sit back and sulk about your life until sometimes you feel like dying. If you've ever felt like this, keep reading, this could keep you from experiencing the fear of burnout.

Usually, one of the main causes of burnout is too many projects on your plate. Although some personalities, like the "Choleric" tend to handle juggling several tasks at once, for most others it can be just too difficult. Too many people are like the two campers that had twenty logs each to build campfires with that would last all night. One camper threw all his logs in the fire at once and, "Wow!" It sure made a big bon-fire for a couple hours, and then it was out. The other camper just threw one log at a time into the fire. His fire was smaller but it lasted the whole night. Let us learn to be marathon runners in the race of life and not sprinters that tire too quickly.

Many of us are weary in life because we don't know where we are going, so we try a little bit of everything, hoping that something succeeds. We're like Supreme Court Justice, Oliver Wendell Holmes who was on a train one day and couldn't find his ticket. He was frantic until the conductor told him that since he was such a man of honor he would trust him to send in the ticket once he found it. But Holmes complained that his problem was that without the ticket, he didn't know where he was going. We must know where we are headed with renewed vision so that we can get rid of unnecessary things that weigh us down.

Rest is not a bad word. In fact, God has commanded that people take one day a week to rejuvenate their lives. Learn to live only one day at a time and get rid of things that only bring minor satisfaction to you. Save the important time of your life for family, time spent with God, and, of course, time spent with just you and your spouse. Recharge your batteries every weekend at a good church that preaches God's truth and allows you to worship him freely. By all means, don't quit!!!!

Daily Verse: "And let us not be weary in well doing: for in due season we shall reap, if we faint not."

Galatians 6:9

FEAR OF DOUBT

Don't forget in the dark what you knew in the light. That's what happened to the greatest Old Testament prophet born of women, an acknowledgement directly from the lips of Jesus. John the Baptist was a very unusual man from birth. He was born to an elderly, presumed barren woman. He was filled with the Holy Spirit while he was still in his mother's womb. He lived in the wilderness, away from all the corruption of city life, until it was time to answer God's call to ministry. He received the awesome privilege of getting to be the one to announce that the Messiah had finally come, who, by the way turned out to be his cousin. John was a man of rock hard conviction, unafraid to speak out against the adultery of King Herod. He was the first to proclaim the need to "repent, for the kingdom of heaven was at hand." Finally, his last pronouncement after Jesus' baptism was, "He must increase, but I must decrease." And decrease he did. Soon afterward, he was arrested by Herod and thrown into a dark dungeon. I'm sure he had no idea he would decrease to the likes of a dungeon. In the dungeon he began to wonder, "Is this guy really the Messiah? After all we played hide and seek together as kids. I sure hope I didn't make a mistake about him. Maybe I better send a couple of my disciples to ask, just to make sure. I don't know how long I'm going to be in this cold place."

So he waits a few days and his followers return with this word, "The blind receive sight, the lame are made to walk, the lepers are cleansed, the deaf can hear, the dead are raised, the gospel is preached to the poor, and blessed is the man who doesn't stumble because of me."

Ouch! What a hard word for a man in prison. But Jesus knew John could take it, after all John's whole ministry up until this point had been an exclamation point. He was a man filled with courage, and confidence, and he wasn't about to give him up to doubt. The fear of doubt occurs in our life when what we expect to happen in our life doesn't happen. I'm sure as you can see from our story, that no one is immune from this terrible fear.

Circumstances surround us, and come in direct conflict with what we believe. This then leads us to waver in our opinion of what we already know to be true. So how do we increase our faith and decrease our doubts? When doubts arise in your heart, begin to concentrate on what you already know to be true, and not on what you don't know. This will lead you to question your doubts and not your faith. Doubt can sometimes paralyze us in the decision making process, so when it occurs, begin to do what Proverbs 3:5 exhorts us to do, "Trust in the Lord with all your heart, and lean not on your own understanding." Trust means that you have faith in God that no matter what happens in your life, you know that God is still in charge, and He knows best. He will speak to your heart, even if your mind is saying something else.

Daily Verse:" Jesus answered and said unto them, verily I say unto you, If you have faith, and not doubt, you shall not only do this which is done to the fig tree, but also if ye shall say unto this mountain, be thou removed, and be cast into the sea; it shall be done."

Matthew 21:21

FEAR OF NUCLEAR THREAT

Since two nuclear bombs fell on Japan ending World War II, most of the world has lived in a constant state of fear over nuclear war. In some parts of the world it has become the most critical, fear-provoking subject. The United States has been largely responsible for creating most of the fear after causing the decimation of two cities to oblivion and conducting 23 nuclear weapons tests during the '50's on a small island known as Bikini Island; all in the name of "National Security." This heightened exposure forced Americans into a state of panic over the possibility of a "cold war" escalating into a nuclear war. It was very fashionable in the fifties to purchase a bomb shelter to protect your life. This was all propagated much like the Y2K scare of 2000. Throughout the sixties and seventies more and more nations began to get nuclear capabilities. The use of bomb-shelters became obsolete, since a full scale nuclear war would leave nothing inhabitable, so who would want to live anyway?

Finally, what everyone had been saying was going to happen took place; a nuclear accident. The fear-stricken press had been warning us of the dangers of nuclear power, and then in Pennsylvania, the "-Three-Mile Island" incident took place. It was exploited as an exaggerated holocaust by many in the press. What many didn't know was that there was more radiation in an old radium watch than in the Three-Mile Island spill. Just when things started to die down in 1986, the Chernobyl nuclear accident took place and frightened the world once again. As for today, our society absorbs everything nuclear with unnecessary paranoia. If the truth is to be known, nuclear power is the safest, cleanest, most environmentally safe source of power in existence today. We have no need to fear the use of it to enrich our lives today. As for a threat, we will always have that hanging over our heads no matter how much nuclear disarmament takes place around our world.

Some may wonder, "What does the Bible have to say about nuclear war?" It isn't silent about the subject. In the book of Revelation, Scripture mentions a time during the great tribulation when "men's flesh will melt from their bones . . . eyes will melt in their sockets." Unfortunately, this is a sign of nuclear fire; a fall-out that will most definitely take place during a time when all men will be in a state of panic. Armageddon will happen as it is recorded in the Scriptures, and God's Word is truth. But, for the Christian, this is a time when we have nothing to fear for God has promised to take care of us. For you who may still have fear, I repeat the words of former president Franklyn Roosevelt, "We have nothing to fear, but fear itself."

Daily Verse: "Say unto them that are of a fearful heart, Be strong, fear not: Behold your God will come with vengeance, even God with recompense: he will come and save you."

Isaiah 35:4

FEAR OF CONFUSION

One of the most confusing things about flying in an airplane is inertia. Did you know that even if the plane turns its wings completely perpendicular to the ground, things will still drop straight to the floor, and you won't even spill your free drink? This was a hazardous problem when man first took to the airways. When a pilot entered a cloud, they couldn't tell whether their wings were tilted or not. Without the horizon in view pilots were at the mercy of inertia. To compensate for this problem, artificial horizons were built and put on the instrument panel. This would keep the plane from plummeting into a sudden dive, ending in a crash. Pilots rejected the artificial horizons at first, because of unbelief. They had more trust in their instinct, than in something artificial. Soon they came around and flying was revolutionized.

Much of our lives are lived driving along in a spiritual fog. We are unable to see what will take place tomorrow in our life. God has given us a life that must completely be lived by faith and not by sight. He has not left us without instruction though. He used several men through-out history to record His plan for us, and give us a blueprint on how we are to live. God's word is a horizon indicator that we can follow in the spiritual fog, to lead us through the trying times of life. God has promised that he is not the "author of confusion." If confusion exists in your life, it's because Satan has planted that seed in you. His plan is to lead you astray as he has so many in the past. He creates "fog" in your life to lead you away from God's plan. If you begin to live by your own wisdom you will most definitely be deceived. Only by God's wisdom, found in his Word, can we see clear enough to do God's will. Fear not the confusion, just remember who the author is, and this should help you get back to the right path.

Daily Verse: "For God is not the author of confusion, but of peace, as in all churches of the saints."

I Corinthians 14:33

FEAR OF DISASTER

The '90's proved to be one of the most profitable times in human history, but history also records something else about that time. It became known as the "decade of disaster." More natural disasters took place during those ten years then in any other decade. Floods, fires, hurricanes, tornadoes, earthquakes, volcanic eruptions, and a host of other fluke incidents in nature dominated the news reports during those ten years. No country in the world was immune from the droughts and impending disasters. Some have speculated the cause to El Nino is a shift in the earth's water currents, but the Bible reader knows the cause without the weatherman. God has, through-out human history, used natural conditions to get man's attention. In the closing times of man's six-thousand years of recorded history something is about to take place. The Bible records that the whole earth is groaning to be delivered from the curse, placed on it from the fall.

It also records that natural disasters of nature would accelerate in the time just before the deliverance. These would be the "beginnings of sorrows" as the Scripture states. We should not allow these disasters to distract us from the real world around us. God's Word says that the real disasters are not fought in flesh and blood, or in the natural elements; listen to Ephesians 6:12,

"For we wrestle not against flesh and blood, but against principalities, against powers, against the rulers of darkness of this world, against spiritual wickedness in the high places." In the book of Job, Satan had approached God's throne and asked permission before he could send a tornado to wipe out Job's house. Did Job lose everything? Yes, everything except his integrity and faith. He maintained them and God was able to restore everything that Satan stole from him twice over. Serving God does not guarantee we will not face disasters in life but what it does guarantee is, like Job learned, we don't face them alone. Our lives are at the mercy of the providence of God, but what do you expect? After all He is God.

Daily Verse: "Be not afraid of sudden fear, neither of the desolation of the wicked, when it cometh."

Proverbs 3:25

FEAR OF MEANINGLESS LIVING

Throughout human history many great men and women have fretted over their meaningless existence; people you would never expect when you look at the contributions they made - Albert Einstein, Abraham Lincoln, Ernest Hemingway, even the father of the modern protestant movement, Martin Luther, slumped into a period of depression over his purpose, in life. Even though he brought great spiritual success to the common man by translating the Bible from Latin to the common language of German, Luther still couldn't find rest in his mind. He suffered so long during one particular period that his wife wore a black armband to breakfast, a common sign of mourning a lost loved one. When Luther inquired as to who died, her comment was that the way he had been carrying on around the house, "God surely must be dead."

Even Solomon in all his wealth, prosperity, wisdom, had this to say about his life; "Then I looked on all the works that my hands had wrought, and on the labor that I had labored to do; and, behold, all was vanity and vexation of spirit, and there was no profit under the sun," (Eccle. 2:11).

What could possibly cause such great men to fall into such a pit of despair about life? It's the everyday sand in our shoes that we have to deal with. A great cross-country runner was asked one time by an interviewer what was the most difficult thing he had to face in a cross-country race. Though the sun was hot and the pavement hard, the runner answered that the most difficult thing was the dreaded sand that gets in your shoes as you're running. It literally wears your feet out over time, step after step until you can't take the pain anymore and you have to clean it out. The sand in our shoes of life - like disappointments, let downs, unreal expectations, losses and such can all contribute to a time of despair. Some new age gurus are teaching that we need to look inside ourselves for the answers to our purpose in life. They say when you get in touch with your inner being then you are beginning to get on the right path in life. Let your "karma" lead you. This is a totally fruitless adventure that is completely contradictory to what the Scriptures teach. The Scriptures teach that man is "inherently wicked," and his "heart" is quite capable of "deceiving" him. In fact, it even teaches that if there wasn't a devil to deceive us, we would still find a way to do wrong. And you want to follow that? No, I think not. Rather I would follow the leading of God, since He seems to have things under control. He promises to give us more than we can expect if we will submit and follow Him; "For I know the thoughts (plans) that I think toward you, thoughts (plans) of peace, and not evil, to give you an expected (prosperous) end," (Jer.29:11). If God has plans on making us prosperous in life, wouldn't it to be foolish to live our lives without him at the helm? Solomon found this out later in his life when he penned these words as to man's whole purpose for existence. "Let us hear the conclusion of the whole matter: Fear God, and keep his commandments: for this is the whole duty of man," (Eccle. 12:13).

Daily Verse: "He hath shewed thee, O man, what is good; and what doth the Lord require of thee, but to do justly, and to love mercy, and to walk humbly with thy God."

Micah 5:8

FEAR OF DISCONTENTMENT

Discontentment is a powerful force that has distracted many people away from what's important in life, in pursuit of what some people may call pipe-dreams. Many mothers have sacrificed their family's well-being for the sake of a "real job." Today's youth are turned into latchkey kids so mom can find satisfaction and fulfillment in life. Don't get me wrong, I realize that there are legitimate reasons for a mother to work outside the home, but for the most part a new car is not worth the sacrifice. As for my family, my wife and I decided early on in our marriage that she would be a stay-at-home mom. And since she stayed at home with the children, (four by the way), we decided to teach them at home to assure they received a proper education. At the time of this writing we are left with only one child at home, and he's fifteen years old. My wife went on to school to pursue a dream of hers, and now she happily works everyday as a nurse.

This decision to wait on a career for her was not an easy decision for us to make. We sure had some lean times in those early years of marriage. But now I look at how our children have turned out to be caring individuals fulfilling their dreams in life and I can't help but give Susie, my wife, all the credit for deciding to stay at home with them in those formative years.

The fear of discontentment has caused many to develop a "keep up with the Jones mentality." (Sorry Mom, that's her new married name). People will do just about anything to feel a season of contentment in their life. They will cheat, lie, or steal for a few moments of peace. The problem is those suffering from the fear of discontentment are looking for relief in all the wrong places. Paul, the writer of two-thirds of the New Testament, revealed that only through a relationship with Jesus Christ can we really be content. If you think a new job will give it to you you're wrong. Moving to a new city doesn't promise it either. Having a baby might seem fulfilling, but will not bring lasting contentment. Only when you decide to get to know Jesus, one on one, will you find what you're looking for.

Daily Verse: "Let your conversations be without covetousness; and be content with such things as you have: for he hath said, I will never leave thee, nor forsake thee."

Hebrews 13:5

FEAR OF THREATS

All was quiet at the UCLA Medical Center in Los Angeles on a particularly boring Monday, when suddenly, the door burst open, and in walks an irate woman by the name of Sophia White. There she stood waving a .38-caliber handgun threatening to shoot one of the nurses. She quickly fired off six rounds hitting a woman by the name of Elizabeth Staten twice. "I'm going to kill you, you husband stealer," were her words of threat to Staten. Staten, with two slugs already in her and bleeding profusely began to run into the emergency room for safety. But a determined White pursued Staten firing off another round. Then, from seemingly out of nowhere, stepped up a very brave Joan Black who was another nurse who worked in the hospital who without hesitation, calmly walked up and hugged the angry White and offered some encouraging words of comfort. Finally, after a few consoling words about the pain she was suffering, White willingly gave Black the gun, and sobbed over her shoulder. It's amazing what a little understanding and comfort can do in this world.

We live in a world that is in extreme pain. But nobody wants to accept the responsibility for causing the pain. It's always somebody else's fault things went wrong. "My dad didn't spend any time with me." "My mother didn't kiss me enough." "I come from a dysfunctional family," are some of the many excuses today. Hey! Guess what? We've been a dysfunctional family since Adam and Eve! Show me a family that doesn't have problems. It's not the threats that count, it's how you handle them that matters. The Bible records a time in the Apostle Paul's life when he "breathed out threats against the church." He was punishing the church of Jesus Christ by having Christians arrested and killed in some cases, as with Stephen, the first martyr. He was doing all this evil work in the name of God. How did the church respond to his threats? They kept on spreading the Word and growing as a sect. In today's society there's a lot of hostility toward Christians and the church; rightly so for all that has been done in the name of God in these past years. However, we must still hold up the banner of the blood-stained symbol of our Christian faith - which is love. Only true love can set those free who are bound by hostility and hatred. Let us be that Love.

Daily Verse: "He brought me to the banqueting house, and his banner over me is love."

Song of Solomon 2:4

FEAR OF COWARDICE

Throughout human history many men and women have rose to the challenge of the moment; performing uncompromising feats of pure bravery in the midst of trial. They willingly gave their lives for the life of others. In 1996 another such feat was performed by Andrew Meekens, an elder of a local church. What would you do if you knew you only have three minutes to live? How would you respond to such terrifying news? The story begins as a plane is hijacked and on it's way to Africa. The plane finally ran out of fuel around the Comoros Islands. The pilot told the passengers they were about to make an emergency landing, so they were told to brace themselves. According to one of the few survivors, Andrew stood to his feet and presented the gospel of Jesus Christ to people aboard the plane. He invited them to accept Christ and twenty people quickly accepted Him as their Savior. As I read that story, I don't know about you, but I'm a little embarrassed about the opportunities I've had in the past to share Christ, and I shunned them. Once I was at a grocery store to pick up some milk or some small item when I noticed a gentleman who once had attended our church. At one time he was a very anointed man, who loved God with all his heart, but something snapped in him, and now he was a casualty of war, with no concern for Christ, church, or anything spiritual. I wondered, "Should I witness to him about Christ?" As I was wondering, and praying about whether I should witness to him or not, another line opened up in the store, and he quickly went to that line. He went from the back to the front in a couple of seconds. As I was debating about witnessing to him, he was already checking out; he was just picking up a video tape for his family. As he walked past me, I was completely disgusted when I happened to notice the movie he had chosen to watch - a movie titled, "Witness." God spoke to me and told me that I had just missed an opportunity. Now, in hindsight, which is always 20/20 vision by the way, my prayers were offered because of cowardice. I wanted some divine mandate to assure me my labor would not be in vain. Instead of stepping out in faith, and doing as God commands at least five times in the Scriptures, "preach the gospel to every creature." So where does the boldness come from to share our faith like the early disciples in the early church? It comes from the same place they got it. Read today's daily verse, and pray the same prayer they prayed that led them to a life of boldness.

Daily Verse "And now, Lord, behold their threatening: and grant unto thy servants that with all boldness they may speak thy word."

Acts 4:29

FEAR OF DEFEAT

"If you think your beaten you are,
If you think you can't you won't?
Life's battles, aren't always won by the
Stronger or faster man,
But true winners are,
Those who believe they can."

This is known by so many as the "Winners Pledge." This pledge was taped to my locker in school. It was taped to our football helmets during practice. It was written in our notebooks for school. And here I am, twenty-eight years after graduation, still remembering what it takes to be a winner.

That pledge had meaning to my team. Six of our eight victories my senior year came from 4th. Quarter rallies, as we huddled together and recited that pledge. It restored our energy. It brought us renewed faith, and a determination to not give up. "We will not be defeated" was our attitude. This is the attitude of a winner. A person that finishes what they start, without reservation. It's the same attitude Sir Ernest Shackle ford had as he began his 2,100-mile trek across Antarctica, in the early part of the twentieth century. He dreamed of crossing the frozen wasteland by dogsled. His dreams were cut short though by a massive ice pack, which sank his ship two-hundred miles from land. He and his men loaded nearly a ton of supplies into a lifeboat from the sinking ship, and pulled it across the frozen ice floes nearly 1200 hundred miles to the nearest outpost. At one time they reached a body of water; they had to cross waves of over ninety feet that threatened to sink their small lifeboat. Finally, after seven of months of dragging across the cruel wasteland, they reached their destination, which was the starting point for their trip across Antarctica. They were so worn out, that nobody even recognized them, yet they kept going, because winners never quit. Winners never admit defeat, they just "keep on keeping on," no matter what the circumstances. They believe that every situation that occurs in life is a learning experience for them.

Don't fear the agony of defeat, which will leave you wishing you, would have done something. How many things would you attempt to do, if you knew you couldn't fail at them? God has promised in his Word to help us in all things we attempt for him if we'll include him in the decision making process. Make God your senior partner in your life, and he will always vote right.

Daily Verse: "I can do all things through Christ which strengthens me."

Philippians 4:13

FEAR OF LOSS OF JOY

How many of you have ever helped your child build a volcano for a science fair project? First, you mold the clay into a small mountain, and then you hollow out the center with your hand. Then after some patience and a few days, the clay finally hardens. Now you're ready for the experiment. You fill the belly of the project with baking soda. Add just a touch of red food coloring to the vinegar, and your ready for the test. Pour an equal amount of vinegar, into the top of the volcano and get out of the way. Stand back and watch the red lava pour out the top of your homemade natural disaster. That eruption you're watching is exactly what God wants our joy to be like. He wants it to bubble over in our lives, so our joy can affect others around us. He wants us to have joy when things are good, and when things are bad. Joy is not the same as happiness; joy comes from the inside, and is a product from being in the presence of God. Happiness is determined by your circumstances. If everything is going alright in your life, you are happy, but you let adversity take place, and your happiness goes out the window. Joy has nothing at all to do with success. It is everywhere God's presence is. Happiness is external; joy is internal. Happiness has its roots in chance; joy is based on making a confident choice. Happiness is based on the circumstances of your life, but joy is based on a relationship with Christ.

It's interesting to note that in the Eskimo language they have no word for joy. This made translating the Bible quite a challenge for some translators who were working on making it available for them. They did some research, and found out that for Eskimos, the happiest time of the day is when they allowed their sled dogs to come into the hut for their nightly feeding. Everybody gets excited. The dogs jump up and bark, the children laugh, and squeal. Even neighbors would stop over to share in the nightly ritual from time to time.

This event was used to convey how joyful the disciples were when they saw Jesus after his resurrection. It would read in our English Bible like this; "And when the disciples saw Jesus, they wagged their tails." Whatever the translation, real joy has everything to do with God's presence. When we want joy we must find a way to get into the presence of God. Whether by meditation, prayer, Bible reading, worship, whichever you desire for the day, get into God's presence today. He is able to take a frown and turn it upside down.

Daily Verse: "Thou wilt show me the path of life; in thy presence is fullness of joy; at thy right hand there are pleasures for evermore."

Psalm 16:11

FEAR OF DOUBLE-MINDEDNESS

Get out of the middle of the road. If you stand in the middle of the road too long, you take a chance of being hit by traffic, coming from both directions. If you allow indecision to dominate your life, you will actually die before your dead. Indecision feeds on itself and can become so habit forming, that it will become the main portion of your whole life. James put it this way; "A double-minded man is unstable in all his ways."

Double-mindedness is not unbelief, but it isn't faith either. It wavers between faith, and doubt, unable to make up its mind. It's like the lonely hitchhiker who can't make up his mind which way he wants to go, so he sticks up both thumbs and takes the first one that gives him a ride. James 1:6–8 also gives us some characteristics of a double-minded man. It says he's "like a ship tossed to and fro by every wind that comes along." Emotionally, the double-minded person is up one moment, then down the next. Being around someone like this very long makes me seasick. Outside forces are always directing them here and there, when the Bible clearly says we are to be guided by faith on the inside. Double-minded people aren't sure what they believe. They don't have a firm grasp on their spirituality. In fact, they aren't quite sure that they have salvation, because they live in a 'yes' and 'no' mentality. They live a confused life, not quite sure which way is right.

Once there was a snake born with two heads and when it was studied, scientists noticed a strange behavior. One minute it would crawl one direction, then in just a couple minutes time it would begin to crawl an entirely different direction. This serpent was the picture of a creature that was truly double-minded. In the same way a person who suffers from this fear lacks any direction that they can put confidence in. They are forever wondering which the right way to go is.

If this sounds like you, get off the confusing yo-yo. Begin to trust in the Lord with your heart, and not your head. This is an easy statement to make, but can be quite a challenge to accomplish at times. When logic knocks on the door of your mind, turn your entire heart over to God. Learn to trust your internal instruments much the way a pilot trusts his instrument panel while he's thirty-thousand feet in the air. When the days are clear and sunny, the pilot doesn't need the instruments. But most of their flying is done in the clouds, and at night. In the same way most of our lives are lived in the dark, not knowing what tomorrow holds. Trust God even if some of the decisions you make in life are wrong; He is able to get you back on the right path.

Daily Verse: "That we henceforth be no more children, tossed to and fro, and carried about by every of doctrine, by the sleight of men, and cunning craftiness, whereby they lie in wait to deceive."

Ephesians 4:14

FEAR OF BLOOD

Blood is a very strange and mysterious substance. Some people can work around it - like in slaughter houses. They can be up to their elbows in it, with it flowing down big drains, others faint at the site of a rug burn. People pay hundreds of dollars for tickets to watch boxers beat opponent's faces until the blood begins to flow. It seems that our human nature side enjoys the site of blood, while our spiritual side favors the more humane life, and is repulsed by the site of it.

While the Bible does not give us the chemical composition of blood, it does give us some understanding of this mysterious substance. It states; " . . . the life of every living creature is in its blood." For the life of the flesh is in the blood. When God breathed into the first man the breath of life, he also breathed the chemical composition of blood into him. That blood carries the life. The blood isn't the life, it only carries the life. Life itself is spiritual, and blood is only the carrier of that spiritual life. When someone dies, the spiritual life leaves the physical carrier, which is the blood. Another unique fact about blood is that apart from a few variations in blood types, all blood is the same, no matter what color the skin.

I am convinced that many Christians live miserable lives fighting sickness, and recurring sins because they fear the blood. Which blood do they fear? Why the blood of Jesus, of course. They have a passive theology about what the blood can do for them, and for such, it is powerless. A person with an active faith, full of vitality, will use it, sprinkle it, plead it, and apply it to themselves and their family. The Bible claims that our victory over Satan is by the blood of Jesus and when we apply it to everything involved in our life, he is powerless over us. It's a mystery to me that we all know that salvation by the blood is not automatic, but we think healing by the blood is. All the promises of God are conditional. You must apply faith to them, to receive them.

The book of Zechariah declares; that when Jesus died on the cross he opened a fountain (river) that would flow forever and ever. This river flows continually available for us to plunge in daily to wash away our sins, sicknesses, and sorrows. It is time to put away your fears and swim freely in his river of power available to His children.

Daily Verse: "And when I see the blood, I will pass over you, and the plague shall not be upon you to destroy you."
Exodus 12:13b

FEAR OF BEARING A DEFORMED CHILD

I've been asked on several occasions while witnessing to people," If God is such a good God why does he allow suffering?" "Why does he let little children be born deformed?" "Why does He let small babies live with pain?" These questions and a host of others are often asked in this world of pain in which we live. Some give canned answers, like, "Well, man sinned, and all the suffering was caused by the fall." This is mostly true, yet I personally don't have an answer to most of the questions about the suffering and pain. In fact, I don't think anyone but the Creator knows for sure the answer. All I know for sure is, if God the father saw it fit to allow His only begotten Son to suffer an unjust death for my sins, who am I to question the small amount of suffering I may be forced to endure?

The late Dr. Barnhouse, who pastored the Tenth Presbyterian Church of Philadelphia, Pennsylvania for thirty-three years, was holding a series of meetings for a young pastor friend. The young pastor and his wife were expecting their first child any day and were filled with excitement. On the last day of the meeting, the young pastor didn't show up to start the service. Dr. Barnhouse assumed that this must be the big day so he went on with the service as scheduled. Before the service ended he noticed that the pastor slipped in at the back and quietly sat in the pew. When the service ended, the pastor made his way to his office and asked Dr. Barnhouse to speak to him for a few minutes. As the pastor shut the door to his office he burst into tears and blurted out, "Dr. Barnhouse, our child was born with Down Syndrome. What am I going to do? I haven't got the heart to tell my wife."

Dr. Barnhouse, in all his wisdom, immediately replied; "Friend, this is of the Lord," as he took his Bible and began searching for a Scripture. He went on to read this passage from Exodus 4; "And the Lord said unto him, 'Who has made man's mouth? Or who makes him dumb or deaf, or seeing or blind? Is it not I the Lord?'" As the Bible was closed the young man thanked the wise, older pastor and excused himself so he could go see his wife.

When he entered his wife's room, he could see panic on her face because she had not seen her precious newborn yet. The brave young pastor took his wife by the hand and quoted the scripture from Exodus 4, then informed his wife that God had blessed them with a beautiful Down syndrome baby. They cried and wept as he showed her the Scripture from the Bible. News of the birth spread through the hospital like a wildfire. Some people were even listening in on their telephone conversations. In one particular conversation between the wife, and her mother one woman was amazed, that they called this little baby a "blessing" from God. She was the hospital gossip, and soon was telling everyone in the hospital that these people weren't falling apart, but were calling the child a "blessing from God." The following Sunday an amazing thing happened as the young pastor stood behind his pulpit. Seventy hospital staff members attended the service that morning and as he finished his sermon, thirty of them came forward in response to the invitation and gave their hearts to Christ.

The question remains: Would God allow one of his people to have a handicapped child for the sake of thirty souls? You decide for yourself.

Daily Verse: "For our light affliction, which is but for a moment, worketh for us a far more exceeding and eternal weight of glory."

II Corinthians 4:17

FEAR OF HATRED

The bitter venom of hatred is much like the digestive juices of spiders. You see spiders have been created in a unique way from other creatures in God's kingdom. They are born without stomachs; which means, they don't have the ability to eat something, and then digest it like everything else. They must inject enzymes, and digestive juices into their prey, then sit back and wait until the juices dissolve the organs, nerves, and tissues, of the quarry. After everything inside has cooked down like a soup, then the spider once again sucks the life out of his meal only leaving a shell of what was once there. Have you ever seen someone years after they allowed the bitter fear of hatred to have control of their life? Their life shows the scars of guilt, humiliation, and anger as it so progressively ages the individual. Hatred is listed in the "big seventeen," of Galatians 5:19–21, adamantly stating that those who practice the works of the flesh have no place in the inheritance of the kingdom of God. Knowing these things - what type of people should we strive to be?

Hatred is defined as having a strong dislike, for something or someone. The Bible also exhorts us to love what is good, and hate what is evil. It never gives us permission to hate anybody, but to only hate the evil things of this world. But please don't fight the war against evil with "white-out." Someone in the state of Oregon, went to the public library, and decided to be a self-appointed, censor. They took a bottle of correction fluid called, "White-out," and whitened over words in books that spoke of sexually explicit material, and swear words. Although this person may have thought they were doing right, God never gives us permission to destroy someone else's property in the name of "right." Instead, God would rather we wage the war on the inside. Allow no hatred to take root in your life, and grow into bitterness. Learn to forgive peoples sins against you quickly.

"Let not the sun go down on your wrath," the Bible demands. But instead seek restitution against wrongs while you are still in the person's presence.

Daily Verse: "Hatred stirreth up strifes; but love covereth all sins."

Proverbs 10:12

FEAR OF DIFFERENT RACES

The words of the famous speech, "I have a dream" still ring today in the ears of many people. Many like Martin Luther King were ready to give their lives in the sixties, to see our country honor it's constitution, "that all men were created equal," despite the bitter opposition from people, even people holding government offices. George Wallace, the governor of Alabama, bitterly opposed allowing African-Americans into the University of Alabama. In fact, in 1963 he refused entrance of a young African-American woman named Vivian Jones. Then in 1996 Jones became the first to receive the prestigious Lurleen B. Wallace Award for Courage. The now former governor, Wallace presented the award, along with a public apology for the 63 incident. Jones in turn extended a hand of forgiveness and reconciliation began for them that day.

Why is it we fear people who aren't just like us? Did you know that in the late sixties when a federal judge ordered that African-Americans be allowed in public school with whites, everyone seemed to protest, everyone except the parents of six year old Ruby Bridges. With a police escort, everyday that little girl walked by herself through mobs of screaming people on her way to the New Orleans school. The whites wouldn't send their kids to school with blacks, and the blacks were too afraid to go, so everyone stayed home, but little Ruby. Everyday she had the whole school all to herself, just she and the teachers. I'm sure glad we have overcome such behavior, or have we?

Are people still afraid of people who have different colored skin, or those who speak differently? I think you will agree that the answer is "yes." Is there anything we can do about such prejudices?

First, let's practice what the Bible teaches about the subject. Peter, one of Jesus' first Apostles learned that prejudices against races had to be removed from his belief system. In Acts 10:28 it reads; "Ye know how that it is an unlawful thing for a man that is a Jew to keep company, or come unto one of another nation; but God hath shewed me that I should not call ANY man common or unclean." In the eyes of God, all men are equal regardless of race or position in life. God does not discriminate, and neither should we. Let us not discriminate against people like many in the past who have stained our history, but let us love one another.

Daily Verse: "For he is our peace, who had made both one, and hath broken down the middle wall of partition between us."

Ephesians 2:14

FEAR OF LOSS OF GOOD REPUTATION

Solomon, the last king of the united kingdom of Israel, made this statement in Proverb 22:1, "A good name is rather to be chosen than great riches, and loving favor rather than silver or gold."

You can replace gold and silver, but a tarnished name is spotted forever. With this in mind listen to how a mother fought for the honor of her son after the close of the Vietnam War.

A private first class by the name of Alan Barton was found missing in action. Meanwhile a body was found that had been killed by a land mine a short distance from home base. The remains were unable to be identified so they were shipped back to the states unlabeled. For some unknown reason the army never made a connection between Barton, and the body, so they labeled Barton as a deserter. This devastated his family, especially since his father was a retired war veteran. Since his mother was sure her son wasn't a deserter, she would not allow the unidentified body to be buried. For thirteen years the body remained in a military morgue in Hawaii, until finally in 1983 the army identified the body as the remains of Alan Barton. He was then given the proper military funeral, with a "21 gun salute," and a bugler playing "Taps." His mother wept quietly, realizing for the first time since the wars end her son's precious name was cleared.

Many in God's army have been wrongly accused, and have had their name ruined by the enemy. Remember that God promises to clear everyone's name, either at this time or at the final judgment on the last day. Our duty today is to fight to hold up our honor, so that our God will not be dishonored by our behavior. When someone thinks about you, what comes to their mind?

What type of person are you? Are you stingy, greedy, selfish, or are you kind, gentle, and giving? The best way to determine what type of person you want to be remembered as is to go ahead right now, and write your epitaph. Describe precisely how you would want to be remembered. Then strive to be that person, and I'm sure you'll see a change take place in your behavior.

Daily Verse: "And see if there is any wicked way in me, and lead me in the way of everlasting."

Psalm 139:24

FEAR OF OFFENSE

Everyone alive today has been guilty of offending others. Also we've all experienced offenses from time to time. Jesus said that, "offenses must come." So we must learn how to handle these minor injustices, (in most cases) if we are to live lasting fruitful lives. How do we define the word offense? It is when you feel as though you have been insulted, or slighted. Maybe someone has treated you unfairly and you became resentful over the issue.

The Greek word for offense in our New Testament is "the device used to trigger a trap to catch an animal." So an offense is something designed to set off a trap that will restrain us from movement.

Offenses simply are anything that puts a hindrance or stumbling block in our way, or someone else's way. Since none of us have reached perfection, we should be as careful as we can not to allow our tongues to run freely. Our tongue is the most common instrument used to offend others. Oftentimes people will hold a grudge, or nurse a grievance over something that is said years prior. Jesus exhorted us that as Christians, we were to live a life ready to forgive, even if we had to as much as 490 times in a single day. Now don't get me wrong, there are people who are "set up" to be offended. They take offense over the slightest little wrong. Mark's Gospel says "immediately they are offended." These people who have touchy feelings, and are overly-sensitive make me nervous to be around. My personality type clashes with them very easily. These people suffer from an imbalance that needs to be corrected, but since most find nothing wrong with their behavior, it is good for us to be extra careful around these people. After all; the Bible does say that a "brother who has been offended is harder to win than a strong city."

So how should we conduct ourselves so that we don't live with the fear of offence? Matthew 18:15 says; "Moreover if your brother sins against you . . ." I think it is best to determine if an offense has actually occurred or not. Some people are overly sensitive as we have stated, so check your attitude, and motives for saying what you said. If an offense has occurred then go to the person alone and discuss it with them. Don't needlessly drag others into the situation unless they are already involved. In most cases this will clear up any misunderstanding between the two of you. You then are reconciled to your brother and will be on your way to serving God with a clean heart. Our goal should always be like Job's - to not offend anyone.

Daily Verse: "Surely it is meet to be said unto God, I have borne chastisement, I will not offend anymore."

Job 34:3

FEAR OF INJURY

In Corrie Ten Boom's book entitled "The Hiding Place," she writes of a time in her life when she was getting rather inquisitive about life. One day as a young girl, when her father had just returned from a business trip on a train. They sat there waiting to get off the train, and she asked her father what it meant to have sex sin. He being the wise old father he was, just calmly stood up, and lifted the case from its overhead rack, where it had been traveling in. He then placed it on the floor, and asked Corrie to carry it for him. She tried to pick it up, but what she didn't know that it was stuffed full of old watch parts he had purchased that day for his business. Corrie tried to pick up the case, but it was entirely too heavy. She hollered, "It's too heavy for me too carry," as she tried to drag it along.

"Yes it is," her dad said, "and only a pretty bad father would try to get his child to carry such a load."

Just as the knowledge of what sex sin is all about, it's too heavy for you to carry, and it could injure you to try to carry it at your age. As I read that story of Corrie's wise father, I'm reminded of how Our Heavenly Father keeps the knowledge of things from me until that last possible moment. Oh, sometimes I'm impatient, and complain about not having the clear guidance I so desire. But always keep in mind, it's all for our own good to avoid the injury of carrying something too heavy.

In the Garden of Eden, God with held the knowledge of good and evil from Adam and Eve; all to protect them from personal injury. But once they disobeyed God, they let the Pandora of evil out of the box. Later their firstborn son, the one they loved so much, used that knowledge to become the first recorded murderer, by taking the life of his brother over proper worship styles.

So if you're having problems finding peace over questions you may have, just remember our heavenly Father may be keeping the answers from you to protect you from injury.

Daily Verse: "For the Lord God is a sun and shield; the Lord will give grace and glory; no good thing will he withhold from them that walk uprightly."

Psalm 84:11

FEAR OF THE IMAGINATION

In the book of Revelation chapter twelve the Bible talks of a future war to take place between the devil, and God's archangel Michael. It gives us a description of four different faces the devil would use against us in those days. "And the great dragon was cast out, that old serpent, called the devil, and Satan, which deceiveth the whole world: he was cast out into the earth, and his angels were cast out with him." Rev.12:9. Each one of these names tells us something of his future tactics to use against us. The devil means "deceiver," and he will try to deceive you into believing a lie. The name Satan means accuser, or slanderer. He is constantly accusing you before the father in heaven day, and night according to the scriptures. The term old serpent signifies his work he did in the garden to evoke doubt in the mind of Eve, about God's intentions for them. He will always try to get you to doubt God's word. And finally, it speaks of a dragon. Just what is a dragon? History has given us much information in the form of drawings of creatures that breathed fire from their nostrils. Men of the middle ages were given credit for slaying these giant creatures with swords, and spears. But besides all this, nobody really knows for sure if they ever did exist, except in the imagination of the writers. In the same way, Satan in these last days will attempt to use your imagination against you. Those who are plagued by chronic fears that will never happen are prone to letting their imaginations run wild.

Worry is your most horrible enemy. It seeks to rob you of your future, while stealing your today. Worry is the magnet that attracts negative faith, into your life. It sets up your imagination to believe in an unpleasant future. It tells your imagination of disasters that don't exist. It acts like a spiritual fog that hangs over your life. Those who have this fear live their life in the fog. Did you ever notice how creepy it is to walk all alone on a foggy night? It has been reported that a dense fog thick enough to completely cover seven city blocks, more than one hundred feet thick only contains about a cup of actual water. The imagination does all the rest.

One way to control your fear is to think back to a year ago. Do you remember anything you feared about? How many of those things have happened that were once causing you to lose sleep? God never created us to hold tomorrow's anxieties today. Let us cast all of our cares unto him, for he is always thinking about us and caring for us. He is the only one built to handle the stresses of this life.

Daily Verse: "In God I will praise his word, in God I have put my trust; I will not fear what flesh can do to me."

Psalm 56:4

FEAR OF RESENTMENT

Have you ever wanted to get back at someone really good for the things they did wrong to you? Vindictive thoughts haunt you when you try to sleep. You stare blankly at the ceiling of your bedroom dreaming up subtle ways to embarrass them, without you getting too much blame. If these symptoms sound like you, you suffer from the fear of resentment.

Once there was a man who was an excellent contractor. His boss would always give the toughest jobs to him, for he knew he could handle them. He was able to take impossible situations, and come out under budget, without skipping on quality. I guess he just had a knack for it. He worked for the same boss for over thirty years, and on the outside everything was ok. But on the inside a seed of resentment had been allowed to grow. He loved working for his boss, for his boss was a fair man, but he felt after all this service he should have been rewarded more. Over the years, he had seen his boss reward other employees with great gifts of appreciation, but he had yet to reward him. Then one day the boss came to him, and told him he had a special friend, he was going to build a house for, free of charge. He was assigning him to contract the job, because he was the best he had, and he knew he would keep a careful watch on the budget. Here are the plans to the house; I want this house to be special, for my friend is special to me. I want you to not cut any expenses on this house. Go ahead and feel free to put any extras in, that you think would make the house better. In fact I want you to treat this project as though you were going to be the one living in this house, and you surely wouldn't want any cuts if that's the case.

The man walked away with the plans in his hand, feeling a little excited, and sad at the same time. He was excited to build such a house, for he loved a good challenge. But he was sad that his employer never thought of him, after all those years of faithful service. As he pondered, his resentment was allowed to feed, and then it began to grow. "I'll show him," the man said as he walked away. "This is going to be my last house I'm building for that ungrateful xxxxxx. I'm going to cut every corner I can cut on this house." He used cheap low grade dimension lumber and cheap, inferior fixtures on the inside. In fact on every code, he cut it to the bare minimum, just so it what be passing inspection. In no time at all, he was finished, and had his boss come and take a look. He didn't fear his boss would notice anything, for all the inferiors were hidden under a protective cover and everything looked good on the outside. When his boss met with him, he asked how everything had gone. "Everything went fine sir." was his reply. "Good, now tell me, did you build this house with all the extras, and just like you would be living in it?" "Yes, sir," answered the contractor. "Very well, then here's the keys, I built this house to reward you for all the years of faithful service you've given me. You saved me so much money over the years I just wanted to give some of it back to you." What's the moral of this story? If there's anything inferior on the inside of you, you've allowed resentment to put it there.

Daily Verse: "That thine alms may be in secret; and thy Father which seeth in secret himself shall reward thee openly."
                                                        Matthew 6:4

FEAR OF CHURCH

From the beginning of its existence people have feared the church. Many have used their fear to lash back at the church with persecutions and threatening. Saul, who later became Paul, hated the church, and everything it stood for. He was one of the early churches greatest threats, going from city to city arresting everyone known as the "way." Later on, Nero the emperor, burned his own city, and blamed it on Christians so people would hate the church. Despite all the attacks in the last two-thousand years, the church of Jesus Christ has stood the test. Even when monuments are erected prematurely, like the one that's erected on Diocletian's grave. He was a cruel emperor of Rome, who received credit for extinguishing Christianity during his rein as emperor. As you can plainly see, we are far from being extinguished. In fact, Christianity is one of the fastest growing faiths worldwide. Jesus promised that even the gates of hell would not be able to prevail against his church .I think the biggest fear against the church is it's uniqueness to accept a diversity of different nationalities of people. This tends to make people nervous, when you get a bunch of people together who look different, talk different, but all have the same goal, which is to worship the Almighty Creator of the universe. The bond of Christian fellowship is so real around the world, that people can't believe such a volunteer network can work together so good. Jesus Christ does remove the barriers of race and nationality, while destroying all the hatreds that are so common with these differences. Each person is considered an individual, valuable part of Christ's body, using their gifts and talents to the fullest, to please their God. We as God's people must not squabble over issues in the church that have no eternal value. Let us keep our focus on pleasing our Maker, and not on being our brother's judge.

Daily Verse: "For by one spirit were we all baptized into one body, whether we be Jews or Greeks, whether we be bond or free; and have been all made to drink into one spirit."

I Corinthians 12:13

FEAR OF CONTAMINATION

There is a disorder known today as the Obsessive Compulsive Disorder, or (OCD). People suffering from this disorder have a compulsive fear of contamination. They fear they will catch a disease such as aids, or be infected by some germ. Outside they may look normal, but inside, they have images, and senseless obsessions that can cause their behavior to be anything but normal. These people can be found chronically washing their hands, and bathing abnormally. They will be found wearing rubber gloves to do even the most menial tasks. People suffering from this disease also have a compulsion to check the doors at night more than once. They inspect everything in their houses more frequently than needed for they fear a burglary, or fire. If this fear is allowed to persist without check, it will lead to unnecessary distress, low self-esteem, and incapability to work properly. People may find themselves avoiding social contact to prevent unwanted contamination. It is no doubt that the late Howard Hughes, one of the riches men in our countries history suffered from this fear. In his later years, he lived in the top floor of his penthouse apartment complex. He had hair below his shoulders, for he feared getting it cut, and receiving an infection from a barber. His fingernails were six inches long for fear of infection. He wore bags on both hands, and feet, and walked on newspapers all around his apartment. He ate with sterilized plastic silverware to avoid contamination. The ironic ending to this whole story is that he finally died from the disease of hepatitis. The thing that he focused on surely came upon him.

If you suffer from this fear, you must learn to abstain from the compulsive thoughts that are creating this fear. Some need artificial means, such as medication to find balance in their thinking patterns. It is noticed that when this balance is found people begin to return to a more normal existence. The goal is to bring about a reduction in the anxiety level that you suffer from not washing your hands compulsively.

Daily Verse: "They shall take up serpents; and if they drink any deadly thing, it shall not harm them . . ."

Mark 16:18a

FEAR OF BACKSLIDING

The issue of backsliding is quite a controversial subject to many. It need not be a problem, if we sincerely respond to the scriptures with an open heart. Some people wrestle with the subject, and find themselves in a perpetual pattern of backsliding. Others believe there condition to be permanent, and give up all hope of recovery. In a biblical sense the term backslider relates to someone who has made a willful decision to turn away from their faith, and retreated to their old beggarly affections and pursuits of this world. A backslider abandons his loyalty, dedication, and enthusiasm for Christianity. Let us be sober toward the awesome results of unrepentant backsliding. Several Bible authors warned us with Scriptures like Heb. 3:12, "Beware, brethren, lest there be in any of you have an evil heart of unbelief in departing from the living God." II Pet. 3:17, " . . . beware lest you also fall from your own steadfastness, being led away with the error of the wicked;" I Tim. 1:19, "Holding faith, and a good conscience; which some having put away concerning faith have made shipwreck." These scriptures along with many others teach us that people can fall into a spiritual apathy which will result in a falling away from the faith.

Several bible illustrations show us examples of backsliding heroes. Sampson chose spiritual compromise which led him away from God. David chose an adulterous affair with Bathsheba which led him into a deep sinking sin. Solomon his son turned his heart away from God and served idols to the point where he was even weary of life. All these men and many others temporarily left their first love, which was God, but soon found their way back. Yes, there is hope for the backslider. Through genuine repentance, and a willingness to change, they can receive complete restoration, and recovery.

You must stop your feeble attempts to justify your sin, and blaming others for your actions. Take responsibility for your actions, and confess your sins completely. Decide to strive for a Godly change in your heart. This in turn will lead to a determination to forsake all sin in your life. Commit yourself to make the changes necessary to live a Godly lifestyle, putting away all filthiness of the flesh. Finally establish

Godly relationships with other committed Christians who will reinforce and strengthen your walk with God. This fellowship will assure that you will not repeat the same destructive habits they led you away before.

Daily Verse: "A just man falleth seven times, and riseth up again."

Proverbs 24:16

FEAR OF ACCIDENTS

One day there was two young boys born to a Kansas farmer. They had the awesome responsibility of keeping the fire burning in the one room school house they attended. One particularly cold day they were in a hurry to get the fire burning, before the other kids got there, so they poured kerosene on live coals. The stove blew sky high, and set the schoolhouse on fire.

The blast blew one of the boys away from the fire, toward the door, his name was Glenn Cunningham. The other boy, his brother was caught in the fire. Glenn quickly rushed back into the burning building to save his brother, but in the process suffered severe burns on both legs. His brother later died, and he was hospitalized with severe leg burns. As he lay in the hospital bed, his dreams of being a track star seemed to slip away. The doctors approached him with distressing news a few days later, when they told him to the best of their opinion it looked like his injuries were so severe, they had doubts he would ever walk again.

Glenn being the determined young man he was, decided not to accept the report of the doctors as the gospel truth. When he finally healed, he was sent home, where everyday he would wheel his wheelchair down to the corral they had on the farm. It was not much more than a circular fence. He would struggle for hours at first to pull himself up out of the wheelchair, and onto the fence. Then he would proceed to drag his legs around the fence with brute force, all the time telling his legs to walk. At first when people saw him, then would sigh in sorrow for his determination. Glenn kept up this behavior daily, until he had a rut around the fence from dragging his legs behind him. Them one day it finally happened, his legs began to take off. And to make a long story short, Glenn Cunningham went on to hold the international world record for distance running in his time. In fact he kept breaking records as he ran more and more.

Are you afraid of what might happen to you if you try new

things? Accidents are all apart of our everyday life. We must not allow them to cripple us from attempting big things for God. Glenn wasn't willing to give up on his dream, because of the opinion of others. He knew it would take determination, and hard work to make it happen, but his dream was bigger than the scars he received from the accident. Don't let the scars of yesterday paralyze you from accomplishing your goals in life.

Daily Verse: "And David said to Solomon his son, Be strong and of good courage, and do it, fear not, nor be dismayed; for the Lord God, will be with thee."

I Chronicles 29:20

FEAR OF DREAMS

What do you dream of doing with your life? Is there anything you would attempt to do for God if you knew you wouldn't fail? A dream is a picture of your future that dominates your mind. Though it may seem unattainable now, if given time to develop, the seed-picture will become a reality in your life. Once God plants desires, or photographs into our hearts, these seeds begin to grow in us. These small invisible seeds sometimes take a whole lifetime before they fully develop enough for others to see them. And sometimes people uproot them by disobedience to God's will, thus leaving a crop that can't be harvested.

Many people spend their whole lives trying to leave a lasting legacy on this earth. Their lifetime dream is to leave something on this earth to be remembered by. Instead, they should focus on not what people think of their life, but what does God think of your life? As in Bible days, Paul said, people strive to win, so they can have a perishable crown, but instead we should strive to get a crown that doesn't perish; a crown of life. Those trophies you work so hard to get, all the countless hours of training ,just to achieve a medal, when given enough time ,they will all be thrown in the trash. Men dream of amassing great fortunes of wealth, all to die, and leave them to people who probably won't appreciate all the sacrifice you made for them. Your earthly treasures will be sorted out, and trinkets will be given to family members, while the rest will be sold, and portioned out in small lumps. All those sacrifice for what? Just to leave a legacy behind? To have something nice said about us at our funeral. Why not decide today, to set your dreams to a higher standard, and don't be afraid to dream big. Let God choose for you, what he would have you to do for him. Decide today that you are not going to live carelessly anymore, but instead you're going to make sure you understand what the master wants from your life. Don't allow people who don't see your dream to shake you from accomplishing it. This was how Joseph the eleventh son of Jacob fulfilled his dream God had for his life. Everyone, including his whole family was against his dream. But he knew it was God-given, and he was not going to allow any person or circumstance to rob it from him. For the most part keep your dream to yourself, and don't share it with people that it is not intended for. Allow it to become your obsession, and it will soon become your possession.

Daily Verse: Where there is no vision the people perish;

Proverb 29:18

FEAR OF FATIGUE

The Old Testament tells the story of one of Gods most colorful bible characters. His name was Elijah the Tishbite, whatever a Tishbite is. On one of his many escapades for righteousness he single-handedly took on 450 baal prophets. It was to be a showdown to top all. It was to prove once and for all who the real true God was. Elijah had hoped this display of Jehovah's awesome power would be enough to draw Israel's, lukewarm people back to God. So with stage set, they go to the top of Mt. Carmel, and begin building their altars of sacrifice. Baal's prophets get first bids, and the pick of the sacrifices. All day they spend dancing, cutting themselves, shouting, and nothing happens. Finally, after Elijah quits having his fun with them, by harassing them, it's the time of the evening sacrifice, so he single-handedly builds an altar, then completely cuts up a bull all by himself, then has several barrels of water poured on the sacrifice, during a drought I might add .He raises his hands, and calls on the one true God to answer by fire. That was the challenge whoever's God was real, let him answer by fire. Jehovah does send the fire in a mighty way, and completely consumes everything, even the water. Then in the excitement of everything Elijah decides to single-handedly wipe out false worship from the land of Israel. He takes a sword and kills all the prophets of baal by himself. A little while later he outran the kings horses on the way back to town, because now he knows revival will breakout in Israel. The next picture we have in the scriptures of him is him patiently waiting outside of town for the revival to break loose. Does it happen as he expected? Does anything in life happen as we expect it? Instead he gets a message brought to him from Queen Jezebel, informing him that he would be a dead man in twenty-four hours for killing all her prophets. So what's the next move by the man of faith, and power? He ran for his life. You'd think it was the attack of the fifty-foot woman or something like that. He ran for miles, until finally he collapsed under a juniper tree, and since he was the only prophet of God left, so he thought, he might as well die, and go on to heaven to.

This story is a textbook example of a man of fatigue. It all begins when you think you're all alone, and you have to do everything by yourself. This complex can drain you of all sense of God's presence, protection, and provision. When fatigue sets into your life it becomes meaningless. You feel as though the situation of your life is hopeless. At times you can even feel forsaken by your loved ones, in fact you're no longer thinking clearly. Your enemies will become stronger to you as you become weaker. Your tired eyes can no longer see the fresh vision God has given you to accomplish.

So how do you escape from the fear of fatigue? In the story God sent an angel to minister to Elijah. First realize that God is not far. He never went anywhere, you did. Elijah needed refueled he was running on empty, skipping meals and sleep for the cause of revival. If you don't shut down, then you will shut down. You need to schedule refueling points though out your day to allow your mind to rest, and your body to rebuild itself. Jesus understood this, as you read today's daily verse think of ways you can apart.

Daily Verse: "And he said to them, come ye yourselves apart into a desert place, and rest a while; for there were many coming and going, and they had no leisure so much as to eat."

Mark 6:31

FEAR OF CROWDS OR PUBLIC

Agoraphobia is the scientific name given to this fear. It is a fear that affects some 850,000 Americans according to the ADA association in Washington. A total of some 13% of our U.S. population suffers chronically from this fear. Some reports of people who suffer from this fear, have been unable to leave the refuge of their home for months and even years. Many in my own family have been plagued by this culprit. One Bostonian woman was reported as being so fearful that she cut herself on the head, and bleed profusely for more than 36 hours before a visiting health aide found her, and got her assistance. One reason it is so hard to help these people, many legislatures say, is because they are always so homebound, that it is hard to find them. Symptoms for this sickness range from panic attacks, to all forms of social disorders. Those who have reoccurring nightmares and dreams that horrify them in their sleep, as well as give them a sense of helplessness. Most people who have this fear are treated with medication, or behavior therapy. They are taught that although their fear may be frightening, it is not necessarily dangerous.

Here are some simple steps that a person could follow to relieve some of the pressures of this fear. Set some minor goals for yourself. Start by leaving your house to go to a tree, or fence in your yard. Then you might start by looking at people as they walk past you in the eyes. Say simple things like hello. Strive to be released from your prison by attempting new things every so often. Of course you may need cognitive therapy, or medication to help you get this problem under control. Whichever you do, always remain positive, and allow God his time to work with you. God wants us to fellowship one with another, to reinforce his strength in our life. He truly is a friend who sticks closer than a brother.

Daily Verse: "Not forsaking the assembling of ourselves together, as the manner of some is; but exhorting one another; and so much more, as ye see the day approaching."

Hebrews 10:25

FEAR OF FLOODS

Floods occur in almost all parts of our globe. To some they are a welcome treat, for they replenish valuable nutrients in the soil that may be lost to over cropping. To others they are very damaging to their lives, causing millions of dollars worth of damages yearly. Some people loose homes, livelihoods, and even their lives to these devastating acts of nature. All through human history God has been getting the blame for these natural disasters. When in reality he only instituted one flood as the Bible records; a flood of floods, one that devastated the entire earth by encompassing the whole earth under a blanket of flood waters. The flood of Noah's day was so widespread that it wiped out the entire human and animal population. All human life was gone, except for the eight souls that found grace in Noah's family. Over a hundred years they spent building an ARK that would save them from God's impending judgment on sinful mankind. Forty days and forty nights God opened the flood gates of heaven, and poured out so much water that it would take them almost six months of floating around, before the waters would subside enough that they could safely leave the ark.

Whether today's floods are, "Acts of God," as they are called by newscasters and insurance companies, or just random acts of nature we do have this confidence given to us by God's word.

Daily Verse: "And I will establish my covenant with you; neither shall all flesh be cut off anymore by the waters of a flood; neither shall there any more be a flood to destroy the earth."

Genesis 9:11

FEAR OF SEXUAL LOVE

Many times when I speak to teenagers I am amazingly surprised at how embarrassed they get when you talk about sexual love or intimacy in church. For some reason they see this topic as too taboo to talk about in church. Many are completely surprised when I tell them that God created sex. He intentionally made it to be pleasurable. He wanted a man and a woman to explore each others bodies in sexual intimacy. It was his way of propagating the earth with people. His ultimate plan was that he would be assured that men and women would be attracted to each other, and not the same sex.

If circumstances in your life have caused you to have a fear about sexual intimacy, I want to be delicate with you. I know you may feel awkward or uncomfortable talking about the subject, but let's explore God's word together, and see his opinion on the subject.

Marriage is honorable among all, AND THE BED UNDE-FILED," (Heb. 13:4). God is not a Victorian prude about sexual love, in fact in Songs of Solomon he mentions things like allowing a wife's breasts to please her husband at all times. And that the husband should have so much sexual desire for his wife, it should be as though he was intoxicated. God's attitude toward sexual love is pro, so long as it is enjoyed under the confines of a marriage covenant. In fact the marriage covenant is the only proper sanctuary for sexual gratification. Not that God is a killjoy, but that man's enjoyment in sex would be satisfied by his own mate. This would safeguard against the transmission of sexually transmitted diseases, and other unhealthy practices. I Corinthians 7: 2 states; "Nevertheless, because of sexual immorality, let each man have his own wife, and let each woman have her own husband."

One last point we should cover, is the subject of virginity. Virginity has lost much of its virtue and sacredness in today's society. The desire to keep oneself sexually pure for the marriage bed is frowned on today, and considered old fashioned. Don't you believe it young person! According to scriptures, keeping oneself sexually undefiled before marriage is an ultimate act of glorifying God with our bodies. So once you find your soul mate and follow thru with holy matrimony, gently enjoy each others sexual intimacy and receive the sexual fulfillment God intended for you.

Daily Verse: Flee fornication. Every sin that a man doeth is without the body; but he that committeth fornication sinneth against his own body.

1Ccorinthians 6:18

FEAR OF SCIENCE

Men all through the history of mankind have had an obsession with the unknown. They have been able to take their God-given minds and expand on their knowledge beyond our wildest dreams. Most people who were ahead of their time in technology have been persecuted as being workers of the devil or, branded as a witch. Many suffered at the hands of narrow-minded prosecutors. Men like Galileo, Newton, and even Columbus were considered mad by many. The rapid increase in knowledge is just sure sign that we are truly living in the closing pages of human history. The book of Daniel, a prophetic book that reveals what will happen in the last days tells us in Daniel 12:4, " But thou, O Daniel, shut up the words, and seal the book, even to the time of the end: many shall run to and fro, and knowledge shall be increased." All our scientific knowledge is a result of living in the last days.

In recent years science has done the unthinkable. Many fear it has overstepped its boundaries. Scientists are now practicing human gene splicing. Some have said it is our best hope, or our worst nightmare. Others against the practice of science have said we shouldn't be messing around with human design. "Those scientists are playing God," are the quotes critics are claiming. The purpose of this devotion is not to debate over the morality of human cloning, or other scientific discoveries. But instead, to put you at ease that God is still very much in control of his creation. Whether we have a power hungry scientist, or researchers that stretch the boundaries of human morality, God promises that every soul that is conceived in the womb, is under his watchful eye.

Instead of taking a defensive attitude toward science, let's remember what life was like before vaccines, flu shots, and of course treatments for sicknesses. Remember what life was like before automobiles, air planes, electricity, water sanitation, and what would our life be like without computers. No science is our friend, leading us into the quality of life that God intends for his creation to live. It has been properly quoted; "We have nothing to fear, except fear itself."

Daily Verse: "O Timothy, keep that which is committed to thy trust, avoiding profane and vain babblings, and oppositions of science falsely called; which some professing have erred concerning the faith . . ."

I Timothy 6:20&21

FEAR OF HEAVEN

Have you ever sat and thought about what heaven will be like? Can you see the streets of gold, and the beautiful gem laden walls? The bible records trees, grass, rivers, mountains, and such beauty that would stretch the human mind. Some theologians of the past, such as Finis Dake, have speculated that heaven is a planet in the farthest point north of our cosmos. Scripture reveals that it is a place of peace, and happiness, unparalleled by anything or anyplace on this earth. Many have rejected the idea of heaven altogether, and this is fine for we each are entitled to our own opinion. Be careful though, because Jesus was one of those who believed in heaven. I personally think the reason people doubt about the existence of heaven, is because they fear it. They fear that there may be a place that they are going to miss, when their life is over. Many who claim heaven to not be real, also say that hell is a farce. Friend, listen to me, just because you doubt the existence of these two places, does not change a thing. Someday each and every one of us on this earth is going to experience one or the other.

So let's assume heaven is a real place. How do I get there then? Here is where the confusion sets in on peoples lives. Some have falsely believed that suffering is the key, so they live a life of abasement to the flesh. Some well known televangelist's have made statements like," all the Jews who were killed in the Holocaust went to heaven," reasoning that since their suffering was so great, God would overlook their past sins. Some believe morality is the key to heavens gate so they live pure, wholesome, lives promoting family health and well-being. Others unknowingly think that salvation is wrapped up in a bunch of religious practices such as baptism, speaking in tongues, proper dress code, etc. Friend listen to me, although most of the things I've talked about are important, they by themselves will not open heaven's gates for you.

Jesus gave us the proper entrance exam in John14:6; "I am the way, the truth, and the life; no man comes to the father, but by me." Then the Apostle Peter reinforced the idea a few years later in Acts

4:12, "Neither is there salvation; for there is no other name under heaven given among men, whereby we must be saved." So cast aside all your preconceived ideas about entering heaven by any other way. Only a life lived out in repentance in the name of Jesus gets entry. It does matter that you were baptized when you were young, that won't work. You can't have access because of your parents, or social status. And you certainly can't live moral enough to deserve it, but only when you will confess your sins to Christ, and decide from this day forward that the life you will live, will be lived in God's will, and not your own ,then do you have access to heaven. If you haven't yet, pray to him right now he's listening.

Daily Verse: "In my Father's house are many mansions; if it were not so, I would have told you. I go to prepare a place for you."

John 14:2

FEAR OF HELL

Do you believe in the existence of hell? If you say no, then you are saying that the bible is a hoax. You are saying that over forty authors conspired together over a period of about three thousand years to write a canon of books, sixty-six in all, just to deceive you about the existence of hell. Now if you believe that, your farther gone than I thought. Don't get me wrong, if I could remove any doctrine from the bible, it would be the doctrine of hell. But I can't, so we must live with it. Now on the flip side, some of you fear the place called hell. And you have good reason I might add, listen to the description of a certain rich man in hell in Luke 16. He had full consciousness of what was going on. He said, "I am tormented in this flame," so he must have felt pain. He was thirsty, and asked for just a drop from a fingertip, and was denied. Other descriptions of hell are; a place of unquenchable fire, everlasting punishment, weeping, gnashing of teeth, a place of shame, and everlasting contempt, away from the presence of the Lord, eternal fire and darkness. All these, and many others, are descriptions of a place that I wish to avoid.

Some have asked, "If God is so good, why would he send anyone to such a terrible place?" The answer is quite simple; he doesn't send anybody to hell. We send ourselves there, by rejecting the way he's made for us to be saved from the awful place. You see, hell was never created for man anyway. Hell was created for the devil and his fallen angels. Hell became a holding place of torment until the last judgment, when those who are punished will be sent to the lake of fire, which is the second death. Hell is the place where God separates his children that have an incurable disease known as sin, from those who have been healed from it with pardon of their sins by accepting the work God's son did on the cross. God, like any other good father, just separates the healthy from the unhealthy, by allowing the unhealthy to go to a place where he is sure no one will want to visit. In fact God tells us in the last chapter of Isaiah that on the new earth, there will be a place where man can go look down into hell ,and see those who are in torments. They will be able to see what the punishment is for rebelling against his plan.

Now if you have accepted Christ into your life, and have received Him as your personal Lord and Savior then you have no need to fear hell. The good news is none of us have to go to the place of torment. Right now decide to forsake your old life, and ask for God to give you a new one in Christ. He will take away the old heart of stone, and replace it with a new heart of flesh, and compassion. He will forever write your name in the Lambs Book of Life, which the angel will read out loud in the last day, to assure your place in glory. Don't wait, do it now.

Daily Verse: "It is a fearful thing to fall into the hands of the living God."

Hebrews 10:31

FEAR OF HEIGHTS

People, who suffer from this fear, have such a terrible time in this world. It seems that there are varying degrees of this fear. My wife, who is one, suffers to some degree from this fear, got in an airplane, and confidently looked out the window with no fear at all. I guess when you look at things from God's perspective everything looks pretty small. Others who suffer from the fear of heights sit at the local swimming pools, secretly dreaming of being able to jump from the high dive. Others avoid elevators, tall buildings, amusement park rides, anywhere that their fear may flare up. I personally suffered from this fear at one time in my life. I used to cover my fear with a joke by misquoting the last half of Matthew 28:20, where Jesus commanded, "LO, I am with you always." To tell the truth, I believe my fear came from my childhood, when a bunch of us teenagers were just hanging out at the local strip pit. It was a place that had been mined for coal, back before the strict reclamation laws, and they just left these big high walls filled with water that made ideal swimming holes for a bunch of hot summer teens.

Once, not wanting to be the odd man out, I decided to jump from the cliffs, the way all my friends were doing.

I ran up to the cliff, and just as I went to jump it broke sending me crashing into about six inches of water from about thirty-feet up. The fall knocked me unconscious, and the next thing I remember I was laying on the bank, with my friends around me, wondering if I was going to be alright. Now let me tell you, I was the nose tackle on our football team, the tough guy, and I was not going to let anybody know how much I hurt, so as soon as I came to my senses, I jumped back up and was ready to swim some more. In reality, I hurt like crazy inside. From that day forward, nobody jumped from the high walls any more, for they were just too unstable. But I walked away with a fear of getting close to edges and looking down. This fear carried me well into my adult years, to the point that on a visit to the Grand Canyon, in Arizona I couldn't even enjoy its wonder, for I was too afraid to look over the edge. I drove six hours out of the way to get to it, and when I got there, I looked for about thirty seconds, and said;" that's nice let's go." I don't exactly know when I conquered my fear, I just slowly did. I would walk across high bridges, and look down. I would go up next to cliffs, and look down. The more I did these things the more rational my thinking became. I would just relax, and let my heart calm down until the fear would subside. So in my opinion the best way to defeat the fear of heights is confront it on your terms. Pick a place where you know you will be safe, and begin looking over the side. Repeat it until it just gets easier and easier.

Daily Verse: "Thou hast thrust sore at me that I might fall; but the Lord helped me."

Psalm 118:13

FEAR OF LOST PLEASURE

I've heard several people in my life say that they would never serve God, because he takes away all your fun. They claim that if they become a Christian, they will never be allowed to have pleasure again. All they get to do is sit around at church, and read their Bibles and other spiritual things like that. Nothing could be further from the truth. I can honestly say that since I've been a Christian, and rapidly approaching seventeen years, I've had more pleasure and enjoyment, than in the previous twenty-eight years before Christ. You must learn to differentiate between good pleasure, and bad pleasure. It's like the subject of cholesterol. Everyone in the health kick these days is running around claiming that we should watch closely our cholesterol level. But medical studies have shown that there is good cholesterol, and bad cholesterol. Good cholesterol has a high density of HDLS, which seem to carry the bad cholesterol or LDLS out of the coronary-artery walls. This prevents artery walls from being blocked and thus causing a heart attack. Studies have even shown that the risk of heart disease drops when we raise the levels of good cholesterol in our body. So since all cholesterol is not the same, neither is all pleasure the same. The Bible gives us clear pictures of the difference. I am so tired of Christians living life in the defensive mentality. My son and I were just at a bible book store today, and I happened to notice a book in the clearance rack, (I always check there first,) warning parents about the dangers of the internet. Come on mom and dad do we really need warned about the internet. A lot of Christians are going to miss out on a move of God, while they are still trying to figure out whether God can use the internet or not. We did the same thing with Television in the 1950s and Satan was allowed free access to it. Let's learn from our mistakes and not take a defensive attitude about all the new technology coming around today. Let's realize that although some things are in need of moderation that doesn't make them wrong. I looked at my son in the store and said, "If you accidentally click up a website full of pornography, what would you do?" He said, "I'd get rid of it with a click."

As far as pleasure goes the bible warns us against any self-indulgent, addictive behavior as being wrong. You decide with your own conscience which of these you should avoid. A good rule of thumb to follow is to avoid any behavior that is disobedient to God's word.

Daily Verse: "For we ourselves also were sometimes foolish, disobedient, deceived, serving divers lusts and pleasures, living in malice and envy, hateful, and hating one another."

Titus 3:3

FEAR OF KNOWLEDGE

Some people live with the mistaken belief that if they don't know something, they can't be held accountable for it. Others have used the excuse to avoid knowledge because it produces pride, and they use scripture to back up their claim; " . . . we know that we have knowledge. Knowledge puffeth up . . . , (I Cor. 8:1) sadly to say, both of these excuses won't hold water on judgment day.

In reality the major reason people fear knowledge, is because warfare in your life begins when you learn something. As long as you remain passive about your learning, you have nothing to fear, but as soon as you make a stand to grow, and seek the kingdom, then Satan pulls out the arsenal to try to discourage you. Satan is not intimidated by who you are, he shutters in fear about what you know. He knows that faith is the accumulation of facts. It is not some blind leap in the dark like some disappointed people have found out. Real "now" faith is when you hear Jesus speak, and act on the words He commands. You receive instructions in the form of knowledge, and then step into realm of faith by acting on that knowledge. If you don't have the knowledge then you can't use your faith. Knowledge is for the hungry, not the haughty. It slams the door on the deception of the enemy, and allows him no entrance into your life. Knowledge can produce incredible increase in your life if you will pursue it. Satan wants to keep you in the dark about what you already possess. This way he can rob you of the many blessing you already have. For instance let's say your spouse tucked away some extra money for you in your wallet or purse just to surprise you. Then on your way to work you ran out of gas in your car. Suddenly you look in your wallet, and notice that you're broke, so you think. If only you had known about the stash in the secret pocket, put there by your loving spouse, you wouldn't have had to walk home or get a tow. This is what God has done for us with his word. He has placed a secret stash for us, all we have to do is search for it, and use the knowledge we gain to walk the life of faith.

Proverbs 1:7 tells us that; "The fear of the Lord is the beginning of knowledge; but fools despise wisdom and instruction." Let us not fear accumulating knowledge about God, for it truly is the way to wisdom.

Daily Verse: "My people are destroyed for lack of knowledge. . ."

Hosea 4:6

FEAR OF LOVE

Love is more than a feeling, it's a command. It's even more than a command; it's a way of life. God says in his word, that saying we love someone is cheap. Instead he demands that we show our love to others, in order to reflect, what he has done for us. Of all the qualities God wants us to show as his children, love is his most powerful virtue. Some fear showing real love, because they are fooled into thinking that lust is love. Lust is the desire to please you; love is more concerned about the needs of someone else. You will never accidentally love someone. You must make a conscious decision to love someone, and then sacrifice to prove it.

Of course God showed his love for us by sending his son Jesus to die on a cross for our sins. But listen to this modern day love story that took place in late 1994. A San Diego couple, by the name of Randy and Victoria fell deeply in love with each other. They had planned on getting married that year but Randy's diabetes, which he suffered from, took a turn for the worst. Apparently the forty-six year old man was in desperate need of a kidney transplant right away to save his life. Odds were not in his favor since he was at the bottom of a very long list of transplants. Things got worse when all his family members tested negative for possible donors. Before he would consider pursuing the relationship with Victoria any farther, he took her to the doctor, and allowed him to tell her the sorrow of the situation. She was heartbroken, but insisted that she be tested for a possible match. Nothing short of a miracle, with all odds against it, she was found to be a perfect match. So in October of that year they became man and wife, then one month to the day they were both wheeled into the operating room to undergo a five and a half hour surgery to save Randy's life. Victoria gave her new husband her left kidney to prove her love for him, and save his life.

The day Jesus willingly faced the cross, was the day he demonstrated his love for you and me. He didn't have to go to the cross but he chose to. In the same spirit we must choose everyday to love those God puts in our path. Let us not fear to do as he commands.

Daily Verse: "My little children let us not love in word, neither in tongue; but in deed and truth."

I John 3:18

FEAR OF OCEANS

So many people are too nervous to go into the water. I guess one of the main reasons is because of movies like Jaws, and all the host of other, "shark attack" movies being made these days.

Terror-seeking promoters of these movies start with words like; "Just when you thought it was safe to go back in the water, NOW . . ." If the truth is to be known, it is safe to go back into the water, since there are only about 58 shark attacks a year worldwide, and very few are fatal. Now when you consider how many people are playing in these great bodies of water everyday, you probably have more of a chance to get hit by a semi-truck while checking the mail, than being bitten by a shark. Others are not a big fan of the ocean, because of its vast expanse of other aquatic, marine life other than sharks. I remember a couple years ago my wife, Susie, and I were on a Caribbean cruise with a couple families who are best friends of ours. One of the ports of call was to a small island owned by the cruise line, "Cococa," was its name. We arrived in the morning and had to take a tender boat to shore to enjoy the islands activities for the day. My friend Duane and I decided we were going to try our hand at ocean kayaking. So were secured the tickets for the trip, and met each other on the island. With a brief explanation of what we were going to do on the trip the crew, about thirty of us were off two to a kayak. Everyone pretty much got the hang of it that is except me and Duane. The kayak was just to small for us well fed preacher boys, every time, and I do mean every time a wave of any size hit that little kayak, water would come rushing over the side fill the kayak, and over we'd go. Time after time our little unseaworthy craft would flip, and over we'd go. It was kind of fun the first ten times we laughed until our sides hurt, but then twenty, thirty, times later it quickly quit becoming fun. We would raise our heads up, and look out, and all the rest of the people in our crew are sitting in their little kayaks waiting on us to get to them. Finally, after about a half hour of battling the waves we got to them, and they took off again, all rested up. Duane and I were wiped out, my hands and legs were stinging like fire from falling into jellyfish along the way, and Duane's hand was on fire from ramming it into a starfish in one of our tumbles. We sat in that little kayak watching everyone leave quickly, when suddenly; a waterspout came up from the water. The waterspout came up from the direction we were heading. The staff very quickly closed the island down and sent a pair of wave-runners out to rescue me and my friend. Later I had people from the kayak crew; thank me for holding them up by flipping the kayak so much, because if we would have been on time our whole crew would have been in the middle of that waterspout. Isn't it amazing how God can use the silliest things to get his will accomplished? We truly are led by the Spirit of God.

Daily Verse: "He hath compassed the water with bounds, until the day and night come to an end."

Job 26:10

FEAR OF SLEEP

It is estimated that more than one hundred million Americans fail to get a good nights sleep each night. And with now more than 84 different sleep disorders coming against them, it's no wonder. Some people have the mistaken idea, that sleep is just a "time out" in life. I too had this opinion for a major part of my life. I would hate to go to sleep for fear that I would miss something important in life while I was wasting my time asleep. Instead now I realize that sleep, is your body's way of renewing your mental and physical health. Actually sleep is a very complicated process your body goes through each night. You begin by feeling drowsy, then you dose off into a light sleep, if undisturbed you will drift off into deep sleep, and just before you wake, you will enter dream sleep. Do you have problems entering these different stages during the night, if so you probably have some disorder disrupting your sleeping patterns? Aside from some medical problem, and there are a host of them from snoring excessively, sleep apnea, insomnia, narcolepsy, nightmares, jet lag, etc. God's word in the book of Proverbs chapter three gives us one of the best prescriptions for sleep I believe we can take.

"My son let not them {God's laws} depart from thine eyes; keep sound wisdom (God's} and discretion: so shall they be life unto thy soul, and grace to thy neck. Then shalt thou walk in thy way safely, and thy foot shall not stumble. When thou liest down, thou shalt not be afraid; yea thou shalt lie down, AND THY SLEEP SHALL BE SWEET."

Do you have trouble sleeping at night? Maybe you need to add God's wisdom to your life. Maybe you fear that you won't wake up like the three thousand estimated deaths that take place every night in our land, while people sleep. God's prescription for a good nights sleep is not some sleeping pill, but a good dose of the "Gos-PILL." (Gospel): A life that is lived in accordance to the scriptures, and not spent trying to cheat to get ahead, or carousing most of the time on pornographic websites. Let God's law rule your life and he promises your sleep will be sweet.

Daily Verse: "It is vain for you to rise up early, to sit up late, to eat the bread of sorrows; for he giveth his beloved sleep."

Psalm 127:2

FEAR OF SNAKES

Some polls show that this fear is the number one fear people have today. It is said that as high as 36% of all US citizens are afraid of snakes. I personally believe this is part of the curse God put on man when he put enmity between the serpent (Satan) and the woman, (Eve). Although this fear, "ophidiophobia" as it is called, is the most popular fear, in truth most snakes are quite harmless. People fear these slithery creatures for nothing. Many victims can't even look at a picture of a serpent without experiencing some form of an anxiety attack. I remember once after my wife and I were first married, I was asleep during the day, for I worked the midnight shift, when I heard a bloodcurdling scream come from the room right next door. It was a very small bathroom in a very small trailer home. I jumped from the bed and swung open the door only to find my wife in terror. She was pointing to the bathroom. I looked in and there was a twelve inch long garter snake beside the bathtub. You know I can almost feel some of you shaking at just the thought of finding a snake in your bathroom.

They tell me that they have medication that will help people get back to enjoying nature, if your fear is so severe that you won't even venture outside your home. If you want to snake-free your home just make sure that there are no rocks, logs, ground hugging shrubs, or any-place that might be a convenient place for one to hide. Although most snake-free yards look rather plain. I think I would rather put up with an occasional snake or two, than to live with a pool table looking yard.

God has promised that his last day people would be allowed to tread on serpents without receiving harm, "Behold I give you all the power to tread upon serpents and scorpions, and over all the power of the enemy; and nothing shall by any means hurt you." Luke 10: 19. Of course the serpents this verse is referring to is a type of the enemy, "the devil." Satan appeared to Eve in the garden in the form of a serpent, and notice she was not afraid of him at all. In fact, I think if I was standing looking at a tree, and all the sudden a snake started talking to me from a limb, I don't think I would have stayed around long enough to be tempted, and I'm not afraid of snakes at all. But Eve wasn't afraid and this fact leads me to believe that the fear came after the fall.

We need not fear natural snakes or spiritual snakes, (devils), for with either case God has promised to give us a refuge in him. And in HIM we can defeat anything that can come against us, even serpents.

Daily Verse: "They shall take up serpents; . . . and it shall not hurt them."

Mark 16:18

FEAR OF TAKING TESTS

I understand that everyone has a certain amount of anxiety before taking tests. This is quite normal, but some people suffer from irrational fear, and excessive anxiety, over the thought of taking one. Even when they are sure they are prepared for the test, they tend to clam up under the pressure. There mind goes dry, so to speak, leaving them void of the answers.

If this sounds like you, here's some practical advice that could help you not feel crippled at the exam table. First get plenty of rest, the night before the exam. Fatigue often reduces your ability to perform your best; this is why it is not a good idea to spend the night before, doing late night cramming. Always listen carefully to your teachers instructions about the test, and follow them to the letter. Avoid listening to what people say about the tests. Tests are always difficult for people who don't prepare. When studying for tests always pay close attention to the meanings of italicized words, these words are usually used for the preparation of several tests. By all means don't wait until the last minute to begin with your preparation for the exam. This type of pro-crastination behavior only leads to excessive anxiety. Also, don't allow your thoughts to daydream into failure. Scripture informs us that "as a man thinks in his heart, so is he." If you concentrate on failure, it's sure to find its way to your front door. Instead substitute negative, worry thought for thoughts of success. Begin to see yourself not only passing the test, but also getting one of the highest grades in the class. Soon you will displace the ideas of failure, with pleasant ones.

Finally, in all tests, there will be questions that you can't answer. Don't panic, skip them and move on to the ones you do know. After you finish all the ones you know, then go back and do the harder questions.

Remember God is a God of preparation. He prepared the plants then he sent the bees to pollinate them. He prepared the plan of salvation before the creation of the world, and the first sin. He sent Jesus to prepare for us a place in heaven, and he also is preparing to send him back to receive his people in heaven. If we will prepare ourselves, God will reward us by bringing back to our remembrance the things we have studied for.

Daily Verse: "The preparations of the heart in man, and the answer of the tongue, is from the Lord."

Proverbs 16:1

FEAR OF WORDS

Do you remember when you were a child, you used to say a simple phrase when someone said something bad about you? Maybe your mom taught you to say it, in order to ease the pain those words caused. "Sticks and stones may break my bones, but words will never hurt me." Nothing could be further from the truth. Not that your parents were intentionally lying to you, but they did not quite understand the power of words. Words are the very framework of all things that exist. The Bible informs us that because of God's Word, "the earth holds its place in orbit." God spoke, and everything came into existence. In the same way our words frame our lives, within a circle of either faith or doubt.

Jesus told us in Matthew that words are more important to us than any other single feature in our life. "For by thy words thou shalt be justified, and by thy words thou shalt be condemned." Our words either make us, or break us, in other words, the words we spoke yesterday, have made the life, we are living today. Jesus also told us that we can have whatever, we speak. In Mark 11:23 it says; " . . . he shall have whatsoever he saith." With this in mind, should we not be more careful what words we allow to come from our lips. In moments of anger, or fear, should we not hold our tongue until the situation calms down?

Some people have lived crippled lives from their childhood. Unsuspecting parents have spoke sharp piercing words to them when they were young, and those words haunted them ever since.

Proverbs informs us that "There is that speaketh like the piercing of a sword; but the tongue of the wise is health." Begin to speak the type of future you wish to have. Change your words from the negative confessions that you tend to allow to flow freely, to a positive confession of faith and victory. Listen to how words can shape your life from this incident that took place in the lives of two young men. Each boy was serving faithfully as an altar boy. Each boy's responsibility was to serve the cruet of wine at communion, during the weekly mass. And each boy so clumsily dropped the cruet of wine sending it shattering during the sacred moment. One priest went into a fit of rage, striking the boy on the cheek, and demanding he leave the church forever for being so careless. That boy became Tito, the communist leader of

Yugoslavia for many decades. Now when the other boy dropped the cruet, instead a sharp reprimand, the wise priest looked at the boy, and smiled. With a wink he reassured the boy that some day he would make a fine priest.

That boy was Archbishop Fulton Sheen, who became one of the first preachers to grace the television set. Our words really do make us or break us.

Daily Verse: "But I say unto you, that ever idle word that men shall speak, they shall give account thereof in the Day of Judgment."

Matthew 12:36

FEAR OF BEING A HOMOSEXUAL

This is a very delicate subject to talk about these days. Since the release of this lifestyle from the closet, they have seemed to receive much sympathy for their depravity. Schools across this great land of ours are teaching, "The Rainbow Curriculum," as an alternative lifestyle to that of heterosexuals. Television networks are adding more shows to their Primetime schedules, involving homosexuals in hopes of showing another way of life. Laws are now being passed to allow the legal marriage of two same sex partners. We have even stooped to the all time low, of ordaining Bishops in churches who are known homosexuals to serve as pastors. Where will it all end? Only father God knows for sure. Today speaking out against this sin has become unpopular. You are branded as a "gay-basher" in today's society.

With all the negative, let me assure you that you are not a homosexual because you have depraved tendencies. Satan has sold the people the lie that they were born homosexual. So they feel that since God made them this way, that's what they must settle for. This is just a half truth, as he is so good at spreading. We were all born with the tendency to be a homosexual, and a fornicator, and to commit adultery, and any other depravity of the fleshy human nature. In fact we must strive, and go against the flow of society to be otherwise. The easy way is to accept your depraved nature, and go with the flow. The bible speaking of people that choose the lesser base of their human nature, are willingly ignorant. Do you know what that means? They decided to be dumb on purpose. Do you want to be dumb on purpose? Then reject that lifestyle today, and receive forgiveness now, as many have done to be part of God's kingdom. Listen to how God feels about those who reject his forgiveness, and persist with their depraved state. "For this cause God gave them up to vile affections; for even their women did change the natural use into that which is against nature; And likewise also the men, leaving the natural use of a woman, burned in their lust toward another; men with men working that which is unseemly, and receiving in themselves that recompense of error which was meet," (Romans 1:26&27). Friend abandon thoughts of this lifestyle today, and serve the living God. God is able to wash away all sins even this one. God loves the sinner, but hates the sin. In the same way, we as Christ's body should follow his example of loving these deceived people into the kingdom.

Daily Verse: "Every way of man is right in his own eyes; but the Lord ponders the hearts."

Proverbs 21:2

FEAR OF PERFECTION

"I am the Almighty God; walk before me, and be thou perfect," (Gen. 17:1). "Be ye therefore perfect, even as your Father which is in heaven is perfect" (Matt. 5:48). What is God demanding from us in these scriptures? Some would say he is being unreasonable, asking man to be perfect. Didn't Jesus say that there was only one perfect person, and that was his Father in heaven? The answer is yes, God is perfect, and he demands that we walk in perfection. But Christian perfection and human perfection are not one and the same. Christian perfection is only attainable by having a close, living, and walking relationship with Jesus Christ, through the power of the Holy Spirit. Christian perfection is displayed in the lives of those who have matured in Christ, by testing their faith, and allowing God free movement in their life. When God speaks mature Christians listen. I've heard well meaning Christian teachers teach that it is God's will for you never to be sick, and if you get sick, you must be out of his perfect will. Listen to me, Scriptures claim it was God's will to bruise his only begotten son, who am I to think I am too good to not be bruised by him also. The mature Christian knows his God, and his ways, and doesn't fear him, but deeply reveres him. Human perfection would try to keep a list of rules and regulations to make himself holy; while Christian perfection, lives in a liberty that allows God to remove the unwanted desires from his life. I've commonly stated that I have the right to drink all the alcohol I choose to. I can do anything I choose to do. Christian perfection deals with your chooser. He takes out the old wants and desires and replaces them with more of him.

Some people desire human perfection in this world. This is completely impossible.

Once a woman in my church came to me, and said that the Christian life she was trying to live was hard. I looked at her, and without blinking commented that it isn't hard, it's impossible. You can't live like a Christian. You have to let Christ live through you. You have to remain fastened to the vine, and allow him to live through you. Only Christ was able to walk the perfect life in the flesh, so we must die to our own desires and allow him to resurrect us in the power of the spirit. He will take you to the place He wants you, and if you fail, don't fret, just fall on His grace and let Him restore you.

Daily Verse: "Not that I have already attained, or am already perfect."

Philippians 3:12

FEAR OF AMNESIA

If a mind is to function properly, it has to learn to forget most of the sensory inputs it encounters in any given day. People, who have learned to tap into the power of the mind and to memorize incredible amounts of data, do so by forgetting the words, in order to grasp the meanings of them.

A textbook definition of the fear of amnesia would be to have a memory loss do to a psychological trauma. There are many different types of amnesia according to psychologists. Some have short term, long term, semantic, which is having a general knowledge of things going on around them, procedural, which means you know how to do certain things, and don't know why. There is a host of other types that I'll let go for now, for the sake of not getting too technical. The mind is actually the most powerful computer in existence today. It has been said that if you could build a computer that would house all the knowledge the mind can store, you would build a build a building as tall as the Empire State Building, which would take up an entire city block. You would also have to run all the water that the Mississippi River flows in a day right through it, to keep it cool. Your mind is a powerful thing. God has so created us to be beings quite capable of housing incredible amounts of information. Although researchers estimate that the average human doesn't quite use ten % of their brain potential. Can you imagine what God has in store for us when this is all over, and we release everything that God has put in us?

The bible is entirely silent about trauma induced amnesia. But

Don Nicely

God gives us several scriptures that relate to self induced. Listen to what God commands us to do in Hebrews 13:2; "Be not forgetful to entertain strangers; for thereby some have entertained angels unawares." God has been known to send strangers in the path of his people in human form, who were really his angels testing us. Also in James it reads; "But whoso looketh into the perfect law of liberty, and continueth therein, he being not a forgetful hearer, but a doer of the work, this man shall be blessed in his deed." He that remembers what God's Word says and doesn't forget to do it shall live the blessed life. Since I'm not a medical doctor, I don't have any advice for someone suffering from accidentally induced amnesia, but let us not practice spiritually induced amnesia, except for today's daily verse given to us by Paul.

Daily Verse: " . . . but this one thing I do, forgetting those things which are behind, and reaching forth unto those things which are before."

Philippians 3:13

FEAR OF TRAVEL

The fear of travel is a very complex fear. For most people this fear associates itself with modes of transportation, like airplanes, automobiles, trains, etc. Of course, the fear's of strange places, and meeting strange people works their way into this fear. This fear has recently reached record levels since the September 11th attack on the world trade centers. Defense programs unlike any in history have been put in place, since the wake up call Americans received that dreaded day.

The truth is, our world is not a safe place in which to live or travel. With the increase of technology, people are quite capable of blowing up city blocks with a bomb the size of a wristwatch. Although our governments are doing their best to keep us safe, I take comfort in my favorite Psalm. This Psalm promises to keep us safe no matter what the situation is around us. It promises us a safe refuge in the midst of a raging storm. David penned this Psalm as he was fleeing for his life, from his jealous father in law, Saul. He found refuge in his fearful world, by securing his life in the breast of Jehovah. "He that dwelleth in the secret place of the most High shall abide under the shadow of the Almighty. I will say of the Lord, He is my refuge and my fortress; my God; in him will I trust," (Psalm 91:1&2). David found his security was wrapped up in declaring with his mouth, that God was his refuge, and fortress. Two keys are seen in this passage that assured David of his protection. First he learned to dwell in the secret place. The word "dwell" means several things. It means to take up residence, then to settle a claim, build fences, dig a well, then finally to drive away claim stealers. When you dwell in the secret place of God, you live with him day in and day out, twenty-four seven, with no time off for holidays. You allow the perimeters of God's word to build fences in your life to keep your property, (your heart) safe. Sometimes you must dig deep into the wells of salvation, in order to draw from it the water of life. When David said he learned to "abide under the shadow of the Almighty," that meant he learned to live under the mercy seat which was part of the Ark of the Covenant. We are able to fall on the mercy seat of God, and allow him to protect us with his presence. No one would dare approach God's ark, for fear that they would drop dead from God's presence.

The writer of Hebrews exhorts us to approach God's throne with boldness every time we need it. Let us not fear, but follow this instruction.

Daily Verse: "Let us therefore come boldly unto the throne of grace that we may obtain mercy, and find grace to help in time of need."

Hebrews 4:16

FEAR OF LOSING YOUR VIRGINITY

Although virginity has lost most of its honor and sacredness in today's promiscuous society of free love, and free sex, it still is the highest virtue you can bestow one's soul mate. Some feel it's a little old-fashioned to "Save one's self," sexually for marriage, but God never changed his mind about it according to his word. Some people don't understand that God is not only interested in the purity of one's soul, and spirit, but also of the chastity and purity of our bodies. I Cor. 6:13 reminds us, "Meats for the belly, and the belly for the meats; but God shall destroy both it and them. Now the body is not for fornication, but for the Lord; and the Lord for the body." Our body belongs to the Lord to do with as he sees fit. So he informs us, that to keep our self for the one person that will become our spouse is his first choice. He also goes on to inform us that if we decide to not marry, we can stay a virgin forever without sinning. But if we decide to marry that's ok too, for as long as there is a marriage, there is no sin.

The sacredness of virginity is more than just a physical deed performed by a willing individual. It carries a strong spiritual significance as well. God is all about covenants. A covenant is a contract between two parties that promises unity. All covenants were sealed with blood. Without the shedding of blood the covenant was considered null and void. God's ultimate covenant was when he cut covenant with man, by shedding his son's blood on a cross. This consummated the marriage between Jesus and his bride the church. In the same way he wants our covenant in marriage to be consummated with blood. The male penis was to be circumcised, this would shed blood, and then when his seed would pass through it into the woman's virgin vagina it would break her hymen, and also shed her blood. This act of shedding mutual blood between the two parties would form a covenant in blood, that can't ever be broken. Believe me marriage in God's eyes is way more than just a piece of paper, as some believe. So don't fear losing your virginity to your mate, it is God's will for your life.

Also let's say you've already made a mistake, and lost your virginity. The Lord says in his word that he considers a born-again Christian to be like a virgin. Look at today's daily verse, and take comfort in its promise.

Daily Verse: "If any one is in Christ, he is a new creation; old things have passed away; behold, all things have become new."

II Corinthians 5:17

FEAR OF WATER

The victory over any fear comes by the willingness to face it, and the determination to overcome it. Many people have overcome great fears that plagued them for decades, by finally facing them head on, and becoming the victor. Today as you face your fear, allow the words of Franklin D. Roosevelt to ring loudly in your ears. "Let me assert my firm belief that the only thing we have to fear is fear itself." If you suffer from the fear of water, don't feel alone, surveys have shown that more than 36 % of the adult USA population has a fear of submerging their face underwater, even in the bathtub! The secret to overcoming this fear is not by ignoring it, but by patiently dealing with it, systematically, and steadily. A fearful person needs an experienced instructor to work with them. If the person is able to trust the instructor, they are able to overcome this fear quickly. I remember when our children were young. We used to take them to a beach at a state park, a few miles away from where we lived. Every one of our kids, at one time in their life deeply feared the water. I would patiently wade around in the shallows with them holding my hands under their bellies as they practiced swimming. We would do this for hours, and just before we would go home for the day, I would pick them up, and throw them in the air. They would go down under the water, and come back up kicking. This was to teach them how to get their head wet. If you don't learn to stick your head under the water, you will never learn how to swim. My actions to some would look cruel, although I never threw them in water that was too deep for them. They acted as though they didn't like it, but years later they told me that those tosses in the air helped them to learn how to swim. Once you gain confidence, swimming is a simple task. In fact the body will naturally float if you just hold your breath.

God chooses for his people to swim in his love, at the mercy of his water. In the natural, the key to becoming a good swimmer is to allow the natural buoyancy of the human body to float with the surface tension of the water. Once you stop fighting the water, you begin to float. Stillness is the key to using the surface tension to your favor. Let your body go to the mercy of the water. In the same way allow your life to be at the mercy of God's love, and don't resist him at all. He will keep you in his stillness, with perfect peace. Good swimming.

Daily Verse: "And I knew him not; but that he should be made manifest to Israel, therefore am I come baptizing with water."
John 1:31

FEAR OF WEALTH

The two big questions being asked by many people today are these; "Does the Lord want Christians to be wealthy?" and, "Is there anything morally wrong with being rich?" I think the best way to answer those questions is to take a look at the financial conditions of our spiritual ancestors. You will notice that the "fathers of our faith" were not only rich but some, like Abraham, were very rich; "And Abraham was very rich in cattle, in silver, and in gold," (Gen.13:2). Some have even had the mistaken idea that Jesus was poor, barely making ends meet; "For ye know the grace of our Lord Jesus Christ, that, though he was RICH, yet for your sakes he became POOR, that ye through his poverty might be RICH," (II Cor. 6:9). In all actuality, Jesus was very wealthy, but He chose the life of a carpenter turned preacher, to demonstrate His love

Scripture informs us that it is God's will that we produce wealth in our life. "But thou shalt remember the Lord thy God; for it is he that giveth thee power to get WEALTH, that he may establish his covenant which he swear unto thy fathers, as it is this day," (Deut. 8:18). I don't believe God would have given you the power, if he didn't want you to use it. So the decision to live in poverty or prosperity is entirely up to you. You already know God's vote on the subject, He votes yes. Today forsake the lie that you should not have wealth. And make a life-changing decision to choose prosperity so that you may help finance God's end time harvest.

The only way Satan can stop you from receiving your God-ordained wealth is by making you fearful about the subject. He feeds you lies that will make you afraid to try new things that could produce wealth in your life. God is constantly feeding his people God-ideas that will give them a step above, but most of the time they aren't listening. Instead they are listening to the lies of the enemy telling them not to try new things for fear of failure. Let today be the day you choose faith over fear. Allow God to counteract Satan's lies about your finances by letting your faith talk for you. Take a step of faith now, and position yourself to receive God's blessings in your life.

Daily Verse: "If therefore ye have not been faithful in the unrighteous mammon, who will commit to your trust the true riches?"

Luke 16:11

FEAR OF POISONS

Various forms of poisons have been used throughout human history by the unscrupulous to kill people; some poisons have been used for capital punishment or have been the cause of death for countless premeditated murders. Poison has been used to "get rid" of someone who was "in the way." At one time there was even a person who taught wives how to poison their husbands if they became too much trouble. Emperors and other rulers used this means to further their ambitions or kingdoms when another heir threatened them. By nature, this type of killing is premeditated and very secret, but the true horror is that poison usually remains completely undetected until too late.

The study of the aspect of poisons is known as toxicology. The origin for this word has its roots in Greek culture, as so many of our English words do. It is the product of two root words. The Greek word "toxin," means, "a bow for shooting arrows," and "logos," which means, "the science of . . ." Since ancient times the tips of arrows were tipped with poison, to assure the kill factor, thus the word "toxicos" came into being. When you combine the two meanings, you can see the powerful word story for the word "toxicology." About 40–90 AD, a

Greek physician, named Diocorides, classified all poisons into three major categories: Animal poisons, mineral poisons, and plant poisons. This classification is still recognized to some point even today.

Even in the time of Christ poisons were very much a part of culture, used often for capital punishment. In fact, when Jesus prayed in the Garden to His Father, about letting the cup pass from Him, He referred to a form of capital punishment used in those days. It was custom to line up a group of condemned men on death row. Then each man was to take a small drink from the same cup; a "bitter" cup containing poison. There was only enough poison placed in the cup for the condemned men. But as custom would have it, if the first man would drink the entire cup, then all the rest of the men could walk away "scot-free." The government felt justice was served once the cup was emptied. This is what Jesus did for us. We were all condemned to a punishment of death, but Jesus drank the bitter cup of death for us all, so that now anyone who accepts Christ as their personal Savior need not drink the cup of punishment, for He drank it once and for all.

We need not fear poisoning ourselves today. God has made provisions in his Word. He exhorts us to pray over our food and give thanks, receiving it with a gracious heart. He promises to keep us in the last days from unnecessary harm. He even said that they would drink deadly things and not be harmed by them.

Daily Verse: " . . . and if they drink any deadly thing, it shall not hurt them. . . ."

Mark 16:18b

FEAR OF JUSTICE

Do you fear that justice won't be served in our society today? It has been said "Don't ask God for justice - you might be surprised if He gives it to you." I am amazed at times at the hypocritical nature of human beings. Many scream they want justice served but when God serves justice, they think He is being unfair. Some suppose that God will overlook sin on the Day of Judgment for the sake of good works. Many in our world think today that if they are a good person and help people, God will just let them into Heaven on their own merit. Some wonder, "Why if God is such a good God, as Christians say, would He send anyone to an awful place like Hell?" Many in our land today worship a God who is a figment of their imagination. Hollywood movies and television series portray a God who rewards us for our own goodwill and merit. Some say, "Just believe in God and everything will be alright."

Dear friend, if you just believe in God, that puts you in the same standing as a devil, and we know they can't have salvation. James says; "Thou believest there is one God; thou doest well; the devils also believe, and tremble." Instead we must look at our God as a great God of justice. Let's not suppose Him to be any less than our earthly judges.

If you're a parent, let me put you in a hypothetical situation. Say your child is riding a bicycle down the back quiet street where you live. It's a beautiful summer day, and everyone is out mowing their grass and enjoying the wonders of God's blessing. Suddenly along comes the local market clerk in her automobile and she's watching for "garage sale" signs, not paying attention to the street, when, without intention, she strikes your baby on the bicycle and kills her. Whose fault was the accident? Some would argue it was the child's fault for riding on the street. But most would agree it was the fault of the driver for not paying attention. She's essentially a good person, works hard everyday at the market, has two children of her own, and is a member of the local PTA. But she killed your little girl. Does she deserve punishment? So the court date arrives. You attend the hearing to see what the judge will do. You don't hate the woman, but you feel she should pay for her wrong-doing. So you sit in the court room, and you can't believe what the defense attorney is saying. "Oh, judge, we know you are a good judge; you have such a compassionate, loving heart. And we know that since you're such a loving person, you wouldn't send anyone as good as my client to prison. Your honor, she is a member of the PTA, she works hard for her family everyday, she is a mother; she is what we would call a "model citizen." Now I know she made one little mistake, but I think all her good should well out-weigh that one little mistake." You sit there in that courtroom ready to explode. You want justice, and you won't settle for anything less. That one little mistake cost your only daughter her life. What would you do if the judge said, "Since you've been such a good person, I'll let you off this time?" You would protest. You'd shout, "Unfair, this judge is unjust." Yet in the world we live in today, that is exactly what people want our God to do. They want him to overlook their wrongs, (sins) and judge them by their good works alone. Friend, no earthly judge would intentionally let someone who is guilty go free, and neither will our heavenly Judge. Because He is so good, He will judge each of us by our relationship with His son. So before you leave this world, let Jesus become your Advocate in the courtroom by accepting Him as your Savior.

Daily Verse: "In the day when God shall judge the secrets of men by Jesus Christ according to my gospel."

Romans 2:16

FEAR OF LEARNING

It has been said that failure and discouragement are the two surest stepping stones up the ladder of success. No other two elements a man can have in his life will teach him like these two. But you must be willing to study them, and learn from them. Some people have such a problem with learning these days. The most common cause is they're inability to keep their mouth shut. Proverbs tells us if we learn to keep our mouth closed we will avoid lots of trouble. As you go through life you will be given plenty of opportunities to keep your mouth shut. Take advantage of them as much as possible. Most great opportunities knock very softly on our life, so if we learn to listen, we will be able to take advantage of them.

Henry Ford soon learned that even mistakes can turn out to be worthwhile achievements. If you can learn to fail intelligently you will be on the pathway to greatness, like many of the great achievers in our history's past.

Paul tells us in his writings to his young protègè Timothy, that in the last days before the coming of the Lord, there would be a group of people who were ever learning, and never able to come to the knowledge of the truth. II Tim. 3:7. He said these people were going to be like the group that withstood Moses from completing his mission of leading God's people out of Egypt. They will distort the truth with trickery to try to lead others astray. Today our land is full of supposed intelligent theologians who are distorting God's word, and leading many astray. They are disputing such doctrines as ,the virgin birth of Christ, the blood of Jesus, and whether or not the bible is the inspired word of God, just to name a few. Listen dear friend, you need not fear learning, God was able to handle these deceivers in the Old Testament, and he will do the same today. He will not allow his word to be destroyed, or return to him void. It will accomplish its intended purpose for which he sent it. Let us become students of God's word, workman that can be proud of our heritage. Let's learn from mistakes, and go from failure to failure allowing God's word to lead the way.

Daily Verse: "A wise man will hear and increase in learning; and a man of understanding shall attain wise council."

Proverbs 1:5

FEAR OF TAKING MEDICINE

For some reason some people think that God is against medical science. Cult groups like Jehovah Witnesses reject the use of blood transfusions, even when lives are in danger, claiming it is against Scripture. Of course this is crazy since there wasn't any such thing as a blood transfusion when scripture was written. Others of so called "Faith movements," have allowed their children to die, since they're beliefs went against the use of science for healing. Don't misunderstand me, I'm a faith preacher. I believe that God still can perform a miracle in my life if I need one. But miracles come from hearing the spoken Word of God, (rhema) and if God is not speaking a "rhema" Word to me, I'm going to take my medicine. Just because I'm a faith preacher, doesn't mean I'm a stupid preacher. A couple years ago, I had my thyroid gland removed, because it was found to be cancerous. Everyday I have to take this little green pill that replaces the thyroxin. I would be stupid to say I believe God can heal me so I'm not going to take my medicine anymore. You can't make God do anything that He has not spoken to you personally; no matter how much you claim it. He is still sovereign, and he will make the decision who he responds to. I've heard people claim that if you declare something enough God will respond. I've only saw in the scripture, where God responded to the faith of someone which he already spoke to about touching. When the angel came to Mary to tell of her virgin birth of the Messiah, she received the "rhema" to fulfill the task by hearing the spoken work of God to her. Faith does come by hearing Jesus speak. But what about taking medication? Should a Christian take medication, and does this show a lack of faith on our part? The answer is yes, and no. Let me illustrate, by relaying a story of a very special woman whom we'll call Kathy.

She came to church with her husband Joe (not his real name) and their two children. They were good church going people. But something happened early in their marriage that caused Kathy's mind to slip. A spirit of Fear gripped her mind rendering her unable to cope with life as we know it. She was perceived as a threat to her children, as well as her husband. The diagnosis was I believe Paranoid Schizophrenia. Treatment was heavy doses of medication daily to help keep the mind in check. And that is what Kathy did, she took I believe more than twenty pills a day, that is, until she got a "rhema" from God. One Sunday night church service was going as usual, when suddenly Kathy heard God speak to her. She cautiously approached the altar for prayer.

I prayed for her, but not really understanding what I was praying for. Immediately joy irrupted all over Kathy, and she told me, and I quote: "Pastor God just told me to not take anymore medication for he has healed me." I looked at her and wisely said, "Sister, you do as you feel you have to." I was not going to instruct her in anyway against her medication. Because I know I'm not God, and I have no ability to heal anyone. Kathy went home, and flushed her medication down the toilet. And to this day she is fear free.

The miracle was so noted that she later had to refrain from receiving Social Security for being disabled. So dear one don't fear medical science, but allow God room to work also.

Daily Verse "A merry heart doeth good like a medicine;"

Proverb 17:22

FEAR OF MEAT

I'm not a dietitian nor do I play one on TV. Just kidding, I've always wanted to use that term. So today I'm not going to make great claims of being highly educated in the area of food sources. However we live in an age that is loaded down with information just a fingers click away on the web. Although I do believe that a lot of the illnesses today are directly related to our eating habits. It seems to be that about half the people I come in contact with are overweight, myself included, so I'm not throwing any stones. And this is probably due to excessive eating. Some have gone the route of avoiding meats for fear of gaining weight, or eating animal flesh. They feel that an all vegetarian diet is God's choice. This isn't true. Before the flood of Noah man did only eat grains and fruits. But after the flood the curse was in full effect, and man began to live shorter life-spans. The earth quit yielding its total nutrition, and thus God then permitted man to eat animal flesh. He put a fear in the animals to protect them from senseless slaughter, and made all flesh editable to us.

Some in the early church had considered themselves to be more," holy," because of their certain consecration practices of abstaining from meats. Paul quickly addressed this falsehood in his letter to Timothy. He wrote, "Now the Spirit speaketh expressly, that in the latter times some shall depart from the faith . . . and commanding to abstain from meats, which God hath created to be received with thanksgiving of them which believe and know the truth. For EVERY creature of God is good, and nothing to be refused, IF it be received with thanksgiving; for it is sanctified by the word of God and prayer. God has made all things to be received with gratitude. We have the right under the New Covenant to eat whatever we choose, if we do so with a gracious heart, not failing to sanctify it by prayer.

Daily Verse: "And put a knife to thy throat, if though be given to appetite."

Proverbs 23:2

FEAR OF RAIN

Rain can be the farmer's friend, or his worst enemy. Too much of it can cause excessive flooding and crop damage, while too little can lead to expensive, and difficult irrigation. Every year reports total in the millions of dollars of losses due to rain. If the flooding or drought doesn't get the crops, the lack of pollination will, for bees won't fly around in the rain. Rain is probably the single most important element in God's plan of nature. In the Old Testament rain was God's way of judging nations, and getting his people back on track. We see in Genesis how God fulfilled his plan to raise Joseph to his place in life, by withholding rain on all the land, and causing a drought.

Again in Elijah's ministry rain was withheld to get Israel's attention off false worship. Most of the people were following the lead of their leaders king Ahab, and Queen Jezebel. These two were devoted worshipers of Baal. Baal was the false God of the weather. So when Elijah appeared before the king, and informed him that it wouldn't rain again until he said so, he was telling him that Jehovah was more powerful than his god of the weather Baal. And his God was, for it didn't rain for 32 years. Not until Elijah was ready to have a showdown with all the false prophets of Baal. Today I believe God is still very much in charge of our weather. I personally believe he withholds rains from nations that have stooped into gross idolatry. Many nations that have lived for centuries worshiping false Gods, rejecting any knowledge of the true God Jehovah; have suffered droughts, plagues, and all the other calamities, associated with God's judgments.

Scripture also uses the analogy of rain in associated with the outpouring of the Holy Spirit on our land. He said in Joel 2:23; "Be glad then ye children of Zion, and rejoice in the Lord your God: for he hath given you the former rain moderately, and he will cause to come down for you the rain, the former rain, and the latter rain in the first month." God was promising us that he would pour out his Holy spirit as rain in the early days, and in the latter days. Let us not fear when God sends rain in our lives. But let us close our spiritual umbrellas and enjoy his presence.

> *Daily Verse: "Be patient therefore, brethren, unto the coming of the Lord. Behold, the husbandman waiteth for the precious fruit of the earth, and hath long patience for it, until he receive the early and latter rain."*
>
> *James 5:7*

FEAR OF BEING HURT

A natural human response is to retract from pain, or anything that inflicts pain on us. It would be unnatural to like to be hurt. Some people take this natural human response to the extremes though. They avoid any type of adverse conditions that could perhaps cause pain. Dear friend, listen to me, feeling pain, and getting hurt from time to time, is all a part of growing up. Every little boy has bruises on his knees. Every little girl has scars on them from childhood cat fights as they are often called. These scars remind us of the pains we suffered, helping us not to repeat the actions that caused the pain in the first place.

As parents we often have the unfortunate duty of watching our children get hurt. We would much rather take their pain for them than to sit back, and watch them go through it. Having six kids around the house gave my wife and me our fair shares of emergency room visits. From cutting off fingers, to poking sticks into their head, to breaking bones, and of course let's not forget the time my youngest daughter Elizabeth rode her tricycle down over a bank, and hit a step on a travel trailer with her face, and sliced the fat part of her cheek wide open. I can still see the doctors shoving that needle up under the fat part of her face to try to get a good stitch on it. Although they all have their growing scars, they all survived, and are doing quite well physically.

Whenever I shrink back from a challenge for fear of being hurt I try to decide if the pain is worth the results. Some things are worth a minor amount of suffering. Those who are involved in weight training realize that you must first break the body down, before you can build it up. They have a little phrase that brings light to this principle. "NO PAIN, NO GAIN." Jesus was willing to suffer the pain of the cross, and the scars of the crucifixion, to bring about redemption for mankind. Did he want to go through the pain of the cross? No, but he weighed the results of those six hours of suffering, and decided to face the fear of being hurt, for the good of mankind. HIS PAIN, OUR GAIN.

Let's not fear a few scars from living for him.
Daily Verse: "For I reckon that the sufferings of this present time are not worthy to be compared with the glory which shall be revealed in us."

Romans 8:18

FEAR OF POVERTY

Although living in natural poverty is not of the will of God. Living in spiritual poverty is very much a part of his plan. In fact, in Jesus' great teaching on the Sermon on the Mount, he taught that spiritual poverty is the doorway into the kingdom of God. "Blessed are the poor in spirit, for theirs is the kingdom of God." Many people are so self-sufficient that they fear the thought of any form of poverty in their lives. Most of the disciples began their walk with Jesus with this attitude. He had to take each one through their own personalized training to rid these attitudes from their lives. Peter for instance was a very strong-willed robust individual. He was quite successful in his fishing partnership with three of the other disciples. One night after a long nights fishing, Peter was coming in from an unfruitful nights venture. Jesus was on the shore, and he informed the disciples that he wanted to use their boat as a preaching platform. At first Peter was going to object, for they had already fished all night. But because he respected Jesus' authority he chose to obey. They launched out into the deep, and Jesus told them to cast their nets over the other side of the boat. When they obeyed, they had such a catch that it took two boats to fill up the fish. Suddenly, this illustrated sermon taught Peter his spiritual poverty, and gained him access into the kingdom of God. Peter's next course of action was to fall on his knees, and plead with Jesus to depart from him, for he was a sinful man. In the presence of God's display of power, Peter realized his own poverty.

The first principle in the kingdom of God is not possessions, or making decisions for Jesus, it is having a complete sense of absolute futility about your own ability to secure your life. Once you finally sense your poverty, and admit that you are unable to help yourself, and then God can begin to bring you to your proper place in life where you can accomplish his will. When we realize our spiritual poverty we will begin to take off our blinders that keep us in natural poverty.

James said, "If any among you lacks wisdom, let him ask of God." The word "ask" means to beg. He goes on to say that most of our asking is for our own lusts. He tells us to ask out of our poverty. A pauper does not ask for anything they can get for themselves. They realize their need and hopelessness so they ask out of the painful condition of their poverty. If you are too ashamed to beg, you will receive very little from the Lord.

Many years ago, after I first received Christ, I had a terrible time controlling my language. Words that I no longer wanted to say kept flowing from my lips. I was sickened by my lack of self-control, and one night I sat, and looked up at the stars. My inability to control my tongue had me feeling particularly sad that night, and as I looked up in the sky, I asked God to forgive me, and help me control my tongue. Almost at once I felt a warm sense of his presence in my heart, it was as if he was saying to me, "Finally he's asking my help." From that day until now, I have never had that problem. He was only waiting for me to see my poverty and beg for his assistance.

Daily Verse: "For everyone that asketh receiveth; and he that seeketh findeth; and to him that knocketh it shall be opened."
Luke 11:10

FEAR OF ENEMIES

An enemy is essentially anyone who is against you. Someone who is stern in their opposition against your ideas, and constantly criticizing you, may be considered an enemy. Most enemies are quite evident for they show their rejection openly. But Jesus warned us we would face enemies who were not so obvious. "For I come to set a man at variance against his father, and a daughter against her mother, and a daughter-in -law against her mother-in -law. And a man's FOES shall be they of his whole household." Then he gives us a careful warning in the next verse, "He that loveth father or mother more than me is not worthy of me; and he that loveth son or daughter more than me is not worthy of me." Jesus was warning us that he was coming to this earth to force people to make a choice in life. We would either choose him, and his way of life, or perish. He said that members of our own family would not agree with us, but if we compromised we weren't worthy of his kingdom. If we chose to give in to our unsaved family members wishes, rather than Christ's we would be rejected by him.

Did you know that your family and friends can also be used by Satan to stop you from completing your mission God gave you to do? Listen to this beautiful gesture made by Peter after Jesus finished telling his disciples what his mission was. "From that time forth began Jesus to shew unto his disciples, how that he must go unto Jerusalem, and suffer many things of the elders and chief priests and scribes, and be killed, and be raised again the third day. Then Peter took him and began to rebuke him, saying, be it far from thee, Lord; this shall not be unto thee." Now doesn't that sound like a friendly comment of concern from a good friend? In essence he was saying Lord; I'm not going to let them do that to you, I'll be here to protect you. But look and see where the root of that friendly gesture come from in the next verse, 23; "But he (Jesus) turned, and said unto Peter, Get thee behind me, Satan; Thou art an offence unto me; For thou savourest not the things that be of God, but those that are of men." Wow! Satan was using Jesus' friend, Peter to try to stop Him from completing the mission His father gave Him to do.

In the same way when we go to our well-meaning friends and family and tell them our plans or dreams, how many times do they try to discourage us? Many times since they know you, they look at your limitations, and can't believe you could ever accomplish great things. You tell your mother of your plans to start a business and she responds that you need to keep your secure job that has health benefits. At that time she becomes an enemy of your vision.

This is probably the reason why God demanded that Abraham leave his home country and all his family members. He didn't want that negative influence of family members to stop him from fulfilling his mission for his life. If you're going to be a person that will change the world, you must be immune from other people's expectations.

Daily Verse: "But love ye your enemies, and do good, and lend, hoping for nothing again; and your reward we be great."

Luke 6:35

FEAR OF REJECTION

The fear of rejection has many faces. It can be as simple as a sarcastic smile or a flippant remark by a well-meaning friend. Bitter silence and just a total denial is a couple of other faces of rejection you might see from time to time. Rejection will be much easier to handle if you remember this one thing: It is not the end of a matter, but only the beginning. Rejection is simply another person's opinion about a matter, and certainly not sealed in cement. If visionaries like Walt Disney would have allowed rejection to have its way, there wouldn't be a Disney empire today. Walt was fired from a newspaper job when he was a young man for not being creative enough. Has anyone on this earth ever been as creative as Walt Disney? But he wasn't willing to let the opinions of someone else steal his dream. He even approached all his friends with business propositions to include them in his dream, but most thought he was crazy, and wanted nothing to do with it. Walt died before the completion of Magic Mountain, and at the Grand Opening ceremony, many felt sorry that Walt never got to see its completion. They were all comforted when Walt's wife took the microphone, and assured everyone that Walt saw the mountain long before anyone else got to see it. Yes, Walt knew rejection, but instead of it being a wall, he used it as a "door" to his next season in life.

Some allow rejection to put a stop to their future goals. Life is full of obstacles, but a clear vision is what will see you through in spite of them. Richard Bach, the writer of a ten thousand word story about a soaring seagull would not accept rejection as the last word. In fact, he had to deal with eighteen of them before MacMillan published his little book entitled Jonathan Livingston Seagull. In five years time that little book sold more than seven million copies in the United States alone. The opinion of eighteen publishers didn't stop Richard from seeing his dream fulfilled. Many famous writers chose to self-publish their own works after being rejected repeatedly.

Rejection only has the power to affect your feelings, not your future. Feed your dream as much as possible, so rejection's voice will be so quiet you will hardly hear it.

The best way to overcome rejections is to stop talking about them. The more you play them over in your mind, the more they resurface with the pain that you felt. Instead, put them aside and ask God to help you go on without fear. Get a clear mental image of the desired result, and hang on until you complete it. If you feel like you're at the end of your rope, tie a knot in it, to help you hang on.

Daily Verse: "And have ye not read this scripture; the stone which the builders rejected is become the chief cornerstone."

Mark 12:10

FEAR OF TRAGEDY

Have you ever heard the statement, "And now you know - the rest of the story." Yes, that is the familiar by-line of Paul Harvey, a famous radio and television personality. He specializes in telling stories about heroic people who have gone from rags to riches, or have turned tragedies into triumphs. Today's daily verse is the Christian's "rest of the story." It is a popular verse, because it tells the Christian how his life is going to work out. It informs us that although life is like a big jigsaw puzzle, God has seen the end, and he is able to take things, and make them work out for his good. Once a young college student went to the wise theologian Charles Spurgeon, with a very troubling question. He asked; "I don't understand why bad things happen to good people, it just doesn't seem fair to me." Spurgeon answered. "Young man, you must give God credit for knowing some things we don't."

I think the main problem we humans suffer from is we think God in all His power causes bad things to happen. Earthquakes, hurricanes, tornadoes, are all blamed on God being called, "Acts of God." God doesn't cause all things to happen, but He is in control of all things that happen. To cause something to happen means, "To initiate." To control something that does happen means, "to have a hand upon it." When Satan goes to God to ask permission to tempt you, God sets the perimeters of how far he can go. This way He can make a way out of every temptation for us. God does not cause temptations to happen, but He is definitely in control of all of them. He is able to take all the tragedies of our life, and "work them together for our good." Read what Paul wrote to the Corinthian church about the purpose of tragedy in our life: "For our light affliction, which is but for a moment, worketh for us a far more exceeding and eternal weight in glory," (II Cor. 4:17). God is using these problems in our life to refine us and make us more into his Son's image.

The key to overcoming this fear is to trust that God will fit all the pieces together, somehow, even though we can't see an end in sight. The story is told of the cruel father who didn't want to spend any time with his children. One day while he was working at his desk, his young son came into his office and asked if his dad would go outside and throw a baseball with him. Impatiently, the busy father looked over and saw a map of the world laying on a stand. He quickly tore the map into small pieces, and told his son, "When you get the map back together, we will go outside and play." The son, excited with anticipation that his father would play ball, quickly met the challenge by grabbing the handful of pieces and fleeing the room. In what seemed like only a few minutes the little boy was back in the room with the map crudely taped back together. His dad was amazed that the boy could do something so difficult in such a short time, so he asked his son how he had done it so fast. The boy commented, "Dad, there was a picture of a MAN on the other side. All I did was look at the man as I put it back together and when I put him back together, so was the world." This little story helps us to realize that during any tragedy in our life we must keep our eyes on God's man, Jesus. And trust him to put our world back together.

Daily Verse: "And we know that all things work together for good to them that love God, to them who are called according to his purpose."

Romans 8: 2

FEAR OF PROBLEMS

It has been wisely stated that problems are just opportunities wrapped in difficulty. Problems are the catalysts for our creativity. Every problem you have ever encountered was for the sole purpose of promoting you to another level. Let me illustrate with these few people. The world had a darkness problem, so Thomas Edison solved it. People had a transportation problem, until along came Henry Ford. Getting across the ocean was a problem until the Wright brothers made our world much smaller with the airplane. Every problem that exists is for the purpose of promotion. Israel was stuck in the valley for forty days during which there had been no progress all because they had this big problem named Goliath standing in their way. And trust me, he was a big problem - being anywhere from ten to thirteen feet tall. Suddenly, along comes an anointed shepherd boy named David who looked at the problem, and seized it as an opportunity for promotion. Whenever a problem exists, realize that you might be someone's solution to their problem.

Once a Christian couple whom we'll call Jo and Mike found out just what a solution they could be too little Jeremy's problem. They were foster parents and had decided to take in a "problem child" as Jeremy was known. The truth is he had been seriously neglected to the point where he couldn't feed or dress himself and he wasn't even potty-trained. Miraculously in just a short three months he had made incredible strides under the tender loving care of his foster parents. He gained some weight and was even beginning to talk, when suddenly, the state sent him to live with his grandparents. As the couple watched the little boy leave they began to question why they even did what did. A short time later they got they're answer as they attended a church service and the pastor read the passage where Jesus took a small child and placed him on his lap, and instructed that anyone who "welcomes a little child welcomes Me." When we take the time to solve someone's problem, even if it is a temporary solution, it's as though we are solving a problem for Christ.

You are necessary for someone, somewhere, today. Don't get so preoccupied with your own fear that you miss these golden opportunities for promotion.

Daily verse: "Then said the Lord unto me, Thou hast well seen: for I will hasten my word to perform it."

Jeremiah 1:12

THE FEAR CYCLE

You may be asking yourself, "What is the fear cycle?" It is a self-producing cycle that causes your fears to grow at increasing rates, without much outside stimuli. Your mind becomes so preoccupied with your fear that you think very little about anything else. If this cycle is allowed to operate without resistance on our part, most of the time we end up creating the thing we feared. Job learned this principle the hard way - read what he said in Job 3: 25, "For the thing which I greatly feared is come upon me and that which I was afraid of is come unto me." Job feared he would loose everything, making his motives for worshiping his God daily, selfish; and that was all Satan needed to get into his life and try to destroy him with the fear cycle.

Let me briefly explain how the fear cycle works. First, you have some bad experience in your life that causes you pain or hurt. Then without warning you begin to fear it will happen again. Soon your mind becomes preoccupied with your condition; your attention leaves the solution which is God, to the fear that hasn't even happened again yet. This disables your faith, and, almost out of nowhere, comes another bad experience. Now your fear is really enlarged because you have unknowingly encouraged this fear to take place. Your mind is now confused and you are unable to separate fear from facts. Everything begins to seem to work into your fear until it has its grip on your life almost completely. You take measures to avoid the experience from happening again until you feel as though you are a prisoner to your fear. This cycle usually takes a period of time to develop, sometimes even years. If allowed to persist it will send its victim into a debilitating life experience, not enjoying the fullness that God has prepared for us.

So how do you break the fear cycle? You willingly face your enemy head on in the power of Christ and depend on Him for help. Turn your attention from the problem to the problem solver. Your preoccupation has made it what it is in your life so it won't give up easily. Keep your mind on God's Word that promises the victory of being free. Learn to center your love on God and not yourself so that you will learn to not act so selfishly. This will redirect your faith into your circumstances and

allow God's truth to take hold of our life. If you confidently believe that
you belong to Christ, and trust him whole-heartedly with your life you
will break the fear cycle from your life. Job learned this in the last chapter where it says that God removed the captivity of Job when he prayed
for his friends. He got his mind off his fear and God was able to release
him from his captivity. He learned to worship God with a pure heart and
closed the devils door in his life.

   *Daily Verse: "And the Lord turned the captivity of Job, when he
   prayed for his friends;"*

                                                              Job 42:10a

FEAR OF MAKING A MISTAKE

   One of the greatest mistakes we human beings can make in life
is to live in the dreaded fear that we will make a mistake. We must not
be afraid to fail in order to achieve great things. Too many people waste
an incredible amount of energy trying to cover up mistakes. Failure is a
sure sign that you're on the pathway to success. Failure has often been
called a detour, not a dead-end street. Many times in life we will find
ourselves going the wrong way, and have to make an adjustment to get
things back on track, kind of like, "wrong way Riegels," as he's been so
often called. This guy committed perhaps the greatest goof in football
history.
   It was New Years Day in the 1929 Rose Bowl game, UCLA
against Georgia Tech. Sometime during the first half Riegels recovered
a fumble and ran sixty-five yards until he was finally tackled by one of
his own players somewhere around his own five yard line. In all the
excitement of recovering a fumble he somehow got turned around, and
ran in the opposite direction. To make matters worse UCLA was forced
to punt a few plays later, resulting in a blocked punt that led to a safety.
The team was completely humiliated by those mistakes. During half-
time Riegels was ready to quit because of his dumb mistake which
obviously put his team behind. Coach Price in his great wisdom put his
hand on the young man's shoulder and said, "Roy, get up, and get on
the field, the game is only half over." So Riegels got up from his seat of
pity, went back out and played a great second half. Friend, when we
make mistakes that completely paralyze us with fear let us remember
that the game of life is only half over. We still have a whole second half
of God's infinite mercy we can use as our comfort.
   Anyone who is doing anything in life is going to make mistakes.
The strike-out king, Babe Ruth once said, "Never let the fear of strik-

ing out get in your way." We should be people that seek excellence rather than frustrated people chasing after perfection. The pursuit of perfection is often times frustrating at best, while the pursuit of excellence can be very gratifying, and rewarding. The truth is, most people are like tea bags, and their strength is never really brought out until they're placed in hot water. It has been stated that the best way to speed up your successes in life is to double your failure rate. Learn to fail forward, and fail intelligently, which allows you to develop success from failure. Now no matter how many mistakes you make in life you can always start over. Jesus promised all of us the opportunity for a new beginning in John 3. So let's turn our mistakes into stepping stones of success.

Daily Verse: "Though he fall, he shall not be utterly cast down: for the Lord upholdeth him with his hand."

Psalm 37:24

FEAR OF THE EMPTY NEST

Empty-nest syndrome is the name given to the host of feelings many parents experience when their last child leaves home. They no longer have a baby "chick" in their nest, so to speak. Think for a moment: You have just spent the last two decades as a parent so it is very reasonable to expect some changes to take place in your life. And some of those changes prove quite difficult at times. For many, particularly Mom, a sadness and fear take over as they question their role in life now. Each day finds its own challenges as major adjustments are made in marriage, relationships, and social life. No longer is that child always with you, all the time. Now, for the first time in several years you and your spouse are left alone. Many marriages get to this point and realize they have allowed stagnation to set in, and once the kids are gone, there's nothing left to hold the marriage together. Instead of planning a future together, these couples see no reason for remaining married. Take a very important step right now before your nest gets empty; try to re-establish romance in your marriage. This will assure that you will enjoy the years ahead, your privacy, and the thrill of having the run of the house again.

Today, as I write this book, my wife, Susie and I only have one child in the nest, and he's only three years from turning eighteen. We've spent time with all our kids, all were home schooled to assure that they got a good education. My wife waited until she was in her mid-thirties before she pursued her career as a nurse. This latter decision has taken some of the financial pressure off and released me to fulfill some of my dreams, such as writing, speaking, etc. In fact, we are planning a Hawaiian cruise once all the kids are gone; a time just for us.

Today, sit down and make a dream list of things you and your spouse want to do once all the kids are gone. It could be anything from travel, to school, to a change in careers. Maybe you've always wanted to write a book. I believe everyone should write at least one book to leave some ideas that you've learned in life to the next generation. Don't make a whole bunch of big changes right away, like selling the house, or moving to another state. Many times this kind of major change can lead to depression, and a feeling that your life is over. Don't go around expecting others to understand what you are going through. Some will think you're only being silly. If you must talk to someone, talk to your spouse, or someone else who has recently experienced the same thing; they will have more compassion than others who haven't experienced the "empty nest."

One final note today, make sure you prepare your child for life. So many parents do everything for their children instead of teaching them how to cook, do laundry, just the basic things in life. Prepare your children for the time when they are no longer in your care, then you won't be sitting around worrying whether they are making it. When the time comes to let them go, they will be well prepared for life and you will be proud of the good parenting job you have done.

Daily Verse: "Lo, children are a heritage of the Lord: and the fruit of the womb is his reward."

Psalm 127:3

FEAR OF BEING LOST

Although some people have made a decision to serve Christ, they feel that their spiritual life is at a stand still. They have stopped studying the Word, stopped finding quiet time with Him, and would even rather stay home from church, and watch the ball game on television, if they would be honest with themselves. These people have a desire to serve God, but they suffer from a deep feeling of being lost. They cry when they hear songs that say what they are feeling. Somewhere along the way they didn't learn how to totally give their life over to God. They plead, "If only He would speak to me, so I would know what to do." They feel God is silent. Soon they begin to dream up things that they say God is telling them when really it's their own conscience talking through their own lusts. They can't really get in touch with the throne, because they have allowed doubt of their salvation to build a door they can't open. They become impatient for they know the answer is in Christ, but they want a resolve from their situation now. They don't want to wait for him to build them up over time, for they feel they will perish before He is finished, and ready to release them to service. And they know that if they don't serve, they won't hear on the last day, "Well done good and faithful servant," from the Master's lips. Don't get me wrong these people truly want to serve God; they just don't know if they can continue, spiritually, that is.

Does this scenario sound like you? I think this experience is quite common, although it is not good. What people don't understand about Christianity is that it all centers on the cross. We begin at the cross, but for some reason drift away in pursuit of a more sophisticated method of growth. Let me explain with this example. When you become a Christian you become joined to Christ as His bride. So if you have become an unfaithful bride, the only hope for an unfaithful bride is to go back to her groom and depend on his grace and mercy for forgiveness. Believe me dear one, God's love for you well outweigh your unfaithfulness. Many people who suffer from the fear of being lost have not learned the true meaning of Luke 9:23. "If any man will come after me, let him deny himself, and take up his cross daily, and follow me." They have no idea at all, of what the cross represents in their life. They think it means having to put up with persecution by fellow employees at work. Some would even believe a cranky mother-in-law to be a cross. Others even think that bearing some sickness in their body is a cross. No, a cross is not a burden we bear. A cross is an instrument of death. If Jesus were talking to modern Christians he would say, "Unless you deny yourself, and take up your electric chair daily, and follow me." You must die. Your problem lies in the fact that there is too much of you alive. If you are to follow Him you must go to the electric chair with your desires and die. You must get up in the morning and decide to make Him the absolute Lord of your life or not at all. He won't force you, that's why you've been having such a struggle. When you give control over to Him, you don't have to study God's Word and pray, you get to. It becomes a delight in your life instead of a religious duty. And God will help, I promise because he promised to finish what He began in us if we will only allow Him to do so.

Daily Verse: "Being confident of this one thing, that he which hath begun a good work in you will perform it until the day of Jesus Christ."

Philippians 1:6

FEAR OF PATIENCE

Many people are satisfied with just entering the Christian life. They want assurance that they have enough "fire insurance" to keep them out of hell. Luke 21:19 makes a very difficult statement for quite a few Christians; "By your patience possess your souls." It actually means to take control, or possession of your soul through patience. We are sometimes foolish to blame many things in our life to demonic activity, when it's really just stubborn flesh still alive in our life. You can't pray away moodiness, or bad attitudes. You have to determine in your heart to get rid of them now. I've often threatened to preach a sermon sometimes, entitled; "It's Not the Devil, Stupid, it's You!" You are to blame for your undisciplined behavior. The Christian life is one miserable life to live in the flesh, when it's not submitted to the cross.

So what is the fear of patience? It's when we are so absorbed with our own life that we cry about any trial that may come our way, even though the trial is intended to perfect us. James 1:4 says; "Let patience have its perfect work, that you may be perfect and complete, lacking nothing." God wants us to be people of patience, because they always win. When you demonstrate patience in your life you are telling God that you are willing to progress at His pace, which by the way is step by step, and not leap by leap. I'm a firm believer in putting deadlines to goals in life, but also I believe we must be willing to rearrange our deadlines if God tells us to.

Maybe you have dreams of becoming some business executive someday, but instead you're the one who makes the coffee for the office. Then be the best coffee maker that office has ever seen, and soon you will be recognized for it; and, oh yeah, that's soon in His time, not your time. One important quality that I have personally learned about God is that he NEVER promotes anyone until they are over-qualified for their present position.

Scripture instructs us that a patient person is stronger than a mighty person in Proverb 16:32, "He that is slow to anger (patient) is better than the mighty: and he that ruleth his spirit (patient) than he that taketh a city." When people act against you, they're waiting for a response, then, when you don't respond, they don't know what to do. When Pilate was breathing the threats and accusations the people were making against Jesus, Jesus was just standing there not saying a word. Pilate didn't quite know what to do with Him. What was Jesus doing by remaining silent? He was conquering the strongman. When he hung on the cross, and wouldn't defend Himself as they mocked Him, what was He doing? He was defeating the enemy and taking the city back for His father. So don't cast away your confidence at the first sign of trouble, but remain steadfast and you shall reap if you "faint not."

Daily Verse: "For you have need of patience, that, after ye have done the will of God, ye might receive the promise."

Hebrews 10:36

FEAR OF DECEPTION

As I began to talk about this fear, I was having a tough time deciding which way to go. There are many deceptions in this world that people fear. In fact deception has been often called one of the devil's four deadly D's. So I have decided to approach this fear in the spiritual realm. I believe one of the enemy's greatest deceptions is to blind people to the real war that is going on. Some unknowing individuals consider the spiritual battle to be God against the devil. And some well-meaning writers of yesteryear published this fact. But think for a minute, who can pose any threat against God? He is all-knowing, all-powerful, and the Almighty; no enemy can overpower God in anything. The war is not a battle for dominance of "good versus evil," but rather a battle between those who choose to rebel against Him, and those who want to serve Him. Some see themselves as pawns in this big, giant cosmic chess game, doing as the victor makes their next move. But instead, we are all living, breathing participants in a real war, with the ability to choose which side we want to be on. When we decide to live in rebellion against God we line ourselves up with Satan, and permit him to exercise his authority over our lives. But if we choose to be restored back to God, He gives us the peace and harmony for which we so often hunger.

Our battles are not against people. It's so difficult to keep this fact in mind when you're experiencing one disappointment after another in life. We tend to want to blame someone for life's injustices. If you have to blame someone, then go ahead and blame the devil. Look at what Ephesians 6:12 says: "For we do not wrestle against flesh and blood (natural) but against principalities, against powers, against the rulers of the darkness of this age, against spiritual hosts of wickedness in the heavenly places." We're all in this battle together, and nobody is immune. We all must engage in the spiritual warfare whether we want to acknowledge it exists or not. No one can just stand back and remain neutral. There is no place of indecision, you're either on God's side or the devils, and it's that simple.

James also gives us information about the possibility of deceiving yourself in the battle against the fear of deception. He goes on to say in James 1:22; "But be doers of the Word, and not hearers only, DECEIVING your own self." When we don't act on the known Word that God gives us, we become our own worst enemy. We deceive our self into believing a lie, and soon are led down a pathway to destruction. So put aside your fear, and stand with a willing heart, ready to fight on the side of the Master who is the winner.

Daily Verse: "Be not deceived; God is not mocked; for whatsoever a man soweth, that shall he reap."

Galatians 6:7

FEAR OF PARENTHOOD

I personally think that no other single thing in an adult's life can be quite like parenting. It truly is the toughest job, you'll ever love. It is filled with challenges and fears that tempt us everyday of our lives. As Christian parents we are called to a very special mission. We are given the responsibility to raise our children to be responsible adults. Parenting is simply loving your kids enough to teach them to do right. Sometimes it's tough to stick to your guns, but that is the only way your child will learn right from wrong. I think the best way to approach parenthood is to follow God's pattern for being a good father. He has a three step process he uses on each of us. The three essential items every child needs to grow and develop properly are: love, discipline, and teaching. If we will follow this three step pattern we will be employing the proper method of raising children in the likeness of God. One of the greatest ways to love your children is to spend time with them. Once a 19th Century diplomat named Charles Francis Adams was asked by his son, Brook, to go fishing with him. He obliged the boy, but later wrote in his journal concerning his time spent with his son; "Today went fishing with my son, a day totally wasted." His boy wanting to please his father, also kept a dairy, his entry for that day was completely different: "Went fishing with my father today, it was the most wonderful day of my life." You never know just how those moments you spend with your child can mold them. When we spend genuine time with our kids it conveys your love to them.

The successful Christian home is characterized by an atmosphere of love. It is important that as responsible parents, we keep our homes sacred not turning them into penal colonies, and courtrooms. Dad, don't fall into the role of policeman, trying to protect them from all the rigors of the cruel world around them. I made that mistake at one time in my early parenthood days. Since then I've learned to be more relaxed, and use more peaceable means to show the kids around the house that this world that is controlled by the Anti-Christ system. I've learned to enjoy doing more fun things with them, spending time just enjoying each other's company.

Parents don't fear taking on this duty; it is God's purpose for creating the human family unit on this earth. Just enjoy the gift of children and thank God everyday for them.

Daily Verse: "And he will turn the hearts of the fathers to the children, and the hearts of the children to their fathers."
Malachi 4:6

FEAR OF ENEMY ATTACKS

Identifying the enemy in the spiritual war can be a very difficult process. This is mainly because the forces of evil aren't clothed in human flesh. Only with the aid of God's word are we able to identify the enemy's nature and his strategies against us. Some people live their lives shadow-boxing the enemy. They attribute all the events that happen in their lives to demon activity. We must at all costs avoid the "-demon-this, demon-that" mentality. In fact most of the problems in our lives are a result of human activity, and not demon activity. Nowhere in Scripture can we find where Satan or his demons are responsible for all the earths' evils. If Satan was responsible for all the sin in the world, God would not hold man accountable for his sin.

Today let's look at the four primary attacks we can expect to take place in our lives. First, demons tempt people. The Bible informs us that no one is immune from this attack. Even Jesus in Luke 4 was led up into the wilderness to be tempted of the devil for forty days.

Next they deceive mankind. Revelation 12:9; "So the great dragon was cast out, the serpent of old, called the devil and Satan, who deceives the whole world;" Then Scripture informs us that the devil oppresses people; "Jesus of Nazareth . . . went about doing good, and healing all who were oppressed of the devil," (Acts 10:38).

Then, finally, Satan brings people into the bondage of FEAR. Heb.2:15; "And deliver them who through fear of death were all their lifetime subject to bondage." The work that Christ performed on the cross released us from the fear of death. Although, Satan's troops con-

tinue to fight on this earth influencing men and women to do evil, God
has empowered His people, the church, to stop these forces dead in their
tracks. He has given us authority to trample on the enemy, without the
slightest fear of being hurt by the enemy. Should we fear the enemy's
attacks on our life? Absolutely not, as long as we remain in our realm
of proper spiritual authority.

When Satan came to this earth, he only possessed "angelic"
authority. Soon he stole from Adam, through deception, his, "Adamic"
authority, which was superior to "angelic" authority. But the reason
Satan hates believers so much is because we are "in Christ." Scripture
encourages us that we are "seated in the heaven lies" with Christ Jesus,
which means now we have "Christ's" authority. And He has given us
all-power over everything because of His obedient act on the cross. So
now when Satan comes at you with a temptation, just resist his influence in the power of Christ, and he must flee from you. Don't fear the
devil.

*Daily Verse: "Behold I give you the authority to trample on ser-
pents and scorpions, and over all the power of the enemy, and
nothing shall by any means hurt you."*

Luke 10:19

FEAR OF LOSING

Nobody likes to lose a fight. As a matter of fact, I myself have
become quite competitive throughout my lifetime. Think for a moment;
is there movement without resistance? If you don't ever want to have
problems in life, I have your answer for you. Don't do anything, just sit
around like a bump on a log and waste away. But when you're ready to
move ahead expect some trouble, and don't be surprised by it. You must
decide if what you want out of life is worth the effort, and be persistent
in your pursuit of it. Jesus was given what seemed like an impossible
task. He was to live a human life clothed in weak human flesh, and obey
God's law to the letter. His obedience would assure that he would be an
acceptable sacrifice for our sins. Was the task difficult? You bet, but
Jesus is no loser. He faced the opposition head on, defeated the flesh,
the devil, and went to the cross as God's spotless lamb. He won the battle, in the final hour in the Garden when He felt like giving up, but He
courageously put to death his own desires and submitted to the will of
His father. "Not my will, but thine be done," were the words of victory.

Personally I love stories of victory. That is why I enjoy watching the old Rocky movies. No matter how hard it gets for him, Rocky

draws strength from some unseen source to come back and beat the "tar" out of the opposition. He's like Jacob of old, when he grabbed the angel, and said, "I won't let you go until you bless me." Where did that come from? He would have the power to fight against an angel, when in one battle in the Old Testament one angel struck down 185,000 men in one night! And here's Jacob, one lone old man wrestling with one all night long. I'll tell you where it came from. It's the desire to win; the tenacity to see the victory at all costs. We draw our strength from realizing that "greater is he that is in me, than is in the world." Although life can be tough at times, get back up and start throwing your blows, and sooner or later some of those punches will connect and you will be victorious. Don't accept a loss as the final answer. Life is not the game show "Who Wants to be a Millionaire?" So you stumble a little, back up into your corner of life, rub your eyes, then take a fresh drink from the water of life, find some encouragement, and get back in the ring. If God didn't want you to be a fighter, He would have given you the victory medal without you having to fight. But Revelation 12 states that "they overcame him (Satan) by the blood of the Lamb, and the Word of their testimony." Do you have a testimony? You can't have a testimony without a test. Stay in the fight, and allow God to pull you through.

Daily Verse: "And having spoiled principalities and powers, he (Jesus) made a shew of them openly, triumphing over them in it."

Colossians 2:15

FEAR OF MISUNDERSTANDING

Many of life's little woes can be attributed to some misunderstanding somewhere along the way. In Jesus' time, the main reason Jesus was not accepted by the religious group was because He didn't come in the way they had envisioned. They had thought He would enter the world riding a white steed in all His glory, to overthrow the Roman government and establish His earthly Kingdom. They completely missed His first coming, because Jesus came as a suffering servant. They had presumed that the Messiah would be born from royalty, not from a meager carpenter's family; a misunderstanding that was very costly to them. Sometimes a misunderstanding can be as simple as the story of the woman who wanted to take a snack break on a long flight overseas, so she bought a newspaper and a package of cookies then went to the lounge. As she was reading her paper, she heard a tearing noise from across the bar. She lowered her paper, and to her surprise there was a man tearing her package of cookies open. She watched as he smiled at her, took a few, and set the rest on the bar. Being a woman of character, and not wanting to make a scene, she just reached over and took a few for herself. As she ate the cookies she became more upset as she could hear him taking more cookies from the package. Quickly, she grabbed a few more before they were all gone. Then, adding insult to injury, she was amazed when the man got to the last cookie, politely broke it in half and placed the half for her back in the package. She picked the package up and tossed it in the wastebasket beside her and decided she'd had enough, so she grabbed her purse, and was about to get a drink and go back to her seat, when to her surprise, in the top of her purse was the package of cookies she had purchased. She had forgotten to take them out of her purse when she sat down. Can you see how easy it is to be led astray when you don't know the whole story?

One way to avoid being caught in some big misunderstanding is by refusing to act on things until you get the whole story. Don't just take someone's word for something. Be sure before you take an action that might be considered vengeful. Gather all the facts of the circumstances and then make a rational decision. When you've done that, you can be sure that you won't be the cause of some big disagreement.

Daily Verse: "In the lips of him that hath understanding wisdom is found; but the rod is for the back of him that is void of understanding."

Proverbs 10:13

FEAR OF DEPENDENCY

Some people have DPD or "Dependent Personality Disorder," so bad that it has restricted them from even functioning on their own. This disorder usually revolves around people being so overly dependent on someone else that they actually lose the ability to take care of themselves. On the flip side, some suffer from the burden of having total responsibility for another. They fear that they won't be capable of caring for someone else properly. This fear affects many different people in many different ways. Some become workaholics, depending on their job for their self-esteem. Teenagers become overly dependent on always listening to music. And still some become addicts of things like sports, TV, sex, exercise, cleaning, clothes, and so on. I think that feeling so inadequate that you can't handle life without a pill or an activity must be a terrible feeling.

Dependent people are experts in the art, or shall I say, witchcraft, of manipulation. They often appear helpless just for the sake of forcing someone else to care for them. Listen dear friend, if you're the type of person who receives a great reward for helping people, just remember, if you are allowing a dependent person to use you, it isn't helping them at all. Although being compassionate is commendable, it must strengthen the weak, not further them along in their fear. Jesus wept for these people as he saw them as "sheep without a shepherd." We must learn to strengthen ourselves by becoming more dependent on God and not the "arm of the flesh." Dear dependent one, you need no other help except from the Lord. Don't resist giving up your dependency on someone else–rely on the Lord. Draw your strength from the greatest self-help book that was ever written, the Bible, God's holy Word. It has often been said, "If God wrote a love letter to you would you read it?" Well, He did, and He wants us to find all our answers to life's problems from His book. When you sit down with God's Word, and invite Him to come and speak to you from the book, you are asking the Creator of all existence to be your help and guide. Let us learn today "where our help comes from" as we fall on the Rock, His Son, Christ.

Daily Verse: "My help cometh from the Lord, which made the heaven and the earth."

Psalm 121:2

FEAR OF THE DAILY GRIND

What is the daily grind you may ask? It's LIFE. Some people are on a constant search for "utopia." They want to have a place to live that will be the perfect place; you know where the temperature is seventy degrees at all times, and they never have a weather disturbance of any kind. This place would be much like the new Walgreen's drug store commercials, "A land called perfect." Wake up! That kind of place doesn't just exist on this side of Heaven. You want to live in Heaven on earth. We haven't made it to Heaven yet. The earth is not supposed to be Heaven, this is the training ground, the place of testing, and it's not going to be a Sunday picnic on a battle field. Get those crazy ideas out of your head and start living realistically in the daily grind. God wants you to start developing good habits that will carry you through the grind, and make you successful in life. These habits will determine your future. You can't allow any fear to dominate you. You have a purpose you must fulfill, for no one else can do it but you. Get a picture of a desired future you want, and begin to pursue it. Start by making prayer part of your daily habits. Many Bible characters that did great things for God used this habit to gain great successes. David prayed seven times a day, Daniel prayed three, Nehemiah often is quoted for praying specific target prayers over the needs of God's people. Trust me; God wants to give you His will more than you probably want to receive it. Have you ever thought about planning you're day ahead of time?

Mary Kay Ash, the secretary turned cosmetic multimillionaire, planned each day with a list of the six most important things to do for the day. She worked from the top, and did not move on until she had the list completed. If she couldn't complete the list, then she placed unfinished projects at the top of tomorrow's list. She did this for years, and it was one of her keys to being so successful. You see, your day doesn't seem so long when you know where you're going. Many people live such a meager existence, playing video games all day or watching television from sunup to sundown. Then they wonder why they get bored so easily. They wonder why life is so void of satisfaction. Get out from the front of someone else's vision, and start living one of your own and you will find the satisfaction you so long for.

Daily Verse: "Every day will I bless thee; and I will praise thy name forever and ever."

Psalm 145:2

FEAR OF PERSECUTION

Since Christ walked the earth in human form, man has been suffering persecution for His faith. Christ was the first martyr, soon followed by Stephen, then on to most of the original disciples, then Apostle Paul who came along and gave his head (life) for the cause. This spawned an epidemic of persecution, including the martyr of famous people like John Bunyan - the writer of Pilgrim's Progress, to brave women such as Joan of Ark. Also, some not so famous people unto this day where it is conservatively estimated that some 100,000 people willingly give their lives for the cause of Christ around this world we live in each year. Persecution is a fearful thing for most people. In the New Testament Jesus gave us some comfort when He put this word at the close of His great teaching on the mount; "Blessed are ye, when men shall revile you, and persecute you, and shall say all manner of evil against you falsely, for my sake. Rejoice and be exceedingly glad; for GREAT is your reward in heaven." I ask you today, "Can you stand to be blessed?"

Joseph Ton, the pastor of the Second Baptist Church of Oradea,

Rumania felt he could run away from Rumania to study theology at Oxford in the late sixties. In the early seventies he wanted to take back his knowledge and do a work in his native country. Although many advised against it, he went ahead and met the challenge. It is told that he preached uninhibitedly like a wildfire, that is, until he was finally arrested. During interrogation he was threatened with death for preaching the Gospel. He further invited death by telling his captures; "Go ahead, take my life, you will seal my message in blood. I have preached all over this country; if you kill me you will prove my dedication to my cause." They decided he was right, and later released him. Actually, in a later report he told of his discouragement at being released. Ton was ready to die, and receive the supreme honor due a martyr of the faith, but he couldn't find anyone to oblige him. Later in 1981 he was exiled from the country altogether. This story illustrates the power of God who is able to remove all fear from our heart when we need it. FEAR NOT.

> *Daily Verse: "But I say unto you, Love your enemies, bless them that curse you, do good to them that hate you, and pray for them which despitefully use you, and persecute you."*
>
> *Matthew 5:44*

FEAR OF PARALYSIS

God's Word declares in Deuteronomy 30:19; "I call heaven and earth to record this day against you, that I have set before you life and death, blessing and CURSING: therefore choose life that both thou and thy seed may live." Jehovah gave a strong warning that day to His people, Israel. It's interesting to note that He gives them a choice, and in His never-dying love, affirms which choice they should make. "Choose life," He says. In that same passage God also explains the cause of some of the woes of our existence. He encourages us that some of our days would be filled with blessing, but without taking a breath, He also informs us that some would be affected by the curse. This was so His people wouldn't be deceived into believing that because they had God on their side they would be free from the earth's curse. Did God put the curse on us? Absolutely not! The whole human race was affected by the sins of Adam and Eve. Today many look around, and unknowingly judge God as unjust because of all the heartaches of our world. Some would say; "If God was so good, why did this happen to me?" Listen friend, God is not the cause of all the earth's problems. We, (Adam & Eve), gave Satan the power to be the prince of this world, also called the "god of this world system" according to the Scriptures. So if you fear becoming disabled in some way, always remember God is not the cause of your problem, He is the answer.

Listen to this beautiful story of two elderly ladies, and how they didn't let the fear of paralysis be the deciding factor in their lives. Both ladies lived in the same retirement home, and became very good friends. One of the main reasons for their friendship was their common passion for playing the piano. Both loved to play the piano more than anything else. They would rather play the piano than eat. Then both ladies suffered incapacitating strokes that left one side of their bodies completely paralyzed. One lady was unable to use the left side of her body; the other lady lost the use of her right side. Both were devastated because each was now unable to play the piano. Then one day a unique idea came to one of the ladies. "Why don't we sit on the piano bench together, and you play the right handed notes and I will play the left handed notes?" So a long bench was brought in, and they attempted to form a team. It worked wonderfully for them. Not only did they begin to play beautiful music together, but their friendship grew increasingly. Don't let this fear hold you back from accomplishing your heart's desires.

Daily Verse: "Then saith he to the man, Stretch forth thine hand. And he stretched it forth; and it was restored whole, like as the other."

Matthew 12:13

FEAR OF INSUFFICIENCY

Jesus once made a claim that puts all of our inclination to worry to shame. In Matthew 6 He taught that His people were to live the Kingdom-life. He addressed areas such as giving, praying, forgiving, saving, working, and even an item that's not a part of His kingdom - worrying. Look at what He said in verse 34; "Take therefore no thought for the morrow; for the morrow shall take thought for the things of itself. Sufficient unto the day is the evil thereof."

Was Jesus claiming that planning a future was wrong? Was He claiming that we should just live day by day, and have no concern for what we will do once we reach retirement age, and can't produce any-more? No, that's not what He was teaching at all. He was speaking against the laziness of mankind. If He had wanted you to be lazy, He wouldn't have used the analogy of the birds in verse 26. He spoke of birds being cared for by the heavenly Father without storing things up for the future. How does the heavenly Father care for the birds? By making everything they need (to sustain their life) available to them, and yet they have to go out and work their tail feathers off to get it. He was speaking against the man in the parable of the rich fool in Luke 12 who had gained such abundance in resources that he felt he could take it easy in life. He reasoned that he finally had enough. All he had to do was build barns that would be big enough to hold all his earthly wealth, and then he could sit back and take it easy.

What was God's response to this self-sufficient attitude? "THOU FOOL, this night thy soul shall be required of thee: then whose shall all these things be, which thou hast provide?" God's desire for His people is that they be a people of dependence. We must need God everyday of their life. He cares not whether we use careful planning to provide for our futures. He just doesn't want us to believe that we can make it one day without His help. God's idea of sufficiency is found in the Lord's Prayer; "Give us this day . . ." Our sufficiency can only be found in Him, and that is an everyday experience. He desires us to need Him - to look to Him to provide for us everyday so we don't think we can make it without Him. Fear not–you're sufficiency is in Christ - only place your dependence in Him.

Daily Verse: "Sufficient unto the day is the evil thereof."

Matthew 6:34

FEAR OF ROMANCE

One of the most humorous tasks a pastor is called on to perform, is to counsel young people before they get married. Don't get me wrong, I'm not taking the responsibility lightly or making marriage out to be a joke. But I'm talking about how most couples don't understand the difference between men and women. If we understand that we were created very different we will be on our way to living a happy success-ful marriage. For instance, women need to understand that men don't care what's on television; they just want to know what else is on. They want to control the remote so they don't have to watch commercials. Men, you need to understand that women live for details. They don't care that you worked today, they want to know how, where, when, and what you did that day. Some people actually fear romance, particularly men, since they are not well equipped for the task.

Another difference; women love to talk. It has been proven that women use twice as many words each day as men. Sometimes this can be a problem with romance, since its roots are in communication. Speaking tenderly and light touching are two key elements involved in real romance. Contrary to what young, soon-to-be married believe, the most important room in the house is not the bedroom. It's whatever room in which you and your spouse communicate. Our passions for sex may wane, but a deep, meaningful, relationship will last forever. The longer a couple is married the better their friendship should become.

My wife and I have little things we do for each other. Although I have to admit she puts me to shame in the romance department, I've been known from time to time to redeem myself with some pretty clever ideas. Once I bought a dozen cards and started mailing them to her on my way to work twelve days before our anniversary. Each included an interesting little poem relating to our marriage. Then on the big day I gave her a giant three foot card, letting her know how much she means to me. Be creative, and go out on dates together. One of the strengths of our marriage has been that we do our best to maintain a weekly date time, just to show each other how much we care for each other. Don't settle for a second rate marriage, do your best to relate to each other in personal ways; ways that only the two of you can recognize.

Daily Verse: " . . . be thou ravished always with her love."
Proverbs 5:19

FEAR OF FALSEHOOD

It has been said that truth is always true, no matter how false it looks, and falsehood is always false no matter how true it looks. Don't ever use anything to your advantage that will cause you to compromise your word. Scripture informs us that we are only as good as our word. It amazes me how shocked people are when they see honesty these days. It's as though it is some great virtue, when in reality it should be the norm. Thomas Jefferson was known for saying, "If wisdom were a book, honesty would be the first chapter." Truth, by its essence is the source of all freedom. Apostle turned Gospel writer, John, said it this way in John 8:32; "You shall know the truth, and the truth shall set you free." Anytime we try to stretch the truth, others can see through it. What most people don't understand is that if they stretch the truth it could snap back and hit them! If we become a person who makes our word, our bond, then people will trust us in all our dealings with them.

Even if truth is ignored, it does not cease to exist. Truth stands on its own merit whether we believe it or not. Truth never depends on the majority vote to be right. The day Jesus was tried in a Roman court for tax evasion, the majority called Him a man who perverts nations, when in reality He was the way, the TRUTH, and the life. He never ceased being the Son of God, no matter how many people doubted or lied about Him.

Truth never needs a crutch to carry it, so if something is said to you, and you see it limping around, it probably is a lie. Lies only stand on one leg, while truth always stands on two. Truth is the only solid foundation upon which we can stand.

People who claim to only tell white lies, soon find themselves "color-blind." For lies are always black. Every lie we tell will soon come back to punish us. The story is told of the little boy who always cried "Wolf!" Three times he told the townspeople that the wolf was invading the flocks. Three times they went out to fight the wolf. All they saw was the little boy laughing at them. Then one day the wolf really did attack the flock, and the little boy cried: "Wolf!" but nobody came to the rescue because they didn't believe him. The flock was destroyed by the wolf. The moral of the story is that our lies always hurt the innocent. Let us be a people who are known by our TRUTH.

Daily Verse: "The lip of truth shall be established forever; but a lying tongue is but for a moment."

Proverbs 12:19

FEAR OF ABANDONMENT

So many people in our world today fear abandonment. I'm not talking about living a reckless life running here and there looking for the next thrill-ride. I'm talking about giving God complete control; placing your life, lock, stock, and barrel into the hands of the Master. Some people will recklessly surrender complete control of their lives to a crisis. When a crisis takes place they search for some spiritual meaning to life, but as soon as the crisis passes, so does the search. It's much like the movie where the man thought he had an incurable disease, so instead of waiting it out, he thought he would take his own life by drowning. In the scene, he quietly walks off in the ocean, trying to get over his head so he will quickly drown. Once he reaches the point of no return, he reasons that he will just quit swimming and that will be sufficient. So he closes his eyes, and gives himself to the waves. But after a couple of minutes without air, the will to live kicks in, and he begins to plead with God to help him make it back to shore. In one of the scenes, he promises that if God would save him, he would go to church every Sunday. But as he is pulled closer to shore, realizing that he will be saved, the less and less his promises become until he says, "You don't expect me to go to church during football season, now do you, God? Is this not the way most people treat God. They are God-chasers in crisis, but run from Him when all goes well. God desires that we will remove ourselves from the superficial experience with Him. Let's not forget that He is the Almighty. He is able to draw from the deep wells of hurt that lie in your heart, and comfort you with His healing balm. Sometimes we are such poor examples of Christianity because we haven't abandoned ourselves to Him totally. We struggle to reach the bottoms of our own well only to find them empty and useless; within lays the water of incompleteness and unsatisfying thirst. If only you would get your eyes off yourself, and look toward Him, then you can find peace from your fear.

Ask yourself these questions; "Do I really love him? How does He know I love Him? Do I show my adoring love to Him everyday? These questions can all be answered in one word: "separation." The message of abandonment is to separate myself to Him. If we place our trust in our own goodness the waves of judgment will take us under in times of testing. But if we place our trust in Christ's' redemption, and abandon our desire to Him, He promises to make holiness a reality in our lives. So surrender today, and live for God with purpose.

Daily Verse: "Paul a servant of Jesus Christ, called to be an apostle, separated unto the gospel of God."

Romans 1:1

FEAR OF EXHAUSTION

Do you know that we serve a God, who never grows weary or tired? That is such good news to think about in our many times of weariness. Many times God's people use all their vital energies to the point where they feel totally worn out and exhausted. This spiritual exhaustion does not come from sin, but from spiritual service. If you feel this fear in your Christian experience, then you need to change where you're shopping for supplies. Some people shop in news papers, magazines, videos and, of course, TV. These are all okay means of entertainment, but should not be the source of our "meat." Notice what Jesus said about His food in John's Gospel. "But he said unto them, I have meat to eat that ye know not of. . . . My meat is to do the will of him that sent me, and finish his work." He said He was drawing His nutrition from His service to God. Notice on one occasion just before Jesus departed up into heaven, He gave the instruction to Peter to "feed his sheep." The interesting thing is that He left no food with which to feed them. Jesus was depending on Peter to be their food. They must eat from him in order to grow and sustain life. In the same way, God expects His people to be the nourishment for other people's souls. We are to be the broken bread, and poured-out wine that people need. But we must be so careful not to completely drain our supply of food to the last drop. If we do, then we will become spiritually exhausted. Friend you are someone's supply of food until they learn to get nourishment on their own.

Have you ever completely drained yourself of supply by serving God? If so don't remain in need by sinking in the pit of weariness. Instead, rekindle, and renew your desires for Him. Search for your reasons for serving Him in the first place. Is the main reason to avoid the judgment? Or is it out of a heart of love for Him, wishing to please Him at all costs? Stop serving Him from selfish motives and begin to form your foundation again on love and dependence while remembering that He is your source of power. It's okay to be exhausted for God as long as you remember where your source comes from. Listen to what David said in today's daily verse.

Daily Verse: "As well the singers as well the players on instruments shall be there: all my SPRINGS are in thee."

Psalm 87:7

FEAR OF CONDEMNATION

Condemnation is a fear that we all encounter from time to time. Christian's are particularly susceptible to this problem for some reason or another. Sometimes I don't understand why they are, but they are. Think for a minute; we've been forgiven, cleansed, and completely reconciled back to God. Yet, those who suffer from condemnation have a deep sense of irreversible punishment. Condemnation is a hard taskmaster which by its very nature demands punishment for the offender. It carries an air of finality and doom, as if to say there is no longer any hope for those caught in its grasp. Condemnation turns a deaf ear to mercy, drowning out all cries for grace with its loud banging of the gavel of judgment. People who suffer from this fear live with a deep sense of guilt, feeling that they are beat down by society's struggles. Soon they learn to live under a cloud of frustration, insecurity, defeat, discouragement, and of course hopelessness. They have no joy for life for they can only see the woes of life, and none of the good.

Scripture informs us that there are primarily two sources for this fear. The first is, of course, our old enemy, the devil. He takes great pleasure in attacking our minds with his fiery darts of criticism, and condemnation, while all the time accusing you before the throne of God. But he isn't our only problem. I John 3:20 states; "For if our heart condemns us . . ." Without really trying, we are able to build quite a self-condemning case against ourselves in our own mind, with our very own heart. If fact, some people can be very hard on themselves. If they don't measure up to their own expectations or standards they have set, they retaliate with an attitude of condemnation. You may be one of these people who are suffering from this fear right now, and you want to know if there is any hope to get rid of this fear from your life. Yes, listen to Gods promise in I John 3:20 as we complete the verse; "For if our heart condemns us, God is greater than our heart, and knows all things." God gives us the assurance in His word that He is greater than any problem we may face and able to release us from them right away. You must challenge the lie that condemnation is tolerable for God's people, and give proper council to God's word on the subject. Stand on solid statements from his Word like: "If our heart does not condemn us, we have confidence toward God," then we can trust him completely when we read, "He who believes in him is not condemned," which leads us to "THEREFORE THERE IS NO CONDEMNATION TO THOSE WHO ARE IN CHRIST."

Begin today to develop a Godly self-esteem which will cure any attitude of condemnation. You must realize that there was only one perfect man who walked the earth and his name was Jesus. Remember the old adage "Christians aren't perfect, just forgiven," so as you grow to perfection, you will be able to handle any of the short-comings that may take place in your life. Please bury your slip-ups right away and don't wallow in them, but do as Paul said; "Forgetting those things which are BEHIND." So what is the behind, he was talking about? Why it's yesterday, my friend.

Daily Verse: "There is therefore now no condemnation to them which are in Christ Jesus, who walk not after the flesh, but after the spirit."

Romans 8:1.

FEAR OF AN UNSOUND MIND

God's word informs us that every human has primarily two kinds of minds. The carnal, fleshly mind that seeks after its own interests and the spiritual mind which is hungry for more of God. Romans 8:6 says; "For to be carnally minded is death, but to be spiritually minded is life and peace." It also informs us that the mind is the battle-field. All spiritual warfare is engaged in the mind, primarily because the mind is where all of man's reasoning, thinking, understanding, and of course, remembering takes place. Satan knows if he can make our carnal mind take over then he can keep us hindered from progressing spiritually. He knows that our carnal mind is what keeps us away from God. All the while our spiritual mind is what seeks deep communion with its creator. Satan knows that the way we think affects the way we act, "for as a man thinks in his heart, so is he." Satan's main ploy of offence is to get God's people thinking with an unsound mind. That is where you become filled with fear instead of faith. You begin to respond by what you see, instead of what you know. His fiery darts of doubt, deception, and despair begin to shake, and agitate your thoughts until you become what the Apostle Paul called "shaken in mind."

In the natural if you take a hold of something and shake it, you have control over it, so Satan knows if he can shake up your mind, he can control your mind. He wants to plant seeds of false doctrines, and such into your mind in hopes of causing enough doubt that you will soon depart from the faith, and chase after doctrines of demons. If he is successful at capturing your mind he can even cause Christians to serve God with the wrong motive. God is always more concerned with our motive than our ministry. He created human beings not human doings. So how we to wage this all out war with our minds? Read on my friend.

God has provided us several strategies to overcome Satan's fiery attacks. The psalmist cried; "Search me, O God, and know my heart. . . . . . . see if there is any wicked way in me." We should submit to God's magnifying glass of His Word, and allow Him to reveal any thing that we need to act upon immediately. Then claim that it is God's will for you to have a sound mind. Ask God's Holy Spirit to keep your mind in perfect peace, as you take "every thought captive to the obedience of Christ." This means when a shaking thought comes to your mind, search to see what God's Word has to say about it before you act on it. Learn to strengthen your mind for action like Peter says in I Peter 1:13. Finally be constantly in the "mind renewal process." Prayer and a constant soaking of the mind in God's Word will keep it in the positive mind set. The more you soak the mind in the proper thoughts, the stronger it will become, soon eliminating tormenting thoughts of anxieties and worries. Soon you will begin to meditate on happy thoughts of peace and prosperity.

Daily Verse: "For God hath not given us the spirit of fear; but of power, and of love, and a sound mind."

II Timothy 1:7

FEAR OF UNBALANCED LIFE

The quest today is commonly called, "The search for a balanced life." Listen friend, ask yourself this question: Does history record the achievements of a balanced person? Were men such as Edison, Einstein, Ford, Bell, and, of course, let's not forget Jesus Christ, balanced? I think not, in the terms that people use today. These men were men of passion who gave their lives for an all-consuming cause. They desired accomplishment over balance. Now don't get me wrong; I'm not advocating a careless wasting of time. I think a life lived without consideration, and planning is a life spent in waste; especially since we all must give account for the way we used our allotted days on this planet, I think we should make a wise investment in the way we spend our time. Time is like money, you can invest it in wise things and see a good return, or you can squander it on foolish interests that bring no lasting satisfaction.

Today so many people carry so many burdens it's like being weighed down with excess luggage. Soon the weight becomes unbearable and the physical load begins to take a toll on their physical well-being, then someone runs around and screams "unbalanced." Although none of us are exempt from having problems, there is absolutely no excuse for the Christian to be burdened with worry. We must learn to let go of the invisible weights that so easily cause us to strain at life. I personally believe that most unbalance today is really overburdened. We feel we have to do more to make up for our lack of restraint. Unconsciously we think that the more we succeed the more we will please God. This is such wrong and dangerous thinking. The reason it's dangerous, is because it can lead a person into all kinds of unreal expectations thus causing a burnout effect when things don't workout. And the reason it's wrong? Look at what Jesus, our example for humanity, did to please His Father, which was God himself. Matthew 3:17; and lo a voice from heaven, "saying, this is my beloved son, in whom I am well PLEASED." Now what wonderful, mighty act did Jesus perform before His baptism to make His Father pleased with Him? Nothing - not one single incredible act. He was just His Father's Son—and that pleased God. All God wants is to be included in our everyday lives, and He will help us make all the other things fit. He doesn't really make any demands on us besides the Great Commandment which is to "love the Lord thy God with all your heart, mind, soul, and strength." When we put God on the top of our list, He somehow makes all the other pieces fit together. An interesting thing that not many people take note of is that most great men and women of history who have made wonderful contributions to society, were Christians. They had learned to juggle their busy existence by placing God on the top of the list. Let us do like-wise, and I believe we will soon see the fear of unbalance fade from our life.

Daily Verse: "He that findeth his life shall lose it; and he that loseth his life for my sake shall find it."

Matthew 10:39

FEAR OF COMMUNICATION TROUBLE

Communication has been described as the ability to take people on trips from where they are, into where they need to be. It is difficult to get your point across to some people; like the man who had the frus-trated teller grab him by the ears and make him listen. The story is told of a man who went into a bank, and asked the teller to give him some money. She politely said she would oblige the man if he would sign a check for the money and give it to her. But he took offense to the lady and said, "He would not sign a check." Thus the lady refused to give him any money, so he angrily left the bank, and went across the street to another bank. Diligently, he approached another teller, and demanded that she give him some money. Like the first teller, she also asked for a signed check. Once again the man quickly refused to sign a check. So instead of reasoning with the man again, the teller reached across the counter, grabbed the man by the ears, and banged his head off the counter three times. The man then stood up, and without hesitation, grabbed the pen off the counter and signed a check for which he received his money. Then he took his money and went back across the street to inform the first teller that the bank across the street had explained the need for signing a check much better than she, so he signed one.

If we are to become better communicators we must learn to say in one word, what others take a whole sentence to say. Calmly allow your mind to carefully think about what your loaded gun, which is your mouth, will say, before the trigger of your tongue is allowed to speak. Many people dig ditches with their words, for which they later fall into and are trapped. While others who are wiser, build high platforms for which to stand among the sinking sands of persecutions. I believe that some people who are foolish, would be wise to "keep their mouth shut and remove everyone's doubt," as the saying goes. We can change someone's life with just a word, so let us choose that word carefully. Let us follow these simple steps to make our communication easier with others. If you have something to say, keep your message a simple one. Don't fill it with a bunch of fluff. Keep it clear and concise, so that even a child can comprehend what you are saying. Know something about whom you are talking to, so that you will be able to understand where they are coming from. Then make sure what you're talking about is a part of your experience. People can tell if you believe in what you are saying. If they perceive that you are honest, they will take action in response to your words, and this is the ultimate goal of all communication. Remember Winston Churchill's famous speech to his war torn nation–"Never Give UP!" He repeated those three words three times, and then sat down to a standing ovation. Communication need not be complicated, only from the heart.

Daily Verse: "Let no corrupt communication proceed out of your mouth, but that which is good to use of edifying."

Ephesians 4:29

FEAR OF FLYING

Since the beginning of aviation in American in 1793, when Jean Pierre Blanchard and his flying companion, a small black dog, entered a hot air balloon launched from Philadelphia to New Jersey, people have been held captive by the fear of flying. Studies show that one in every six adults suffers from 'Aerophobia' as it is technically called. For this reason we should not be ashamed of our fear, as it is quite common. Actually, fearing the unknown is quite natural among us humans. Listen to some of the disturbing questions that have been asked by those suffering from the fear of flying. What will happen to the plane if it hits an air pocket? Where does air turbulence come from? Which seats on the plane are the safest seats to sit in? What will happen to the plane if an engine fails? Just how common are plane crashes? These and many others are commonly asked by those suffering from this fear.

One unusual characteristic about this fear is that it usually is demonstrated in people who are older. It seems that as people get older, life seems more precious and this fear often develops to the point where they will avoid any form of air travel.

This fear takes on many symptoms, from sleepless nights to just mild discomfort. Others will have extreme panic or even terror. Don't allow this fear to plague you any longer if these symptoms fit your life. Studies show that fearful flyers need one thing to alleviate their fears–information; information about the way airplanes operate. They should seek reassurance from studying and talking with people who are experienced in the field. Seek guidance from reading the proper material that will give you the assurance you need. Then by all means conquer your fear by facing it head on, and board an airplane for a short trip somewhere. The most common way to defeat this fear, like many others, is to accomplish it. Once you have become a flyer, this fear will soon quiet down, and a great big world will open up to you. The world of air travel is convenient, exciting, and fast. I pray that God will assist you in removing this phobia from your life, as you remember that He is always with you.

Daily Verse: "So that I may boldly say, The Lord is my helper, and I will not fear what man shall do unto me."

Hebrews 13:6

FEAR OF WRONG RELATIONSHIPS

The main difference between Christianity and religion is 'relationship.' Religious people have a form of godliness because they follow a ritual, while Christians have a relationship with their God which transforms them into an example of godliness. Some relationships are good and should be developed, and some are harmful and should be severed before permanent damage is done to your life. Every time God wants to create something great in your life, He births a relationship in which to allow the deed to work, and of course every time the enemy is planning an attack against you he sends a destroyer into your life to harm you. But always remember that the multiplication factor in which God wants to work in your life is never possible until you face opposition. People are constantly watching us; and we become known for the people we avoid, as much as for the ones we hang with. We must learn to choose our friends wisely else they will lead us astray. It has been stated that "one can't choose the family we were born to, but we can choose who our friends are." God has made humans quite interesting. He created us to need each other in order for us to succeed in life. With the proper relationships we can become anything He wants us to be. Some of these relationships are for motivation, some are for education, others are for love, and of course some will be for correction. Now don't forget there is an enemy who is attempting to "sow tares" into

your life. These are the relationships that may look like the genuine article but in reality they are just fakes carefully designed to drain the life
from you. The Apostle Paul commonly faced two-faced friends at one
time when he wrote to Timothy, "Demus has forsaken me, loving this
present world more than Christ." In Acts 20:31 Paul warns; "Therefore
watch, and remember, that by the space of three years I ceased not to
warn every night and day with tears." Warn of what you may ask? Bad
relationships sent from the enemy. Notice verses 29–30 of the same
chapter. "For I know this that after my departing shall grievous wolves
enter in among you, not sparing the flock. Also of your own selves shall
men arise, speaking perverse things, to draw away disciples after
them." Paul was warning that bad relationships would develop even in
the leadership designed to have a harmful effect on God's people. For
this reason we must learn to be careful who we allow into our circle of
love. Be cautious with who you associate with on an intimate level.
This way you will be sure to not become the dumping ground of other
peoples' trash.

*Daily Verse: "Be ye not unequally yoked together with unbeliev-
ers; for what fellowship hath righteousness with unrighteousness?"*

II Corinthians 6:14

FEAR OF THREATS

Have you ever been threatened, or pushed around by some
bully? Maybe someone got angry with you once and pushed you, and
threatened to harm someone you love. As a child I grew up in down-
town Akron, Ohio during the sixties. These were very fearful times for
me, because of all the racial rioting going on in the world at that time.
I remember in the particular neighborhood where I lived, everyday, just
before dark, the police had to shoot off tear gas bombs just to clear the
streets, and make it safe enough for people returning home from work
that day. Otherwise, these people would be dragged out of their cars and
beat up. Living with threats was a way of life for us. And here we are
in the twenty-first century, supposed to be so much more advanced, and
nothing has changed, except for the characters in the drama. These days
it's road rage, school rage, postal worker rage, and just about every
other kind of rage you can think of. People are still spewing out hatred,
and threats to one another because of their differences. In my personal
experience I've learned that we really don't need to fear the bullies. In
reality most of the time, if not all the time, bullies are really covering a

fear of their own with their anger. Most of the bullies I've encountered in my life were really cowards, seeking to intimidate me. David knew this, that's why when people approached him with threats he let them go. In fact, David was so dependent of God for His help, He often let people reproach, and threaten him in hopes of inciting God to take action in His favor. Friend, don't fear the threats of your enemies. Always remember that there are more on our side than there are with them. Elisha, the prophet knew this when he prayed that his "servant's eyes would be opened." As it is written in 2 Kings one of Elisha's enemies surrounded his home in hopes of destroying him. His servant went out to fetch some water from the well and saw the great army surrounding the house, threatening to destroy the prophet. The servant quickly ran back into the house in fear. Elisha never went outside; he just prayed, "Lord open his eyes that he may see." Now when the servant went outside, he could see the natural army surrounding the house, but also the army of the Lord in flaming chariots of fire surrounding them. His fear was removed as he realized that there was more on his side than there was on the enemy's side. Let us take comfort in that fact, since God's army has not been depleted in the slightest.

Daily Verse: "And now, Lord, behold their threatenings: and grant unto thy servants, that with all boldness they may speak thy word."

Acts 4:29

FEAR OF AUTHORITY

God has placed a delegated authority in everyone's life for three main purposes. They are for our protection, provision, and our preparation. But for some reason people dread and even fear authority. Listen to what Romans 12:1–3 has to say about authority. "Let every soul be subject unto higher powers. For there is no power but of God; the powers that be are ordained of God. Whosoever therefore resisteth the power resisteth the ordinance of God: and they that resist shall receive to themselves damnation. For rulers are not terrors to good works, but to evil. Wilt thou then not be afraid of the power? Do that which is good, and thou shalt have praise of the same." God has set in motion the governments of authority of this world. He rises up all authorities and has the power to remove them as well. Each serves His purpose. He informs us in the above passage that these governing authorities are only a threat to those who break the law. Anyone who is a law abiding citizen has nothing to fear from God's delegated authority. This fear was the cause for the very first sin to ever be committed. Satan looked at himself, and saw that he was reflecting God's glory, so pride entered his heart. He then decided to be like God and seek glory for himself. He resisted God's authority, and stepped out of his proper rank. This was a direct violation of God's pattern for things. So in violating God's order, he also rebelled against God's plan. This turned him into the "usurper" of all humanity. Anyone who rejects God's plan for their life can find their root motives from Satan. It makes no difference how much we sacrifice for the cause if rebellion is in our motive. The Scripture states about Jesus that "obedience is much better than sacrifice." In order for us to totally grasp the power of authority, we must also see the two most important forces at work today. We must completely trust God's plan of salvation. And we must obey his supreme authority. "Trust and obey–For there's no other way," as the old hymn writer said. If we completely trust God with the fullness of our lives, then obedience to His authorities is easy. It's when we lack in the trust or faith department, that we find it difficult to obey His complete plan.

Obedience to God's authorities is also God's way of sending blessing into our life. When we line up in his authority we are saying," Lord I'm willing to accept whatever you send my way." David understood this principle that's why every time Saul, his enemy, was delivered into his hand, he would take no action against him. He repeatedly said; "Can anyone touch the Lord's anointed and be guiltless?" He waited for God to remove the authority from his life, before he progressed in his own. And God did indeed remove Saul in His time and placed David to rule in his stead. So let us not fear our governing authorities but let us "trust and obey."

Daily Verse: "And Jesus came and spake unto them saying, All power is given unto me in heaven and in the earth."
                                                                Matthew 28:18

FEAR OF LEADERSHIP

Leadership is the ability to lead someone where you have already been, instead of ordering them to go where you're not willing to go yourself. As John Maxwell, former pastor turned leadership expert, always says, "Leadership is influence." If you're not influencing someone else's life then you're probably not a leader. Many people fear leaders for they have been consistently hurt or deceived by them; most unintentionally I'm sure, but some probably on purpose. History has recorded the feats of many great leaders and of course many not so great. The story is told of the time when Alexander the Great and his army were on the verge of capturing the entire known world for Greece. At one time he was almost defeated. They found themselves entrenched with just a small amount of water in supply. His entire army was parched for lack of water. As Alexander was surveying his troops from horseback, the last remaining drop of water was brought to him. He took the water in his hand and looked at his thirsty, exhausted troops as they carefully watched their leader's every move. Instead of drinking the water, he poured it out in the name of victory, and declared that he would not drink again until he and all his men could drink together in victory. That one act of honor was enough to light another fire in his men, inspired them to march on, and led to their next victory. Leadership is truly the ability to motivate everyone to do something, instead of a few to do everything. Leaders don't have to force anyone to follow them, they just motivate and the followers soon come. As a leader's ability to lead develops, the more people submit to their leadership. A leader's main task is to prepare their followers for the future. A leader prepares others to take initiative and act on their own.

For some people just the thought of being a leader terrifies them. All of us are made to be leaders. Yes, some are more natural because of their personality type, but all of us are created to be leaders. Parents are designed to lead and motivate their children. We all must take our role. I see our children sometimes do the same thing to their kids that we did to them. I remember our oldest daughter Melinda, one time after she had received a spanking for doing something she shouldn't have, looked up at me and said; "When I get children, I won't spank them, because it's wrong." Now every time I see her take after one of the grandbabies I remind her of her comments to me as a young girl. Usually she just looks at me and smiles. Leadership is so necessary today. Let's become the leaders that God intended us to be and learn from our mistakes instead of being just a follower who lives with them.

Daily Verse: "And these things that thou hast heard of me among many witnesses, the same commit thou to faithful men, who shall be able to teach also."

II Timothy 2:2

FEAR OF BEING OVERLOOKED

Have you ever felt like you were just put on a shelf and forgotten? Promotion time came and went but you were overlooked. In fact, in most cases nobody even considered you for the job. It's like always being the last one to get picked for a team. You feel like you shouldn't even play, because no one really wants you, but since they're being nice they let you play. David, the second king of Israel, had these same feelings. Listen to how he describes them in Psalm 102:6; "I am like a pelican in the wilderness; I am like an owl in the desert." What could be anymore alone, or out of place than a pelican in the wilderness? Pelicans live around water, where they can scoop down, and get fish by the mouthful, something that is in short supply in the wilderness. And what about an owl in the desert? Who in the world ever sees an owl in the desert? Owls only come out at night, and roaming around the desert at night would be far too dangerous. David was saying, "Here I am, alive in this world but nobody even knows I exist." Do you ever feel this way–"I am the overlooked human being in this world. I only exist, and that is it, in fact, if I would cease to exist today, nobody would probably even know about it."

Some people who suffer from this fear are always trying to make their life appear to be significant. When they go to prayer meeting, they make sure everyone knows about their financial problem, just in case God wants to use someone in the church to alleviate their problem. They are always trying to plan how God can get them from here to there in life. Dear one I've learned that all of us get put on a shelf from time to time. This is how God builds the character that He so desires in our life. When we don't see His hand operating in our life then we must allow our faith to see us through. Remember that God promised to always make Himself aware of the affairs of His children. When He is ready, after you have passed the test, then He will lift you up to the status He desires for you. Just learn to be patient and wait of Him.

Daily Verse: "For promotion cometh neither from the east, nor the west, nor from the south. But God is the judge; he putteth down one, and setteth up another."

Psalm 75: 6–7

FEAR OF DISGRACE

Fear, like pain, can let us know if we have a problem in our life that needs our immediate attention. For instance, if we should place our hand on a hot stove we will know the next time to fear placing our hand on a hot stove. If there was no pain, we might leave our hand on the stove until the flesh is burned from our hand. In the same way God can use this fear to keep us realizing who we are in Christ. Regardless of how everyone else is behaving, we are a people of another standard, a people who has an image to preserve without being displayed as a "holier than thou." Other people may live a wild and crazy existence, but we have a name to uphold, and that name is Christ. The fear of shame, embarrassment, or disgrace can become a somewhat very valuable fear. Most of us live behind closed doors in our soul. We let no one see into the depths of our hearts. We keep our weaker side to ourselves. Nobody is allowed to see the problems we inwardly face, or the imperfections that secretly haunt us. The fear of disgrace keeps us secretly screaming for help without anyone hearing. When I think of this fear I think of the prophet Jonah. He seemed to be filled with this fear. Although he was a great patriot of his homeland Israel, as we've already discussed in another lesson, he also was willing to let as many as 120,000 people suffer God's wrath and judgment just to spare his reputation. Like Jonah, many people who suffer from the fear of disgrace worship a false God or an idol. What's the idol they worship you may ask? It's the idol of pride. It took three days and three nights in the belly of a whale for the idol of pride to be sacrificed, before Jonah was ready to be used by God again. What is the "whale's belly" experience God is using on you? Is it a passed up promotion? Or maybe a humbling experience where you get left holding the bag, while everyone else laughs? Maybe God has placed you all alone, where you can get to see the real you for a change. Whichever, this fear has a powerful contrast. Think for a moment what the word dis-grace means. It means to be removed from grace, or to fall out of favor . . . to be bankrupt from honor.

Friend, favor with only one person really matters–Jesus Christ. Two thousand years ago Jesus, too, faced the disgrace of the cross for us, so that we could once again fall into God's good grace. Now that we've been brought back, after being purchased by the blood, let's not continue to live in this fear, but instead let's allow our never dying love for the Master to take over instead. One day as Jesus was in the temple the Pharisees brought him a woman whom they said had been taken in the "very act of adultery." So here's a woman probably naked, since most people don't commit adultery with their clothes on, lying at the feet of Jesus as he sat on the ground, writing in the sand. She's weeping, ashamed, and probably afraid since the punishment for this offense was death by stoning. He, seeing through they're hypocrisy, since the law demanded both offending parties to be involved in the stoning, said; "He that is without sin, cast the first stone." When he finally looked up, he inquired to the harlot, as to where her accusers were. She informed him that there were none. Jesus said that He would not become one either, as long as she would stop sinning. Let this be our lesson also.

> *Daily Verse: ". . . who for the joy that was before him endured the cross, despising the shame, and is set down at the right hand of the throne of God."*
>
> *Hebrews 12:2b*

FEAR OF DIVORCE

Fifty years is considered the golden anniversary for marriage, and I'm sorry to say that not very many survive that long. Why? Because our land today is infected with a "me generation."

I heard a story of a man whose wife was diagnosed with terminal cancer, so he quickly divorced her. Today's "ME" generation, is so obsessed with self. They pamper their bodies to the extreme - lifting, running, shaping, tanning, sculpting, rubbing, whatever you can do, they have thought of it. Anything that brings instant gratification and pleasure has been dreamed up, regardless of the eternal consequences. "If someone does not help you grow, divorce them," they say. Some claim a spouse has not kept up with their own intellectual growth, therefore divorce is in order to allow the smarter spouse to excel beyond where they are presently. Some just want a new, younger model (wife/husband) that isn't sagging, or turning gray. Today it doesn't matter how faithful a partner is, as long as MY needs are satisfied. In all the need to satisfy self, children are left holding the bag, full of fragmented lives - today one in every two marriages end in divorce.

With these insurmountable odds so against us, let's take a look and see what God has to say to the "ME" generation from His Word. The scene is another teaching from our Lord Jesus as He was instructing the people on the need for forgiveness. Suddenly the Pharisees thought that they may trip him up so they began to question him on the subject of divorce, since Moses allowed them to divorce in the law. Jesus responded, telling them it was because they were hard-hearted that Moses permitted them to divorce, but in God's eyes divorced couples were still one flesh. Then he went on to give the only true concession for divorce according to God in Matthew 19:9; "And I say unto you, Whosoever shall put away his wife, EXCEPT it be for fornication, and shall marry another, committed adultery; and whosoever marrieth her which is put away commit adultery." What was the disciples' response to those hard words? The next verse says; "If the case of the man be so with his wife, it is not good to marry." Now I know what some of you are thinking, how can something that is so prevalent today be so wrong? It is wrong, my dear friend. To God, marriage is the greatest covenant a man and woman can share with him - the covenant of two becoming one. The same thing happens with us, when we allow Him to come into our heart, and become our spiritual "husband." Now if you are one of the unfortunates that have experienced divorce, perhaps even before you were saved, don't live a life filled with condemnation. As with all sin; repent, and move forward in Christ. The Apostle Paul understood what a tough time it was going to be so in his writings to the Corinthian Church he included a concession that if you were married to an unbeliever, and they left you because of Christ, let them go and live in peace. For then you have not sinned, in such a case. If you are a victim of an unfortunate divorce, don't live a condemned life, for you are not held accountable for the actions of others, only for your response to them.

Daily Verse: "Wherefore they are no more twain, but one flesh. What therefore God hath joined together, let not man put asunder."

Matthew 19:6

FEAR OF PROMOTION

The word "promote" means to move forward in rank, or to rise to a higher position. It's hard for me to imagine that anyone would have trouble being promoted. But the fact remains, that they do. I know a young man who is a good, devoted worker and every place he works his employers soon recognize this and want to promote him. He has had employers who promoted him to foreman, for he is rather sharp, and a quick thinker on his feet. But as soon as this happens it seems like this fear, the fear of promotion kicks in and he soon quits and looks for another job.

Others fear that life will pass them by, and they won't receive the full rewards they deserve. If this sounds like you, and you are always trying to get a promotion, read this story of a hard working man who preferred his brother over himself and soon received a great promotion in his job. The man's name was Thomas Samson, and with a Bible name like that, he lived up to its reputation. He was a hard working miner, who spent many years in the belly of the earth digging out her treasures. One day a foreman noticed how hard Thomas was working and decided to offer him a promotion to work on the surface with a large pay increase. Today it's the same - there are so many average workers out there that when one gives 100 %, they will soon be recognized. Well, Thomas was excited about the promotion, but he asked that the promotion be given to a friend of his that was having a difficult time working down below–in fact, Thomas feared for the friend's life should he continue trying to fulfill the daily quota. The foreman was deeply moved by the generosity of Thomas, so he gave the position to his friend, and when another above ground position opened up Thomas was the first to receive it. The two went on to be lifetime friends for over twenty years. What did Thomas receive besides a big promotion? He received the most valuable thing there is in all existence, a friend. Let us not be so cut-throat in our quest to get ahead that we forget the little guy on the way up. One man said that you better keep your friends you make on the way up, because you're going to need them again as friends when you're on your way down.

Daily Verse: "His lord said unto him, Well done, thou good and faithful servant: thou hast been faithful over a few things, I will make thee ruler over many things: enter now into the joy of thy lord."

Matthew 25:21

FEAR OF SEPARATION

This fear is more commonly called SAD or Separation Anxiety Disorder. Some of the symptoms include the following; distress over being detached from your current home, or excessive anxiety over losing a prominent family figure, worrying about a reoccurring nightmare involving the theme of being separated from the family. It can also be the fear of getting lost, or kidnapped. Some who suffer from this fear have had micro-chip transmitters implanted and had their children and pets implanted so they could be rescued in case such an event takes place. Others may refuse to sleep away from home, or without an authority figure in the house. As children, these people won't participate in even the simplest task or game without a parent or someone they trust helping them, and participating also. They often refuse to go to school, faking some sickness or other reason for not wanting to go.

As you can see, this serious fear, if not dealt with at a young age can leave its captives living a life filled with dread over just everyday tasks.

I remember when we left our children for the first time, and my wife suffered the whole weekend for fear that they would not be safe. Now she rather welcomes the opportunity to get away and we enjoy each others company without having to fill the role of a parent. Although she didn't suffer from this fear, I told you that story to prove a point. One of the best ways to overcome any fear is by simply doing it. If your child is always attached to your hip, and won't even do the simplest tasks without your help, you're not helping them by doing things for them. You must now take action while they are young and help them to get along without you. Insist they spend the night with friends that aren't family. Ask these friends if they will assist you in helping your children grow out of this fear before they end up trapped. Most fears are learned responses, so you should check your own life, to see if you have over-dependence on someone else.

God wants to be our source of protection. His desire is for us to depend on Him for even the simplest pleasures. Teach your children that God is always with them, watching over them to protect them. "Even when mommy and daddy aren't here God is here." Let them see in the Scriptures where it says that "nothing shall separate them from the love of God."

Daily Verse: " . . . nor height, nor depth, nor any other creature, shall be able to separate us from the love of God, which is in Christ Jesus our Lord."

Romans 8:39

FEAR OF CONFRONTATION

Many people live paralyzed lives, at just the thought of facing any form of confrontation. They are consistently just giving in to the whims of others in order to avoid confrontation. Any type of face to face conflict scares them considerably. The truth is we were created for confrontation. It is by confrontation that we grow if we use it to our favor, and don't allow it to destroy us. Don't allow things to stick to you, and you'll be able to use conflict in your favor. As a pastor I'm amazed at how many people live everyday of their lives with yesterday attached to them. They carry around all this unnecessary weight that soon slows them down in their progression with God. For example, let's say a sixth grade teacher made a critical statement to you about your errors on a math test. So instantly, you feel you are no good at math, and unable to comprehend its concepts. Don't give just anyone the right to speak into your life. You must learn to qualify people to be able to speak to you about your future. In confrontation you don't always have to win to be a winner. There is such a thing as winning a battle while losing the war. Good constructive speech is where everyone walks away a winner.

When everyone feels as though something was accomplished, you've had a good confrontation.

If a conflict turns into a disagreement, be the first to forgive. Living a life of unforgiveness is like driving your car with the parking brake on. No matter how hard you push on the gas, you can't seem to get any momentum; you just spin your tires and rev up your motor. Soon your back gets tired from carrying around a sack full of grudges and hurts. I think the most pathetic thing in life is to see a person live an entire life having the deep-seated cancer (a grudge) eating away at them. There was a wrong that was conceived in a moment of confrontation that was allowed to fester until it turned into a grudge. Don't waste your effort, dear one; release all your hurts and grudges and let God free you up at once.

Daily Verse: "To whom ye forgive anything, I forgive also: for if I forgave anything, to whom I forgave it, for your sakes forgave I it in the person of Christ."

II Corinthians 2:10

FEAR OF OUT OF CONTROL

The fear of losing control is a real fear. There is something about us as humans - we have to always feel like we are making things happen in our lives. We spend thousands of dollars on an education that we believe will put us in the driver's seat of life. For some reason we feel that we know best. I remember when my kids were growing up they all used to tell me of their great aspirations and goals for life. One wanted to be a teacher, another a policeman and our youngest wants to be anything from a professional skateboarder to a real estate tycoon. I would just tell them, that these goals were fine as long as that's what God wanted them to do. Then I would ask; "What does God want you to do with your life?" I could see the disappointment in their eyes, it's like they were saying to me; "You mean I have to let Him decide what I should do with my life?" They wanted to be in control. If this sounds like you, rest at ease, that's human nature. Human nature always wants to decide its own destiny. The natural side of man always wants to be in control of one's own life. Think for a moment, what do your kids do when you tell them not to do something? They go ahead and do it anyway. They want to be in charge, even if their action is wrong, and potentially harmful to them. You see, that's the difference between the unbeliever and the believer. They are both sinners, but the believer has relinquished all control of his life over to his Lord. He no longer sits on the throne of his life, but Jesus has that position now.

Over the past few decades there has been a gospel preached telling man that salvation is all a sole act of Christ, and no response of obedience is required of man. This message is just not true. In fact, without obedience on man's part, there is no salvation. Until man decides to make Jesus Lord of his life there is no Savior either. He's Lord of all, or not at all. Listen to what the writer of Hebrews has to say about the demand of obedience even required from God's own son.

"Though he were a son, yet learned he obedience by the thing which he suffered. And being made perfect, he became the author of eternal salvation unto ALL them that OBEY him." Do you see that obedience is required for eternal salvation to be genuine? Unless we are willing to turn over the reins of our life to God, and do as He commands, we cannot possess salvation. So instead of worrying about controlling your own life, seek God, and let Him make the decision for you.

Daily Verse: "And he trembling and astonished said, 'Lord, what wilt thou have me to do?'"

Acts 9:6a

FEAR OF BEING VULNERABLE

Phobias are terrible things. It's been reported that women out number men two to one in the "phobia" department. Also phobias are three times higher in African Americans and Hispanics than they are in whites, leading us to believe that the economic background of poorer, struggling people in our country may play a part in developing certain fears; only God knows for sure. All of us, no matter what color the skin, feel vulnerable from time to time. For some reason, we think we should just coast thru life with no worries at all. This is the way America used to be, she was fat, her stock market was flourishing, spending was rampant, then BANG, September 11th 2001 changed all that. Now she really sees how vulnerable she is. In fact, no one would have believed that terrorists could bomb our military headquarters using one of own planes as the weapon. Instead of people waking up and taking positive action, many have done just the opposite. Instead of Americans leaning on the everlasting arms of God, we've resorted to leaning on the arm of the flesh. It was reported that after the disaster of 9/11, church attendance went up over 50% in some areas. But now three years later, where are the people? I believe many of these people were just responding to the "fear of vulnerability." And the Bible says that "fear has torment," in I John 4:18. In truth, I believe this fear was tormenting people, and standing in their way of their relationship with God. They were afraid and hurt emotionally. Many were too frightened to continue daily routines because of anthrax scares, and reported threats of repeated attacks on the horizon. Some couldn't function in the normal, so they turned to religion; which left many empty, because they lacked relationship. Their motives were all wrong so they didn't receive the faith they were looking for.

The opposite of fear is faith. They didn't want to be vulnerable, because they feared being hurt. Most of America's citizens are really on some pride trip in this country. They feel if they get hurt, it will show their vulnerability, and most interpret vulnerability as weakness, and to appear weak really does something to their prideful ego. For some reason they have to feel like they're super-human, able to take any pain without shedding a tear. Friend, God accepts your vulnerabilities and weaknesses. He takes you just the way you are. It is not a sin to be vulnerable. We all must face living in the uncharted territory known as life, and yes, I know it can be scary at times not knowing what the future holds. But let us rest in the arms of God, knowing that He has already mapped out this thing known as life and He has seen the end of the book. God wants you to be happy, and the guidelines He has set for us, is for that very purpose. Please don't let pride and fear rob you of your God-given privileges. Don't let hurt deprive you of the love and satisfaction in life God has in store for you. Just live in peace with Him.

Daily Verse: "Fear not, little flock; for it is your father's good pleasure to give you the kingdom."

Luke 12:32

FEAR OF EXPOSURE

To expose something according to the dictionary means "to make something known, or to reveal a secret . . . to bring to light something that has been kept secret." Most people, whether we are a Christian or not, have a hidden skeleton or two in the closet. Many feel that if these things are revealed, their embarrassment will be too much to handle. Child of God, there is nothing in your life that God doesn't know about. He knows about your past, present, and future. That's the beautiful thing about our God; He knows all about us, and still chooses to love us. It has been said that the definition of a real friend is someone who knows the real you and still wants to be your friend. God truly is a real friend to us. In fact, Scripture records that he is a "friend who sticks closer than a brother."

Scandals today are a big part of our everyday existence. The news media for some reason feel they are the self-appointed watch dogs for society. They feel that they must catch all the evils of our world. In the quest for the best ratings for the week, they are hunting daily for the biggest scandal. No one is exempt. One news outlet even went after a restaurant chain who was charging 99 cents for a drink, instead of a dollar - claiming them to be deceptive; as if the company worth billions is really concerned about some people saying; "Just keep the penny." They have also decided to catch EVERY crooked preacher that preaches from a pulpit. Like any profession, there are some bad apples in all, but that doesn't make every preacher bad. Teachers every day in this great land of ours are exposed for some type of malicious charge, but do you keep your children home from school branding all teachers as bad? Of course you wouldn't. Police officers are exposed all the time for taking bribes, and doing illegal things, but does that stop you from calling one when you hear a prowler downstairs in your house at night? With this same thinking, we should not be afraid to believe the man that stands behind the sacred desk speaking the oracles of God. We should not stop attending church, just because one preacher has been exposed for some sin. I believe that God is the righteous judge, and he knows how to judge his own. I also believe that God uses exposure to get people to the place he wants them to be in life. Think for a moment of David, the second king of Israel. He committed a terrible wrong - stealing a man's wife and having her husband killed to cover up his own sin. He lived for several months out of the will of God, failing to repent. But when God spoke to the prophet Nathan about David's sin, he instructed him to approach David and restore him. Nathan went to David with a story about a man who only had one lamb, and had it stolen by a man who had many lambs. He asked David what he thought should be done to the man? Although David was living in sin and unable to see his own hypocrisy, he said that the man should be punished for his wrong. At that, the prophet Nathan pointed his boney finger at David and said; "Thou art the man." What was David's response to this exposure? He fell to his knees and repented immediately. God had used the exposure of his sin to his benefit. And he'll do the same with us if we will allow him.

Daily Verse: "For nothing is secret that shall not be made man ifest; neither anything hid, that shall not be known and come abroad."

Luke 8:17

FEAR OF BROKEN RELATIONSHIPS

God's Word is revelation to our soul. In it we find the desires of our Master for His people. He firmly expresses His desires for His servants, and then it is entirely up to us to respond in his favor. If we want to move ahead in our spiritual experience then we must follow His instructions to the letter. In so doing we will guarantee His powerful presence in our endeavors. Christianity is all about relationships. It begins with man entering a relationship with his Creator God, and becoming established in the faith by believing in the work of the cross performed by God's only Son, Jesus Christ. Then, it quickly progresses to one another. Christianity is all about one another. God says; "How can a man say he loves God, which he can't see, while he hates his brother, which he can see?" I don't know about you, but it makes sense to me. You may ask, "What is God's desire for me?" I think He made it pretty plain when He said, "Love the Lord your God with all your heart, mind, soul, and strength, and love your neighbor as yourself." God's plan is simply all about relationship. God says that our relationships with others should be so deep that we would be willing to lay down our life for our fellow man; to crucify all our needs and selfish desires and quests that only benefit us, and prefer our fellow man. History records people who have done just that. Servants such as Mother Teresa, Pastor Damien, David Livingstone, and Jim Elliot; all gave the ultimate price–their lives - for His cause, and who learned that true Christianity is all about restoring relationships.

Scripture makes it every Christian's responsibility when they see another believer fall. Galatians 6:1 says, "Brethren, if a man be overtaken in a fault, ye which are spiritual, (US) restore such a one in the spirit of meekness; considering thyself, lest thou also be tempted." We must stop praying about what we should do, and go to that person, and restore them with love. It was Jesus' mission, and He's left it up to us. Genuine loves takes action, and believe me genuine love and compassion, will go a long way to removing the fear from someone's life. We can make a difference, if we will just do what the Bible commands us to do. We should be bold enough to go and confront another about their faults. Make it plain, and also go with an answer to the problem. Our test of spiritually is our ability to expose sin, while at the same time restoring the offender in love and meekness. Will this work? More times than not. In fact, one man was even quoted as saying, "Christianity? It might work if we would only give it a chance."

Daily Verse: "Blessed is every one that feareth the Lord; that walketh in his ways."

Psalm 128:1

FEAR OF SELFISHNESS

Today many Christians are like the survivors of the Titanic disaster of April 15, 1912. They are safe in their little comfortable lifeboat, (church) unwilling to face people who are drowning in treacherous waters. They fear they might be hurt in the process should they become involved. History records that although there were twenty lifeboats watching from a distance, as the disaster takes place, only Lifeboat #14 was willing to take the risk of being swamped by drowning swimmers, maneuvering its way in and out of the floating bodies, looking for survivors. Although very few were found, they took the chance. Some people fear their action will be so insignificant it wouldn't matter anyway.

One day there was an old man who decided to go to the beach and catch up on his reading. As he sat in the comfort of his beach chair with a cold soda in his hand, he couldn't help noticing the action of a young boy down the beach from him. The boy seemed to picking up something, and tossing it back into the ocean. The old man's curiosity got the best of him, so he put his book down and slowly meandered down the beach toward the boy. As he got closer, and could see what the boy was doing, he couldn't believe his eyes. The boy was picking up live starfish with his hands and tossing them back in the ocean. It seems that the tide had brought in thousands of the little critters, and they were dying on the beach. The old man yelled to the boy, "What are you doing, son?" He saw the boy's task as fruitless, because as the boy was throwing some starfish back, the powerful waves were bringing that many, if not more, back to the shore. The boy replied, "I'm rescuing these starfish sir, for they are dying on the beach." The old man, supposing he was the wiser said; "Son, do you really think what you are doing matters? Look at all the starfish here are on this beach?" In response, the boy reached down, picked up a starfish from between the old man's legs and tossed it back into the sea, then he looked up at the old man and said; "It matters to that one." Any unselfish deed matters to God. He sees our every action, when others don't. He knows if our motives are pure, or if we are trying to manipulate someone into some response. Let us today put the fear of selfishness to silence by deciding to live our life for the good of our fellow man. Every deed we do, let's do in the name of Christ, so He will receive the credit for our selfless living.

Daily Verse: "Look not every man to his own things, but every man also on the things of others."

Philippians 2:4

FEAR OF ISOLATION

This fear has been called man's greatest fear, and Satan's most powerful weapon. The fear of isolation is simply the belief that no one loves us or cares about us–we feel utterly separated, alone. This fear can lead to other fears like, loneliness, depression, despair, betrayal, etc. Satan, through the years has traumatized many lives with this fear. The stories are always the same, the person felt lonely, they assumed that nobody cared so they enter into a life of seclusion, or worse, they decide to end what they consider a miserable existence by attempting some form of suicide. Believe me isolation was never God's plan for man. Listen to what God says about the subject in his Word; "It is not good that man should be alone." For this reason He created for man a help-mate, which later became his wife. God has pre-programmed every human being to desire communion and companionship. In Adam's case God created Eve completely perfect for Adam in every way. She was created as someone with an equal share of God's image. She was some-one who was similar enough that they could have companionship with one another, yet different enough that they could enjoy a lasting rela-tionship with each other. Everything was great for the couple until they sinned and began to feel isolated. They began to blame others and even each other for their wrongdoing. Adam even tried to blame God for not "making" Eve right. Guilt, shame, resentment; all led this couple into the fear of isolation. Not just this couple, but many of whom we call Bible heroes, suffered from periods of "isolation fear." Samson sat alone in prison wondering if he would ever be used by God again, since he had failed him so miserably the first time. Elijah, Solomon, and David all went thru feelings of being totally alone; isolated. But David had a revelation that not many experienced. He knew that God is Jehovah Shammah, or the "Lord is always there." He knew that he was never completely alone; that God says that he will "always be with him." Do you believe that friend? If you are feeling alone right now, take comfort in knowing that you have the Most High God, as an audience. He is completely aware of your affairs and wants to bring you restoration if you will allow Him. He can free you up from feelings of isolation and fear. He will place you in right standing, in your rightful place seated beside him in the heaven lies. Let these word's of the Master bring courage and comfort today; "I will NEVER leave you or forsake you."

Daily Verse: "When my father and my mother forsake me, then the Lord will take me up."

Psalm 27:10

FEAR OF UN-FULFILLMENT

What a sad meaningless existence it is to live a life of un-fulfillment. To know that you have some duty to perform, yet this fear keeps you from completing it. Many search for fulfillment in all the wrong places. A young girl who lives with an authoritarian father, who never shares his love with her, soon finds herself seeking what she thinks is love with some young man in the backseat of his car somewhere, thinking that will lead to fulfillment. Another hardworking man is passed up, year after year for promotion, simply because he lacks the confidence needed to get the promotion. He then turns to an affair with his secretary, and a bottle of scotch to find fulfillment. What these people and a host of others don't understand is that fulfillment can't be found outside of the person of Jesus Christ. God has, in his omniscience, placed an empty spot in each of us; that place represents the need man has to worship. If you leave man alone on a deserted island outside the boundaries of organized religion, and come back in thirty years, you'll find that he has found something to worship. It may be a rock, a tree, a bird or the sun and the moon, but he will find something to make into a god. This is in the heart of every man and he can't help it. Many today who suffer from the fear of un-fulfillment simply need to surrender to the plan of God for their life. If they will give Him what existence they have left, and let Him direct their future paths, then they will find that fulfillment they so desire. It can't be found in a bottle, pill, or wrapped in paper, but only in Christ. I know in my own life, as a young man, I was always chasing after an impossible dream. I had the belief that I could make it without God. I believed that He was responsible for all the problems I had growing up as a child. And just take my word for it; I had more problems than most teenage boys. I foolishly reasoned that I had made it twenty-eight years without Jesus; why should I need him now? Then I heard His voice, the same voice I heard when I was about eighteen, and had rejected. But this time it was different, He loved me, even after all I said and done . . . He still loved me. Wow, I was overwhelmed with His love. I quickly responded by giving Him complete control of my life. That was many years ago, and I've never regretted that day once. In fact, I feel kind of stupid that I didn't do it sooner, and remove all those wasted years of trying to find fulfillment without Christ in my life. Today Christ speaks to me regularly, and gives me the direction I need to heighten my fulfillment in Him. I pray that this will be your testimony also.

Daily Verse: "Peace I leave with you, my peace I give unto you: not as the world giveth, give I unto you. Let not your heart be troubled, neither be afraid."

John 14:27

FEAR OF A BAD HEART

One day I was standing looking at a special news report on television. They were giving the latest statistics for causes of death for men and women. I was not amazed to find out that the leading cause of death in males is heart failure. But I was completely surprised to find out that today woman suffer from the same fate. Yes, the leading cause for death is heart disease in woman also. Just as I heard that report my mind raced back to a Scripture in Luke where Jesus prophesied that in the last days "men's hearts would fail them . . ." for the things coming on this world. As I pondered this report, the Holy Spirit spoke to my heart about writing a book that would give people, particularly His people assurance that He cares and is very aware of their fears.

He directed me to write the book you are reading now, A YEAR WITHOUT FEAR. Will this book make you a fearless individual? Absolutely not! And I make no such claims, but what it will do, is give you God's perspective on most of the fears that plague us today. The fact is, that fear and stress is killing us. Even God's people are living only half-lives, running around suffering from fears from which God has richly freed them.

If you have a history of heart problems, then by all means have regular check-ups from a good doctor, but don't live a life dreading the awful fear of having a heart attack. We are so concerned these days with the condition of our natural heart, but God is concerned about our spiritual heart. He has filled the pages of his Word with instructions about the heart. He tells us to guard it, watch it, care for it, and protect what we put in it. He even informs us that it is the "well-spring of all life . . .

from it comes blessing, or cursing . . . out of the abundance (of its reservoirs) the mouth speaks." In short, what comes out of our mouth is in our heart. Our spiritual heart is what determines whether we are clean in the eyes of God or not. If our heart is filthy then chances are, so is our life. If you have not been to the Master for a "heart transplant," then by all means don't put it off any longer. In the Old Testament, God took out Saul's "heart of stone," and replaced it with a "heart of flesh." His ultimate desire is for us to allow him the right to take His spirit, and write His laws on our hearts, so we will refrain from sinning and breaking the enjoyment of fellowship we have with Him. So, clean up your heart today.

> *Daily Verse: "A good man out of the good treasure of his heart bringeth forth good things, and an evil man out of the evil treasure bringeth forth evil."*
>
> Matthew 12:35

THE FEAR OF THE ELDERLY

What do you think is the elderly biggest fear? I think it's pretty safe to say it's not getting old. I'm sure many suffer with fears of loneliness, bouts of depression, and host of other losses, but I personally believe the biggest fear the elderly face today, is the fear of being forgotten. So many people just go through life, without any concern about who paved the way for them. Today we live with many modern conveniences that were only made possible by the sacrifices of those of the past, while our churches are filled with dear saints who feel that even God has forgotten them. Even in our churches many well-meaning people have abandoned these dear saint's songs for the sake of a new beat. Don't get me wrong, I'm not against speeding up the tempo, and singing modern praise music, but let us not abandon our roots, and those who paved the way for us. Let us become more sensitive to peoples needs, and those who are valuable to God's kingdom. Yes, I believe it's time to remember our heritage, and assure the elderly that they are still of value. The Bible says that a "man's crown is his gray hair." Along with those gray hairs comes much wisdom and knowledge. Elderly people could save us years of trial and error if we would only listen to them, and follow their advice. Instead of treating our elderly like old worn carpet that we put in the back room somewhere, let's give them the top billing they deserve. Remember unless the death angel visits your dwelling before the age of seventy, you too will face this time.

Daily Verse: "The glory of young men is their strength; and the beauty of old men is the grey head."

Proverbs 20:29

FEAR OF BEING SINGLE

In today's society, a single individual is often perceived as a carefree swinger, moving from one big adventure to another. Our media often glamorizes the single lifestyle portraying it as being filled with fun and gusto. However, the truth is that many singles live very lonely lives filled with the fear that they will never find a mate. It is estimated that one in every three adults is single; approximately forty-million people. This figure includes almost twenty-five million who have never experienced matrimony. If you find yourself single, be assured you are not alone. An incredible number of people are in the same state. If you are a Christian, you have an enormous advantage over those who aren't. Why you may ask? Even though you don't have a mate, you have a unique relationship with Jesus Christ. You must believe that you are single for a purpose and God can use this time in your life greatly.

Satan loves to promote insecurities in Christian singles about their status. Peace will only come when we accept our place in life before God. We must believe that God can be trusted to guide us through all the details and times of our lives. It is not wrong to desire to be married, but we should not allow our mind to be consumed with the thought so much that we lose our joy every time we think about it. God's goal for singles is to live a life of fruitful productive service to others. We must learn to "find contentment in whatever state we are in" whether married or single. In my own personal experience, I found satisfaction in truly being in love with Christ. I needed no mate to feel complete. When my love for Christ was at its peak, then God could share me with someone else, so He directed me to my wife, and I fell in love. Only when I didn't need a wife, did he give me one. That's how God works with us - when our identity and security is in Christ then we have something to share with someone else. Singles should meet the need for companionship by developing close and intimate friendships with other believers. These friendships can be very rewarding, and fulfilling when experienced in the proper context. If you are single don't restrict your friendships to only those of the same sex. Although there are some restrictions for your friendships, allow God to use you as He sees fit.

Some singles have the constant haunting fear that they will

never get married. They worry that they will be alone for the rest of their lives. If these fears haunt you, rest assured that there is nothing wrong with you. Chances are you will find a mate and get married. Just use your singleness now as a way of blessing God's kingdom with your freedom. Become a wise steward of your time now, and be the Lord's servant.

Daily Verse: "Whoso findeth a wife findeth a good thing, and obtaineth favor of the Lord."

Proverbs 18:22

FEAR OF LIGHTNING

Lightning is simply a giant spark that jumps between pools of positive and negative currents. In ancient times lightning controlled the lives of many. The Persians believed that the god, Seth caused lightning streaks with a huge iron spear. Greek culture's claimed Zeus was thought to be the god responsible for the lightning and thunderbolts seen in the sky. Greeks determined lightning was a sign to warn them against enemies. Scandinavian mythology gave credit to Thor, the red-haired Norse god who sent sparks flying as he swung his big hammer. These beliefs and fears continued until about the Middle Ages, when people began to shake their dreaded fear of lightning. Actually that's when church bells came into existence. Many believed the ringing of church bells would cause the lightning to cease so bell-ringers were sent to the towers during storms, causing 103 deaths to bell ringers from 386 lightning strikes to bell towers during a 33 year period. In fact, churches were the target of several lightning strikes, resulting in fires that destroyed them completely. Finally in 1766, a Christian printer by the name of Benjamin Franklin installed the first lightning rod to avoid this trouble. By the way even though there's a legend that says that Franklin flew a kite with a key attached to prove that lightning was electrical there is no written proof to documenting the event. However, one Christmas day he nearly electrocuted himself while attempting to cook a holiday turkey with a pair of charged glass jars.

Although no one really knows for sure, it is estimated that lightning is 30'000 degrees Celsius - six times hotter than the sun. Most lightning strikes take place from cloud to cloud, but when it does strike cloud to earth it sends a pencil wide bolt at the speed of 60,000 miles per second, back and forth between the two pools. Yes, lightning is a feat of nature to be respected, but not feared. In spite of the Saturday morning cartoon depictions, victims of lightning strikes do not burst into flames and become a crispy critter when such a fate happens to them. There are variables, but being struck by lightning may not mean sudden death, although someone who knows CPR might have to revive you. Many lightning victims only suffer minor burns. One man became known as the "human lightning rod," after he was struck for the seventh time in 1977. Twice his hair was burnt completely off and he had several burn scars on his body, but he didn't die. Lightning is something we should definitely respect, but not necessarily fear.

Daily Verse: "When he uttereth his voice, there is a multitude of waters in the heavens, and he causes the vapors to ascend from the ends of the earth; He maketh lightnings with rain, and bringeth forth the wind out of his treasures."

Jeremiah 10:13

FEAR OF EATING FOOD

I've often considered those who suffer from this fear to be very unfortunate, since there are so many delicious treats to try in this world. The fear of food produces several different responses in people. Some have "bulimia nervosa," the eating disorder that causes one to binge (gorge themselves with food), then purge (vomit the food) so as not to gain weight. Others suffer from self-inflicted hunger strikes which means they don't eat at all, this is known as "anorexia." You may be wondering what has caused this fear to take such a hold in our land, - to force people to take such drastic measures. Some believe it all began with "Twiggy." Who in the world is Twiggy? She was the pencil-thin teen that came on the modeling scene in the mid-sixty's. Shortly after her arrival she became a famous supermodel from England. Quickly, attitudes over weight and curves changed to slim and trim. Since then a whole generation has grown up watching parents fret and diet to control their weight, many with no success. This has spawned a whole new generation that is exercise crazy, and completely self-conscience about their body, because they don't look like a Barbie or Ken doll.

On the other side of the spectrum, there are those who are compulsive eaters, who have a strong emotional attachment to eating. Most of these people feel ashamed, and do their best to hide their fear, but it shows in their waistline.

I think the main problem with those who suffer from eating fears is that they don't see eating for what it is. It is simply God's way of refueling our bodies. Our bodies are nothing more than machines in need of fuel - and that is it. You are simply a spirit that lives in a body. That body is not the real you, it only houses your spirit.

If you feel your fear is out of control, and you are considering getting help, or you decide to stay at a treatment center, get ready to empty your purse. Prices can range from $15,000 to $100,000 for two months stay at these centers. Before you take the bank account plunge consider if you really have a problem or not. You must realize that each one us is uniquely designed by God, and some are larger boned than others. Remember that God never created Barbie, man did.

Each of us should find happiness within our self, not with what someone else thinks about us. Be more concerned about your diet, and not your size. Take vitamins, and enjoy your life that God so graciously gave you. Do not live in fear created by what others think of you.

Daily Verse: "For bodily exercise profiteth little, but godliness is profitable in all things."

I Timothy 4:8a

FEAR OF FRIDAY THE 13TH

Throughout most of human history many people have suffered from "Triskaidekaphobia," which is the fear of the number thirteen. Some of the more famous people were Napoleon, J. Paul Getty, Herbert Hoover, and of course Franklin Delano Roosevelt. Roosevelt went down in history as the most superstitious President in history. He was so afraid of the number thirteen, that anytime he would notice that a dinner party would number thirteen, he would immediately call his secretary to join them, just so the number would be fourteen. Roosevelt's fears even went way beyond the dinner table. He wouldn't travel on the 13th, if circumstances forced him to do so, he would leave on 11:50 P.M. on the 12th, or wait until the wee hours of the morning until the 14th. He unfortunately believed another power was controlling that number.

Many have reasoned the number thirteen unlucky because of its numeric position. It follows the number twelve, which is considered by numerologists to be the complete number. There are 12 months in a year, 12 signs in the zodiac, 12 tribes of Israel, and 12 original apostles of Jesus. They say that since 13 is beyond the number of completeness, it makes people feel uneasy. This then is the basis for fearing Friday the 13th.

So what is the number 13? Quite simply it is nothing more than a prime number. Meaning it is a number that can only be derived by a factor of one by itself. All prime numbers are odd, except for the number 2. Is there anything wrong with the number thirteen? Only in the minds of superstitious people. Listen to what God's Word says about us observing special days. Deuteronomy 18:10, "There shall not be found among you anyone that maketh his son or his daughter pass through the fire, of that useth divination, or an observer of times, or an enchanter, or a witch." Also speaking about one of Judah's most wicked kings, Manasseh, it says he was an "observer of times" and listen to what the last half of II Chronicles 33:6 says about the Lord's attitude toward him. " He wrought much evil in the sight of the Lord, to provoke him to anger." Dear Christian, if you have a fear of this day, please repent right now and forsake your superstition immediately. God is in charge of our days, not some superstition. He is directing everyday of your life. There's no such thing as luck, and we should abstain from any dealings with chance. If you don't believe God is directing every step you take, then you are shortchanging your potential in Him. So forsake this fear today.

Daily Verse: "But refuse profane and old wive's fables, and exercise thyself rather unto godliness."

I Timothy 4:7

FEAR OF BEING DISQUALIFIED

Read these words written by the Apostle Paul to the Corinthian church; "But I keep under my body, and bring it under subjection; lest that by any means, when I have preached to others, I myself should be a castaway." Was Paul actually saying that he feared being disqualified after he had gone through so much for the cause of the Gospel? Yes, that is exactly what he said, and that's exactly what he meant. He was combating an erroneous teaching that we still have very much alive in the church today. It's the teaching that once you say a prayer, and confess Christ, you can never be lost. To teachers of this doctrine you can never backslide. They simply say that those who fall away from the faith never fell forward in the first place. They profess that these sliders in the faith simply had head salvation and not heart salvation. Neither of these terms is found in the Word of God. They are what some people call professors of "Eternal Security," or proponents of the "once saved always saved" doctrine. Don't get me wrong, I believe that once you are saved, you are truly saved, so long as you keep Christ on the throne of your heart. But once you allow anything; be it money, possessions, people, or whatever, to have that place in your heart, you become an idolater, and the Bible is very clear that no idolater has any part of the king-dom of God. Listen to what the writer of Hebrews said to the Jews con-cerning their forefathers the Children of Israel, in Hebrews 3: "For we are made partakers of Christ, (IF) we hold the beginning of our confi-dence steadfast until the END." Then listen to Hebrews 4, "Let us there-fore fear, lest, a promise being left us of entering his rest, any of you should seem to come short of it, For unto us was the gospel preached, as well as to them, but the word preached did not profit them, not being mixed with faith in them that heard it." God is simply saying that these people are our examples, and just because they heard the gospel, and followed God for awhile, that doesn't mean that they obtained salva-tion. They never allowed their faith to become active, so they perished in unbelief. In the same way, if we allow our bodies to rule us, we to will be lost, no matter how much we go to church or pray. God has demanded that our faith be so real that it changes us from the inside out. Without this action it appears that our faith is dead. The fear of disqual-ification is a "good" fear, designed to keep us close to our Savior for it stirs us to obedience. And obedience is necessary in salvation.

Daily Verse: "Wherefore, my beloved, as you have always obeyed, not as in my presence only, but now much more in my absence, work out your own salvation with fear and trembling."
Philippians 2:12

FEAR OF GIANTS

Have you ever felt like David of Israel, up against an impossi-ble giant like Goliath? No I'm not talking about facing a ten to twelve foot tall man. I'm talking about going head on, one on one, against some impossible task. Maybe you have to face a problem, like a disease in your body, or your loved one is suffering physically. Maybe you're facing financial giants, which seem to stand in your way of entering the Promised Land. Everyday bills arrive in the mail that you can't pay, and the giant keeps you at a stand still - like Goliath did with Saul's entire army. Forty days seemed like forty years with that giant strutting back and forth every morning and evening, taunting the Israelites. I'm sure most wanted to run away from the whole situation, but they knew they couldn't escape, the giant - he would have chased after them. Eventually they knew they would have to face Goliath. So what do most people usually do? Like Saul's army, they sit back and ignore the situation for as long as they can, hoping the giant will get tired and go away. But deep down inside they know he won't go away, so they wait.

Friend, if this situation sounds like you, I've got good news for you; David's coming into your camp. David was an Old Testament type of the Lord Jesus Christ. The reason Saul's army couldn't progress was because there was no "anointing" in the camp. Saul's disobedience had caused the Spirit of God to leave Saul, and be placed upon David. So when David entered the camp that day, so did the anointing. And the Bible says that it takes the anointing to break every yoke of bondage.

"And it shall come to pass in that day, that his burden shall be taken away from off thy shoulder, and his yoke from off thy neck, and the yoke shall be destroyed because of the anointing," (Isaiah 10:27). Isaiah was delivering a message that everyone at that time could understand. They used oxen to work their fields. Now and then the ox would reach over and take a bite of the corn as he was pulling things along. This action, over time would cause the ox to get a swelled neck, and then the yoke wouldn't fit their neck anymore, possibly even causing it to break. Thus they remedied the problem by putting a muzzle on the ox. But God's Word says, don't "muzzle the ox that's treading out the corn;" allow the animal to feed for he deserves his reward for his labor. God is saying that He's sending the anointing in our lives, and that anointing is the Lord Jesus Christ - He is the Anointed One. He has promised to break every yoke of bondage if we will only trust Him by obeying His word. That doesn't mean that you will win the battle immediately, but it does mean He will stand in the valley in your place, if you will give him a chance. It takes a life of faith to defeat this fear: faith that God has your best interests at heart. So trust him to fight your giants today.

Daily Verse: "That ye would walk worthy of God, who hath called you unto his kingdom and glory."

I Thessalonians 2:12

FEAR OF BEING A FOOL

I once saw a bumper sticker that read "National Atheist Day is now declared April 1st." And this is the truth according to Psalm 14:1, "The fool hath said in his heart, there is no God." Some worry that they will be branded one of these unfortunate souls. How does the dictionary define "fool?" . . ."One who is destitute of reason . . . commonly refereed to as an idiot . . . one who has a deficiency in intellect, who pursues a course contrary to wisdom, or . . . any person who rejects religious wisdom. According to Webster, a fool is described as any person who knows to do right and refuses, for whatever reason, to do so. The

Bible gives us several illustrations of fools in the form of parables. A parable is a story that tells a heavenly truth with an earthly story. One of those parables is called the "parable of the rich fool." The rich man makes it big, becomes wealthy, but, instead of sharing his wealth with the needy around him, he decided to build bigger barns to store it in, so he could keep it all and live a lazy, carefree life the rest of his days. Which by the way, came very soon, since the story continues to tell how he got his barns full, set back in ease, then he died. What were God's words at this man's funeral? "Thou FOOL, today is thy soul required of thee, now who does all your wealth belong to?"

Another story in Matthew 25 tells of ten virgins who were considered foolish because as they waited for the bridegroom to return for the wedding, they failed to take any oil with them. The oil of course typified the Holy Spirit, and the virgins were the foolish ones in God's church who are trying to serve God without the Holy Spirit living in their heart. They go to church every week faithfully. They are part of the programs and ministries, some probably even read the Bible and pray, but they have never asked God to come into their heart to save them from their sins. These people are depending on their good works to help them get entrance into heaven, and God clearly says in Zechariah 3 that our good works are as "filthy rags." Only by grace through faith in the shed blood of Jesus Christ can we enter heaven. We must put all our trust in what He did on the cross, by confessing our sins to Him and living a repentant lifestyle. Only then do we have access to heaven.

The books of Proverbs and Ecclesiastes are filled with Scriptures that tell us a fool is recognized by his multitude of words; in other words, most fools talk too much which soon gets them in all kinds of trouble. So my advice for you is simple: if you don't want to seem like a fool, then don't talk so much. Learn to control your conversations allowing others to get words in too.

Daily Verse: "Even a fool, when he holdeth his peace, is considered wise: and he that shutteth his lips is esteemed a man of understanding."

Proverbs 17:28

FEAR OF BEING CONNED

The most distressing thing about the fear of being conned or "taken advantage of" is that most of the time it happens without you even knowing it. You think you're getting this deal, and, Bang! You're caught in an elaborate con. Once I was trying to sell a timeshare that my wife and I had purchased. We enjoyed the timeshare very much, but the kids were all growing up, leaving home, and with the responsibilities at the church we were pastoring, we didn't have much time to vacation. Also, we had been taking cruises and preferred those vacations over the timeshare vacation. One evening as I was resting, I received a call from a very nice man inquiring about our timeshare advertised on the internet. He was so pleasant, talking to me about his personal history from Hershey, Pennsylvania. He proceeded to tell me his company was very interested in purchasing my timeshare since it was located in south Florida. All he needed was an appraisal on the timeshare to make sure it was worth what we were asking. I knew it was, so I agreed to the appraisal. Then he gave me three phone numbers of appraisers, with the prices each charge for the service. That should have been my red flag. Since the buyer always pays for the appraisal, unless otherwise agreed upon. He then assured me that they would pick up the tab after the deal went through. But I was to use my credit card to cover it now, then they would reimburse at the closing. So I agreed, and called the cheapest appraiser on the list; you don't want to pay too much you know. I spent four hundred dollars for an appraisal which I received a few weeks later in the mail. As for the company that wanted to buy the timeshare, their number was disconnected, and I never heard from them again. I had been "conned" along with a few thousand other people that year. I soon found out later that there is no such thing as an appraisal on a timeshare. I truly felt violated by that nice old grandpa on the phone. This kind of thing goes on everyday. In fact, one of the biggest cons in existence is supported by your very tax dollars. Everyday in America, a false statement is made to thousands of students in our public schools. It says that evolution is science and creation is religion. So this con has people believing that there can be no scientific proof for creation, and since creation is a religion and not a science, it is thus nonsense. This is a con! Hitler himself stated that if you tell a lie long enough people will believe it. If the truth be known, according to the definition of religion, evolution fits the description, hands down. It is truly a "government supported religion." Evolutionists choose to believe in evolution because they don't want to believe in God. The Bible has a term for these people; it says they were "willingly ignorant." That means they were dumb on purpose. You see evolution is easy to believe - if you believe in God you have to do what He says. However, if you believe in evolution, then you can do as you like; deciding that abortion is not murder, or I am my own judge. What is the result of this absurd train of thought? We now live in a crumbling society, with a failed moral system. Forsake these false teachings from the false religion called Evolution, and decide not to be conned anymore. Your very life depends on it!

Daily Verse: "O Timothy, keep that which is committed to thy trust, avoiding profane and vain babblings, and oppositions of science falsely so called: Which some professing have erred concerning the faith."

I Timothy 6:20–21

FEAR OF MAKING FRIENDS

Can you think of any reason why we should have any friends at all? The book of Proverbs warns us against making friends in 18:24. "A man that hath friends must show himself friendly." Or, in other words, if you're going to have friendships, you're going to have to put yourself out for them. Another translation warns that if you have many friends they will soon bring you to ruin. This seems to justify the reason so many people suffer from the fear of making friends. I'm sure that most people will agree that most of the relationships in your life are for some personal gain; either you need something from them, or they need something from you. This is not necessarily what I'm talking about when I say friendship. I'm talking about people with whom you are willing to share your everyday existence. Caring people that you will allow into your own "circle" of love. Today let's consider why we have friends in the first place. Most of us desire to have friends to care for us when we need them; someone to share our hurts, pains, and the unjust things that society throws at us. Most of our reasons are somewhat selfish in nature. If we are to truly have real friends, we must change this motive for developing friends. Instead we need to develop the motive that Christ has toward us. The above verse finishes with, "There is a friend who sticks closer than a brother." Of course, that verse references the coming relationship that all mankind would enjoy with their Creator, Jesus Christ. God desires that we, his people live on a higher plane of existence. We must decide to be like Him, with limitations of course, but seeking to be obedient children, not conforming to our former lusts, of selfishness, and such, but to be holy, as the One who called us is holy. Our holiness will determine which relationships we can pursue as good friendships, and which ones should only be acquaintances.

Any meaningful and appropriate friendship we decide to develop should of course have a pure motive. Our pureness of heart will assure that these friendships will be lasting and true. They must not only benefit you, but be of mutual benefit. We should always seek to be faithful in doing our part, thus God will be faithful in doing His. He assures us from His word, that if we prayerfully develop relationships He will enable us to find the people who are right for us. Don't fear making new friends - just realize that everyone is not right for you as a friend.

Daily Verse: "A friend loves at all times, and a brother is born for adversity."

Proverbs 17:17

FEAR OF THE LIGHT

The power of darkness is not like the power of light. Light is a person, which is God Himself, wrapped up in the personhood of Jesus Christ. Darkness has no substance of its own. It is simply the absence of light. Satan cannot claim the same attribute of darkness that God can claim of light. He is simply one of the many workers of darkness, while God is the absolute power of light. Light possesses the only real power, darkness has only illusionary power. Light is completely self-existent, possessing its own source of energy, while darkness depends solely on deception, and the willingness of men to close their eyes to the truth. Light is the true source of all life, while darkness only produces death, and unfruitful works. Those who fear the light enjoy darkness because their deeds are evil as the Scripture states. At anytime one can choose to see the light, and have the blinders lifted from their eyes. Of course, Satan needs people to do his bidding on this planet, so he doesn't give up without a fight.

I John 1:7 makes the promise that if we will turn to him he will forgive us and remove all darkness. "But if we walk in the light, as He is in the light, we have fellowship one with another, and the blood of Jesus Christ his Son cleanseth us from all sin." Simply, God is light and light is defined as the activity of good done by Him on this planet. If we hide in darkness, we cannot be made clean, and thus we will perish like those who refuse the light, which is the message of salvation. Dear one, if you are still living in darkness I plead with you to step into the light and profess Christ as your Lord and Savior today, it will be the beginning of a bright future.

Daily Verse: "Then this is the message that we have heard of him, and declared unto 'you that God is light, and in him is no darkness at all."

I John 1:5

FEAR OF BEING RIDICULED

Some of you may be asking; "Just what does it mean to be ridiculed?" It means to have someone pick on you with the intent of producing laughter. It's when some one mocks you to make you look like a fool. Jesus was no stranger to this treatment, and so was Colonel George Washington Goethals. Unfamiliar to many, he was the man responsible for completing the Panama Canal. Many obstacles came his way as he undertook the project. Rains, flooding, and hot climate were just a few. But his biggest obstacle to overcome was the constant ridicule from those back home that saw him as a failure. Some even predicted that he would throw in the towel way before the project was ever completed. One of his fellow workers asked Colonel Goethals if he was going to respond to the criticism. He said; "I most certainly am my good friend." "When?" questioned his friend. "As soon as the project is complete," was his confident reply.

This is also the way the Lord Jesus handled his would be cynics. He just ignored them until He completed His work on the cross. Many witnessing the crucifixion that day commanded Him to come down from the cross, and then they would believe Him to be the Messiah. Others were constantly ridiculing him, calling him names, professing him to be a fool to die for such a fruitless cause. Jesus handled the ridicule like Colonel Goethal. He knew what His mission was. Both men possessed a clear vision of what they wanted to complete and they weren't willing to let anyone shake them from accomplishing it. If you are paralyzed with fear over being ridiculed for accomplishing something for the kingdom, just draw strength from knowing what it is you want to do. Don't be afraid to attempt big things for God, for He is a great big God. If He is guiding you into something, He will provide the resources necessary to complete the task. He is faithful ALWAYS, so do not fear.

Daily Verse: "Death and life are in the power of the tongue; and they that love it shall eat the fruit thereof."

Proverbs 18:21

FEAR OF ANTS

Some people suffer a terrible anxiety regarding their size, feeling themselves too small to be successful. Well, the little common ant proves that train of thought to be wrong. They may not look like much, but they are one of the most incredible of all God's creatures. Myrmecophobnia is the technical name for the fear of ants. And with more than 1,000 different species worldwide, there are plenty of them to fear. Despite mankind's best attempts to control these little critters, they seem to always pull through with sheer diligence. I think the biggest fear of these creatures is not necessarily the creature itself, since it by itself serves hardly a match for even the smallest human. But when these little brownish, black critters get together and swarm, they can wipe out everything in their path; man, beast, and all living vegetation. Although most are blind, they use their antennae with incredible results. They smell, explore, and even communicate with their antennae alone. Their greatest threat is their powerful jaws which are called "mandibles." These jaws are able to make even the toughest enemies back down. They can chew through wood, dig through soil, and even bore into living trees with these powerful jaws. It has been said that if ants were the size of dogs, they would become the dominate species on the planet, overtaking the human race by sheer power, and diligence. Most ants are no threat to us; however, the Australian bulldog ant can grow to over one to two inches long. In fact, they are even deadly, for only thirty stings by these creatures can kill a human being. And worst yet, they can jump well over a foot from the ground. So if you're ever in Australia, be careful. Now what does God think of His little handy work- the ant? He gives them high regard in Scripture. Listen to what He says in Proverbs 6; "Go to the ant you sluggard; consider her ways, and be wise; which having no guide, overseer, or ruler, provideth her meat in the summer, and gathereth her food in the harvest." He is saying that the common ant is wiser than a lazy man. The ant doesn't need someone breathing down their neck to get the job done, they use sheer willpower. The Scripture states that the worker ant is female by calling it "her." This is true; because male ants are only used for breeding purposes, then die shortly afterward. Most males only have about a couple weeks life-span, spending the whole time mating with the queen.

Let us not fear this little creature, but let us learn from her diligence. Let's not let an insect be wiser than us. You can be a success in life, just "consider the ant."

Daily Verse: "But God hath chosen the foolish things of the world to confound the wise; and God hath chosen the weak things of the world to confound the things that are mighty."
I Corinthians 1:27

FEAR OF ANGER

Dad gets up late for work and he can't find something, so he takes it out on the rest of the family by yelling, cursing, calling his wife, and kids all kinds of names. The kids hide in their rooms in fear, for they know what is going to take place when he finally leaves. They don't hear mom saying anything to Dad, and they know that means she will take it out on them when he leaves. Instead she remains silent, just crying and waiting on him to finally leave. At last he's gone, and mom calls the kids out, and screams at each of them for making daddy mad.

In another family, little John gets up and throws a temper tantrum; he wants his own way this morning, and being an only child means he's used to getting what he wants. Mom and dad just run all over the house tripping over themselves, trying to please John, just to get him to quiet down. In another family, twelve year old Katie tells mom what she's going to do, and demands that she support the event with her attendance, after all, that's what mom is you know, a "taxi service." Mom instead would like to get lost in a bubble bath, but she knows how mad Katie gets when she doesn't support her activities. What's wrong with this picture? Anger has been allowed to dominate the lives of these dear families. Actually I think for most of us, we see some of these traits in our own families if we will only admit it. So what is a person to do when they are trapped in the fear of anger? First, get a handle on your emotions. When emotions are allowed to dominate our lives we are in big trouble. Now this is not as easy as it seems, since emotions are involuntary, and can't be controlled directly. Yes it's true we can sort of act friendly to people we don't like, but in reality we are actually being a hypocrite.

Instead we should learn to control the things that happen in our lives, instead of reacting to them. For instance you must realize that things really only happen in your head first. We are usually never fearful of the events that happened to us in the past. Only those things in our future stir up a fear in us. This is just the opposite of anger. We are always angry about past events; not future events, that may or may not happen. So why should we let the future, or our past ruin our present? Notice you can't eat an apple in the future or the past. These are only in your thoughts, so why get upset over a worm being in it? God's Word tells us it's okay to be angry as long as we don't let the anger become sin. Read today's verse, and don't allow the past or the future to dominate your present.

Daily Verse: "Be ye angry, and sin not; let not the sun go down on your wrath."

Ephesians 4:26

FEAR OF VOMITING

I had to think twice about including this fear, because of its apparent disgusting qualities, until I found out that some women have actually terminated pregnancies for the fear of "Emetophbia," or the fear of vomiting. For some of these ladies it is their single worst fear. Most, who suffer from this dreaded fear, further display other symptoms; like nausea, heart palpitations, skin rashes, headaches, disorientation, and numbness in their body. This fear can really be a serious problem for some, leaving one unable to think rationally. Dear one listen, it is perfectly normal for a new mother to suffer from morning sickness. Your body is going through all kinds of changes, and hormone overloads at this time.

I remember in my own experience, God had spoken to me specifically about the birth of my son, even before I met my wife to be. He also gave me the name for the child - Jacob. When my wife and I were married I told her of my encounter with God and what he had told me about our son. (He also told me that the next time I was with a woman intimately, Jacob would be conceived). This turned to be true in the first few weeks after our wedding night, when my wife and I were sitting on the couch together enjoying each others company as most newlyweds do, when she jumped to her feet, and hurried to the bathroom. She came back in the room wiping her mouth, and smiling. I looked at her and said; "You have to be kidding." Later that day she had purchased a home pregnancy test which proved to be positive. God was true to his word to me.

The big question is does the Bible have anything to say about this awful thing known as vomiting?

Unfortunately, yes, it does, only not in a light that most of us would care about. It says that there are people in this world that make God sick; so sick that he wants to vomit. Read what Revelation 3 has to say about what God thinks about people living lukewarm lives and not serving God with all their heart; "I know thy works, that thou art neither hot or cold: I would thou wert hot or cold. So then because thou art lukewarm, and neither hot nor cold, I will SPUE, thee out of my mouth." In other words hypocrites, who act as though they are alright, when really they aren't, make God sick enough to vomit. He despises the self-sufficient attitude most people alive exhibit today. Totally, unaware of the need for God to make their lives complete, they say they have need of nothing, when in reality they are living empty, fruitless lives. Whole entire lives are wasted seeking things to make them happy, and all they find is bags with holes in them; all the treasure has fallen out Today let's make a commitment to pursue the things of God, and put aside all our own interests until we know that our actions please Him.

Daily Verse: "But without faith it is impossible to please him: for he who cometh to God must believe that he is, and that he is the rewarder of them that diligently seek him."

Hebrews 11:6

FEAR OF SUNSHINE

I personally think that it's hard to find anything more relaxing that a walk along the lake or beach, or even a stroll in the park or woods. The problem is for most people just being outdoors in the summer can be quite painful due to exposure to the sun. Remember the sun is your friend, sunburn is your enemy. In 1995 alone, the medical community reported the treatment of skin cancers resulting in medical costs of $200,000,000. There are some 700,000 cases of skin cancer per year. The problem comes from most people being unaware that most skin protection products don't protect from the cancer causing rays (UVA) but only the burn causing rays (UVB). So what is the fearful person supposed to do, stay in doors all the time, to avoid being burned? By all means don't do that! Research shows that sunlight reacts with cholesterol inside our body to bring to the surface of our skin, and create vitamin D. This vitamin is necessary to aid our body in absorbing calcium, and other necessary nutrients. Studies show that there is a great vitamin D deficiency in the northern climates during the winter months. This has resulted in a higher rate of heart disease, diabetes, osteoporosis, and colon and breast cancers, among northerners than southerners. All these ailments are because they don't see the sun as much as there southern neighbors. As I said before, yes, the sun is truly our friend. Doctors say that every person should be exposed to at least five or ten minutes of sunlight every day just to secrete the hormones of happiness in their body. Without these hormones many resort to overeating, and depression. Not to mention all the various mood swings that can take place.

Remember when God finished creating the sun and the moon and the stars at the end of the third day he said; "It is good." Just use wisdom in your exposure to its rays by limiting the time you spend out in it, and by making sure you have the proper sun screen protection.

Daily Verse: "And God made two great lights; the greater light to rule by day, and the lesser light to rule by night: he made the stars also."

Genesis 1:16

FEAR OF TORNADOES

There are people who refuse to live in the central part of the United States just because it is called "tornado alley." Their fear for these large black funnel clouds is so intense that just the thought of one being around makes them quake. Listen friend, the Native Americans lived with these terrible twisters long before white men ever came on the scene. There's a lot of confusion as to whether tornados are God's way of judging the sins of a nation or if they are a result of the devil's attack on our lives. I think the answer to that two part question is; both are responsible. Remember God sent a whirlwind down to take up his prophet Elijah into heaven when he was ready to depart this earth. But also Satan used a whirlwind to destroy Job's entire household, all ten of his children were having a feast at the oldest son's house when the great wind blew the house down on top of them, and killed them all. The interesting thing about the story of Job is that when God finally talks to Job when his ordeal is over, listen to what God speaks to him from Job 38:1: "Then the Lord answered Job out of a whirlwind." The very thing that Satan had used to try to destroy Job, God used for a dwelling place. No other Bible character did God ever speak to from a whirlwind. Scripture tells us God scatters with them, even rides on them, but only with Job did he speak from one. I believe he was teaching Job that he was in charge of Job's life, and not the devil. Job must have feared these power works of nature after he lost his family, until God spoke to him not once, but twice from one. He was saying, "Job you don't have to fear the whirlwind, nothing happens in your life that I am not in control of, even a tornado."

If you fear these powerful storms take comfort in the fact that God is in charge. He knows about every storm that is coming. In fact, in Job's case he asked for it. I'm not advocating we become a stormchaser, but instead we should see the beautiful side to these works of nature. Let us wake up our spiritual side to realizing that there may be more to a tornado than meets the natural eye.

Daily Verse: "Behold, the whirlwind of the Lord goeth forth with fury, a continuing whirlwind: it shall fall with pain upon the head of the wicked."

Jeremiah 30:23

FEAR OF STANDING UPRIGHT

The Bible declares to be upright before God means to be in "right standing" with Him. Or it means that you have His righteousness in your life. This is only accomplished by accepting Him as your Lord and Savior. Many people today falsely believe that they have right standing with God, because they are good people. They believe that God will judge them on the basis of their own merit. They practice what we would call righteousness without practicing Christianity. They avoid Christ's beloved church, which He died for, like the plague, believing that if they are good people who don't do too many bad things then everything will work out in the end. These are the same people that while reading a medical report about smoking, see that the article is heading in a negative tone, so they skip it to read something else, believing that if they don't know about it, they can't be held accountable!

A study was done in 1957 that showed conclusively, that after a person bought a new car, they continued to read articles about cars. But only about the one they just recently purchased. Why you may ask? The person wants to justify their action. They believe that if they found a better car for less money, they would feel a deep sense of pain or loss. So for this reason they don't bother looking. Maybe this would explain why Bible reading is not the most popular activity today, even among supposed to be Bible believing Christians. In fact, some surveys show that more than half the people, who attend church, never open their Bible between Sundays. They have the same false assumption that the smokers had, or what they don't know they won't be held accountable for. God has made no such concession for deliberate ignorance in His word. He uses the same measuring stick to judge everyone. That measuring stick, of course, is the life of His one and only Son, Jesus Christ.

Jesus was the only human capable of keeping the law in its fullest. This is why He was born a human; so that He could share God's righteousness with His most prized creation - man. He deeply missed the fellowship once shared in the Garden with Adam, before he sinned, so He sent the last Adam, Christ to restore that fellowship. Please, don't depend on your own righteousness for your judgment, but His alone.

Daily Verse: "And so it is written, the first man Adam was made a living soul; the last Adam (JESUS) was made a quickening spirit."

I Corinthians 15:45

FEAR OF WORK

Some people have a misconception that work is a result of the fall of Adam and Eve. This is certainly not true, since we see that God had commanded them to tend the Garden, long before the fall (sin entering the world.) In fact, the Bible says that one of the reasons God created man was because He had no one to till the ground for Him. Several reasons are apparent today as to why so many people have the fear of working. They see work as a job, when in reality it is what we have to do to be obedient to God. And this obedience is what keeps us in good standing with God.

An old ox found this out one day when he decided to pretend to be sick, instead of working in the field with the plow horse. The ox went to the horse one day and said that they had been working so hard that they needed a break. The horse replied; "We can't miss a day, because the season is so short to plow, that the farmer will get upset with us." So he declined the offer. When the next day came, and the ox did as he said, and pretended to be ill. The farmer left him in the stall, and hooked up the plow horse alone to the plow, and away they went. When evening came, the horse returned dog-tired, from pulling the plow all by itself. Curiously, the ox asked the horse how things had gone that day, and if the farmer seemed mad at him for not working with him that day. The horse answered; "We didn't get much done today, but the farmer didn't seem too upset by it." The ox was relieved and reasoned that he had stumbled on a good thing, so on the following day he decided to pull the same prank again, and pretend to be too sick to work. At the end of the day, once again, he asked the exhausted plow horse how the day had gone, and what the farmer had thought about him not working another day. The plow horse replied; "Well today was much like yesterday - we didn't get much done; but today it was mainly because the farmer spent most of the day on the cell phone talking with the butcher."

The New Testament has much to say about the laziness of God's people, particularly to the young Thessalonica church. These people had received letters that Christ was coming so soon that they had to get ready right away. So many in that church decided to quit work, and sit around waiting on Christ's return. The Apostle often reminded these young Christians how when he was with them he worked night and day to set an example that they needed to follow. He also said that they needed to stay away from anyone who called himself a believer; but then refused to work. The Bible calls the person who is afraid of work, a "sluggard." When you see the work you do as glorifying God, it's easier to put in a full days work, for a full days wage. Ask yourself this question, "Am I glorifying Christ today with my life?" If not, make a change now.

> *Daily Verse: "For even when we were with you, this we commanded you, that if any would not work, neither should they eat."*
>
> *II Thessalonians 3:10.*

FEAR OF BEING SMOTHERED

This fear could be easily defined as a "persistent, irrational fear of choking or being smothered." Surprisingly, more and more people are afflicted by this dreaded fear. Some seek therapies which cost thousands of dollars and take months to complete, before they can see any sign of improvement. Some therapists have been known to use the very cruel (and what I would call crude) method of covering someone's head with a pillow to relieve them of this fear. Also known technically as Pnigerophobia, the fear of being smothered leaves many victims with a poor quality of life because they are unable to use transportation, or ride in closed spaces. Some doctors are quick to recommend drugs to help relieve the stress, but I don't believe drugs are necessary to handle any fear. Drugs are not the cure-all for fear. They only suppress the symptoms giving temporary relief. Don't live your life in fear, missing out on life's priceless experiences. Some only live a shadow of what their life could be because of this problem. Like all fears, this fear is created in the unconscious mind as a protective mechanism, to keep one safe from harm. But the same walls your mind builds to protect you, are the same walls that keep you locked in. Maybe you had a bad experience that birthed this fear in you. It's time today to do some rewiring of your hard drive and get rid of this phobia now.

As with any fear, the only way to completely remove it, is to mix faith with God's Word and you will believe that you are free.

Freedom comes when we meditate on God's Word, until it replaces all the negative stimuli you receive with the positive current of God's truths. As soon as you train yourself to be positive instead of negative you are on your way to removing this fear from your life forever. As soon as you quit replaying the mini series horror movie in your mind starring, "you," you're on your way to a cure. Practice resting in the arms of God, and sitting in your daddy's lap as you let him love you everyday. I promise you if you'll do your part, He'll do His.

Daily Verse: " . . . as the Lord God of thy fathers hath said unto thee; Fear not, neither be discouraged."

Deuteronomy 1:21b

FEAR OF EXCUSES

Many people settle for lives that are filled with excuses. This is the reason so many livelihoods today are in jeopardy. Making excuses such as the economy, or the stock market will not help you, but instead only hinder you. If you work for a successful company they won't accept any excuses for not making sales. They demand that employees find a way to make things happen, and this is how we should live our lives. Think for a moment if you were going to jump out of an airplane. Would you accept any excuses for why your parachute wasn't prepared right? I think not. Then why will you settle for a shoddy existence or allow excuses to make or break your life? Today let's all take the responsibility for our lives, and not allow this fear to be the final word. When God came looking for Adam and Eve after they had sinned, He asked the question, "Where art thou?" It's not that He didn't know where they were, but rather He couldn't understand why they would have broken fellowship with Him for such a lame cause. Listen to the excuses Adam and Eve gave about what they did. "And the man said, the woman whom THOU gavest to be with me, she gave me of the tree and I did eat" (Gen. 3:12).

So Adam used Eve as an excuse but notice that he blamed God for giving him a flawed wife. Now, look at what the woman said in the next verse; "And the Lord God said unto the woman, what is this that thou hast done? And the woman said, the serpent beguiled man, and I did eat." So Adam felt it was God's fault he sinned, and Eve felt it was the devil's fault. Both were unwilling to accept the responsibility for their actions, and that led to the downfall of mankind.

We must learn from this example, and decide today not to follow in the footsteps of our forefathers. Instead of spending time complaining and blaming others, let's look for solutions to problems in our lives from God's Word; it truly is the book of life. His Word has all the solutions to every problem that we may encounter in our life. God always has our best interests at heart because He can see the end from the beginning. Settle in your heart right now that you will let no obstacle get in your way from accomplishing your dream. If you decide to not let excuses rule your life you won't have to worry about taking a nosedive while parachuting through life.

Daily Verse: "For the invisible things of him from the creation of the world are clearly seen, being understood by the things that are made, even his eternal power and Godhead; so they are without excuse."

Romans 1:20

FEAR OF SMALL BEGINNINGS

When I think of someone who was able to conquer the fear of small beginnings, a man comes to mind who was my employer for over nine years of my life. My family and I had planted a church in Coshocton, Ohio, back in the mid Ninety's, so I had to look for a job immediately. My ministerial credentials are aligned with The Church of God, a denominational organization who plants churches by sending pastors into communities who are looking for a church. The pastor must then secure a job to support his family as he works with the people to get the church off the ground. I was privileged to secure a job with the Longaberger Basket Company. It is one of the most prestigious jobs in the community paying salaries well over twenty dollars an hour. While I was there, I learned so much about vision from the company's founder, Dave Longaberger. Dave was an incredible visionary, able to cast a vision on to other people that would live on long after his death. In fact, although he's been dead for several years, his dream, The Longaberger Company is still thriving as a leader in the basket-making industry. I remember the day the company hit the billion dollar sales mark, it was such a milestone for the company. Listen to where the visionary began, and how he was able to take his company from such meager beginnings to what it is today:

Dave never graduated high school on time; I believe he was twenty years old, having to take several grades over before he finally finished. This didn't hinder him from dreaming. He only had an eighth grade reading level, and often stuttered when he talked in public. But he sure was a man of desire. As a youngster, Dave worked many jobs and this would prove to be great experience for him, even though he wasn't the best "book-learner" However, he was a master at hands-on learning. He studied people and quickly learned their behavior, and what it took to please them. He learned ways to make work fun and this became one of his great selling points in business–"every work day should be at least 25% fun." Later, he went to the army where he learned how to become a risk-taker, but not a gambler. One of his first enterprises in business was to open a small restaurant with almost no capital. He started on opening day with $135.00, and after the breakfast rush was over, he would hurry down to the grocery store to purchase the supplies for the lunch menu. Then after lunch he used that money to buy the dinner fixings. He truly wasn't willing to make excuses for not being successful. Every enterprise led him to bigger and better things, until he finally found his dream in basket-making, which was part of his family heritage. If you want to learn more about this incredible company, to which I owe a lot, visit their website at www.longaberger.com.

We must learn that God's system of reward is not based whether we are a good person or not. It is not based on whether there's a need or not. But instead, according to Matthew's gospel 25:14–30, His reward system is based on what you do with what you have. If you are faithful with little he will reward you with much; this is the principle He has set for us to live by. Let us not fear small beginnings, but rather let us be faithful.

Daily Verse: "For who has despised the day of small things?"
Zechariah 4:10

FEAR OF PROCRASTINATION

When my oldest son Derek was growing up, he used to have a favorite saying, "Why do today what you can put off until tomorrow." I'm glad to say that he no longer subscribes to that philosophy of life, but soon learned that if you want to accomplish something in life you have to get started. As soon as he realized he was talking the life of a sluggard, he went to school to be in law enforcement, and now is happily fulfilling his dream, as a full time police officer. It is difficult to defeat the fear of procrastination because it is human nature to put things off. Most of us would rather do our own thing, instead of what we need to do. I find it amazing that I have no energy to do the things I have to do, but energy comes from somewhere to do the things I want to do,; like golfing, hunting, or fishing. We must learn to work with the same enthusiasm as we show the day before we go on vacation. Isn't it amazing to see how much work we can get done when we are going away for a week?

I've learned that when I don't feel like doing something, and I go ahead and get started anyway, a few minutes into the project I begin to feel like doing it. It's just getting started that seems to be impossible at times. The Apostle Paul, found out what a procrastinator King Agrippa could be toward the cause of Christ. Paul knew that his ministry would be to witness to kings and rulers of the gentiles, so he wasted no time to do so when the opportunity arose. He poured out his heart about being a strict enforcer of the law. Then he told of receiving the heavenly visitation from Christ which changed his course in life completely. The "heavenly vision" as he called it, was for the purpose of sending him to into the world to share Christ with all people. Listen to the remarks of a procrastinator which ended the linage of the Herods. Paul said; "King Agrippa believest thou the prophets? I know that thou believest. Then Agrippa said unto Paul, ALMOST thou persuadest me to be a Christian." Almost? What in the world was he waiting for? As you read Acts 26 you can feel the sincerity in Paul's witness. It was so powerful; it almost converted a Herod, a lineage that went all the way back to before the birth of Christ. His great grandfather was the one who wanted to put Christ to death at his birth. Herod Agrippa was the last known Herod. I've often wondered what would have happened to their line, if Agrippa would have not procrastinated away his day of grace. If you decide that you want to begin to experience your life instead of living it from the sidelines, decide to take a stand against procrastination today, and who knows maybe you might like it.

Daily Verse: "He becometh poor that dealeth with a slack hand: but the hand of the diligent maketh rich."

Proverbs 10:4

FEAR OF TALENTS

Many people deny the right to develop their talents in hopes that nothing will be expected of them. They find it very comfortable not doing what they are created to do. They fear that if others see that they are able to do things, they may expect things of them. They are lazy, and often procrastinate in using their gifts. They have this misconception that someday they will do the things they are supposed to do, but unfortunately that someday never comes. They let this fear dominate their lives and decide to play it safe, and do nothing at all. They soon learn to live irresponsible lives and find it comfortable blaming others for not fulfilling the purpose for which God created them.

Jesus in Matthew 25 tells the story of three servants who were given talents to use and to increase while the master was away on a journey. To one he gave five talents, to another he gave two talents and to another he gave one. He left on his journey, which seemed to take some time. When he returned, he called in all his servants for an account of those talents they had been given. One, who had been given five, doubled his talents to ten and greatly pleased the master, as did the one who had been given two. But, the servant who had been given just one talent became afraid, and decided to hide that talent and not develop it. When he came before his master with all his excuses about the honesty of the master, he completely displeased the master. In fact, the master became so hostile with the lazy servant, that he took away the one talent he did have, and cast him out of service, as a wicked and slothful servant. This story tells us that God takes our service to him very seriously. He feels that if we don't develop our talents and use them for his kingdom, then we are depriving someone of their much needed progress. There are ten little two letter words that are absolutely true in fulfilling God's plan for our life. They are; "If it is to be it is up to me." You are the only one with your talents, so begin to develop them today, and use them for the master's kingdom.

Daily Verse: "For the gifts and calling of God are without repentance."

Roman's 11:29

FEAR OF IMPROPER SECURITY

Human beings seem to live for security. Just the thought of taking risks sends some people into a state of panic. It seems we must know that there's no chance of failing before we are willing to launch out into the deep. I remember when all of our kids were young. We had five kids at the time, and the oldest one was eight. Money was pretty scarce in those days. Eating out was nothing more than a bologna sandwich out in the backyard with a bag of potato chips for a second course. For recreation we would drive to a local state park, and allow the kids to walk around with a bag and collect aluminum cans. Anything they collected was theirs, and they had to apply it to the $100 youth camp fee coming up later in the summer. Sometimes we would go to the beach in that same park, and just find a place to be alone, and swim with the kids. One of my favorite things to do with the kids was to grab one of them up in my arms, and start walking out into the deep with them. Slowly I'd whisper in their ears; "It's getting deeper, and deeper." Without hesitation they would clench my neck for dear life. The farther out we went the tighter their grip became. Never at any time did I go over my head. But what used to confuse me, was anyplace in the lake was over most of their heads, except a small portion up close to the shore. So it really didn't matter how far out I went, it was still over their head. What was the reason for their increased anxiety? They were losing their security of the shore. They felt that as long as they were close to the shore, they would be safe from drowning. When they got away from the shore, then dad became their security. Thus the reason for gripping my neck for all they were worth.

God in his infinite wisdom seeks to get us away from the security of the shore. For this reason he creates opportunities of struggle for us. He desires to take us out into the deep, where he can provide miracles for us. When Jesus first met Peter, and desired to use his boat for a preaching platform, he asked Peter to launch out into the deep. Peter was a little hesitant since they had just finished fishing all night without any success. What Peter didn't know was the fish were out in the deep. He was satisfied fishing like everyone else in the shallows, where it's easy. God wants you to get away from the shore like Peter did. When Peter obeyed, and cast his net in the deep, he caught so many fish, that his net almost broke. If we will follow God's prescribed plan for our life, and get rid of our security blankets in life, then we can hold onto his neck without worry, because the waters of trouble never go over his head.

Daily Verse: "I will say of the Lord, He is my refuge and my fortress: my God; in him will I trust."

Psalms 91:2

FEAR OF GOD

The time of the early century church was an amazing time for the church. Scripture is very clear that the early disciples were so committed to the cause of Christ that they did what was necessary to win the lost no matter the cost. Some like Barnabus, one of the first missionaries with the Apostle Paul, were willing to give up their earthly possessions, like real-estate, in order to make sure there was no lack in the body. They would sell the property, and give the money to the church to distribute as the needs arose. I'm not sure this was a good plan since later on we see the church at Jerusalem suffering a great financial hardship, and needing help from gentile churches. But one thing is for sure, there was a deep respect for God, and a holy sold-out group of followers. That is until Acts 5 when along comes a couple in the church that apparently had some clout. This couple, Ananias and Sapphira sold a portion of land and wanted to give some of it to the church to meet its needs. They probably had a reputation in the church as big contributors. I would imagine that this couple gave more than anyone else in the Jerusalem church. And this was good, until they gave an offering from a portion of land that they had sold. They probably had witnessed Barnabus giving his big offering, and didn't want to be outdone, so they sold a bigger portion of land, and gave more than him. Now I don't think that motive of giving pleases God, but I don't think that was their problem. Their problem was that they didn't fear God. They brought their offering to the altar like everyone else, and after a brief encounter with Peter each dropped dead, right their in church. Peter had questioned whether the offering was all that they had received from the land, and when they lied about it and said it was - that was it! God took their lives from them, right then and there. The next verse tells the reason for God's harsh judgment against this couple; "And great fear came upon all the church, and upon as many as heard these things." God will not just sit back and see his people not revere his presence, especially in the forming of the early church. He will not let us be deceived by our sins and do nothing. As soon as this couple fell dead, then the church woke up to the holiness of God. I'm sure that church members were doing a lot of rethinking of things and being thankful that it wasn't them who God took action against.

Peter the one who first hand witnessed God's judgment, later wrote these words in I Peter 1:17, "And if ye call on the father, who without respect of persons judgeth according to every man's work, pass the time of your sojourning here in FEAR." Peter was telling us that each one of us that names the name of God in our life must have a holy "fear" of Him in order to be truly blessed by Him. We must conduct our every day activities with a fear of God. Paul later wrote in his second letter to the Corinthian church; "Knowing therefore, the terror of the Lord, we persuade men. . . ." The holiness of God is an awesome thing, and only when we fear our God are we able to experience it.

Daily Verse: "The secret of the Lord is with them that fear him, and he will shew them his covenant."

Psalm 25:14

FEAR OF BEING SHALLOW

Have you ever taken the time to pick out the lobster you were about to make a meal of. I remember going to this one supermarket where my wife used to shop. They had live lobsters in a tank with their claws wired together. I used to show them to the kids and talk to them about what would happen if the lobster's claws would come un-wired. They are a fierce looking creature; with those big claws that look like they could cut a finger clean off with just one snap. Although we never took one of those confined lobsters home to be a meal, they fascinated us none the less. They may look like a vicious competitor, but lobsters are not as tough as they look. In fact, they go through several stages that make them quite vulnerable to their enemies. One of those stages is called, molting. This is when they out-grow their shell, and must shed the old shell in order to grow a new one. This is a very risky process for them, for they are quite soft bodied at this time, and can be easily torn apart by the smallest of fish. If they decide to not go through the process and play it safe, the shell that was supposed to protect them becomes the casket for which they will soon die - enclosed. I'm sure the lobsters don't want to go through the process of molting, and risk their life for growth, but it is a necessary thing, prepared by God for them. In the same way, God has prepared levels of change for us in order to further us in our growth. We must decide to shed our shells of security and comfort in order to receive His best. It has been often said that "good is the enemy of best." Don't settle for a life that is good, shortchanging what God has for you. He demands that a life lived as one of His disciples is a life lived for him. A life that is sold out to whatever He decides. If we are to grow in Him, let's shed those shells of security, and pride, and with a humble attitude like Isaiah say; "Here am I Lord, send me." Growth comes to those who aren't held prisoner to their past successes and failures. They have learned dependence and obedience through the things they suffered. Don't settle for a shallow life - content with soaking your tired, weary, feet in the water. Jump in and make a commitment to swim with him!

Daily Verse: "For when for the time ye ought to be teachers, ye have need that one teach you again which be the first principles of the oracles of God; and are become such as have need of milk, and not strong milk."

Hebrews 5:12

FEAR OF A WORKAHOLIC

Some of you may be asking yourself, "What is the fear of a workaholic?" Why it's the fear that you won't get every thing done that you have to do. You see I know this, because I'm a recovering workaholic. They are very task oriented people, while non-workaholics tend to be more people-oriented. Workaholics usually try to juggle ten things at once, while the non-workaholic wouldn't even attempt such a crazy thing. One day I was complaining about my schedule to my wife. I was telling her how tired I was, since I had been going for about twelve days straight, without a break, when she looked at me and said; "Don, stop complaining, you're the one who sets your own schedule." I thought for a minute, and realized she was right. It's like the guy who complained every day about getting bologna in his lunch, and when a fellow employee advised him to tell his wife he wanted something else in his lunch bucket, he replied back that he packed his own lunch everyday.

The Bible gives us a great illustration of a very task oriented workaholic, and Jesus' response to her. The setting is the house of Jesus' biggest partners in ministry. This family would support him through anything. There's an uproar in the house because the Master was visiting for dinner. Most of the people are enjoying the moment, just spending time with the Master, hanging on to every word He speaks. While the workaholic, Martha, was in the kitchen preparing the evening meal. She was getting a little upset, that everyone else was enjoying themselves while she was left alone to get everything ready. We see her going into the scene, and complaining to Jesus because her sister, Mary was evidently too lazy to help. Isn't that just like a workaholic, complaining because everyone else doesn't see the urgency of the moment like they do? Workaholics sometimes feel that if they would just get some help, they could rest. This isn't true, because they would usually just find some other urgent task that demands immediate attention. Listen to the answer Jesus gave to Martha in Luke 10:41–42; "And Jesus answered and said to her, Martha, Martha, thou art careful, and troubled about many things . . . But one thing is needful: and Mary hath chosen that good part, which shall not be taken from her." Jesus wasn't criticizing Martha for her fussing about getting the housework done; He was cautioning her about getting her priorities straight. He was informing Martha that sitting at His feet, and listening to His words were just as important as working to please Him - if not more important. I also caution you workaholics about getting your priorities straight. Don't seek to please the Master by serving Him, and then neglect talking to Him. Make time everyday to spend with Him in quiet time. Sitting as His feet is just as important as witnessing for Him, winning the lost for Him, or working for Him. Never does Christ tell us not to work; we just shouldn't make work our number one priority.

Daily Verse: "And to you who are troubled rest with us, when the Lord Jesus shall be revealed from heaven with his mighty angels."

II Thessalonians 1:7

FEAR OF MENTORING

Some people fear mentoring because they have a wrong impression of what it is. It's not some mysterious process between the perfect mentor and the willing protégé. It's not finding someone to connect with, but instead it's discovering whom God is linking you up to. It's the system of passing down knowledge that everyone can enjoy. When God gives you a mentor, its proof that he wants to change your future by giving you a better present. Some have this terrible fear that the person who they are trying to mentor will reject them. Also protègès don't understand why someone would want to put up with them. They fear that the mentor will reject them once they find out who they "really are." They fear they will look awkward, or like a fool, or maybe they will even blow it in the big time. One thing a protègè can do to get rid of their phobic fears is get a clear idea, of exactly what they are looking for in a mentor. Find someone who genuinely cares for you, who you can enjoy being with. A mentor must have more experience than you have, and be happy to share their life with you. Mentors should not be such a friend that they can't correct you when you need it. They must be honest with you for your mentorship to be effective. Friends can encourage you, but they can't help you like a mentor can. Mentors must be transparent, and open enough to be a good teacher and model. If a mentor is deeply committed to you they will share their own personal struggles with you, and allow you to see a side of them that will help you understand that everyone is human. This trust must never be broken, or else mentorship is compromised. Scripture gives us several examples of mentor- protègè relationships. Ruth was the protègè of her mother-in-law Naomi, a mentorship which led Ruth into the lineage of the Lord Jesus Christ. Elisha poured water on the hands of Elijah, which led him into receiving the double portion anointing he so desperately wanted. And finally Moses mentored Joshua who was to take over as

Senior Pastor of the 'Church in the Wilderness.' Joshua witnessed first hand Moses losing it, and being disallowed entry into the Promised Land. But for forty years he faithfully served him, never once mentioning the incident.

Every now and then protègès make plans and decisions that are self-destructive. Mentors will spend extra time with their protègès at this time to assure they not feel rejection. What is the mentors reward for all their responsibility and hard work? To see their protègès achieve their God-given rewards for obeying their mentor. Whether you are a mentor or protègès, fear not this great God-birthed method for passing on traditions and methods for getting God's will accomplished in this earth.

Daily Verse: "And Joshua the son of nun was full of the spirit of wisdom; For Moses had laid hands upon him. . ."

Numbers 34:9

FEAR OF HARD WORK

I know we've already talked about the fear of work, but there's a difference in working for a living, and working hard for a future. Many people find it too easy to give up on their dreams of accomplishing great things for God, so they settle for a meager existence that doesn't satisfy them at all. If you want to be successful in life you must dream big, and persevere through any obstacle that stands in your path. It takes hard work to make life fulfilling. One man once said: "To be successful in life you have to work half days, and it doesn't matter which you choose to work, the first twelve hours, or the last twelve hours of the day." That's what Hispanic born writer Victor Villasenor learned it would take to make his life a success. He had always dreamed of being a writer, the only problem was he was illiterate until he was an adult. It was no fault of his own though; he was born dyslexic and no one at the time knew how to treat the dyslexia. One day he prayed a prayer and asked God to help him accomplish his dreams. Soon he was led to a woman who was able to teach him, with much patience, how to read and write. During this time he worked as a common laborer cleaning houses and digging ditches, and devouring books like a kid in a candy store. It is said that he probably read over five thousand books, wanting to make up for lost time. Each book he would carefully remember an opening line, or an action scene that caught his attention, or maybe particular paragraph that would help him in his own writing career. Finally he started writing, and writing he did, in every spare moment. He wrote like there was no tomorrow. Soon he had compiled sixty-five short stories, ten full length plays, and a whopping nine complete novels. All of which were totally rejected with no hope of resurrection. Victor never let discouragement be his foe, but took on the challenge, and finally after 260 rejection slips he got a publisher to accept his first novel which was called Macho. From there he went on to publish several screen plays and non-fiction works, one of which took him over twelve years to write. It was a two part saga about his own family called Rain of Gold, which soon launched his writing career. I believe God answered Victor's prayer, with a lot of hard work on his part. At anytime during those long years of struggle, Victor could have given up and not seen his dream fulfilled. He could have been like most would be after a half a dozen rejection slips, saying, "Well, it must not be God's will that I be a writer," shortchanging every thing God had planned for him. God has promised that if we will do own part, he will do His part. And He is always faithful, it is we who are quick to quit on our dreams. So today let's follow the famous words of the great Winston Churchill and, "Never give up!"

Daily Verse: "He becometh poor that dealeth with a slack hand: But the hand of the diligent maketh rich."

Proverbs 10:4

FEAR OF FINDING A PROPER ROLE MODEL

Who in the world are you letting your children pattern their lives after? A role model is a person who is inspiring others to be a certain way. As a pastor, I am totally shocked when I visit in a family's home and see all these posters of sports figures and singers hanging on their teenager's, or child's bedroom wall. They allow their children to idolize a sports figure that professes to be a Christian, but has several children out of wed-lock to a woman who isn't even his own wife. Some pop or rock singer's "graven image" is hanging on some child's bedroom wall, which is probably going to die of AIDS because of a promiscuous lifestyle that they live offstage. The old television commercial still sounds true today; "Do you know where your children are?" I might add, do you know who they are hanging out with? Also, do you know who their role model's are? Please don't let your children pattern their lives after some pro-wrestler, and then get upset when they themselves resort to violence to handle the problems they face in life.

I personally believe that every young boy's role model should be their dad, and every young girl should strive to model their mother. I remember how proud I was when my wife showed me something that my oldest son had once written about me. The school project was about best friends, and my son had written that his best friend was his dad, since his dad "didn't treat him like a little child." We had shared many memories together as he was growing up, hunting together, and just hanging out a lot. Positive memories will help forge your child's character for life. Listen to what Titus said about older women in the church being proper role models; "The aged women likewise, that they be in behavior as becometh holiness, not false accusers, not given to much wine, teachers of good things, That they may teach the younger women to be sober, to love their husbands, to love their children, to be discreet, chaste, keepers of the home, good, obedient to their own husbands, that the word of God be not blasphemed" (Titus 2:3–5). God has made the role models for our children to be us, and not some Hollywood star that lives a lifestyle unbecoming a Christian. Please remember that everyone who names the name of Christianity is not necessarily a Christian. So be careful even of singing groups that sing so called "Christian Music," then live a lifestyle contrary to Christian standards. Many singers are switching to the "alternative music" today because the selling life of a song is so much longer than regular music outlets; and worth more money that way. Be aware that they may be poor role models for your children–offering them a watered down form of true Christianity.

Daily Verse: "In all things shewing thyself a pattern of good works;"

Titus 2:7a

FEAR OF RETIREMENT

How do you know when you are old enough to retire? Is it because the government says retirement should come at the magic age of sixty-two or sixty-five? I'm a firm believer that retirement isn't in the word of God. All the Patriarchs retired from service when they "went to be with their fathers," (died). There's no retirement seen in the prophets or the kings. The apostles were killed for the cause of Christ. Even John, as an old man, began writing Epistles and a Gospel. My son just recently asked me, "Dad, when are you going to retire?"

I answered, "When they cover me up with earth."

He said, "I thought you were going to go fishing more, and hunting more."

I replied, "If all had to do was hunt and fish, I would get bored - quick."

I'm not waiting until I'm too tired to do those things. I'm going to do them now. One day I read an amazing statistic that said that most retiree's die within the first ten years of retirement. I decided right then and there that I was never going to retire. I'm going to plug on like Winston Churchill, who began his conflict with Hitler at age sixty-five. When he turned eighty-seven a young reporter interviewed him about the conflict, and commented, "Sir Winston Churchill, I hope to see you well on your 100th birthday." To which Churchill quickly snapped back, "Boy, you might do it, you look rather healthy."

Today the senior citizen population is the fastest growing segment of our society. Many people have such a wrong attitude about senior citizens. I personally believe that by God's grace I will accomplish more in the next twenty years of life, than I did in the last forty-five. How you may ask? I've learned much through years of trial and error; I've learned to work smarter, and not harder. I've learned what it takes to see dreams come to pass, and I'm not waiting until everything lines up before I begin. Many years are wasted in life waiting on the ideal condition to start a project. I truly believe my best years are ahead of me, a time when I can focus on my objectives without worrying about just earning a living. The seniors years are often called the "golden years," when people can finally do the things they have wanted to do, instead of the things they've had to do. But I challenge you to make those years now. Don't wait to live the abundant life that Jesus promised in John 10, live it now! The only mention of what we call retirement in the Bible was referred to as a form of punishment and I'm sorry to say that's what it is for most. They go from doctor visit, to the drugstore for prescriptions. All they have to do in life is remember the past. I'm here to tell you to bury the past, and make your future bright. Live on, carrying the banner of love for which Christ so willingly gave his life. Do your retirement now, and don't leave any stone unturned that you might regret later.

Daily Verse: "The glory of young men is their strength; and the beauty of old men is the gray head."

Proverbs 20:29

FEAR OF CONSCIENCE

Do you live in fear that someone will discover your past? Maybe you worry that some unsuspecting bystander will find those things you've hid in the closet of your conscience. Just what is a conscience? The prefix con means with, and the word science means knowledge. So put them together and you get "with knowledge." The word conscience means "to do something with knowledge." Some people seem to live without a conscience. They are so hardened, that they have lost all sense of right and the ability to function correctly. Men such as Hitler, Mussolini, and Osama Ben Laden are all people that I Timothy 4:2 talks about; "Speaking lies in hypocrisy; having their conscience seared with a hot iron." They are unable to hear the voice of their conscience, which, by the way is the Holy Spirit speaking to us.

The great preacher of yesteryear, Charles Spurgeon once said; "The conscience of a man, when he is really quickened, and awakened by the Holy Spirit, speaks the truth. It rings the great alarm bells in their mind. And if he turns over in his bed, that great alarm bell rings out again and again, 'The wrath to come! The wrath to come! The wrath to come!'" The conscience is where God brings us to the place of surrender, the place where He can begin to work His partnership with us. Many Christians are plagued with their conscience like people who suffer from phantom limb symptoms. Doctors tell us that amputees who lose limbs often suffer sensations and even pain in the limb that no longer exists. They sit helplessly, and watch patients scream in pain, as the person complains about something being wrong in a limb that isn't even there. In the same way, many Christians are haunted by their past failures and shortcomings. For many a false since of guilt lies buried deep in their conscience. They are always bringing up their past so they can beat themselves up again and again. Somehow they have erected barriers to receiving the grace and mercy of God. Over and over they work overtime to prove to God that they are really sorry about their sins. The memory buried in their conscience can even cripple them from performing the ministry that God now has for them.

One way to overcome this fear is to realize that God is the God of the now, not the God of the past or the future. We must use our now faith, as recorded in Hebrews 11, to reach a Now God. When Moses was instructed by God to go back to Egypt and tell Pharaoh to let His people go, Moses asked God His name. "Who will I say has sent me?" God replied, "Tell the children of Israel that I AM sent you." Not I WAS, or I WILL BE, but I AM! He is the God of the NOW. That is the present tense. What do you need from Him now? That is what He can do for you? Don't allow the fears of the past or worrying about the future to rob one more minute from you. Make this the day that you serve the God of the NOW.

Daily Verse: "How much more shall the blood of Christ, who through the eternal Spirit offered himself without spot to God, purge your conscience from dead works to serve the living God."

Hebrews 9:14

FEAR OF AN UNCONTROLLED TEMPER

Our first Biblical encounter with an uncontrolled temper is when Cain loses his temper and slays his brother in the field. Jealousy overpowered him when God accepted Abel's offering and did not find Cain's offering acceptable. This turned him into the first recorded murderer of planet earth.

A father is driving down the road, and he is in a hurry. Suddenly he gets cut off and loses his temper. He decides in a moment of anger, to make the rude person pay, so he pulls up beside the car, and makes a finger gesture with his middle finger. The partially stoned passenger of the rude car pulls out a gun and shoots through the back window of the father's car. Immediately the father pulls away, and thinks he has beat the odds, until he looks in the back seat and sees his child got struck in the face with the stray bullet. His road rage had cost him the life of his son.

Any quick flash of anger could be harmful to your health. It is told that Alexander the Great once lost his temper, and took the life of his best friend in a fit of rage. What a tragic way to end a good friendship. Don't ever do anything when your angry, or I promise it could be the last thing you will ever regret.

The best known way to control your temper is to prevent yourself from getting angry. When it comes to anger, "an ounce of prevention is worth a pound of apologies." Some may say that this is impossible, but the Scripture tells us to practice it, and God's Word would never give us a command that we were not able to keep. James 1:19 says; "Wherefore, my beloved brethren, let every man be swift to hear, slow to speak, slow to wrath. (Anger)" The person who practices an angry life, does not bring about the righteous life that God desires. A lost temper will misfire and cause emotions to erupt, much like lava that pours from the top of an active volcano.

Nahum 1:3 tells us that we have a God who is "slow to anger." Aren't you glad He isn't trigger happy with lightning bolts like some of the humorous commercials portray him? But instead, He is slow to anger, and patient, even when we don't deserve it. God's greatest desire is that we are people who will not stir up other peoples tempers, but instead will love them as He does. We should try to control our tempers to prevent hurts that could lead to souls being lost in hell. You must delay your 'explosions' until you get a few minutes to think about the situation. Some people count to 100, 200, or whatever it takes to cool off. Some people record their hurts and pains in a book in order to prevent them from blowing up. Whatever it takes - do it.

   Daily Verse: "Be not hasty in thy spirit to be angry: for anger resteth in the bosom of fools."

Ecclesiastes 7:9

FEAR OF PESSIMISM

The age old debate, do you see the "glass as half empty, or half full," marches on? If you see it as half full you're considered an optimist' if you view it as half empty then you're a pessimist. Too many of God's people live with negative opinions. They seem to have forgotten that hope is one of the Christian's greatest virtues. They live their lives in misery only focusing on the problems and not giving any consideration to the solution.

Amway President and Founder, Rich DeVos said, "The only thing that stands between a man and what he wants from life is often merely the will to try it, and the faith to believe that it is possible." Do you know what you want from life? Don't allow the negative influences all around you to be the deciding factor over whether you get it or not. When times get dark in the pursuit of your goals, turn on the flashlight of faith, soon you will be able to see and find your way. Every day of your life has two handles, you can either take a hold of the handle of worry, which produces a pessimistic day, or you can grab tightly to the handle of faith, and see your day filled with hope, and success. Scripture informs us that "without faith it is impossible to please God." If your desire in life is to please God you must increase your faith and allow Him to stretch you like a rubber band. Have you ever noticed that a rubber band serves no purpose without being stretched? Once it is stretched from its comfortable position then it can bind any two objects together that need to be. Real faith is not daydreaming about what you want your life to be like: it knows that you already possess your dream in the realm of faith, and deciding what you have to do to see it in the natural realm.

James says we need to possess an active faith that keeps your hands working when your head is saying it can't be done. Real faith is always optimistic about your future because you serve a God that "calls those things that are not, as though they are." You become pregnant with a dream that God places in your heart, and although everything around you seems negative, you can every now and then feel the baby kick, so you know it's still in there waiting on the right day for delivery.

Daily Verse: "The time is fulfilled, and the kingdom of God is at hand: repent ye, and believe the gospel."

Mark 1:15

FEAR OF BEING CALLED TO MINISTRY

Some feel their biggest stress in life over this fear. I remember when I first received Christ as my Savior, I feared that He would make me a missionary and send me off to Africa, or India or some third world country where I didn't want to go. If you've ever suffered from that thought then stress no more. Although God's desire is to save us from our sins, He also desires us to be happy in life. Some people don't understand this about God. They see him as the "cosmic killjoy" out to make their life miserable by forcing them to do something against their will. God is a gentlemen and he will never force you to do anything against your will. The call of God is no different. He will patiently prepare you to do whatever it is He has selected you do in life. Your life, once you receive Christ is not a decision on your part, it's a discovery.

Jesus said in the book of John; "As the father has sent me, even so I send you." Our call into life is to complete the work that Jesus started. Read what Isaiah 61:1–3 says about the coming Messiah, who of course was Jesus; "The Spirit of the Lord is upon me, because the Lord hath anointed me to preach good tidings unto the meek; he hath sent me to bind up the brokenhearted; to proclaim liberty to the captives, and the opening of the prison to them that are bound;

"To proclaim the acceptable year of the Lord, and the day of the vengeance of our God; to comfort all who mourn;

"To APPOINT unto them that mourn in Zion . . ."

There it is our appointment. All these things that were appointed unto Jesus have also been appointed unto us to complete.

Whatever call, to whichever ministry we are to perform for our God, we must remember that it is to complete the list of things in this passage that Jesus began. We must preach the gospel, set free the captives of Satan, heal the brokenhearted, release all the prisoners held captive by sin, and don't forget to tell them that this is God's "year of jubilee." Today many people are suffering in this world of pain; our commission is to comfort those who mourn.

Here's a list of a few things to remember about God and the call to do service for Him. Always remember that wherever God sends you, He goes with you. He has promised to never leave us or forsake us. Also where God guides, He provides. If you are struggling financially with the ministry you are involved in, take notice of why. He always confirms our ministry with works following our obedience. Remember what He did with Moses when Moses faced Pharaoh. God was in complete control of the circumstances before He even sent Moses. He plainly told Moses what to tell Pharaoh, then He told Moses what Pharaoh's reply would be. He gave Pharaoh every chance although, being omniscient, He already knew Pharaoh would not change. God was right there all the time helping Moses with every struggle. And He will be there to help you, too. The key to following God's plan for your life is simply to pray and obey.

Daily Verse: "Wherefore the rather, brethren, give diligence to make your calling and election sure: for if ye do these things, ye shall never fall."

II Peter 1:10

FEAR OF MISSIONS

As I've already stated in another day in this book my biggest fear when I received Christ as my savior was to fear that he would send me off to some foreign country that I didn't want to go to. Now more than sixteen years later, I would sort of welcome the challenge. My how God is able to change us into his likeness. I think one of the biggest reasons people fear missions is they think God has commanded them to go into the harvest and save the lost. That was Jesus' direct mission on this earth; to seek and save those which are lost. But He has given us a command that is much different. He has commissioned us, to go into the world and make disciples, not get decisions. A missionary, by definition, is someone who is sent by God to perform a mission. He is not sent by the needs of a certain people, but instead by the commanding force of creator God. His challenge does not come from the fact that people are indifferent to the gospel, or that there are language barriers that stand in the way of them understanding the message completely. But instead, the greatest challenge is from us having a relationship with Christ that keeps us aware of what is going on around us.

Back in September 1985 a small town in Ohio known as New

Philadelphia, was having a celebration at the local pool. The reason for the celebration was that this was the first summer in history that they had not had a drowning. Hundreds of people attended the gala celebration, including over one hundred certified lifeguards. As the celebration was breaking up, and the people began to clear out, one of the four lifeguards on duty found a horrible thing. There in the deep end of the pool, was a drowned man with all his clothes still on. They retrieved Jerome Moody from the pool, and tried to revive him, but he had been in the pool too long for resuscitation. This man drowned at an event celebrating the fact that there had been no deaths due to drowning; and surrounded by one hundred people who were trained to stop such a tragedy from occurring. What was the cause of the tragedy? Nobody was paying any attention to what was happening. I wonder just how many people are in the pool of life drowning, and all they need is someone to rescue them with the life ring that says; "Jesus Saves."

Although most of us don't have the call to be a missionary, we have been commissioned with the call to "Go therefore . . ."

Daily Verse: "Go ye into all the world, and preach the gospel to every creature."

Mark 16:15

FEAR OF BEING BORED

My children learned real fast growing up to never sit around the house and say they were bored. The concept of being bored has never entered my mind, and if I see someone who is bored, I begin to look for something for them to do. If there's one thing I know for sure from reading the scriptures, it is that Jesus hates idleness. The generation that is being raised today has been raised on high tech computer games, and so much fast paced advertising that it has created an "entertainment minded" bunch of junkies. They feel that they have to be constantly involved in some form of amusement in order to be fully functioning. They don't know what it feels like to get sit under a tree somewhere with a good book, and feed their mind.

When we hear a child say that they are bored, I believe it means something entirely different than what most of us think it means. An adult's concept of being bored means that they are involved in some form of study that they can't comprehend well, it's sort of 'over their head' if I may say. Where as a child's concept of being bored means he doesn't want to do anything except play. It doesn't matter how good or easy the material they are studying is, they would rather be playing a video game, so they say they are bored. Most good parents teach their kids that they must eat their meat and potatoes before they eat the desert, and it's the same way for studies. Repetition has been called the mother of all learning, and it still is the best teacher. Some people say that they hate doing the same lesson over and over again, but that is the only way to get the material embedded in your mind. Personally, I have a library that contains over one thousand books. I also own a two thousand tape library, all of which I have read or listened to at least three times each. Some tapes I have listened to as much as ten times, just to get the material in my mind. It has been said when you get tired of hearing or saying something yourself, then you are finally getting it.

Today educators are trying to develop new ways of teaching the same material, in order to keep the so called gifted children from being bored. It is true that about 2.5 % of all children would fall into what we would call the gifted category. I feel these children should be separated, and taught material on their level, instead of complicating the concepts for the rest of the kids.

The fear of being bored doesn't only apply to learning - it fits into all facets of our lives. Some people fear getting married for they fear they will get bored being with the same person all the time. This is an unfortunate thing for I feel that marriage is one of God's greatest gifts to mankind. Others fear they will get bored when they retire, so they put it off as long as they can. Let me ask you a question. What are most people retiring from? Most work jobs that they can't stand. They can't wait until the weekend so they can drink away their misery after suffering all week. I say find a job that you love, and you won't ever want to retire, so to speak. You might slow down, but you will never get your gold watch and turkey for the holidays. If you feel like you're bored, throw your life into a cause for Christ and He will make sure that you will never be bored again.

Daily Verse: "He becometh poor that dealeth with a slack hand: but the hand of the diligent maketh rich."

Proverbs 10:4

FEAR OF SAYING THE WRONG THING

As a pastor I've been face to face with this fear many times. What do you say to a mother who has just lost her beloved child? How can you comfort someone who has lost a spouse that they shared forty years of their life with? And what about the dreaded birth defect baby, how do you keep from sounding cruel in people's most desperate times of pain? There are some things that are appropriate to say and there are some really stupid things that can be said. I pray this small list will help you rid this fear from your life by disciplining yourself to say the wise things. Remember what Proverbs says when you simply don't know what to say - "Even a fool seems wise when he keeps his mouth shut."

Whatever you do, refrain from telling someone, who has just suffered a great loss that you know how they feel. In reality you can't know how they feel because you're not them. God has uniquely created each of us with our own set of feelings and emotions, so it is impossible to know how someone else feels. If you say this to someone what you are really saying is; "I know you're in pain now, but your pain is really not that bad, because we have all had to suffer the same pain and we have all made it." Instead, we should let them know that we hurt with them by saying; "I feel so sorry for you, is there anything I can do to help?" Also, the wise person would never go to one who is suffering and get theological with them - "Now you know the Bible says that all things work out for the good, of those who love God." Please don't do this. I know this is theologically true, but hurting people don't need theology they need compassion and grace. Don't ever tell a grieving mother who has just lost her precious child that at least she can still have more children. She doesn't want more children at that time; she wants the one that she has just lost, and feels that no other child will ever replace the one she has just lost. What about someone who just lost a parent or grandparent. Don't ever say, "At least they got to live a full life." It would be better to say something like; "I know you're sure going to miss her/him - I'll miss them too." Sometimes when you approach someone in pain you're better off to say nothing; instead give them a hug, and just be there for them.

I recently lost my younger brother, Ricky who had suffered for over a year with terminal cancer. For over twelve months the tumors had made it impossible for him to lie on his back He slept while sitting, bent over in extreme pain, with his head on a table. Every time I saw him my heart would go out to him, for his suffering. Up until about a month before his death he was unsure about the condition of his soul. Finally he decided to accept Christ as his Savior. This gave him assurance to the point where he asked our mother, who cared for him every day, if she would let him go on to heaven. With tears in her eyes she told him she wasn't holding him back. Less than a week later he died. At the funeral I heard well meaning people say that he was better off now in heaven. Although I felt the same way, I didn't say it, because statements like that don't help those that are left behind. Actually, I felt a little guilty because I wasn't grieving; instead, I was so happy that he accepted Christ. I felt so sorry for my mother at the funeral, although at the same time I was proud of the way she handled things. There's a great big world out there that is in pain. Let's be careful what words we use to relieve it.

    Daily Verse: "The words of a wise man's mouth are gracious; but the lips of a fool will swallow up himself."

Ecclesiastes 10:12

FEAR OF LOOKING STUPID

    I think the fear of looking stupid grips us all from time to time. We often fear that we will perform some act that will appear stupid in front of our peers or someone we respect. Today many even fear that the clothes they choose are not fashionable and they will appear less than knowledgeable. Teenagers especially may refuse to wear something different; for fear that they will be laughed at. Let me say this about fashion. Don't get pressed into the world's image of what you should be wearing. I personally don't care if the entire world wears 3, 4, or 10 button suits; I'm not giving up my double-breasted. Someone once told me, "I guess you're going to have to go out and buy all new suits since the double-breasted are out of style now." I quickly replied; "Oh no I'm not, I like double-breasted suits, they make me feel good. And I'm going to wear them if nobody else does." I learned a long time ago, it's not the clothes that make a man; it's who is living inside the man who makes the man. So I choose my clothes, based not on the passing fads, but based on my own tastes.

    So many people die a thousand deaths from the fear of looking foolish in front of the masses. Some try to copy the Hollywood types in hopes that this will help them fit into a particular crowd. Don't do it. Romans chapter 12 tells us to not let the world squeeze us into its mold. Don't be like 'Jello' Christian and just form-fit into any mold in which you are poured , but instead be an original. It's interesting to note that the only paintings that are worth any kind of money are the originals. God made you to be an original, so don't settle for being a copy of someone else. No one else has your DNA, you are the only one with your fingerprints, and God loves you just the way you are.

    One of the biggest reasons this fear grips so many people is because they lack the confidence they need to be an original. This fear can be felt by many employers who have sought to hire individuals that have allowed this fear to dominate their lives.

Employers can smell this fear on you. Once when I was a young man I got trapped in a job that I really hated. All I had to do all night long was stand, and push a button. It left no room for creativity for a person with my abilities, and creativity. I was constantly frustrated, and found myself watching the clock all the time. Then one day it dawned on me, go get another job. So I approached a pipeline company that was installing sewer lines throughout the small communities around where I lived. I asked to speak to the boss and then approached him with confidence. I asked; "Are you doing any hiring?"

He said; "Maybe, what can you do?"

My reply was; "Anything - what do you need me to do?"

He chuckled and said; "We're looking for someone who can fuel, and service our equipment, do you think you can do that?"

"Oh yes," I replied, "I used to work for a coal company, and my job there was to run the service truck." (true story)

He said; "Good, be here Monday to start."

I was excited because that one act of confidence netted me about a $6.00 an hour raise over my previous salary.

Once, Herbert Hoover, (maybe some of you will remember him) approached an employer, and asked if they needed any new employees. They replied that all they needed was a stenographer, and wondered if he could do the job. He answered that he could, but he needed the weekend before he could start. So the employer graciously gave him the weekend, and he hurried out, and rented a typewriter so he could learn how to type before Monday. That's the kind of determination it takes to be successful.

Daily Verse: "Cast not away therefore your confidence, which hath great recompense of reward."

Hebrews 10:35

FEAR OF ASKING QUESTIONS

Thomas Jefferson once said; "Question with boldness even the existence of God, because, if there is one, he must approve of the homage of reason, than that of blind-folded fear." He understood the power of questions. Many fear asking questions for fear that they will appear to be foolish to the people they are asking. The fact is, asking a question is a sign of intelligence. Einstein, one of the most intelligent minds of the twentieth century, developed some of his greatest theories by asking questions. One day while he was being bored to death by his math class, his mind began to wonder as he gazed at a clock on the wall. He asked several question in his mind. "Who knows for sure that the time is right?" "How do we know time moves forward?" "I wonder if it would be possible to go backwards in time." "What if we could travel at the speed of light, I wonder if that would change time." These questions and several more aided him in developing some of his great theories about time.

Just what is a question anyway? It's an interrogation, or an inquiry, about something you don't know. So if you don't know something, don't be afraid to ask. Some fear that if they ask a question about something they will be in trouble with the employer, or teacher, etc. Friend, even God asks questions. Remember when God appeared to aged Abraham and Sarah and told them they were going to have a child - when it was physically impossible for Sarah to conceive one? What did he say in their response to their laughter? "Is anything too hard for the Lord?" He used a question to put faith in his servant Moses about going back to Egypt and setting his people free from Egyptian bondage. He asked Moses; "What's that in your hand?" speaking of Moses' shepherd staff. Once again he used the prophet Elisha to spare a widow woman from certain debtor's prison when he asked her, "What do you have in your house?" - signifying that she had everything she needed when she had God on her side. Yes, God uses questions to teach us the power of his Word.

These are some practical things you can do to help you overcome your fear of asking questions. First, always ask open-ended questions, meaning there really isn't a right or wrong answer, but instead you are seeking information and not promotion. This will put at ease anyone who may be paranoid about your reasons for asking questions. Make sure all your questions are non-threatening in nature. Then if you do have someone who wonders about your motives you can explain your purposes. Finally make sure that all your questions are simple ones, for it does no good at all for you to learn something that you are unable to apply to your life. Always remember that asking questions is no sin. There will be times, when you don't understand what is going on in your life, which you will even want to ask God, "WHY?"

Daily Verse: "And when the Queen of Sheba heard of the fame
of Solomon concerning the name of the Lord, she came to prove
him with hard questions."

I Kings 10:1

FEAR OF JESUS

One thing that I have noticed over the years in witnessing for my faith is that people don't fear your testimony until you add the name Jesus to the conversation. You can talk about God all you want, and they for some reason don't feel threatened. But as soon as you personify the character of God with the name Jesus you can begin to see them get uneasy. You see, most of the world has heard about the character of Jesus. They know of His work that He died on a cross some two thousand years ago. In fact, some of them have even been to church as youngsters, and have heard what He did for them. Jesus puts a face to God. As long as He's some cosmic figure way out in the universe somewhere, we don't feel threatened by His existence. Most might even say they kind of believe in God. But now, Jesus, that's a whole other story. The life of Jesus is a real documented historical fact. If He is God then we might be in trouble because we know He exists. The Bible states that God has given Jesus a name above all names that "at the name of Jesus every knee shall bow." Let me say that again, I said every knee shall bow. Even the "Hitler's" of this world; and bringing it into the current time frame, the "Osama Bin Ladens" of this world, all will bow to the name of Jesus. This is the main reason unbelievers fear the name of Jesus. I've heard testimonies of converted Satanists and they were told as children to never say the name of Jesus. That's because Satan knows that ALL who call on the name of the Lord shall be saved.

Friend if you suffer from a fear of Jesus put your mind to rest. He is a friend that sticks closer to you than a brother. If your mother and your father will forsake you, Jesus promises to take you into His family. He loves you more than you love yourself. He is the one who knew no sin, yet for your sake became sin, and took sin's punishment, so that now we can share in His redemption power. If you will only bow to His throne, and give your life to Him not only as Savior but, as Lord of your life - you will have nothing to fear–EVER!

Daily Verse: "Greater love hath no man than this that a man lay down his life for his friends."

John 15:13

FEAR OF THE RUT

It has been wisely stated that the difference between a rut and a grave is that the rut is nothing more than a grave with both ends knocked out. Perhaps you've heard the saying, "Died - age 25; buried - age 65," it speaks of a person who lived their entire life in a rut, waiting only to make it the grave. How sad. God intended for our lives to be filled with abundance and happiness and He never intended for us to dread our daily existence. Jesus told the story in Matthew 25 of three men who were each given talents to use for their master's service. The first two were faithful and used their gifts to bring about increase for the master's kingdom, but the third was stuck in the rut of life. He feared that the master would not be just with him, so he hid his talent in the earth and did nothing with it. In fact, he even feared putting it in the bank, because he didn't even trust them. He took no risks involving his talent at all. Finally when the master returned and was checking to see how faithful his servants had been, he called each one individually to give account. The first two had used their talents wisely and increased what the master had given them. He was deeply pleased with their work so he gave them everlasting authority; but on the other hand, the servant that hid his talent (in the rut of life), had what was given him, taken away. Then he was cast into everlasting darkness. Don't let this happen to you.

I think people misuse the time they are given. We need to profitably use the time we have before retirement to stretch our God-given talents, and challenge ourselves to go beyond the norm. This will keep us from getting caught in the rut of life. I don't believe anyone was created to sit around in a rocking chair, and talk about the good old days. I believe we were all created to be busy, no matter our age. As long as we have breath, we can be useful. Only Jesus has the ability to take away the fears that keep us frozen, and unable to be productive in life.

When Jesus takes away our sin the only thing we have to focus on is putting the talents he gave us to work for him. Then when this life is all over we will hear; "well done good and faithful servant, enter now in the joy of my rest."

Daily Verse: "But wilt thou know, O vain man, that faith without works is dead."

James 2:20

FEAR OF TAKING A STAND

Read what the Apostle Paul wrote to the Ephesians church about the Christian's only position of victory: "Wherefore take unto you the whole armor of God that ye may be able to withstand in the evil day, and having done all to stand, STAND therefore."

First, he says we must withstand, then stand, and finally stand. Three times in 28 words he says to "stand." So standing is our victory position. When everything is going wrong you have to stand. You look around and see everything falling apart - you still have to stand. When everyone forsakes you - you still have to stand. The armor we wear as Christians only provides protection for the front–to shield us from the enemies flaming arrows. If we turn and run, however, we are exposing our open back side to his attack. Over the years I've witnessed many people shot in the back by Satan's flaming arrows of doubt, despair, and destruction. If they would have only stood their ground a little while longer, I was sure they would've seen the victory.

Someone has wisely said; "The person that's too afraid to stand for something will foolishly fall for anything." God has given us a cause worth dying for, and many have paved the way doing just that. We must, in this time of sinking sand, be the rock on which people can stand. People are looking today for others that believe in a cause. Those who will face opposition head on, and say, "I'm not going to compromise my beliefs for anything."

I think the story of Balaam recorded in Numbers 24 is one of the saddest stories in the entire Bible. Here's a man who had the privilege of prophesying about the Messiah's return, but allowed himself to get side tracked in a pursuit of wealth. Instead of taking a stand for what he knew was right; he compromised his beliefs, and settled for God's permissive will instead of God's perfect will. God had to open the mouth of a donkey to speak in a human language to show Balaam how far he had fallen from God's good grace. If the donkey hadn't seen the angel with the sword drawn, Balaam would have surely died for his weakness. God put such a fear in Balaam after the incident, that Balaam wouldn't dare curse Israel no matter how much money someone offered him to do so. In the same way, our stand for what we believe strikes fear into the heart of the enemy. When Jesus was faced with the opportunity to shrink back from His responsibility -which was to die on the cross for us - he refused to run–He bravely stood during His greatest test. I feel since he was willing to take a stand for me, and die for me, the least I can do is take a stand for him, and LIVE for him.

Daily Verse: "Yea, he shall be holden up: for God is able to make him stand."

Romans 14:4b

FEAR OF FREEDOM

Every July 4th the United States observes a holiday known as Independence Day. It is a day set aside to celebrate our country's freedom - a freedom that has been very costly. Thousands of lives have been lost defending the right to be free in this country. There's hardly a family that hasn't been affected by the cost of our freedom. Sometimes I think we take advantage of freedom that others only dream about. Our daily routines entail such freedom that the rest of the world can hardly imagine it. At the time of this writing I just finished watching the television report of the fall of tyrant-dictator Saddam Hussein in Iraq. I watched the poor, suffering people weep, and cry as they pulled down his graven image that he had erected in his own honor. Just one taste of freedom has changed the course of that entire nation.

God never made good people or bad people, instead he made free people. They were free to choose righteousness or unrighteousness. It wasn't until Adam and Eve sinned that the whole human race lost its freedom. Instead of being free to do his will they were captured in a cage of sin. Now they were slaves to Satan's concentration camp - slaves to do his bidding. Their lord became the driving forces of the natural man; forced to live in an Anti-Christ system of shortage.

Today countless people who live in a free nation have constant fears of going hungry, and not being able to pay the rent. They fear they will be put out in the cold in their old age, or they fear not having a roof over their head. Many Americans today have been robbed of their freedom by two tormenting twins, called bitterness and unforgiveness. Instead of living out their lives in freedom and enjoying a peaceful life, they suffer everyday, a victim of their own hatred. Hatred puts up bars that can't be bent and before they know it they're trapped behind walls that were meant for their protection. Instead of protection, they live, sentenced everyday to prisons with no parole. Friend, don't let your life become like this. Take every advantage of enjoying the freedom that you can have in Christ. Be thankful for the work He did on Calvary and allow Him to exercise your God-given right to be free. Remember it is our responsibility as God's people to show the world the power of Christ's cross and lead them into the new birth experience.

Daily Verse: "For the preaching of the cross is to them that perish foolishness; but unto us which are saved it is the power of God."

I Corinthians 1:18

FEAR OF TOMORROW

Songs have been written about it, poems have been read publicly, and many people who are alive today fear, and even dread it. What is this mystery I'm talking about? Why, it's tomorrow of course. Many people fear that they will be one of the three thousand people in our land that never wake from a nights sleep to see another tomorrow. I personally don't understand all the fretting over tomorrow that people do. It's not here yet, and I don't have the time to worry about it. My motto has always been; "Let tomorrow be tomorrow, just live it today." I had adopted the slogan; "Just do it," long before it became one company's by-word. Let's look and see what the Bible has to say about tomorrow. After Jesus finished his great teaching about the Kingdom during the Sermon of the Mount, he said these words in Matthew 6:33–34: "But seek ye first the kingdom of God, and his righteousness; and all these things shall be added unto you. Take therefore no thought for the morrow; for the morrow shall take thought for the things of itself. Sufficient unto the day is the evil thereof."

Jesus was telling us that worrying about the future was a waste in itself, for we can't change anything. But we should be more concerned about whether or not our righteousness was measuring up with what God was wanting from us. Instead of dreading tomorrow, we should be seeking after God's peace and joy. These are just a few of the things that make up his Kingdom, and these are the things that really matter. He goes so far as to say that constantly scheming to make tomorrow better for you is an evil practice. Do you remember the scriptural example of the rich fool who had built bigger barns to house all his wealth? He was only concerned about what his future would hold. Instead of sharing his prosperity with the suffering and needy of this world, he hoarded it. The next thing we see is God demanding an account of his soul. Apparently after he figured he would have it made in the future, he died. God does not want us so self-sufficient that we don't need His hand at work in our lives daily.

In the prayer that has become known as the "Lord's Prayer," He tells us to pray; "Give us this day our DAILY bread." God is a now God, concerned with our present. Don't misunderstand me, I'm not advocating that we shouldn't make some plans for our future, like retirement investments and possible insurance policies; I'm just stating that the future should not become our focus. The only future thing that is really necessary is the condition of our souls. Have you guaranteed your spot in heaven yet? Or are you too worried about earthly matters? Too many people are too concerned with 401Ks and IRA's and not the least bit concerned about their ASSURANCE policy. If you haven't accepted Christ as your Lord and Savior, do so right now, and I promise you, you'll have no need to worry about tomorrow again.

Daily Verse: "Boast not thyself of the tomorrow; for thou knowest not what a day may bring forth."

Proverbs 27:1

FEAR OF HEREDITY

Thousands of people in the world today are in a constant search to discover details about their family tree. Others would like to take an axe and cut their tree down so nobody could see what's in it! I personally don't think it matters what your family tree consists of. Now don't get me wrong - I know science has revealed to us that certain diseases like cancer and heart disease is sometimes hereditary, but I feel these things are more in the line of family curses, than sicknesses anyway. Let me briefly explain what I'm talking about. In my family lineage they have a long line of cancer victims. Uncles, grandparents, others have all died from cancer. Now I know that cancer is a curse put on fallen generations for their disobedience to God (read Duet. 28). As far as I know, my family tree on my father's side indicates that they were atheists. Nobody has ever told me about anyone from that side of the family ever being saved. They apparently were beer drinkers, and carousers–those were the stories I heard. I believe, as a result, that side of the family suffered the results of cancer at a prolific rate. A couple years ago Satan tried to put that curse on my life. As for my immediate family, we have broken that curse. I was diagnosed with thyroid cancer, it was removed, and that is that. I declare all the time that no family curse will attach itself to my life, because God has given us the power to break the curse.

Listen to what happened to the family of the devout atheist who was mostly responsible for removing prayer from our public schools back in 1962. This story proves it doesn't matter who your genes come from, when Jesus is in your genes. William O'Hare, the son of famous atheist Madelyn Murray O'Hare, is now a fundamentalist preacher of the gospel. He travels preaching God's Word around the globe, and lobbying to get prayer back in public schools. He is a strong supporter of Christian schools because he believes they work; because they have prayer in them. . Don't take his word for it; look at the 4.5 million students attending Christian schools and the school's track record in comparison to public schools. On the average they are two grades ahead of their public school counterparts. William once commented that his mom's three motivations in life were food, sex, and booze. She led a lifestyle that would lead her into an unmarked grave. In 1995 she was found dismembered and burned with fire, in a hole in Texas. Her murderer was captured, who, by the way, was one of her associates in the atheist society who committed the hideous crime for $600,000 worth of gold coins.

Child of God, don't fear what your family's closet has in it. But instead start your own family tree with the blessings of God. Make sure that your children will be picking the leaves of healing for their bodies, while dining on the fruits of righteousness. Only you can determine what your future has in store for the generations to come.

Daily Verse: "Therefore if any man be in Christ, he is a new creature: old things are passed away; behold all things are become new."

II Corinthians 5:17

FEAR OF PRIVACY

Million's of paranoid people live with the constant fear that their fourth amendment right to privacy is going to be violated. Television networks are capitalizing on this paranoia by forcing strangers to live in single houses together, and letting "big brother" watch. Reality TV they call it. Others feel that the government or "big brother" has video cameras in our television sets to watch what happens in our own households from time to time. I am very doubtful that the government is watching me, or even cares about me for that matter. I don't feel I need to put tracking chips in the hands of my kids to keep track of them. Instead I would rather teach them right and let "Big Father" who is always watching, keep track of them.

If you think about it, none of us is ever really alone. God says in his Word that He is always watching over His creation, and is ever attentive to their prayers. Look at what the writer of Hebrews says in chapter twelve about the people of heaven taking notice of the earth's dealings:

"Wherefore seeing we also are compassed about with so great a cloud of witnesses, let us lay aside every weight, and . . . run with patience the race that is set before us." According to God's Word, if you're looking for privacy, the earth is no place to find it. He says that the people of heaven are leaning over the banister rails of glory waiting to witness another victory by us over the devil. He compares this life we are living to a race, which by the way isn't a forty yard dash, but instead a marathon. And the only way we will assure a victory is to lay aside any weight that could stop us from completing the race. Over the years as a pastor I've watched many people walk away from Christianity because of weights too heavy to carry. Many times I've wondered what their lives would be like if they would have only hung in there a little while longer.

Concern yourself no longer over whether your rights are being violated, for Scripture states that we are only passing through this world like a vapor. This world is not our home, and I'm sure most will agree that fretting over lost privacy is pointless. When Jesus was faced with whether he should defend his rights or depend on his Father, he calmly told Pilate, "You have no authority over me except it be given to you by my father in heaven." Yes, we shall depend on him to defend our right to privacy.

Daily Verse: "For the eyes of the Lord run to and fro throughout the whole earth, to shew himself strong in the behalf of them whose heart is perfect toward him."

II Chronicles 16:9a

FEAR OF OVERPOPULATION

In 1968 an article was published called "The Population Bomb." This article, along with the support of several big named philanthropists, was responsible for sending nations around the world into a state of panic. The article stated that by the year 2000 the world would be so over crowded that millions of people would die because of a shortage of food. Millions of dollars was raised at that time to help with the nation's population problem. Now, almost forty years after the article was published, we laugh at the writer's ludicrous predictions. The problem today is not overpopulation but in some instances, the problem is under-population. Countries today in the world are spending millions of dollars on matchmaking services trying to get people to get hooked up and have children. I personally feel that the great population scare was simply a trick of Satan to promote the dreaded sin of abortion. Abortion is simply the murder of the innocent for the sake of convenience. Some countries, like Russia, abort two children to every one that is born. It is said that the average Russian woman will have as many as four abortions in her lifetime. And of course I'm not proud of my own country's statistics about abortion. Currently, mothers of the United States murder a quarter of every baby that's fertilized. That's approximately one in every four pregnancies ending in abortion. Frankly, I get tired of political candidates who say they are against abortion, but do nothing to help remove this awful sin from our society. Stop talking about the issue and do something about it - now.

Actually many nations in the world are in dire straits over the population issue. This issue has begun to affect the way world leaders are managing their defense departments. When the United States President George Bush declared war against Iraq's dictator Hussein, politicians of France and Germany wouldn't join in because they feared the repercussion from their Muslim voters. Why you may ask? It's because they need them desperately to maintain their society. The average Muslim wife has 7.2 children. And the average fertility rate of most of the developed nations of the world is only 1.6; with Germany, Russia, and Italy being the lowest at 1.3. According to the Population Reference Bureau a nation needs a fertility rate of 2.1 in order to have a replacement value. This means that nations below 2.1 fertility rate will have half as many people in the next generation. This causes a host of problems with people living longer, and their being nobody around to put into the social programs, but instead to only withdraw from it. In essence, we have murdered our insurance that there will be someone in our future to take care of us. Now I'm proud to say that the United States is making the minimum requirements with a fertility rate of 2.1. But there's no guarantee that these statistics will hold up in the future. Experts predict that the world's population, which is around 6 billion now, will level out at around 9 billion before it starts to decline.

People, let us not look at sex between a man and a woman as a mere pleasure act to be enjoyed, but instead–it is also God's way to replenish the earth with more of His people.

Daily Verse: "And God blessed them, and said unto them, be fruitful, and multiply, and replenish the earth, and subdue it."
Genesis 1:28a

FEAR OF RIGHTEOUSNESS

"In righteousness shalt thou be established: Thou shalt be far from oppression; for thou shalt not fear: and from terror: for it shall not come near thee." (Isaiah 54:14). Most of us from time to time have feared that our righteousness just wasn't lining up the way it should have. Some who are still lost in sin falsely believe that they have to clean up their act before they can come to Christ for salvation. The world system seeks to manipulate us into its schemes, and we must decide not to follow it. The above Scripture says that we are established by God's righteousness, and if we are to become what He wants us to become we must tell our mind to line up with God's Word. That is the only way we will get on the right track that he wants us to run.

It's interesting to note that Jesus didn't say seek fame, money, power or pleasure. He didn't even say to seek to be prosperous, but instead he said to seek first the kingdom of God and His righteousness . . . and all the other things would be added unto you. God's righteousness is the producer of everything we humans need in life. So you may be asking; "Just what is righteousness, and how do I seek it?" The general meaning for the word means to be in right standing with God, or to be conformed to the revealed will of God. Righteous living simply means to live your life upright before God. You are aware that He is your most important audience, and you live as though He is watching at all times, (and indeed, He is). God's Word declares that we, (His people) are to wear a "breastplate of righteousness" to guard our hearts from the enemies flaming arrows. If these arrows of hate, lust, pride, etc. are allowed to pierce our hearts they may do damage that will hinder us, and perhaps even discourage us from following God.

Man's own righteousness is as "filthy rags" according to the Scriptures - it has no redemptive power at all - it has not paid the ultimate price as Christ has. Listen to what II Corinthians 5:21 has to say about Christ's righteousness; "For He hath made Him to be sin for us, who knew no sin; that we might be made the Righteousness of God in Him." So His righteousness is imputed to us because of our belief in him. When we respond to the clarion call from on high to receive Christ as our Lord and Savior, then we receive Jesus' righteousness. Then we can boldly state; "I am the righteousness in Christ Jesus!" This means that now you have the power to correct your behavior in His strength and power. You can be "perfect as your heavenly father is perfect." You can become an imitator of God, in His strength of course. We can practice righteousness just as He is righteous. This simply means doing what God's Word says. The moment you abide in His Word and His Word abides in you; you are practicing His righteousness which has no limitations.

Daily Verse: "The fear of the wicked, it shall come upon him: but the righteous is an everlasting foundation."

Proverbs 10:24

FEAR OF SIN'S PENALTY

I don't believe there is a greater fear than the fear that comes to a man, on his death bed, which has never been saved. Hebrews 2:15 states; "And deliver them who through fear and death were all their lifetime subject to bondage." The only fear greater than the fear of going to hell is the fear of someone who doesn't know for sure. Because of Adam and Eve's disobedience, the whole human race has been plunged into sin's angry grip. Now we are all guilty in heaven's courts of justice. God looks at all mankind as sinners due His wrath, because of the wickedness of sin.

Jeremiah informs us that all men's hearts are "deceitful above all things and desperately wicked." So what is God's answer to the need for punishment? He imputes grace and mercy on us. Just as an airplane is able to overcome the law of gravity, so is God's grace and mercy able to overcome the law of sin and death. How, you may be asking? By the righteous acts of the man Christ Jesus. God looked at mankind, and He being the lawgiver, decided that any man who could not keep his law (Ten Commandments) was worthy of death. But then His grace and mercy prevailed and He decided that since there was no man capable of keeping the law on this earth, He himself would become a man and do it for them (His creation). Thus Jesus was born the perfect man without sin. He was God Himself wrapped in human flesh. His only purpose in His thirty-three years of life was to buy back mankind from the enemy. So He lived the perfect life without sin, but there was still that matter of justice that needed to be settled. You see justice was crying out from the courts of heaven that there was a sin penalty that needed to be paid. So in the fullness of time Christ went to the cross and satisfied justice with the giving of His life. Now when justice cries out against us we have the right to fall into Jesus' arms and ask for His help. If we have committed our life to Christ, and asked for his forgiveness, when justice cries out against us, it must take into consideration what Jesus, our propitiation, did for us.

Though we were once dead in trespasses and sins, now we are set free as one of God's very own children. The old law has no power over us, because Jesus fulfilled the law for us. If you have not taken the step of faith to commit your life to Christ, do it now. Don't face the wrath of God on your own. Don't allow sin's penalty of eternal hell and death to get its grip on you. Some atheists will say they see no need for God, because there is no God to which we are required to be accountable. Well, to that, I say one thing is for sure; "There are no atheists in HELL." (Of course, I'm being facetious). Believers have no grounds to be fearful of sin's penalty–we are gloriously saved from that awful cost.

Daily Verse: "There is therefore now no condemnation to them which are in Christ Jesus, who walk not after the flesh, but after the spirit."

Romans 8:1

FEAR OF UNCONTROLLED THOUGHTS

Many times I have told people that they can't stop wicked thoughts from coming into their minds, but on the same hand, you don't have to sit down with them and share a cup of coffee. If you entertain negative or sinful thoughts they can send you on a downward spiral that could lead to disaster for you, and those around you. It could be something as innocent as a glance at something that looks harmless, but if left unchecked, before you know it, that glance could turn into a bondage, that can quickly erect prison bars, that will hold you captive.

I'm relieved to say that the Bible clearly shows us a way out of bondage; a way to stop the on-going war between Satan, and your mind. He has a lot a battle material to work with in this media crazed society in which we live today. He is so deceptive, in that he tries to plant small seeds in our mind through our everyday life. He knows within our thought lies the capacity for good and evil. Proverbs 23:7 says; "For as he thinketh in his heart, so is he. . . . . ."

Once the seed is planted Satan quickly tries to water it with reasoning and doubt about God's Word. "Reasoning" is the 'mother' of disaster. She will always take you away from faith, and produce the child of unbelief. Let's face it; the Kingdom of God is an upside down, unreasonable kingdom. It works in direct opposite of the way the natural world works. Let me explain with these few examples. Scripture says that in order to get you must give. You must love those who hate you. Be kind to those who despise you. Forgive those who won't forgive you. Give to those who take from you. You must lose in order to find. Do you get the picture that the kingdom of God is upside down? So if you use reason to make your decisions you will always be out of faith in your decision making. Satan knows that actions flow from thoughts. So he tries to entice you to flirt with your desires. This in turn will produce lusts in you that will soon captivate your mind completely. James 1:15 tells us that when lust conceives it produces a baby that is called "sin." This baby will grow rapidly, and then when it matures its name will be changed to "disillusionment," continuously saying, "I never dreamed it would lead to this." The enemy always blinds our eyes to the consequences of sin, as he sets the traps to catch us. He sends us what I call mind mirages to fill our mind with deceptive delusions of how good things are, and how positive things will work out. Many families have been destroyed by these mind mirages.

Enough of his tactics, it's time to learn how to overcome this fear. Jesus gave us the proper method of controlling our thought life in Luke 4. As this chapter records, Satan came after Christ three times; Jesus used Scripture to tell him to stop it. In the same way we can use the simple acrostic S.T.O.P. to fight against the devils attack on our mind.

First, you must speak out against impure thoughts. That's right say it out loud, "I rebuke you Satan . . . I refuse to allow this sin to stay on my mind." Then Think "God thoughts." Philippians 4 informs us that we must replace sinful thoughts with thoughts of things that are just, true, pure, lovely, honest, praiseworthy, and of a good report. This is only accomplished by meditating in God's Word. Then you must bring every thought into the Obedience of Christ. Order every thought to obey God's word. And finally Practice the process, and never let up, because Satan never will.

Daily Verse: For as he thinketh in his heart, so is he. . . .
Proverbs 23:7

FEAR OF TRANSITIONS

The idea of change sends heart-wrenching fear into the minds of some people. As a whole, most people are traditional, and love the status quo. Most people get so used to the routine that any deviation from the course brings instant opposition. I personally feel we have to look at change, not as an obstacle, but instead as a necessary process in life. For instance if you stayed in diapers until you were twenty-one, and didn't learn how to change the process of that important bodily function, you would be abnormal; strange. That's the way some of our lives are–they stink because we won't change the diapers. I don't feel that change has to be a roadblock to productivity. Some resist any change in the process for they feel it will lead to a setback. Not if the change is managed well. Think for a moment about what our lives consist of. Our lives are nothing more but a series of leaving and entering. This series begins in the womb. We leave the womb, and enter infancy. Then we leave infancy to enter the toddler stage. Then we leave the toddler stage and enter childhood. From childhood we enter adolescence. Then we leave adolescence and enter young adulthood. Then we leave young adulthood to become middle-aged, and then finally we leave the middle-aged phase to become seniors. Do you get the picture?

Our lives consist of constant changes as we grow to full maturity. If we reject any of these stages along the way we soon will become know as a freak of nature. In the same way I feel that God has stages of transition that He wants us to grow through, and we must not resist, or we will be resisting Him. For some reason most feel that God desires to get us to the place where we can get comfortable in life, and settle down for a life of ease. If we don't say this out loud we still think it in our hearts. Friend, this is only a lie of the devil. If anything, God speaks out against living at ease. He is constantly creating growing opportunities for us that come in the form of changes. We must learn to flow with these changes properly and not resist the work of God in our lives. We must let go of some good things, so that we can have God's best. One example of this concerns my wife Susie and me. When we were first married one big thing we thought about was a house. We wanted a home of our own. Since then we have owned three of them, and each time they get better. But just the other day, in a casual conversation we both stated that we were ready to get rid of the one we are living in now if that's what God wants. We will move wherever He sends us, and not look back; even though that would mean giving up our 2500 square foot house with a three car garage and a 25,000 gallon in-ground swimming pool. It doesn't matter, if that is what He wants. Once you understand the need for letting go, then you will allow God to get creative with your life. Don't be afraid to launch out in the world of new beginnings; this is where God is allowed to work miracles in your life for you. But if you refuse to let go, you will remain in a constant state of limbo, half way between God's good and God's best.

Daily Verse: "But we all, with open face beholding as in a glass the glory of the Lord, are changed into the same image from glory to glory, even as by the Spirit of the Lord."

II Corinthians 3:18

FEAR OF RULES

Any good parent soon finds out that rules without love equals rebellion. If you subtract love from any set of commands, you'll soon find a child that doesn't respect you, and will at the first chance jump rank. Even though the rules are good for them, and promise blessing to those who will follow them to the letter. Several years back when Hurricane Andrew devastated the state of Florida, news crews were traveling around filming the aftermath and the reactions of people who had been hit hard by one of nature's most crushing forces. Amidst a pile of devastation and house debris there stood one lone, solitary house among all the debris. This house had apparently been untouched by the storms powerful wind. The news crews were baffled by the sight. How could this house stand when all the other houses had been so badly crushed? Quickly they rushed to the owner of the fortress to hear his comment about all the devastation around him.

They asked how his house stood when all the rest were destroyed. His reply was quite simple. "I followed the rules. When the code called for 2x6 studs I used them, in fact my house was built by my own hands, and I didn't cheat on any code. The code book stated that any house built by this set of codes would be hurricane proof, and I guess the proof is in the pudding." When the news crews looked around they could see all the people who had cheated on the codes. They had intentionally broken the rules for some reason or another and the Scripture came true for them that states, "Be sure your sins will find you out."

God makes rules in order to protect us from harm. Some foolish people see these rules as restrictions placed on them by a cosmic killjoy, but rules are placed in our life to assure that we live productive long lives. He tells us that if we build our lives according to His blueprint, which is His Word, then, when the storms come against us, our house, (lives) will stand. But if we decide to take the easy way out, refuse the teachings of His Word and choose to ignore His blueprint, the storms will come, sending our house crashing down like Andrew upon those who cheated on the building codes of the state of Florida.

Daily Verse: "If ye be willing and obedient, ye shall eat the good of the land."

Isaiah 1:19

FEAR OF LIBERALISM

Many people in our land today believe that any gathering of a group in the name of Jesus to hear a preacher preach a sermon is what constitutes a "church." They feel that if they give money to the group and sing some songs while planning to do some charitable act for the less fortunate, they are a true church of Jesus Christ. There is danger in trying to define a church by religious activity. Some people foolishly

308 *A Year Without Fear*

follow action, believing that God is everywhere the action is. Jesus knew this would happen so, no less than three times in Matthew 24, He tells us to beware that "no man deceive us." Many in our land today criticize fundamental preaching of the gospel, but it truly is the only way to tell the real from the counterfeit. Although everything around us may be changing, God's Word never changes. If Paul said it was wrong for people to be homosexuals in the early church, modern liberals wanting to accept it in the name of love does not make it right. No, we don't hate the homosexual or bisexual, but we're not going to embrace their lifestyle by ordaining them into the ministry and receiving them as pastors. You may turn your head in the name of change or love but I promise you God won't. I warn you today; if you're involved in a church that is debating over whether the Bible is God's inspired word or not, RUN! Don't look back - you may get sucked into God's judgment, like Lot's wife did when she looked back on God's wrath on Sodom and Gomorrah. God punished those two cities for the same things that are going on in churches that bare His name.

Many have embraced the Universalist's opinion of God today. Yes, America is a free country that allows the freedom of religion and I pray she never loses her right to worship freely, but at the same time she has become like Solomon of old. The richest man who ever lived, in his youth was deeply devoted to Jehovah only, but in his old age he married foreign wives and worshiped their gods along with Jehovah. This soon turned his heart away from the true God and left him feeling empty amidst all his successes.

I witnessed a priest during the Presidents Inaugural prayer pray in the name of Allah, Buddha, and of course several others before mentioning Jesus' name and I said to myself, "He should have saved his breath." God was a million miles away from his ritualistic praying, for He still says in His word, "Thou shall have NO other god's before me. I am the Lord and I change NOT." He is a jealous God who will not share His glory with any man-made deity.

Most liberal worship services are more like Rotary club gatherings. They are man centered "get togethers" that focus on what good thing they can do for the community. They have hopes that all their good works done for their fellow man will buy them good standing with whichever God is the true God. Most members are like Solomon, empty, and void of understanding. The messages of these liberal counterparts of true Christianity are more like lectures about how God wants to bless us and how a good God would never punish anyone with the fires of hell. In fact, most call hell, a Christ-less eternity, making it seem a little more twenty-first century. People! Get out now, while there's still time! Don't stay trapped because your great, great (grandmother, etc.) went there. God's Word still says "Come out from among them and be ye separate."

> *Daily Verse: "He shall not alter it, nor change it, a good for a bad, or a bad for a good."*
>
> Leviticus 27:10a

FEAR OF GIVING

We've been sold a bill of false goods. For years people have told us that if you give away what you now have, you will then have less left We have depended on our own resources to make our dreams come true. We are like the strongest baby bird in the nest, which will, without reservation, push the weaklings out of the way to get that extra morsel of meat. All this pursuit of stuff to make our life better has left us feeling empty and undone. For some reason we just can't get a handle on it. We should be satisfied with our two year old car that still smells new, but we can't help looking at the new ads promising to bring more satisfaction than last years model. Instead we waste countless of thousands of dollars a year on interest charges for things that are out-dated after we purchase them. We feel we must get, get, get. Solomon once said with all your getting, "get understanding." So today I want to share with you some understanding in hopes of removing the fear of giving once and for all from your life. First, and foremost, I want you to know that we serve a God that practices what he preaches. He tells us in His word that He loves a cheerful giver. The word cheerful in this passage means hilarious. Or in other words God loves people who live to give. This is because He lives to give! One of the most familiar verses in the entire Bible is of course John 3:16; "For God so loved the world that he gave his only begotten son." He truly is a giver, giving only his best. I once heard a foolish preacher say God loves a cheerful giver, but he'll take it from the grumpy and stingy too. I wanted to stand up and say; "Oh, no he won't. We might take it, but He won't accept it." Have you ever wondered if God was accepting your sacrifices you've been giving Him? The Bible records several people who gave sacrifices to God that were unacceptable, because the offerings weren't given according to His prescribed plan for giving. God did not accept Cain's offering, nor Nadab's and Abihu's, (Aaron's two would-be priest sons). And, of course, let's not forget about Ananias' and Sapphira's offering in Acts 5, for which they dropped dead after placing it in the offering plate. No, the Scripture is very clear that God doesn't accept everything given to Him, especially that which is given with the wrong heart or motive. In Luke 6 the physician gives his version of what has been often called the "Beatitudes." These are principles Christ left us on how to live in the Kingdom of God in this world. From verses 30–38 he tells us to do things like forgive, love, lend, be kind, judge not, condemn not, and of course give. What's interesting is that in verse thirty He begins the teaching with give, and in verse thirty-eight, He ends the teaching with give; almost like He was telling us that we need to focus on giving twice as much as we do any other Kingdom principle. Giving is the only Kingdom principle that includes an incredible promise. Look at what He says about being a giver in Luke 6:38: "Give and it shall be given unto you; good measure, pressed down, and shaken together, and running over, shall men give into your bosom. For with the same measure that ye mete withal it shall be measured to you again."

Daily Verse: "I have shewed you all things, how that so laboring ye ought to support the weak, and to remember the words of the Lord Jesus, how he said, It is more blessed to give than to receive."

Acts 20:35

FEAR OF GOD'S VOICE

I can think of no better example in all the Bible of "fearing God's voice" than when the newly redeemed children of Israel rejected God, by not wanting to hear His voice. God had so graciously redeemed them from Egyptian bondage, as He promised to do some four hundred years prior. He then had plans to give them a land they didn't have to pay for, vineyards they didn't have to plant, even houses they wouldn't have to build; all they had to do was to sanctify themselves, put on new clothes, come up the mountain and fellowship with Him in return.

Instead, when they heard His voice and saw the dark cloud filled with fire, they feared and said; "Moses, why don't you go up the mountain, and talk to God for us, we'll just stay down here where it's safe and let you tell us what he wants to tell us." It would be like if your dad brought a new bicycle home for you, put it into the garage and waited for you to come out and kiss him in order to get it; but instead you send out mom to say; "I'm here to kiss you for Amy; now give me her new bicycle." You'd get upset, and so did God. He did all the miracles for these people, and here they are too afraid of Him to fellowship with Him. God was angry and wanted to destroy all the people except for

Moses that day. But in God's infinite wisdom He picked the right man for the job, for instantly Moses started petitioning God to spare the people for His name's sake. What was the reason for the people's sudden burst of fear? They feared God's voice. Now I will admit, it was quite a display with fire, thunder, and smoke, but their fear only revealed the condition of their hearts.

Today much like then, God wants to speak to us. Oh, He's not using fire and thunder anymore to get His Word to us, but many people even fear the silence required at times to hear His voice over the clamor of the world. Many run around in a constant state of noise and confusion. They only listen to the voice of others, speaking about God and never get to hear Him for themselves. Friend, God dwells in the stillness. His voice is sometimes quiet, yet when He speaks it's as the "voice of many waters" as the Psalmist said.

A few years back, I finally understood that Scripture when my family visited Niagara Falls. I stood there and could see my wife's mouth moving but, unless I got real close to her mouth I couldn't hear a word she was saying. And that's the way it is with God. We need to tune into His frequency, get up real close, and let His voice drown out all the other voices in our head. As you read God's Word allow His spirit to speak to you about the course of your life. Don't just shrug things off as the voice of self, for God speaks most often through the voice of conscience.

This is how He can assure that we will receive the message He has specifically for us, and not someone else. Don't just rely on second hand knowledge from others about what God is saying. But instead get in His presence, and hear for yourself.

Daily Verse: "Behold I stand at the door, and knock; if any man hear my voice, and open the door, I will come in to him, and will sup with him, and he with me."

Revelation 3:20

FEAR OF BLAME

The fear of blame generally follows two courses of action. The blaming of self or blaming someone else. Only the fool goes through life not expecting to be blamed for actions they didn't commit. It's all a part of the fallen nature of man to shift the blame to someone else, rather than take full responsibility. The truth is, we all make errors from time to time and need to know when to accept the responsibility for our actions. But the problem is, some of us fall into the blame trap. This is when we look for reasons to explain away our shortcomings as possibly someone else's fault. Instead of trying to live in a blame-free environment, we should accept the responsibility and move on when truly we are to blame.

Think for a minute at what our Lord Jesus must have suffered at the hands of his cruel executioners. Here's a man who had truly did nothing wrong, yet he was being charged with sedition, cultism, and tax evasion. Let us take this opportunity to learn from the Master's life about accepting blame. He knew He was dead right in His convictions, but what were His words of defense against the charges? Matthew 27:13&14; "Then said Pilate unto him, Hearest thou not how many things they witness against thee? And he answered him to never a word; insomuch that the governor marveled greatly." Jesus' response to the blame trap was - nothing. Don't you realize that you don't have to win every argument to win the war? Instead, Jesus submitted to what He knew to be God's will for His life and let the chips fall where they may. He disciplined His mouth to be silent in order to remain sinless. He accepted the destructive criticism in stride and allowed His work on this earth to be completed. He was so sure of Himself that when they ridiculed Him, as He hung on the cross, He prayed for His executioners and their eternal souls. He was the picture perfect example of a mature Christian. Blaming others is truly a sign of immaturity. I've watched our children grow to the point where they would accept the blame when they are wrong, just to make sure the others don't get punished. This is a big change from when they were young. I remember once when our youngest daughter Kahla told me a lie, and I didn't know how to get the truth from her. Being a new father and very inexperienced in handling those type of situations, I punished all three girls, trying to get one to break and tell me the truth, when, in reality, two of them were telling the truth. It was the youngest who was being sneaky and shifting the blame to someone else. I remember how terrible I felt when I finally did get the truth out of her. I spent a long time apologizing to the two innocent girls for my harsh punishment against them and I never used that method anymore. Well, I guess we're all learning. The youngest, who had been telling the lie all along, was punished accordingly and I'm proud to say that that one incident was the only problem I have ever had with her. Today she's a beautiful young Christian woman, soon to be married to a fine Christian man. She learned her lesson about blaming others, as we all should.

Daily Verse: "Who shall also confirm you until the end, that ye may be blameless in the day of our Lord Jesus Christ." I Corinthians 1:8

FEAR OF LEGALISM

Some may ask, "Just what is legalism?" It's the same problem that the Apostle Paul dealt with in the Galatians church when he said; "I marvel that ye are so soon removed from him that called you into the grace of Christ unto another gospel." Here, false teachers had moved into the church and began teaching a bunch of dos and don'ts, soon placing the Galatians church in religious bondage. We see this same spirit in many churches today; they have the big long list of requirements to be a Christian. You must wear a dress at a certain length, and of course woman aren't allowed to cut their hair, or wear any type of jewelry or makeup. They must all look a certain way for them to be considered "holy." Friend, don't you believe it. Now, I'm not professing that God's people live in extreme liberalism in their dress or mannerisms, but if you're counting on some external act to make you holy, you are in for a rude awakening. I've personally witnessed these "external holiness" people get mad at someone and want to punch them out. Or, I've personally witnessed them steal things and think nothing of it. Jesus, in His short time of ministry made it very clear that holiness is an internal act that affects the external. When a young lady gets right with God, she doesn't want to expose herself, so she automatically wears a longer skirt without some policy being forced on her. The problem with most people, who practice the legalistic lifestyle, is that they are insecure in their relationship with Christ. In my observation, most of them don't know how to rightly divide the Word, but know only portions of its portions that support their legalistic beliefs. If you take the Bible out of context, you can make it say anything. And these propagators of legalism are experts at taking the Bible out of context.

The Bible clearly teaches that we are saved by faith, through grace, and belief in the redeeming work that Christ did at Calvary. No amount of religious practice by itself has the power to save us from our sins. We are free moral agents, able to choose freely what we should do with our life. If we choose our own plan, it will surely lead to eternal death, and hell. But if we should decide to give our life to Jesus, and follow His plan freely, we are promised eternal life, peace, and happiness in heaven; not in this life. In this life we are promised with certainty - afflictions, sufferings, tribulations, but in the end, eternal life. It's your choice, choose God.

Daily Verse: "Stand fast therefore in the liberty wherewith Christ hath made us free, and be not entangled again with the yoke of bondage."

Galatians 5:1

FEAR OF BEING MIDDLE-AGED

Scripture informs us that the "glory of a young man" is his health and physical strength. And the honor of the old man is his "wisdom and experience." The interesting thing about the different ages is when you're young, you look forward to getting older, and when you're old, you look back wishing you were younger, but when you're middle-aged, you look worried. Many people face this time with great fear, and some even get thrown into a crisis tailspin. The age of the mid-lifers, is approximately ages thirty-five through fifty years of age. For men in this age bracket, they grow more hair in their ears than on their head. And, of course some women feel that gravity is a lot more powerful now than it was when they were twenty. These are very stressful times for people, but the aging process is the same for all of us. All we have to do is defuse the middle-aged time bomb, and we will be in for some exciting times ahead.

For some reason mid-life people want to look younger than they are. They finally realize that time is unwinding at a faster pace each year. Many run to and fro looking for a pulse button to slow the process down. Most finally come to the point where they realize that they aren't getting older, they're just getting old. Another problem mid-lifers face is the fact that life seems to be more routine than when they were younger. King Solomon with all his success became bored with his life. In Ecclesiastes 3 this is what he had to say about his life; "The thing that hath been, it is that which shall be; and that which is done is that which shall be done: and there is no new thing under the sun." King Solomon's mid-life crisis led him away from the one true God and into worship of false gods. I thank God that in the end of the book he realized that he was only passing through life and he came back to Jehovah.

I know in my own personal life, I finally realized that if I was to accomplish certain goals, I would have to begin to stop putting them off until next year. Since I made that decision, "next year," is not in my vocabulary. I decided to get a grip on life, stay calm, and face mid-life as a part of God's plan. I decided to not panic, and instead of trying to start life over again, I would keep calm and follow God's plan for my life. This book is a part of my mid-life goals, and I plan on finishing several more that I've been storing up in my mind until I had the time to write them.

Since I overcame my mid-life crisis by setting new goals, and seeking after God's will, I've been able to not regret finding new gray hairs. I now understand that God has made every stage of our life to be full of its own advantages and disadvantages. If you're middle aged, and looking for the secret to happiness, it's deeply imbedded in realizing that your strength is no longer in your back, but instead it's in your head. You can avoid stupid mistakes that you would once make as a young person. When you understand the benefits of your age, you'll stop wanting to be younger, and start learning to be wiser. Learn to make the most of the present, and enjoy the many blessings that God has given you with your wisdom and above all know that God is not finished with you yet.

Daily Verse: "Let us hear the conclusion of the whole matter: Fear God, and keep his commandments: for this is the whole duty of man."

Ecclesiastes 12:13

FEAR OF SPIDERS

The fear of spiders rates high on the list of the most dreaded fears. "Arachnophobia" as it is called, affects everyone from children to women, and, of course, even some men. Maybe some of the comical horror movies contribute to the wide-spread varieties of people who have this fear, but I personally believe it's the fact that spiders are generally creepy looking. As a whole, more people are afraid of spiders than they are bugs. Some are so frightened at the sight of these little eight-legged crawlers that they jump, scream, and even have panic attacks at the touch of one. Many feel that the silk they spin, which is called the web, is gross. Actually even with all the fear, they are one very beneficial critter. Being the great opportunist that they are lands them everywhere on this planet, even in the cleanest of homes. They care not whether you are rich, or poor, if, given a chance, they will find their way into your life. These little predators are perhaps the best agricultural workers for the modern farmer, feasting on some of the farmers worst enemies. Since there are perhaps over 170,000 species of spiders, with the average country acre housing approximately 2.5 million of these little furry fellows, the farmer has lots of help. No, they aren't very beautiful with their multiple eyes, and fangs, but they are the most beneficial arachnid of them all. It's interesting to note that most children, boys especially possess bug collections when they are young, but they tend to fear spiders at a very young age. To help them with this fear and not encourage the fear in the kids, we should teach them that spiders eat bugs not people like the television shows try to teach us. We should teach children that they are more afraid of people than people are of them. Read children books about spiders, highlighting all the beneficial things this little creation of God does for us. And, of course, show children how to avoid being bitten by the creepers when the spider reacts in defense. Spiders can't eat things like you and me; however they inject their prey with an acid that dissolves all the insides of a potential food victim. Then, they suck the soup through a straw-like mouth until all that is left is a shell of what the victim once was. Except for the black widow most North American spiders are completely harmless to humans.

Daily Verse: *"The spider taketh a hold with her hands, and is in king's palaces."*

Proverbs 30:28

FEAR OF UGLINESS

I once heard a comedian who was trying to be funny say; "Beauty is only skin deep, but ugliness goes clear to the bone." Although he was bucking to get laughs with his foolish statement, he really was making a true statement. The only person who can decide whether you are ugly or not is you. Most people who see themselves as ugly stand in their own way of being beautiful; they are their own worst enemy. They constantly beat themselves up over their looks. Listen, the fear you fear is only on the inside of you. It exists nowhere else except in your mind. Yes, I know that some people can be cruel about the way you may look, but the fact is, you determine if you're beautiful or not, by how you respond to their negative comments. Instead of believing the hurtful comments as gospel, see those comments as being from a foolish person with no heart. Don't allow the vicious remarks of a fool to give birth to an internal critic that sees nothing you do as right. Please don't beat yourself up.

Once when I was young, I owned an old style refrigerator. It would constantly build up ice formations around the freezer reducing its freezing capability. I once took out a brand new half gallon of ice cream that was thawed out in the freezer. Quickly I took out a knife, and began to chip away at the ice, removing it layer by layer until the freezer was operating properly again. This is the way a person is when they listen to the harmful remarks of a cruel bully. They can freeze up, and not be effective to anyone. Instead, listen to what God's Word says about Satan who was created to be beautiful; "Thou sealeth up the sum, full of wisdom, and perfect in beauty . . . thine heart was lifted up because of thy beauty, thou hast corrupted thy wisdom by reason of thy brightness;"

Satan was created the picture of perfect beauty, and he let it go to his head to the point where he became corrupted by pride, then, of course, ultimately became the first sinner of the universe. Friend, God has created you just the way you are. Each of us has uniqueness whether we could model fancy clothes or not. God is not concerned with how we look on the outside, but with what our inside looks like. That's why I said in the beginning that what the comedian said about ugliness being to the bone is the truth. It's only on the inside that we are ugly or beautiful. God is looking at our inner man, because He knows that no matter what we look like, some day in a very short time, we will trade in this outside look for a new body that is free from sin; a body that is perfect and without blemish.

Daily Verse: "Favor is deceitful, and beauty is vain, but a woman that feareth the Lord, she shall be praised."

Proverbs 31:30

FEAR OF MATERIALISM

The story is told of the man who worked all his life to be able to buy a new BMW. One day while going home from work to his beautiful mountain villa, he encountered a pounding snow storm. The car slid off the road and was about to go off a cliff when the man quickly unbuckled his seat belt, and leaped out of the car. The car went over the cliff and burst into flames as it hit the canyon floor below. In his state of panic, the man did not realize that he had caught his arm on the door lock and his arm had been completely ripped off. A local "good Samaritan" was following behind and witnessed the accident. He immediately stopped to see if he could be of any help. He rushed over to the man, and was amazed that all he could hear the man doing was crying over his new BMW. "Oh I've lost my new BMW," cried the man, oblivious to the fact that one of his arms was missing. Suddenly the helper noticed that the man's arm was missing, and he quickly commented; "Buddy, you've got bigger problems than your car, one of your arms is missing - let's find it and get you to the hospital- maybe they can still save it." Finally, the man looks at the stub where his arm used to be, and began to scream, "Oh, no, now I've lost my new Rolex, too. Quick help me find my new Rolex."

This may seem like a humorous story, but the truth is, more people are attached to material possessions than we would like to admit. I've always said that God doesn't care if you have stuff, He just doesn't want stuff to have you. When He blesses us materially, it's not so that we can make a shrine to the possession and worship it. But instead it's so we can be a channel to bless someone else. He blesses us to be a blessing. The problem is that most people want to swim in the gravy with God's blessing, and become selfish. In fact, some people serve God just for the things he promised to provide. This was Satan's accusation against Job. In short, Satan told God that the only reason Job served God was because God had blessed him so much. Well, God, knowing the heart of every man, knew that this wasn't true. So He allowed Satan to challenge Job and prove to Satan once and for all that Job was a man of integrity. I know we live in a world filled with the materialistic spirit. People spend five times the amount of money on pet food in this country than they give to the mission field. We allow little children's stomachs to bloat from malnutrition, while we gorge ourselves until we can hardly walk, all in the name of prosperity. Yes, God wants you to be prosperous, but He doesn't want you to be materialistic. Being prosperous means that you have enough of God's wealth to accomplish the work that He wants you to do. It doesn't mean you have enough wealth to buy a new BMW every year. I once asked my congregation when speaking about tithing, "How much of your income belongs to God?" Many gave the canned answer - 10%. And they are right - 10% is the required tithe according to God's Word. However, it doesn't belong to us and we have no right to spend it on our own things. Actually God owns it all 100%, since we are now His bond slaves, bought with the price of His Son's blood. So don't forget who owns you.

Daily Verse: "Let him that stole steal no more, but rather let him labor, working with his hands the thing which is good, that he may have to give to him that needeth."

Ephesians 4:28

FEAR OF NEGLECTING DUTY

Webster's dictionary explains that duty is a "required action by someone in a position - doing something out of moral or legal considerations." All around the world people are shirking their duties. Parents are neglecting their children's God-given rights to be cared for, abandoning them in a world filled with need. Dads are deciding that they don't want to raise their kids, so they get rid of their children's mother, seeking a newer model. Employees steal countless of millions of dollars worth of goods from their employers, forcing consumers to pick up the tab for the losses by increased pricing. Teachers have resorted to becoming babysitters only, not caring whether the kids learn anything or not, as long as they get their paycheck. Politicians go back on their campaign promises, usually within the first few months of office, since they no longer need the votes of the people. And, of course, Christians too act like secret agents when it comes to sharing their faith with the lost and dying of this world. One thing is sure, we can't do much about the woes of neglected duties in this world but, we can make sure we are not part of them. God has entrusted an awesome responsibility to His church; the responsibility of being His body on this earth. We are the only hands that Jesus has now. Nobody will be touched by those wonderful healing hands if we don't reach out and touch others. If He is to go anywhere today, it is to be done with our feet, because our feet are the only feet with which Jesus has to walk. We must carry the good news with us everyday and always be ready to speak His words with our mouth about his healing grace. So many people today are suffering while Christ's body is dormant. It seems as though we've taken Christianity and turned it from a full time service into a one day observance. Most only experience Christianity on Sunday mornings, totally oblivious to the fact that God is with us in all our actions. Many people are so busy with their own lives that they don't even see the tragedies around them.

In 1992 a traffic officer from Los Angeles County wrote out a parking ticket for a man who was illegally parked on "street-sweeping" day. He quickly ran the plates, wrote out the customary $30 dollar ticket, walked up to the car, and tossed the ticket through the rolled down window onto the dashboard of the man's car. Completely ignoring the man who was sitting in the driver's seat, the officer, writing out the ticket, told him to "get it moving." Then, the officer hurried back to his police car and sped away, looking for another violator of the parking laws. What the traffic officer didn't know was that the man couldn't move the car if he had wanted to - he had been shot in the head about twelve hours before and was just sitting their stiff as a board. Today many of us are only concerned with the sins people are committing, and not the least bit concerned with the sinners. People who are imprisoned by the laws of sin and death don't need a citation, they need a Savior - so let's not neglect our duty any longer–Give them Jesus!

Daily Verse: "So likewise ye, when ye shall have done all those things which are commanded you say, we are unprofitable servants: we have done that which was our duty to do."

Luke 17:10

FEAR OF CROSSES

Hollywood for decades has portrayed a group of imaginary people who had a violent fear of the cross. They were the "walking undead," known as "vampires" who suck the blood from their victims. Although we know that these stories are pure fiction–there's no such "-un-dead" among us, still the characteristic the "undead" shared was to be horribly terrified of crosses. Every time someone would hold up a cross, these creatures would scream for fear. Today we face another group of people who are afraid of crosses. They are the unsaved of our society. Many of them hide their fear by wrapping little crosses in gold, and wearing them in their ears. Others wear them around their necks without any understanding about what the cute little trinket is. Friend, the cross is not a piece of jewelry - it's the instrument of death. Many people have been put to death by these torturous painful instruments of death. Some were guilty, and deserved punishment, and some were innocent, and didn't. In fact the greatest testimony of some one dying on an old rugged cross is from our Lord Jesus Christ. This story is quite different from the way it is today. In today's age if someone is important like the president people are willing to step in front of a bullet for them. They even have a group of trained protectors known as the secret service, created just to protect our government officials with their very lives. These agents are willing to do so because the president is an important authority figure in our government. They would gladly die for someone that important, but for some common person they would hardly give their life. Two thousand years ago, Jesus reversed the trend, when an important person decided to die for the common man. The God of Glory laid down his heavenly robes and wrapped himself in human flesh. Then He took upon Himself the punishment of all mankind - on a cross.

This was to satisfy His Father, who stated; "Cursed is everyone that hangs on a tree." You see, the first sin against mankind was when Eve took the fruit of the knowledge of good and evil from the tree in the Garden. So, the last Adam had to come along, who was Jesus, and put the fruit of obedience back on the tree; the fruit Adam took off the tree through his disobedience. In like manner, the cross was the tree that His Father chose to get the job done. Let us not fear the cross for it is the power of God unto salvation. But let's take the cross up daily, and follow God's plan for our lives.

Daily Verse: "And having made peace through the blood of his cross, by him to reconcile all things unto himself; by him, I say, whether they be things in the earth, or things in heaven."

Colossians 1:20

FEAR OF APATHY

Once a professor stood before his class and asked the students to define for him what the words indifference and apathy mean. He looked in the back of the room to a student who paid little attention in class, and said; "John, can you tell me what the words indifference and apathy mean?"

Startled by the request, John commented back sarcastically; "I don't know, and I don't care."

"Excellent, that is correct," replied the professor. Apathy means to not care . . . to be so apathetic about your life that you don't care what happens. It's like the camper who went camping and woke up in the middle of the night to find out that he had put his sleeping bag in the middle of an ant highway. He laid there feeling the ants crawling all over him, but didn't want to turn on the lights and see them. He knew if he actually saw them he would have to do something about them. So it was easier for him to just lay there and let them crawl all over his body. In the same way, many who are in the world know their actions and lifestyle are wrong, but, they fear that if they take some action they will have to change and give up the apathetic lifestyle. It's an easy lifestyle, just ignoring everything and pretending everything is alright even though you know it's not.

In the same way many in the church are living lives of apathy. In Revelation 3 Jesus addressed the church in Laodicea about their lukewarm, apathetic lifestyle. This church made no waves in society, but instead was the great church of compromise not wanting to offend anyone. Many in today's modern church have gone the way of the Laodicea church with their methods of watering down the gospel so as to not offend the sinner when they attend church. They have multiple thousands of people who attend Sunday services every week but don't have a born again experience with Christ, because they have yet to be challenged with the Gospel. Jesus specifically stated that the world hated him, and would hate us to if we were truly of Him. Many in the church are asleep, like the man in the ant bed, and they don't want to turn on the light of the gospel and see what is crawling all over them.

Once I preached a message on the four major diseases attacking the church today. I called it spiritual AIDS. Neither one alone is deadly, but when you have all four in your life, they will weaken your immune system much like natural AIDS does, to the point a common cold could kill you. The "A" stands for Apathy, "I" is Indifference, "D" is Deception, and the "S" is Stubbornness. First, you develop a rebellious attitude about something, which leads you into an "I don't care" mentality. If allowed to persist it will quickly turn you into just an average thinker who thinks they are right all the time, but in reality are dead wrong. Soon, you will begin to deceive yourself by your apathetic attitude into believing everyone else is wrong and only you are right. This was the lukewarm church that Jesus addressed when He told them he was standing and knocking on the door of the church and no one was allowing Him in. He wants to be in your life too, so don't leave Him outside trying to get in. Open the door and let Him give you the cure for spiritual AIDS.

Daily Verse: "Slothfulness casteth into a deep sleep; and an idle soul shall suffer hunger."

Proverbs 19:15

FEAR OF HUMANISM

The famous Gloria Steinem once said; "I hope by the year 2000 we will have our kids believing in their own potential, and not God's." Sorry Gloria, Y2K is passed, and God the Father is still on the throne. Don't get me wrong, the humanists have made a valiant effort to the point where they have almost turned our public schools into a humanist training camp. The big difference is that God always has a remnant to work through. Although the school system teaches that man is the center of things and you must get a hold of your true self to see things accomplished in your life, God's people are still combating these teachings, spreading the word that only Jesus can claim the divine title of "I AM." Instead of self-awareness and self-sufficiency concepts taught by humanists, Christians teach the need for surrender, and servant-hood. God's people know that with God all things are possible. Instead of the humanist approach in life, they have sought after the need for humility and humbleness. Christians know that God's power is only effective when they themselves are weak, for the Scripture states, when we are weak, then He is strong.

Throughout most of human history great minds from the Greeks and Latin's have sought to spread their intellectual gospel to mankind. Great philosophers during the middle Ages preached about the ideals of mankind. They believed that man is the center of his own universe and can overcome any obstacle if he only believes he can. They seek to teach that man is a god on the inside, and quite capable of designing his future as he sees fit. Jesus was very aware of this teaching even when He walked the earth - look at how He faced the problem head on in Philippians 2:4–8; "Let this mind be in you, which was also in Christ Jesus: Who, being in the form of God, thought it not robbery to be equal with God: But made himself of no reputation, and took upon him the form of a servant, and was made in the likeness of men: And being found in fashion as a man, he humbled himself, and became obedient unto death, even the death of the cross."

Even though Jesus knew He was God, He emptied himself of His Godhood in order to be like one of us. Now if Jesus who was God left His glory (Godhood) in Heaven to be a mere human being, how can a humanist say that he himself is God? Even though humanists blindly believe that man is the master of all things, and that man's will is what controls the universe, God is still looking for a man that is small enough to use. God frets, not over the humanists, in fact, the scriptures say that God sits in heaven and laughs at the ignorance of man. So don't fear what the humanists have in store for mankind in the future, but instead let's raise our children up in the admonition of the Lord and let him sort out the rest.

Daily Verse: "Jesus said unto them, Verily, verily, I say unto you, before Abraham was, I AM."

John 8:58

FEAR OF PRIDE

Pride is included in the list of the seven abominations of Proverbs 6. God hates pride, because it is the major reason for the fall of Satan, and also the cause for the need of a redemption plan for mankind. Scripture informs us that pride always proceeds a fall. Anytime you see someone with a haughty spirit, you know that it won't be long before they take a fall. Usually pride is evident in the bragging that comes from some proud person's mouth. A proud person just can't stand to not get the credit they feel they deserve. It's like the little turtle who was tired of spending his winters holed up in the ground, so just before winter he approached a couple of geese, and asked them if they would take him south with them when they were to go. They said they would gladly oblige him, but they didn't know how they could carry him. So he came up with the idea of biting unto the middle of a small piece of rope that he had found, and having each goose take a hold of an end with their beaks and then taking off. They flew for hundreds of miles and everything was going fine until someone from the ground saw what they were doing and thought the idea was ingenious. They yelled up from the ground; "Hey you up there, who came up with that idea, it looks great?" The turtle couldn't stand not getting credit for his idea, so he opened his mouth to answer and fell to his death. I told you pride always comes before the fall. Scripture warns us in Proverbs 27:21 that we will be tested by the praise we receive; "As the fining pot for silver and the furnace for gold; so is a man to his praise." It also tells us that we shouldn't blow our own horn in verse 2 of the same chapter. "Let another man praise thee, and not thine own mouth; a stranger, and not thine own lips." It is dangerous for us to begin to brag about our accomplishments in that we tend to exaggerate in the issues. We may say something unintentional that could lead us into a pathway of pride that would then of course lead to a fall in our life. God desires that we keep our pride under control, and not allow it to have free course. Everyone will battle the hindrance of pride. It is a product of the fallen nature of man that will be with us until the return of Christ, and we all receive a new redeemed body. Of course, the best way to overcome the fear of pride is to stay humble in all accounts. Your humility will carry you away from the battle of pride. Pride can't stand humility, they're arch enemies. The humble man beats his chest when he prays, and asks God to forgive him for he is a sinner. And the prideful man thanks God that he has made him so perfect that he is not like the other sinner man. Oh friend, pride comes before a fall, and God has no room for it in His people.

Daily Verse: "Wherefore let him that thinketh he standeth take heed lest he fall."

I Corinthians 10:12

FEAR OF ORGANIZATION

God is the most organized being that exists. He is a meticulous planner, just look at the human body design, or the intricacy of the animal kingdom, and how everything fits together. Yes, the heavens do "declare the glory of God." In His wisdom He has given mankind time. Each of us has 1,440 chances in a single day to succeed. That's how many minutes we have in a day. The Bible speaks that we can receive great pleasure by making the best use of all of them for the glory of God. Proverbs 13:19 says; "The desire accomplished is sweet to the soul . . ." We shall find much satisfaction in clearing out the clutter in our lives and doing God's will. That's where organization comes in. Some fear that if they organized things, their lives will be too structured. But, I say, if you don't organize things others will structure your life for you. Disorder produces pain, and if you live with disorder, you will live with the pain that comes from it. You will always seem to be running to the urgent, just because you have left things out of order. Until you get tired of the cluttered lifestyle you will live with disorder. But when you finally make the first step toward organization, you'll see just how out of place things really are. All organization begins with seeing the ending, and not just the beginning. It's quite easy to organize things and another thing to keep them that way. I personally feel that every minute counts, and you can't be effective and waste any of them looking for things that you have misplaced because of disorder. It has been said that the average person spends over three years of their life just looking for things that they've misplaced. What a waste, of a good life.

One of the best ways to begin to organize your life is to prioritize things. Priorities clear out what is good to make room for what is best. They allow you to commit the precious time that God has given you to doing the things He wants you to do. However if you try to hold unto all things, you will soon find your life is like a pressure cooker, with you about ready to pop your lid. The enemy would like to fill your life full of good things so that you will walk around in confusion, and a constant state of frustration. It pays to first commit your day to the Lord, and then allow Him to help you organize the rest of it.

I believe the best way to organize your life is to have a plan for every day. Take a careful look at your schedule, and plan a whole week. Then, the day before, go over the next day's list so you know what you're going to do the following day. I keep a calendar that has my days scheduled on it. I go over it all the time to see if I really need to do everything on the list. If I have a task that seems to overwhelm me, I take small bites until it's done. Some people recommend that you keep a detailed list of what you're going to do for the day, hour by hour, but I've found that I work better with a more flexible schedule. Whichever you choose - learn to structure your time around what works best for you, who you are, and where you are in life.

Daily Verse: "For God is not the author of confusion, but of peace, as in all the churches of the saints."

I Corinthians 14:33

FEAR OF CARRYING EXCESS BAGGAGE

Jesus in Matthew's Gospel urged each and every person carrying a heavy burden to come and give it to him to carry for them; "Come unto me, all ye that labor and are heavy laden, and I will give you rest." He promised that if we would yoke up with Him, He would help us carry the luggage of life. A humorous story is told of the Christian who became tired of carrying his cross, so he looked for a store to trade his heavy one in for a lighter one. To his amazement one day, he found a store with a sign out front that offered the opportunity to trade crosses. So he quickly went in to the store and handed the store owner his cross. The store owner politely took the cross from him, and told him to take a look around to see if he could find one better to fit him. So the man began to pick up the crosses, and try them on for size. He was looking for one that would not be too heavy, and would be more comfortable on his shoulders than the previous one. He went from cross to cross and each one seemed heavier than the last, finally when he got to the last cross he picked it up and said; "Now this is a cross, it's just right. I'll gladly trade my old cross for this one," the man offered.

"But sir," the owner replied, " . . . that's the same cross you brought in here." When we think our burdens are too heavy, all we need to do is compare them to the burdens many carried before us. Even though our burden is not noticeable in the natural realm, it still is very real in the spiritual realm. These invisible weights tend to make us feel very weak and vulnerable in life.

Carrying excess baggage can be dangerous. Even airplanes have been known to crash from the excess weight of too much luggage. As we travel through life we must discover ways to leave our baggage for someone else to carry.

I remember our first trip my wife and I took on an airplane. We had all kinds of heavy bags, with which we rushed around, trying to carry them and stay in line. That was several years ago, and we have since learned about air travel. For our last trip we took the bare necessities. This, in turn, relieved all the stress in travel because we didn't have all the excess luggage. God wants His people to give Him all the past regrets, difficulties, and stresses that we encounter in our everyday life. He wonders why we carry around marital problems, work related stress, overdue bills, and the heavy baggage of responsibilities. One thing I noticed about the airport was that if I didn't want to carry my bags I could either leave them and not claim them, or I could have someone carry them for me. God wants us to not claim the things that we don't need, and let Him carry the rest. Don't just hand them to God, because as long as you are touching them, you have the ability to take them back. He wants us to cast them onto Him, - that way we have to let go.

Once a little boy got his hand stuck in a hole in a tree in his backyard. He screamed for his dad to come and help him. Quickly his dad came to his rescue. His dad tried to pull his hand out carefully, but it wouldn't budge. He got some oil from the garage, and tried to grease up his son's arm, but it wouldn't budge. Finally as a last resort, he retrieved a saw from the garage to cut the tree down, but before he made the first stroke with the saw, he asked the little boy if he had anything in his hand. The boy answered that he had an acorn in his hand, and he was holding it tight. His father instructed him to let go of the acorn, and as soon as the boy loosened his grip on the acorn, his hand came right out of the hole. Let's follow his example, and let go of worthless things.

Daily Verse "Casting all your care upon him; for he careth for you."

I Peter 5:7

FEAR OF VISION

Vision has become a by-word in the modern world we live in. Over the last few years of researching the subject I've noticed that very few people possess one. A vision is simply a picture you have in your mind of a desired future. It's what you want your life to turn out like. Most just wing it, when it comes to life. They mistakenly believe whatever will be, will be. Thousands, maybe millions of people wander year after year without a clue of what life holds for them. It's true we don't know every snare or trap that Satan has set up to catch us, but at the same time we should have some idea of where we will be five years from now. I believe that living without a vision can be dangerous, because Scripture informs us that people who have no vision are candidates to perish. In fact, we should have a detailed list of what we plan to do for the next ten years if the Lord should tarry.

The Bible is filled with illustrations about men and women of God that have lived out their visions. Others have been overtaken by great fears because of the lack of vision. Tucked away in the book of Kings is the story of a man who possessed great spiritual vision, but his servant was just the opposite. He lived by sight, and not by faith. In this story, a pagan king is tired of his enemy, Israel, knowing what his every move was. He had suspected that he had a spy within his own camp. But one of his leaders came to him, and said that the only spy was Israel's powerful God, for He was the spy seeing and telling information to Israel's prophet Elisha, who lived in Dothan. Elisha, in turn, would tell the king of Israel of the enemy's battle plans, and they would use the inside information to prepare to defend themselves. Well, the pagan king couldn't do anything about Israel's God, but he felt he could destroy Elisha, and thus break the flow of information. So, he rounded up a huge army, and completely surrounded Elisha's house. Bright and early, Elisha's servant went to fetch some water for the morning coffee, and looked around the house and saw the huge Syrian army totally surrounding the house. Instantly, fear gripped his heart. You see, people who lack vision, are prone to fear. Quickly the servant dropped the pale and ran back in the house and said; "Alas, my master, how shall we go?" I love Elisha's response recorded in II Kings 6:16&17; "And he answered, fear not! For they that be with us are more that they that be with them. And Elisha prayed, and said, Lord, I pray thee, open his eyes, that he may see. And the Lord opened the eyes of the young man; and he saw: and behold; the mountain was full of horses and chariots of fire round about Elisha." In this story we notice a few interesting things about vision. First, people who have a vision don't have to see it in the natural to know it exists in the spiritual. Elisha never went outside to see the Lord's army; he just knew it was there, because God had promised He'd be there. Next, all spiritual vision comes from the Lord. And the ability to cast the vision that you possess is only done after careful praying, and asking God to help them receive it. Once the servant received the vision, then his fear left, and he was able pray right along with Elisha against the enemies that threatened their lives. Don't allow the fear of no vision to rob you of a happy life, pray right now and ask God to give you a vision today.

Daily Verse: "Where there is no vision, the people perish;"
Proverbs 29:18a

FEAR OF INGRATITUDE

Sometimes we have to search the world over to find one person who is thankful. Even as children, there's a constant quest to get more. Some people are like hogs in a feed trough at dinnertime. They just bury their heads in their plate without ever thinking for one minute where the food came from. When our kids were small we used to always sit down to the evening meal together; this was just one of our family traditions. Each night we would take turns saying grace. Occasionally, one of the kids would be hungry and start eating before we had a chance to say grace. Instantly, the rest of the family would start saying real loud, "Oink, oink, oink," until the guilty party would understand that we were calling them a pig for eating without first thanking God for providing the meal. It was so funny - they would stop chewing instantly, and not know what to do with food that was in their mouth. Finally, we would pray, and they would swallow. Some might argue that this is being a little picky. Surely God isn't concerned about whether our kids say grace every time they eat, is He? I beg to differ with you. Once Jesus was entering the city, and he was startled by the yelling of ten leprous men. It was the law at that time that if you were a leper, you were an outcast who was not allowed around healthy people. In fact, you were obligated to scream real loud the word, "Unclean!" three times. This would warn others of your presence, and they could respond accordingly. In this particular instance the lepers took advantage of Jesus being in their city. They immediately begged that He would have mercy on them. Reports had spread all over of His incredible mercy showed toward lepers. Jesus responded by telling them to go and show themselves to the priests. And they quickly acted in faith to His command. As they went on their way they noticed that something had happened to them. Their leprosy had left their bodies, and they were totally healed. In a moment of gratitude, only one of the lepers returned to give God thanks for what had been done for him. Instead of Jesus being elated about the one who returned to give thanks, look at what he said in Luke 17:17 "Were there not ten cleansed? But where are the nine?" The other nine just took the healing, and went on their way without the slightest concern for thanking God who gave the healing. Jesus was worried about where the other nine were. He was dissatisfied with the ungrateful behavior the other nine lepers displayed. And He still is, for that matter. But look at the reward the one who returned received for showing gratitude for his healing in verse 19. "And he said unto him, Arise, go thy way, thy faith hath made thee whole." He not only received a healing from his leprosy, but he also had the parts of his body that the leprosy destroyed to grow back. He was made completely whole. Today people are divided into two separate categories. Ungrateful people who always see the bad in every situation and grateful people who always see the good in every bad situation. Which category describes you?

Daily Verse: "And let the peace of God rule in your hearts, to the which also ye are called in one body; and be thankful."

Colossians 3:15

FEAR OF UNITY

Jesus warned us in several passages to beware of ravenous wolves that would attack weak, lonely sheep. Paul reinforced the teaching by telling the churches of those days he knew wolves were just waiting for his departure, so they could attack the defenseless flock. What were they warning us about? Were they really worried about wolves, or were they trying to teach us something more important? In most of the passage, they teach us that there is power in unity. Some people are afraid to agree with others. Yet, Jesus taught us that the most powerful force we could use was the force of agreement. When we unite together in His name, nothing can stand against us. Even nature teaches us that there is great strength in unity. When arctic wolves gang-up together to attack one of their favorite quarries, the musk-oxen, the musk-oxen protect their calves by surrounding them and forming an impenetrable circle. Wolves won't attack full grown musk-oxen, but they love their calves. So these oxen circle, heads-in toward their young with their heels out, ready to kick the brains out of any wolf that dares to try to enter the circle. The wolves keep on the attack for hours if need be, until they can get one musk-ox to break the unity of the ring. Once they get one to break unity, they immediately charge the broken rank until they send all the musk-oxen fleeing in a rush of confusion. Finally, the wolves have what they want; calves left to the mercy of the wolves. Before the musk-oxen can figure out what has happened and recuperate, the wolves will have quickly slaughtered all the calves and carried them away for lunch.

Likewise, Satan is attempting to attack the church on all sides, leaving no stone unturned. His wolves are attacking it by ordaining so-called homosexual bishops. Self proclaimed theologians are attempting to rewrite the Word of God, leaving such important doctrines out; such as, the divinity of Christ, the virgin birth, and, of course, the power of the blood of Jesus alone to redeem us from our sins. Some wolves have crept into the flock to lead millions away with their cultish beliefs. Groups like Jehovah Witnesses, Mormons, Christian Science, and a few hundred others are leading people to Hell with a Bible in their hands. The ironic thing about it is most of these don't even believe in the existence of Hell. This is a great tragedy, and I really feel for these religious people who are so deeply deceived.

As believers today in this final hour of God's prophetic clock, we must not break ranks, and thus let the weak become easy prey for the enemy. These wolves won't spare any in the flock if they are allowed just one hole from any of us. We are not very powerful as one, but we can have great gain if we join together, and find common ground in the assignments that God has given each of us to do. In the early church great revival broke out not because they all believed the same thing, but because they all wanted the same thing. This is true unity when people separate their personalities and differences and all work together for the common good. Today is not the time for churches to fight over their disagreements and doctrinal differences, but instead to join together and win the lost to Christ.

Daily Verse: " . . . Behold, how good and how pleasant it is for Brethren to dwell together in unity."

Psalms 133:1

FEAR OF LEISURE TIME

In the early part of the 20th Century, many historians predicted that with the advancement of technology by the 1980's the average work day would only be about 2 hours in length. They felt that people wouldn't have to work more than 10 hours in a week to earn a living. Instead, by the end of the century Americans were putting in some of the longest work weeks in history, with the average professional working more than fifty hours a week, and most work more than that. The motto for the hour has become, "Work, More Work, Work Everlasting." There are those who work Saturdays, Sundays, all three shifts, some seven days a week with no leisure in sight. Some people are so afraid of unstructured leisure that they have allowed themselves to be defined only by their work. Work has become the 21st century religion. Many Americans find their meaning and identity for living in their job. This is too bad because Jesus never called us to be human doings, but instead human beings. He is more concerned with who you are, and not what you do. Many people are so anxious to do something that they are like the unnamed runner who begged to run back a message of the battle back to the king. David was patiently waiting for a runner to bring him a message. The century on the wall yelled that a runner was coming, and then suddenly, he announced that there was not only one runner, but two. The one messenger who begged to go, was faster than the one that had the true message. He arrived and the king asked, "How goes the battle, is my son Absalom alright?" The messenger looked up at the king breathing hard from the run, and said that he had no idea what was going on in the battle. In other words he had run for nothing. He had got his pleasure from just running, not fulfilling God's will. I learned a long time ago, that activity doesn't always produce accomplishment.

A few little caterpillars were placed on the rim of a saucer. In the middle of the saucer was placed their favorite food, pine needles. These caterpillars went around and around nose to tail for days until they starved to death just a few inches from their favorite food. The scientist named them processionary caterpillars, because they followed each other to their death, not willing to stop for one second to eat. In the same way we must take our example from God when he says "six days shall thou work, but thou shall rest on the seventh." He even modeled this pattern for us in creation. Do you think God got tired from creation? I think not, He was only giving us an example to follow in our lives. We should all take a break every week. Also, I'm a firm believer in vacations, not to stay around the house and paint the house or clean out the garage, but to get away and rest from your labors. Remember, if you don't take care of yourself nobody else will. So make a start today and learn that no man on his death bed ever wished he could spend one more day at the office.

Daily Verse: "For in six days the Lord made the heaven and earth, the sea, and all that in them is, and rested the seventh day; wherefore the Lord blessed the Sabbath day, and hallowed it."

Exodus 20:11

FEAR OF CHEMICAL DEPENDANCY

Research data indicates that there is a large percentage of violent crimes that are committed by people under the influence of drugs or alcohol. As many as 2/3 of all crimes have been committed by these people. With this type of data, you don't have to be a rocket scientist to figure out that we have a drug and alcohol problem in this country. Today we're going to discuss the chemical dependency problem, and later we're going to deal with the fear of alcohol. Some have the misconception that if they can work with the abuse problem then they won't have to deal with the violence problem, because it will take care of itself. Actually, the opposite is true - violence follows drug use and attaches itself to a person's life like a leech; slowing sucking the life blood from a dependant person's life until they aren't even sure that they want to continue. Friend, they need our help.

Webster defines a drug as, "A substance that affects the nervous system, such as a stimulant, or a depressant. Use could lead to an addiction." Although we're not really discussing alcohol in this devotion, the only real difference between cocaine, pot, and alcohol is that you can legally use alcohol at a certain age, whereas the other two you cannot. The term "chemicals" can be used to describe any mood altering substance from pot, cocaine, speed, downers, prescription tranquilizers, etc. These substances are very addicting, and dangerous to ones health. People turn to drugs for a multitude of reasons. Maybe a factory worker loses his job and doesn't know how he's going to support his family. An office executive makes over a quarter of a million dollars a year and can't cope with all the stress she's having on the job. Possibly some young person is at a party and wants to experiment with her friends. Most of the teenage pregnancies in our country can be attributed to some young lady who got under the influence and lowered her standards. These substances give you the illusion that you are calming down, when in reality you are really speeding up. They put you in a state where you're unable to think clearly, and you make rash decisions based on emotions and feelings.

No matter which drug is used - they are all poison to your body. People die regularly from overdose, acute physical reactions, and totally irresponsible behavior while under the influence. Some have been known to think they could fly as they leaped to their death. Others not thinking clearly have become totally paranoid to the point where they load their pistol and shoot a friend or even a spouse to death while under the influence. Others, believe it or not, have died from sucking on a toad to get a buzz from certain toxins the toad releases when it is afraid (bizarre, yes). Chemical addiction is here to stay and will not go away any time soon, so it is our duty to warn the next generation of the dangers in participating in the drug culture.

Scriptures are silent about the use of mood altering drugs other than the fact that it rebukes us for wasting money on anything besides food. It also is adamant in explaining to us that our body is the temple of the Holy Spirit, and He lives in it. If you suffer from chemical dependency please seek help now while there's still time. Fall on the grace of God and ask Him to assist you in being delivered from the dependency of any addiction, other than God. The Bible tells us the only thing we should be addicted to is the ministry to which God has called us.

Daily Verse: *"Know ye not that ye are the temple of God, and the spirit of God dwelleth in you."*

I Corinthians 3:16

FEAR OF ALCOHOL

As we talked about yesterday, there's very little difference between alcohol dependancy and chemical dependancy other than the legalities. Alcohol is much the same as any drug in its ability to alter your thinking capacities. Even though alcohol is legal , it doesn't mean it's good for you. In fact it is quite the contrary, leading to addictions, and the disease of alcoholism. American attitudes toward alcohol is paradoxical, they focus almost exclusively on teaching the abstinence problem. Spending as much as 2 million dollars a year on fancy advertising to try to get people to not start drinking. While on the flip side of the coin they spend over ten million days a year to rehabilitate people who can't handle their liquor. Statistics show us that all the media ads are causing people to drink less these days, but instead now they are drinking worse. The volume of consumption is less, down some 20 %, but the number of drinkers has increased and the number of problem drinkers has increased. Mostly among today's youth. As many as two out of every ten teenagers today have a drinking problem. I believe the main reason is the rapid increase in social drinkers even among Christians. A large portion of the Christian church sees nothing wrong with a little toddy for the body as they call it. Friend, with so many people who have a drinking problem, can we afford to let our good be evil spoken of? We should not allow our liberty we have in Christ to be a stumbling block for those who are weak. I learned this lesson with a painful experience I had back when I first received Christ. A good friend and I had decided to go visit another friend and witness to him of our new found faith in Christ. At the time he was living with a young lady who was not his wife. But we knew that Christ could save him in any situation. When we arrived he was very cordial with us, although we made it clear that we were now servants of God ,and no longer involved with the beer drinking culture. His girlfriend wanted to prepare for us a very special dinner, so she cooked us each our own quail and all the roasted potato fixin's that goes with it. Our friend wanted to get something for us all to drink so he asked us, if we would drink wine with our meal. He used the excuse that even Jesus drank wine. Being new to the faith, we didn't know that the wine Jesus drank wasn't fermented with all the additives that they put in wine today. In fact it would take 22 glasses of wine from the "bible days" to equal the alcohol content of two modern day martinis. So we looked at each other, and said, "Sure we'll drink a glass of wine with dinner." So he went out, and purchased this great big gallon jug of wine. The dinner was great, and we each drank a small glass of wine with dinner, that is all of us except our friend, for he drank the whole gallon by himself, and got drunk. He got so drunk that we couldn't talk to him about Christ, and as my friend and myself left we both looked at each other, and realized that we had blown it. We had allowed the liberty that we had in Christ to cause our friend to sin. Just because we said we would socially drink with him, he used it as an occasion to get intoxicated. It is said that every year, college students drink an equivalent of 100 Olympic sized swimming pools full of alcohol during the course of a school term. Yes, we must address this problem with our children, and plant the seeds of abstinence in them.

Daily verse *"If any man defile the temple of God, him shall God destroy; for the temple of God is holy, which temple ye are."*

I Corinthians 3:17

FEAR OF ACCOUNTABILITY

For most people in our land the idea of being accountable is a good idea, but they don't see any reason to be concerned about it. Accountability is not promoted in the public sector. This is a mystery to me, why don't we hold politicians accountable for their campaign promises? Why don't we hold the Federal Government accountable for the federal debt, shared by tax-payers. Millions, even billions, and now trillions of dollars are thrown around like pocket change. Do you have any idea what a billion dollars looks like? If you took a million dollars worth of one thousand dollar bills and stacked them on top of one another, you would have a stack of about 18 inches in height. But if you made a stack of a billion dollars with the same one thousand dollar bills it would be 100 feet higher than the Washington monument. And I don't want to begin to even talk about a trillion dollars. Yes, a billion dollars is a lot of money and those who spend it like water should be held accountable. Accountability is what makes the world go round. If a business wants to succeed the first thing it does is set up a regimen for accountability. They know that their very chance for survival is to make sure everyone is accountable to someone. In the same way, each of us in the business of life, must be accountable to someone in order to find success. Children are accountable to parents in their behavior, and at the same time parents are accountable to their children for a good example. Jesus taught us about accountability when he approached John the Baptist to be baptized. John was confused when Jesus requested that John baptize Him. After all, Jesus Himself was the baptizer sent from heaven. But Christ's remark to him was to do this as an example for all men to follow. He was being accountable to all who would follow after. Incompetence is the child of "lack of accountability." Today we should birth systems of accountability that help each of us live happy productive lives. Most of the people who fear accountability are living in the dark side of life with something to hide. They fear should their past be revealed that they would have to pay for their crimes. God desires that each of us admit our wrongs and pursue Him with a measure of accountability. When I think of those who have the fear of accountability I'm always reminded of Cain's response to God when God asked him where his brother Abel was. Cain said; "Am I my brother's keeper?" Cain had just murdered his brother, leaving him in the field for the wild dogs to devour his body. God immediately set in order a level of accountability in "the Adam's family" that day. He placed a mark on Cain's forehead and from that day forward he would be branded as a murderer. Accountability is not a bad thing, in as much as God is going to hold each of us accountable as to how we used the gifts and talents that He has placed in our lives. You won't be accountable for something that you don't have, but only for what you do have.

> *Daily Verse: "So then every one of us shall give account to himself to God."*
>
> *Romans 14:12*

FEAR OF GREED

In God's third wisdom book in the poetry writings, Proverb 1:19, instruction is given to those who are captured by the fear of greed. Listen to what God's instruction is; "So are the ways of everyone that is greedy for gain; which taketh away the life of their owners thereof." He instructs us through His word that if we allow greed to overtake our life, greed, in turn will take our life back from us. Greed is a powerful force in the days we live. In reality, it has always had its paws wrapped around most of human history. We can see it at work in the life of ancient kings when several murdered their own brothers to get the throne. A grandmother named Athaliah even killed her own grandchildren to assure that she would be able to keep the power of the throne. Elisha's servant Gehazi lost out with God after several faithful years of service, all because greed got a stronghold in his life and caused him to lie to his master, so he could put away things for his future. Greed is the culprit that caused Achan's entire family to be stoned to death all because he coveted, and stole some of Jericho's riches which were God's tithe for the Promised Land Greed is what caused Ananias and Sapphira to drop dead after they placed a large offering in the collection plate in Acts 5. This terrible sin is what caused Judas to betray a man that he had lived with for over three and a half years; a man that on repeated occasions had called him His friend. And of course today greed is going to be responsible for sending countless of millions of people to Hell, because they couldn't trust God to provide their every need. You may be asking; " why does God hate greed so much?" Why has God punished people in the past so harshly for the sin of greed? The answer can be found in Colossians 3:5 ; "Mortify (put to death) therefore your members which are upon the earth; fornication, uncleanness, inordinate affection, (lust) evil concupiscence, and covetousness (greed) which is idolatry. There it is - the main reason why God hates greed so much is not only that it breaks the tenth commandment, "thou shalt not covet," but it breaks the first commandment that "thou shalt have no other God's before me." Greed is in essence placing your needs on an altar before God, thus making it a god before him. And Jehovah says with His own words that He is a "jealous God" that will not share you with anyone or anything else. He wants you to desire Him alone, and Him only will you serve. Anytime we allow greed to operate in our life, we are telling God that we don't trust Him to be our provider. I feel it is foolishness to admit that I trust God with something as precious as my soul, but not trust Him with something that is temporal like my money. This is why the Bible says that He created the principle of tithing to be followed by people all through the ages. He tells us that the tithe is what keeps us from becoming greedy. Every time we place God's tithe in the offering plate, we're telling the spirit of greed that it has no control in our lives. So decide today to not fear greed anymore, and give God your best.

Daily Verse: "He coveteth greedily all the day long; but the righteous giveth and spareth not."

Proverbs 21:26

FEAR OF BUSY-NESS

When it comes to busy-ness many of us have mixed emotions. On one hand we know that being busy is what produces success in life. Scripture even exhorts us to remain busy if we want to see our goals accomplished. The Bible says, the hands of the diligent shall be made rich, but on the other hand, Scripture also tells us to be balanced in life. I personally believe that busy-ness indicates that a person is full of industry and energy. I don't want anyone ever saying that I live a complacent life resting on my laurels and past accomplishments. I don't believe any person alive can squeeze more out of a day than me. Most nights I fall asleep with a book in my hand in the late night hours just trying to feed my mind a little bit more. I understand that Scripture exhorts us that knowledge is one of the three biggest things that every person should pursue if they want their lives to be successful. We should pursue wisdom, knowledge, and understanding above all other worldly pursuits. These three elements of life is where all true success originates. Some people complain about their commute to work–friend, if you drive 30 minutes each day back and forth to work you can put in a years worth of school every year on tape. You can listen to the whole Bible on tape every sixty days, without ever turning the pages of your Bible at home. You can purchase leadership tapes and raise the scale of your leadership level in just a short amount of time. I personally always carry a book with me everywhere I go. Oftentimes I get stuck in traffic and squeeze a few pages in. If I take my son to the dentist, I just sit there and read and don't complain how long it's taking. We like to attend a few professional baseball games every year. We always get there ahead of time so our son will have a chance to catch a few balls from batting practice. I just sit there and read a book, enjoying every minute of that extra time to read. Don't waste your life away just sitting places. Don't allow your mind to wander aimlessly without filling it with some type of resource. I feel that most people's busy-ness is not actually busy-ness, but instead is "catch up" from lack of proper planning. They don't plan things to happen, but instead just respond to the happening of things. I once heard a preacher say that if you fail to plan, you plan to fail, and that stuck with me all these days. If you call me on the telephone and ask me; "What are you doing?" You will never hear me say,

"Nothing." I'm always doing something. Don't get me wrong - I don't think that just because your busy, you'll be successful, but I do know that if you aren't busy, you surely won't.

Daily Verse: "Seest thou a man diligent in his business? He shall stand before kings; he shall not stand before mean men."

Proverbs 22:29

FEAR OF COUNTERFEITS

Today, with modern technology, counterfeiting has become quite an art. My wife and I the other day were noticing just how beautiful our money is becoming with all the different features and colors added to try and thwart the counterfeiter's efforts. Also the gem industry has been hit hard by various counterfeiters who are very good at what they are doing. They smoke stones to make them look more valuable than they really are. They have learned how to add colors, oils, and chemicals to stones to make them look like the real thing. Experts advise buyers of precious stones to have any stone examined by a professional before making any major purchase just to assure that the stone is the genuine article. Anything that is valuable will be counterfeited. This is why Satan has created counterfeit religions in the world, to try to fool people into thinking they have an original when really all they possess is a copy. Bank tellers are taught to tell counterfeit money from the real money by handling only real money. They never touch counterfeit money. As they handle the thousands of real bills, as soon as a fake bill comes into their hands, immediately they know something is wrong. It just doesn't feel right to them. Then as they look at what is in their hand they can tell it is a fake. This is how we tell the counterfeits of Christianity today. We will surely never fall victim of a heretic if we will make our Bible our guide. Stop believing everything that preachers tell you, and be as the Bereans that Paul praised for being students of God's Word. These people would go to church, and hear a great sermon from the pastor, then go home and research what the pastor taught, to see if their spirit would bear witness with the teaching. This would assure them that they would never fall into heresy. There are those false teachers who prey on the fact that people don't read the Bible for themselves. If you are to stand against all the counterfeits that are coming against you today, you are going to have to make a commitment to become a student of God's Word. His truth will always bear witness to our spirit if we have the Holy Spirit living inside us. Although I believe in the whole Bible rightly divided, which means that I still believe that all God's spiritual gifts are in operation for this very hour in which we live.

I was in a service once where the preacher was teaching about the value of having the Holy Spirit in your life. People were agreeing with him wholeheartedly, then he went into heresy. He said that if you don't speak in tongues you're not saved. It was like someone threw a bucket of cold water on the congregation. Most of the mature believers were praying that the false doctrine this man was saying would not take root in anyone's life. I happen to believe in speaking in tongues, but not as an element of salvation. The Bible says we are saved by grace through faith alone; faith in the shed blood of God's Passover Lamb, Jesus Christ. Please study the truth to assure you that you won't be fooled by the counterfeits. I once thought that if I studied everything about the cults I would be able to distinguish them easier, and God told me to study His Word and then I would recognize a cult when I saw one.

Daily Verse: "Study to shew thyself approved unto God, a workman that needeth not to be ashamed, rightly dividing the word of truth."

II Timothy 2:15

FEAR OF NOISE

Noise is a serious problem in America and noise pollution is getting worse everyday. In the last decade alone noise levels have increased six-fold in most of the major cities of our land. According to the US Census Bureau, it is the number one complaint people have about their neighborhoods. It's even the top reason given for moving around from residence to residence. Reports show that 50% of our population changes residences every five years, and noise is the top reason.

Health educators say that excessive noise levels can cause serious health issues ranging from sleep disturbances to elevations in blood pressure, to gastrointestinal problems. Noise pollution, as it is called, is even responsible for many mental health issues like anger, tension, and just plain frustration with life in general. Doctors say that anything over 85 decibels is considered potentially harmful. This is most disturbing since even a common household blow- dryer pumps out 90 decibels. If we want to assure that we don't suffer from hearing loss at an early age we must make sure that we wear ear-plugs anytime we attend anything like car or motorcycle racing, concerts, or do anything noisy, from operating a lawnmower to a leaf blower. These things all put out potentially harmful decibels of sound.

Anti-noise activists are trying to get a message out loud and clear; turn down, the bass-bumping, heart thumping car stereos that young people have playing in their cars these days. Their argument is a valid one in that it puts our cities at risk from terrorist's attacks, since these noise-making car stereos rumble and shake the ground much like a bomb going off next door. People inside their houses, have rushed outside to see what is exploding only to see some young person riding down the street destroying his or her hearing.

Cities like New York City have begun to implement laws and programs like "Operation Silent Night" that measures the sound of excessive noise from five of its boroughs. Officers use meters to measure the volume coming from cars and tow them at the owners' expense if they violate the law. In the first two months of existence they issued over 624 noise citations.

As far as God's word is concerned - the only "acceptable" noise is the sound God's people make while praising Him from His Holy temple. In the book of Nehemiah it's recorded that the people shouted so loud in their worship of Jehovah that it could be heard in the neighboring city. What few people understand about God is that most of the time He speaks with a still small voice, and if we have too much noise around us we will surely miss His instruction.

Daily Verse: "For thus saith the Lord God, the Holy One of Israel; In returning and rest shall ye be saved; in quietness and in confidence shall be your strength."

Isaiah 30:15

FEAR OF TECHNOLOGY

There's a growing number of people who have developed "technophobia," the fear of the information age in which we live today. You can't hide your head in the sand any longer. The industrial age is passed, and so has the agricultural age. Today people are investing all their money in the information industry and by-products. Computers and technology have added so much to our lives. You no longer have to leave your house to do anything. You can go from High School to College and never once set foot in a real classroom.

According to a survey done by the Dell Computer Corporation, 55% of the nations population harbor some form of fear of the technologies being produced these days. One-third of these people break out in cold sweats and suffer from a nauseating stomach at the thought of sitting in front of a computer.

The fear of technology dates back far into the past. As early as 1801 many men committed sabotage on factories to prevent the modernization of companies. They feared if these companies were allowed to modernize, their jobs were in jeopardy; they could be replaced with machines. For the most part, their fears have come true. The computer has become the inevitable evil. They completely run the world today, increasing in advancement every day. Employers have found that the best thing about them is that they demand no pay raises and never go on strike for being worked too hard. Computers have revolutionized the future of employment. But before you worry about being replaced by a machine, think about what life was like before all the advancement we now enjoy. My son is always telling me about how he wants all these old cars to fix up and drive. I tell him, "You can have them!" You see, I remember having to ride around in those old buckets of junk with seats that hurt your back from being too hard, dash boards that were pure metal and the slightest bit of braking would send your face crashing into it. They had windows that leaked air in the winter and froze you half to death in the front seat, let alone those poor freezing "popsicle" kids in the backseat, of which I was one in those days. Yes, give me my nice comfortable 2004 vehicle any day and I don't care what model or make - they're all better than the cars of the old days.

Think for a moment how technology has paved new pathways for our lives. Now we have refrigeration, and indoor plumbing (YEA!); alarm clocks to wake us up, and cars to comfortably get us speedily to where we're going. If we want to travel overseas it doesn't have to take months, its just a few short hours. Today we can eat breakfast in Miami, Florida, lunch in Columbus, Ohio, and dinner in San Francisco, California, all in the same day because of technology. No, we need not fear the advancements that mankind is making, for God is the author of all human advancement. Rest assured that no matter what man attempts, God is still watching over what man is up to, like he did in Genesis 11. He stopped the building of the tower of Babel because man wasn't ready in those days for that type of advancement.

Daily Verse: "But thou, O Daniel, shut up the words, and seal the book, even to the time of the end; many shall run to fro, and knowledge shall be increased."

Daniel 12:4

FEAR OF BEING ROBBED

Gone are the days when people leave their doors unlocked at night as they sleep. Today we very routinely lock our doors, turn on the alarm systems, and make sure all the motion activated spotlights outside of our homes are working properly. Many buy thief insurance against unwanted break ins, and join forces in neighborhood watch programs to assure that their children will be looked after as they are in transit to and from their daily activities. All of us take some form of precautions to assure that our home will not be broken into. I've even heard of people who were too afraid to go on much needed vacations because of the fear of being robbed. There is a fear about what we may lose materially if we are robbed in the physical sense. But what about the robbery that may be taking place in a spiritual realm? Many of us are robbed daily without the slightest hint that it is taking place. This villain's name? His name is "distraction," and he is far more wary than any natural criminal. His subtle craftiness is so much a part of our daily life that many don't even recognize how much time he has stolen. He comes in the form of idle talk, and frivolous reading material. Television and video games can be used to rob you of your very soul, if left unchecked. Young people can sit for hours upon hours living their entire lives just trying to defeat some imaginary dragon and release a queen. I once heard an advertisement from one of the most popular video game producers which stated that their product was one of America's biggest "wasters of time." Of course they were trying to promote it in a positive light, but the fact is, it is the biggest waste of time and creativity. Today "distraction" can attach itself to a person transforming them into a news addict or a sports junkie. Some are easily distracted by their careers; others have this chronic fitness fetish, and they become totally preoccupied by what they look like or what they eat. All these distractions and others are the main cause for the wandering minds we encounter when we try to unite our self with God in prayer. As soon as we bow our head and mention the name of God we instantly remember the grocery list, or that we have to stop at the butcher on the way home. Suddenly, thoughts of the day begin to flood our minds until most people just give up, and get started without finishing the morning's devotions. I once heard a man say that every time the enemy would put a distraction in his mind while he prayed he would just thank the enemy, and write down the chore that had to be done as soon as he was finished with his devotions. He said he used the devil as his daily planner, until one day he noticed that distraction wasn't coming during his prayer time anymore.

If you are one of those who are constantly being robbed by distractions rest assured that you are not alone in this fight. Instead of fretting over the matter, determine in your mind now to defeat this subtle foe. Pray to God aloud and keep your mind in His Word during your devotions. Turn on praise and worship music that inspires you during your quiet reflections. Contemplate what your life would be like if you got to the end of it, and heard the master say; "Depart from me I never knew you." Samuel Johnson once said, "The prospect of death, has a way of concentrating the mind."

Daily Verse: "Faithful are the wounds of a friend; but the kisses of the enemy are deceitful."

Proverbs 27:6

FEAR OF DISAPPROVAL

At times people feel like they are stalled because of other people's opinions. Some may feel that the objections are valid and that they lack the sufficient resources to make their dreams come true. You must not abandon your dream because of others, but instead find a way around the barriers their objections have erected against you. The biggest cause of the fear of disapproval is the feeling that everyone must like you. Please listen, you will waste countless hours and days of your life if you try to please everyone. Jesus, the Son of God, couldn't perform that task and He was the greatest miracle-worker to ever walk the planet. Jesus understood that most of the people who disapproved of Him, or his mission, were insignificant to Him fulfilling God's will. So He didn't fret over their disapproval, but instead just calmly prayed for them. Such should be our example to follow when we face opposition head-on against what we know to be God's will for us. Jesus developed a support team to aid Him in times of trouble, until God was able to under gird him with His strength. We see Him seeking the affirmation of who He was in Matthew 16 when He asked, "Who do you say I am?" The affirmation came when Peter jumped up and said; "Thou art the Christ, the Son of the living God." This was all the support Jesus needed to build on. Finally, He was getting the message across to his hardheaded disciples. He was about to be rejected by the very people that he had just spent the last three and half years helping, yet, He knew He was the Christ. I used to think that Jesus had His whole life's story recorded just for us. But sometimes I think maybe He received satisfaction from knowing that He would help so many people in His short ministry on earth. John goes on to tell us that the world couldn't hold the books of all the people Jesus helped in those short three and a half years. It's like all the little notes I have that little children have given to me over the years as we are leaving church. Nothing blesses a pastor's heart anymore than a little picture of Jesus on the cross that some little child has drawn especially for you during your sermon. I once had a young girl bring me a picture of a birthday cake that she had drawn at home and colored for my birthday. Every now and then I still get those things out of the file so I can remember why I do the work of the ministry. I look at all the notes of people that have written to thank me for my help, and remember why I am a preacher of the gospel. Yes, I know in my heart that the Bible is a book of remembrance for God.

Daily Verse: "For he that is in these things serveth Christ is acceptable to God, and approved of men."

Romans 14:18

FEAR OF SUCCESS

The fear of success is one of the sneakiest, biggest obstacles to reaching our goals. Have you ever stopped to think about what you would do if you did get want you wanted in life? Many people, if God would ask them what they wanted him to do for them, they wouldn't have the foggiest idea. It's interesting to note that God is only able to grant you what you know you want. Once when Jesus was entering Jericho, a blind man pleaded for His attention. The crowd told him to shut up and not bother the Master. But the blind man knew what he wanted, so he pleaded all that much louder. Finally he was called out and received an audience with Jesus. The blind man jumped to his feet, threw his begging robe aside, and went to Jesus. When he stood in front of Jesus, listen to Jesus' question; "What do you want me to do for you?" Immediately, the blind man replied; "Lord that I might receive my sight." Now think for a moment, do you really believe that Jesus didn't know the guy was blind? Of course, He knew, but wanted to know if the man knew what he wanted. And because the man had a clear picture in his mind of what he wanted, Jesus was able to give it to him.

Sometimes people get so close to accomplishing what they want in life, then they make some mistake that will set them back in accomplishing their goal. It seems they possess some self destructive attitude that keeps them just arms length from the brass ring. When we get stuck in life we have to ask ourselves the question, "What will my life be like if I don't succeed?" Some people unconsciously trip themselves up by not identifying correctly the childhood beliefs that our parents have instilled in us. Maybe a parent called you stupid, and told you repeatedly that you would never amount to anything in life. This in turn becomes imbedded in your subconscious mind, and later returns to haunt you with feelings of inferiority and a poor self image. Maybe you grew up with an absentee father (away on business trips, perhaps) and subconsciously you feel that if you're successful, you'll become like your father, spending long periods away from your family. This could indirectly affect your ability to become a success. Whatever your problem may be, you must identify it, and take measures to offset its hindrance. Take the time to identify the assumptions that may be hindering your thinking. God's purpose for you is t hat you are successful in whatever endeavor to which you feel called. Five times in the Joshua 1 God gives us the principles that we need to be a success for Him. He tells us to be strong and courageous. It takes guts to be a success in life, so allow God to work through you, and He will guarantee your success.

Daily Verse: "This book of the law shall not depart out of thy mouth; but thou shalt meditate therein day and night, that thou mayest observe to do according to all that was written therein; for THEN thou shalt make thy way prosperous, and then thou shalt have good success."

Joshua 1:8

FEAR OF STOLEN IDENTITY

Who would have thought that one of the greatest crimes of the 21st century would be "identity theft." Identity theft most often occurs when someone steals the credit information from another and uses it to purchase items. Most people in this world we live in don't even know who they are themselves, yet alone someone else impersonating them. These identity thieves have been aided in their plot by the recent advancements in computer technology. Experts believe that unless this problem is eradicated soon, it will put the hurt to online purchases. There is another thief robbing people of their identities - ourselves. Many change their identities to become someone else, either because of the opinions of others or because they are just afraid they would not be accepted for who they are. Have you ever heard of Billy Tipton? He was a fabulous pianist and saxophonist who began way back in the 1930's when the big bands were the hit thing. Friends that knew him always considered him to be a little weird, maybe even a little eccentric. He wouldn't play and swim with his adopted sons, or go to the doctor even when he was deathly sick. Finally, at age 74, Billy died and the whole world found out why he was so different. When the funeral director was doing his preparations for burial he found out that Billy was really a woman. He had lived his entire life in a lie because of the sexism that existed when he began in the music industry. During the big band era women were not accepted as musicians, so Billy decided to become a man. For over a half a century he lost his identity for fear of what people would think of him. Then there's the story of John Griffin, a man who gave up his identity to understand the suffering of others. During the late 50's John used sun lamps, medication and various plant stains to darken his skin so he could live among the black man of the south and understand them better. During his journeys in the south he was humiliated and looked down upon by his fellow white man. He learned of the tremendous suffering the African-American has had to endure just because of a difference in skin color. Later he revealed his findings in a book, Black Like Me, that helped bridge the segregation gap. When I think of what John did for the black man I'm reminded of what Jesus Christ did for all mankind. He laid down His heavenly identity and took up the identity of a servant; so we would know that God understands what it is like to be human, and be tempted, and tricked by the enemy. He found out what even the lowliest of mankind know; what it is like to be rejected and despised for who you are. He was no stranger to human pain either, for He endured the pain of a slave's beating before He had large spikes driven through His hands and feet. The next time you sing the song," To Be Like Jesus," make sure you count the cost of the words before you say them.

Daily Verse: "I am crucified with Christ; nevertheless I live; yet not I, but Christ liveth in me; and the life which I now live in the flesh I live by the faith of the son of God, who loved me, and gave himself for me."

Galatians 2:20

FEAR OF HOSTILITY

Have you ever heard of the, "hostility index?" It's a method that uses questions to rate how hostile a particular city's residents are becoming. When the index was created, Philadelphia, Chicago, New York, Cleveland, and Detroit were among the top five most hostile cities in the nation. The interesting thing about these cities is that they also have a higher death rate than other cities. This just goes to prove what the Bible warns us against; that anger, if left unchecked, has the power to kill its victims. Look at how Paul instructs the Ephesians church in Ephesians 4:26, "Be ye angry, and sin not; let not the sun go down upon your wrath." He understood what medical researchers are just finding out; that more than 50% of all sicknesses we are encountering these days can be traced to anger; people harboring a grudge against someone. Unforgiveness has been allowed to take root to the point where it is producing bitterness and people begin to suffer physically as a result of their sins.

In Matthew 18:21–35 there is the story of a man who was forgiven a great debt, one of which he could work his entire life without being able to pay. He begged for the master's forgiveness, and the master, being the compassionate man that he was, readily forgave him of the entire debt. That man then went back to his normal life, relieved of the pressure; the debt was no longer hanging over his head. Soon he bumped into a friend of his that owed him a few bucks. He demanded that the man give him his money. The original debtor did not see that his friend was as he once was - in debt without a means to pay it. The friend pleaded for time and promised the debt would be paid in full. But the forgiven man was not as compassionate as his master. He grabbed the man by the neck and demanded to be paid immediately, and when the man couldn't pay, he had him thrown into a debtor's prison. Now off in the distance were two servants of the master watching the whole ordeal. They quickly reported the actions of the forgiven man to the master, and the master immediately was angry with the forgiven servant and demanded that he be brought to him at once. When the forgiven servant was standing before the master once again, the master expressed his disgust over the servant's lack of compassion toward a fellow servant. Listen to what the master said to him in verses 33&34; "Shouldest not thou also have had compassion on thy fellow servant, even as I had pity on thee? And the lord was wroth, and delivered him to the tormentors, till he should pay all that was due unto him." Now read this solemn warning from Jesus in verse 35; "So likewise shall my heavenly Father do also unto you, if ye from your hearts forgive not every one his brother their trespasses." Wow, that will make you think, won't it? People are being delivered to the "tormentors" because of all the unruly anger they possess against their fellow man. With this in mind, can you really afford to have one hostile day toward someone else? Please forgive them today.

Daily Verse: "But I say unto you, that whosoever is angry with

his brother without cause shall be in danger of the judge-
ment. . ."

Matthew 5:22a

FEAR OF FAMILIARITY

We must be very cautious as not to give this fear, the fear of familiarity, much room in our lives. This fear has the power to take incredible things, and make them seem as though they are not that special. Tourist guides of awesome wonders like The Grand Canyon, and Yellowstone National Park where "Old Faithful," the famous nature-born geyser resides, soon tire of these wonders because of familiarity. There's an old saying that says "familiarity breeds contempt," and I have experienced first-hand, the meaning of that saying in respect to the people who live with me daily in the same house. We tend to take the ones we love for granted because of familiarity. Also familiarity causes us to sometimes take God's presence for granted, which can be very dangerous to your health. Scriptures tell a story about David, the King of Israel who wanted to restore the Ark of God back to Jerusalem. It had been in the home of Abinidab for over twenty years. Abinidab had two sons named Ahio and Uzzah. I can only imagine that these two boys grew up around the Ark probably playing hide and seek behind it. You see the Ark was only a box. It was only the representation of God's glory, and not God's glory itself. God didn't sit in that box for over twenty years waiting for someone to rescue Him. But as soon as David decided to do something about the Ark, it once again got God's attention. So those incharge of transporting the Ark did as the Philistines had done, and placed the Ark on a new cart to begin the journey back to Jerusalem. Ahio, led the way, and Uzzah, brought up the rear. Everything was going just fine until they got to the place of Nachon's threshing floor and the ox pulling the cart stumbled, and Uzzah reached his hand out to steady the ark. Suddenly, God struck him dead right there on the spot. The Bible says that David was upset with the Lord because he killed Uzzah, even to the point that he became afraid of God that day. You see the sacred Ark had become common to Uzzah because it had been in his house so long. He thought nothing of disobeying the commandment of God, (the Ark was not to be touched by human hands). This is why the ark had long poles running along side it, so man would not have to touch it as it was being carried. Today, I believe many Christians are like Uzzah; they have become so familiar with God that He is more like a friend or a brother to them instead of a God. People let's not lose our holy fear of God because we have become familiar with His ways. As soon as you feel you have God figured out, He'll change the playing field until you don't understand the game anymore. Make a commitment today to never take His presence for granted.

  Daily Verse: "Yea mine own familiar friend, in whom I trusted, which did eat of my bread, hath lifted up his heel against me."

Psalm 41:9

FEAR OF EXORCISM

   Hollywood in all its glamour, whether intentional or not, has shaped peoples' opinions of demon possession. Movies with heads spinning in circles and spitting green vomit have caused many to just dismiss reports of demonic activity as the work of an overactive imagination. But friend, listen to me; today demonic activity in humans is a very real thing. I go as far as to say if someone doesn't have the Spirit of God living in their spirit, then they likely have a demonic spirit in residence. Jesus told us that there was no middle road, no home base where we could hide and sort things out. If you're not with Him, then you're against Him, and we know who the "commander" of the army of the enemy is. But, what about this thing called "demon possession?" Can demons actually possess the life of a human being? I personally believe that demon control is perhaps one of the greatest areas of misunderstanding in the church today. First, and foremost, let's get one thing straight from the start - even though we use the term "possession," that doesn't mean that the demon can own anything or anyone. God owns every human life, and He's not ready to give up that position. Yet, when a demon enters a person's spirit their strong influence controls the person. If the person has the Holy Spirit living in their spirit then the demon's influence is very minimal, although the demon can still vex the soul of a Christian. This is why the Bible tells us we must "resist the devil," after we have submitted to God. The Holy Spirit is always a perfect gentleman and never forces His will on any of us, so we must willfully decide to submit to the Lordship of Jesus Christ, and actively engage in a warfare against the devil's influence. When we choose to deny sin and self, and obey the teaching of God's Word, then we are minimizing the influence that demon spirits can have over us. Many Christians who attend church every week need to be delivered from the influence of demons. Some of these people even appear to be possessed. They have allowed the enemy to work for so long in their souls without renewing their soul with the Word of God, that now he has a stronghold in their mind that must be tore down before they can ever hope to progress in their walk with God. Although Christ still lives in their spirit, demons have control of their souls and these demons are relentless; doing to these poor people the same things that they do to unbelievers. When you feel the compulsive urge to be hostile toward someone, resist. Don't allow resentment or animosity toward someone to persist, but instead resist. Resist any driving forces like hatred, jealousy, envy, criticism, backbiting, bitterness, negativism, pride, lying, or any form of sin that has pain as a consequence. In severe cases, you may have to have other believers help you get free by having them bind together to break the power of the enemies influence over your life through intercessory prayer. I caution you though, that just because you may manifest some of the symptoms of demonic oppression, that doesn't necessarily mean a demon is at work. Allow the Holy Spirit to help you discern.

Daily Verse: "For ye are bought with a price; therefore glorify God in your body, and in spirit, which are God's." I
Corinthians 6:20

FEAR OF CONSEQUENCES

Back in the late 1930's the story is told of a London, Texas School Board that tried to cut the cost of their winter heating bills by having a local oil company supply them with natural gas, which is a by product of petroleum production, free of charge. The oil company siphoned the gas to their furnace free of charge. The school board was excited about the savings that is until March 18, 1937, when a pocket of gas that had accumulated in the basement of the school ignited, killing almost three hundred people, most of whom were small children. Since that dreaded event, gas companies have had to put an odorant in the natural gas that they produce, so we can tell if we have a leak anywhere, by its very distinct smell. Even though natural gas is odorless and seems harmless, it is very dangerous, and must be respected or you will pay the consequences. In the same way that the London, Texas School Board tried to cut corners, many today try to cut corners in their Christian walk with God. They ignore the still, small voice of the Holy Spirit when He speaks to them about something of which He wants them to have no part. They do not heed the warning, and then must live with the consequences. Many feel as though their walk with God has become stagnant, wondering if He's even still around anymore. It's like the couple when they were first married, and the wife used to ride right beside her husband in the seat, getting as close to him as possible without interfering with his driving. But as time goes on, and the marriage progresses, she slowly finds her way to the other side of the vehicle with her head against the passenger side window wondering why they aren't close anymore. Lady, the driver hasn't moved. He's still sitting in the same place he was when you first got married. It's you who have scooted away from him. Many are living with the consequences of not having any time to spend with the Master outside of Sunday services. They have made the pursuit of material "stuff" their goal in life, and now they have to spend all their waking hours trying to pay for it. Please understand today that every shortcut you pursue has a consequence. The fear of consequence is a good fear, in place to remind us that God has a stated set of principles to live by, so when we break any of those principles, we will pay the consequences. Did you ever notice that He calls them the Ten Commandments and not the ten suggestions.

Daily Verse: "Pray for us; for we trust we have a good conscience, in all things willing to live honestly."
Hebrews 13:18

FEAR OF SHAME

"Looking unto Jesus, the author and finisher of our faith; who for the joy that was set before him endured the cross, despising the shame and is set down at the right hand of the throne of God" (Hebrews 12:2). I think no other example of shame is more appropriate than to remember what Christ did on the cross for us. Many see him hanging there bleeding with only a loin cloth wrapped around his body. The cross as cruel as it was by itself, was primarily an instrument of shame. Its victims hung stark naked for the onlookers to see; completely exposed. We have cleaned up the act of the crucifixion by dressing our Jesus in a loin cloth in our productions of the event, but that wasn't the case on that day. Jesus hung completely exposed for the whole world to look at. And today He is still an open book to be read by all men. That day in all His shame, Jesus stretched out his arms wide and showed us how much he loved us.

Many today live with heart wrenching guilt and shame over past activities, failures, or mistakes. Child of God, give them to Christ today and fear no more. Not only is He the Lamb of God for all our sins, but He is also the "author and finisher of our faith." He wrote the book on faith and knows how to deliver His children from the taunting of the enemy if they will allow Him to do so. He took all our shame with him on the cross. We no longer have to live our lives worrying whether any-one will find out about our past, for we no longer have one. We live by now faith, and that is in the present, not the past, or the future. What do you need from God now? He desires to give it to you, now. Shame need not be a fear any longer - for Jesus the Son of God despised our shame and bore it all for us.

Daily Verse: "For the scripture saith; Whosoever believeth in him shall not be ashamed."

Romans 10:11

FEAR OF REVENGE

Whoever said "revenge is sweet," never ate much of it for dessert. Revenge is simply the vengeful act of inflicting harm in return for a wrong that has been done to you. Webster calls it a "desire to take vengeance." Many people who have been wronged, lick their wounds with the thought of how they will take vengeance on the one who has wronged them. Their lips smack continually to others about something that may have happened years ago. Every time they see the "guilty as charged" on the street, they replay over and over again in their mind, the judgment they would impute on them if given half a chance. Once again the pain returns as they show a rerun of the full feature film star-ring them as the wrongfully accused. Their mind is filled with the words justice, truth, and conviction. The people on the Island of Malta wit-nessed Paul's encounter with the deadly viper as it wrapped itself around the convicted criminal's wrist, and then bit him with deadly fangs. They secretly hoped that Paul would suffer, and that "justice would finally be served." Friend, if you entertain these thoughts in your heart you're in for a huge "let down." I know we can't help it when peo-ple come against us to hurt us, but we can control how we respond to their attacks. The Apostle Paul, who was certainly not a stranger to per-secution, wrote these words in Romans 12: "Recompense to no man evil for evil. Provide things honest in the sight of all men. If it be pos-sible, as much as lieth in you, live peaceably with all men. Dearly beloved, avenge not yourselves, but rather give place unto wrath: for it is written, Vengeance is mine; I will repay, saith the Lord." Paul was teaching us that if we take our own revenge, it will be limited to what we can do. But, if we allow for God's revenge, and let Him avenge us, it is limitless as to what He can do. Although you might be surprised how He sticks up for you. In verse twenty of the same chapter Paul goes on to say this about our part in taking revenge against those who hurt us. "Therefore if thine enemy hunger, feed him; if he thirst, give him drink; for in so doing thou shalt heap coals of fire on his head." There it is; if you're nice to someone who hurts you, God will burn his head off in hell? No, not exactly, although sometimes it's fun to entertain the idea, (Just kidding). Paul could teach this because he himself was a recipient of this type of behavior before he came to Christ. Stephen, the churches first recorded martyr, was being stoned to death for his witness of Christ to the Jews, and Paul was standing there watching the stoning take place as he held the clothes of the men who were stoning him to death. Paul with his own ears heard Stephen praying for him, and the others, as Stephen was dying from the stoning. "Coals of fire" were being heaped on his head that would eventually lead him to the saving grace of Jesus Christ. Later on, after his conversion, Paul writes that all the vengeful things done to him was only his reaping what he sowed before. Don't allow revenge to eat away at you until not much of you remains, but allow God to repay those who have sinned against you.

Daily Verse: "For we know him that hath said, Vengeance belongeth unto me, I will recompense, saith the Lord. . ."

Hebrews 10:30a

FEAR OF VIOLENCE

Violence can take many forms, from people threatening bodily harm, to just some pushing and shoving. Today we live among people who think nothing of destroying your car in your driveway because you may have cut them off in traffic unknowingly. Today we see violence in the workplace, the schools around our country, the grocery store, our government buildings, and of course on our television sets each night. Today, for some reason, the news media thinks that the negative side of life is more interesting than the positive side. So they resort to covering everything negative from sporting event brawls to wars. Quite frankly, the negative violence does nothing more than frighten our children. Little children today are being exposed to all the violence and, as a result, are feeling the same anxieties as adults.

Instead of worrying about getting caught taking a cookie out of the cookie jar, they worry about being shot or knifed at school. They worry about their houses being blown up by a terrorist attack. Anytime a classmate is mean to them they fear that it could end in a violent attack. Parent, it's time we restore, to our children, a sense of safety. Tell your kids that these acts by terrorists are rare, and people are out there right now guarding against any other attacks. Talk honestly about your feelings with your children; don't be afraid to tell them you don't know something if you don't know the answer. If you notice that your child does not want to sleep alone or has suddenly started wetting the bed at night, these could be signs that they are having some fear of violence. Ask your kids to tell you of any activity at school where they see someone behaving as a bully or talking of doing some act against the school. Teach them that as God's child, God has promised to keep us in His shadow, which means that He will be close by us all the time. I taught our children that each had their own guardian angel who would watch over them all the time, even when they were sleeping at night. Where did I get this from? Right from the Scriptures. Feel free to read today's daily verse often to your kids.

> *Daily Verse: "Take heed that ye despise not one of these little ones; for I say unto you, that in heaven their angels do always behold the face of my father which is in heaven."*
>
> *Matthew 18:10*

FEAR OF WISDOM

What is more valuable than a room full of riches? It's even more valuable than living a long life. In fact, it has more strength than even power and authority. Have you guessed what it is yet? That's right, it's Godly wisdom. One man in the Bible, by the name of Solomon, understood this principle and his life became filled with success. It's an interesting story of how one night as a young man he went to sleep, and God appeared to him and asked what he wanted. Wow, that's like every kids dream; you know, to meet the "one wish" genie. If you could have anything in the world what would it be? I'd like to think I would be as honorable as Solomon, but I can't really say for sure. Solomon asked for an "understanding heart" so that he could lead God's people correctly. He wanted God's wisdom to flow freely in his life. This request impressed God so much that since he didn't ask for selfish things for himself, God was going to give him his request, plus the things he didn't ask for; things like great riches. Solomon became the richest man who ever lived. Then, of course, if you're going to have all that money you need some time to spend it, so God gave him long life to enjoy all his wealth. God also promised that Solomon wouldn't have to worry about enemies trying to steal it so God gave him the life of his enemies as well. Solomon became the most famous, wisest King of Israel, all because he asked God for wisdom.

So just what is wisdom, you may be asking? Wisdom is simply

the ability to apply God's Word to your life. Knowledge takes in God's Word. Then wisdom gives out God's Word. When you begin to apply the knowledge of God's Word to your life, then wisdom will prosper every area of your life. Some who fear the wisdom of God would rather go to the "school of hard knocks" to gain their wisdom, which is fine, but the end result is much more painful. Yes, experience is one teacher you can use in your life, but God would rather you use His Word, and allow Him the privilege of guiding you around the obstacles placed in your path. Many people just depend on their own human wisdom for making decisions. This is very unfortunate, because the best guidance human wisdom has to offer is recollection, but Godly wisdom can give you revelation. Only God possesses all wisdom. Job found this out the hard way and finally said; "And he knoweth the place thereof, for he looketh to the ends of the earth, and seeth under the whole heaven . . . and unto man he said, Behold, the fear of the Lord, that is wisdom; and to depart from evil is understanding." When we begin to fear God, which is the sign that wisdom has come into our life. As we progress and learn more about God's Word, then apply it, wisdom becomes more prominent in us. Soon, the principles are a part of our everyday being; you can't separate 'you' from God's Word. As you begin to think, act and be as God's Word teaches, His wisdom will produce all things it promises. So please " . . . with all your getting, get wisdom."

Daily Verse: "Wisdom is the principal thing; therefore get wisdom: and with all your getting get understanding."

Proverbs 4:7

FEAR OF FAVORITISM

Many people fear that they will be passed up for a promotion, just because they aren't the bosses "favorite." Children are constantly worried that they aren't their parents' "favorite." Some even fear that God has "favorites" in this world, which according to Scripture is not so. He shows no partiality among His children. He's not like Jacob of old who made ten brothers jealous of Joseph by giving only Joseph a special coat of many colors. At one time, when I read that story, I used to say, "Come on guys, get over it, a dad bought a coat for his son." Then I found out what the coat represented and then understood the reason for the jealousy. Do you remember the story of the prodigal son, and how the lost son came home and the father went out to meet him? The first thing the father did was to give his wayward son his coat, or his best robe. In Jewish culture when a father wanted to honor his son, he would give him a coat or a robe of honor, possibly even one he wore himself at one time. This was a sign that the boy was in line for the inheritance. Usually it went to the firstborn, but since Jacob had such scoundrels for boys, he was bypassing all Jewish protocol and tradition, and making a public display over who his chosen pick to succeed him. This in turn, led to intense jealousy from Joseph's brothers, to the point where they were ready to kill him whether he deserved it or not. Favoritism can be a very dangerous thing if we allow it in our families. In the case of Jacob's sons, they did the unspeakable to their brother and sold him as a slave. Then they took the thing that made them most jealous, the robe and dipped it in animal blood, then pretended it was the blood of Joseph on the garment–a result of Joseph being torn to pieces by some vicious beast. This in turn sent Jacob, the father, into a pit of despair over the loss of his favorite son. Yes, favoritism can cause many heartbreaks in a family if left unchecked

Romans 2:11 says this about God; "For there is no respect of persons with God," which means everyone who comes before Him is on the same level. Whether you're rich or poor, smart or average, skinny or fat, black or white; it makes no difference to God. We're all equal in His eyes. You don't have to straighten out your life then come to God. He's not impressed by people who think they have it altogether. In truth, no man has all their "ducks in order" until they submit their life to God. So, if you've feared coming to God, worrying that you're going to be rejected, fear not, for He will always receive you."

Daily Verse: "To have respect of persons is not good: for a piece of bread that man will transgress."

Proverbs 28:21

FEAR OF CRIME

According to studies done on the fear of crime, over 30% of people surveyed said they were either "extremely worried" or "very worried" about crime in our world, as opposed to only 5% that were "not worried" at all. Almost everyone over the age of 18 has been a victim of some sort of crime; either a property theft, or a violent crime which caused long-lasting impact on how they view their everyday life. Some view taking safety measures against crime to be one of their assurances of a good quality of life. Statistically, people fear most having their home broken into, then second, they fear that their car may be stolen. In the surveys it seems that the elderly were more fearful of crime than younger people for obvious reasons; not being able to adequately defend themselves. An interesting thing to note is the more prosperous someone becomes in life, the less fearful they are of crime. Maybe it's because financially secure people tend to be more confident about life than the not so prosperous. Whichever, the crime problem can be solved in one easy step. Now don't get me wrong, I believe that crime is like the poor, it will be "with us always," but history has showed us that the more kids we get into Sunday school, the more the crime rate will go down. This isn't a survey, this is a fact. Studies of history have shown that in the early 1800's crime in England was running rampant. Violence was running its course without restraint. Then, in the late 1800's thru early 1900's something happened to the crime rate. It dropped off drastically as if by some magical force. What happened to cause such a dramatic decline the crime rate during this period? An increase in Sunday school attendance has been proved to be the cause. By the late 1800's more than 75% of England's children were enrolled in some form of Sunday school. This, in turn, changed the children's' character and fewer turned to crime, which resulted in the dropping rate. Friend, tougher gun laws are not the answer to crime. Stricter penalties are not what will keep someone from breaking into your house and stealing your valuables. The only way to prevent crime is to change the character of the criminal. When you take your kids to a good Sunday school you are teaching them something of value. You're instructing them that you believe in God's laws which teach that stealing is wrong. Begin when your children are young and raise them in the nurture and admonition of the Lord. This will assure you that when they are old, as the Bible promises, they will "not depart from it."

Daily Verse: "Let him that stole steal no more; but rather let him labour, working with his hands the thing which is good, that he may have to give to him that needeth."

Ephesians 4:28

FEAR OF COMPLAINING

There are a lot of seats in life that we may not choose for ourselves, but if we accept the fact that God has given each of us an assigned seat, it will make sitting in some of the more uncomfortable ones easier. Paul wrote to the Philippian church that he "thanked God" every time he thought of them. The interesting thing to note was that he wrote that letter from prison, and when he started the Philippian church, he and Silas were beaten and then thrown in jail. In fact, Paul's first converted church member was the warden who had ordered the beating.

I'm sure that if Paul could have had a choice, being severely beaten and incarcerated would not have been on the top of his list of "church planting" strategies. Yet, we never see him complaining about the happenings of his life. You see, Paul knew a very important principle about serving God. There's no such thing as happenstance in the life of a believer. Complaining about the circumstances of life is a waste of time. While Israel wandered in the wilderness, there was constant complaining. They never learned that complaining would not gain them favor with God. The more the Israelites complained, the worse things got. If they had learned to be content with whatever "seat God had assigned them," many would not have died in the wilderness. In the same way, most of us always have to be "right." We will argue and complain against people to get our point across. All this fussing only leaves our lives "stinking" in the nostrils of the world. Have you ever seen a picture of a grizzly bear? They are massive creatures; probably the most fierce animal in God's creation. Just one swipe from a huge massive paw will take a horse's head off before the rider can hit the ground. But do you know what animal the grizzly bear is afraid of? They are terrified of skunks. Just one bad experience with Mr. Skunk, and the bear will not go near one ever again, no matter how hungry they get. The skunk stinks so bad that the bear refuses to go around 'stinking like a skunk' for days after the battle. So it is with someone who must live with a "complainer." The continuous complaining gives off an "odor" so to speak, making it difficult for others to be around. Many people miss out on promotions in life, because they would rather moan about doing a job, instead of just getting the job done, and getting onto another project.

An army general once stated that when he looked to promote someone in rank he would gather the prospective candidates and give each a shovel. He then, took them behind the bunkhouse and ordered them to dig a trench. The instructions were to dig the trench just a few inches deep, several feet long and about three feet wide. The General would then select a place close by where he could watch the action take place. Several men would complain about the job. Others would try to figure out 'why' the general wanted the hole. But the man, or men, who got to work and dug the hole with no questions asked, were the ones that would be promoted. In the same way, God is looking for people who will get to work in His Kingdom, without questioning His motives; people who will get the job done no matter what obstacles get thrown in their path.

Daily Verse: "Let no corrupt communication proceed out of

your mouth, but that which is good to the use of edifying, that it
may minister grace to the hearers."

Ephesians 4:29

FEAR OF DISSENSION

The lists of the seven deadly sins are as follows; "These six things doth the Lord hate: yea, seven are an abomination unto him. A proud look, a lying tongue, and hands that shed innocent blood, an heart that deviseth wicked imaginations, feet that be swift in running to mischief, A false witness that speaketh lies, and he that soweth discord among the brethren" (Proverbs 6:16–19).

Listed in the list of the seven abominations is the "fear of dissension." Dissension is quite simply, disagreeing with someone to the point of argument. "Sowing discord" is when you bring others into the argument. There's nothing wrong with having a disagreement with someone. Each of us are uniquely made to add our own gifts and personalities to any project. But when the disagreement gets out of hand, and becomes a feud between the parties, people start taking sides to line up for battle, then the disagreement becomes "dissension." And if it is not nipped in the bud before a war breaks out between the guilty parties, it will spread like wildfire into full blown discord among the brethren. When it reaches this proportion, then God is greatly displeased to the point where He calls it an "abomination."

After being in the ministry for several years now, I feel that I know what the cause of most dissension is, aside from the obvious, which of course is the devil. I believe that the main problem is the "unbridled tongue." Scripture says; "A fool's lips enter into contention . . . a fool's lips is his destruction, and his lips are the snare for his soul. The words of a talebearer (gossip) are as wounds, and they go down into the innermost parts of the belly" (Proverbs 18:6–8). God gave us the power of words to build others up, however when we use this power to talk about the shortcomings and setbacks of others, we become known as "sowers of discord." If you want to change the way you see things, then stop talking about all the problems and failures in the lives of others, and start focusing on what you can do to be of assistance. Begin looking for creative ways to help people instead of cutting them down. If a friend loses their job don't talk about it, talk is cheap, instead do your best to encourage them, and look for creative ways to solve the problem. Remember every time you talk you're programming your mind and the mind of others around you. Begin today to control your mouth to only say positive things that will lead you into a life of love and not lack. There truly is a miracle in your mouth.

Daily Verse: "Death and life are in the power of the tongue."

Proverbs 18:21a

FEAR OF OBSTACLES

An obstacle is primarily anything that stands in your path of reaching a goal. Many people fear that an obstacle will be able stop them from becoming what they want to become in life. But the truth is the more challenges you face the more alive you become. All of us will, from time to time, encounter obstacles and problems in life. It's how you respond to those obstacles that determine whether your life is a success or failure. God had promised the children of Israel a Promised Land that flowed with milk and honey. All they had to do was successfully navigate for a few weeks through a wilderness until God told them to go in, and possess the land. Instead they let the obstacles look bigger than they were. They viewed the giants as impassable. The cities looked impregnable, and they even lost all self-esteem until they felt as small as a grasshopper.

God sets up some of the obstacles we face to give us stair-steps to success. You've been created by God to become involved in solving other's problems. Think for a moment, what one act did God use to elevate David in the ranks? In one day David went from tending a few dozen sheep in the middle of nowhere, to earning the right to marry the King's daughter. All because he solved a problem for the king, a giant problem you might say (Goliath). That's the way God works in our lives. When David woke up that particular morning everything was business as usual. That is until he arrived in Israel's camp and heard the giant, Goliath, tormenting Israel with words of blasphemy. David then said these words; "What shall be to the man that killeth this Philistine, and taketh away the reproach of Israel?" He was inquiring as to the reward offered for killing the giant. This is the way we should be, always on the lookout for challenges that may promote us. David killed the giant that day, solved Israel's problem, and became the Kings son-in-law shortly after. A successful man will never have a day that doesn't bring its own set of obstacles. Obstacles in your path have the ability to be spiritual flat tires or spiritual elevators, whichever depends on you. Sometimes obstacles tend to make you feel as though God has placed you on a shelf and forgotten about you. But instead He is very much aware of the difficulties of your life and is just waiting to see how you respond to them - to see if He can trust us with more responsibility. The more faithful we are with little things, like problems, the more He will give us to handle. So the next time an obstacle stands in your way, instead of complaining about it and giving up, thank God for it, for it may be a seed to a promotion.

Daily Verse: "These things I have spoken unto you, that in me you might have peace. In the world ye shall have tribulation: but be of good cheer; I have overcome the world."

John 16:33

FEAR OF PROTECTION

People today are masters of developing different types of protection. Our well-being is constantly being threatened these days. No one is safe from the threat of being in harms way. Nations of the world are spending billions in their defense budgets to assure that they will be safe in case of an attack. Even everyday people are coming up with ways to deter attackers. Once a group of sharpshooters surrounded a Rochester, New York automobile. The reason for the caution was that in the backseat of the car was a man armed with a rifle. Police attempted to reason with the man, but he was unwilling to negotiate. After hours of standoff the officers decided to storm the vehicle and attempt to overtake the man in the car. Subtly they overcame the car only to be completely surprised by what they found. The man that they had spent hours trying to reason with was really a mannequin that had been placed there by the owner. The owner had equipped the mannequin complete with a rifle and hat. When asked the reason for positioning the elaborate scarecrow, the owner replied that there had been too many carjackings in his neighborhood lately, and he figured that the mannequin would deter any would-be attackers. Yes, it's true that these are dangerous times in which we live, but God has promised that if we will abide in Him we will have nothing to fear. Psalm 91 claims; "He that dwelleth in the secret place of the most High, shall abide under the shadow of the Almighty. I will say of the Lord, He is my refuge and my fortress; my God; in him will I trust." This entire Psalm promises protection from about any kind of attack that the enemy can throw at you. This Psalm promises God's children will have habitation with Him with complete protection from enemy attack. It even assures you long life just because you set your love upon Him.

Daily Verse: "The name of the Lord is a strong tower; the righteous runneth into it, and is safe."

Proverbs 18:10

FEAR OF WITCHCRAFT

God has placed authority in our lives to help us and protect us. Any type of rebellion against God's delegated authority may be considered "witchcraft." Many think witchcraft is a bunch of silly women who dress up in capes and run around with pointed hats, casting spells on unwary victims. Nothing could be further from the truth. Today, witches are doctors, lawyers, and hosts of other professionals that are far from being "silly." The basic sin of witchcraft is simply a form of rebellion against the commandments of God. Look what I Samuel 15:23 have to say about the subject; "For rebellion is as the sin of witchcraft, and stubbornness is as iniquity and idolatry." This verse tells us that you don't have to ride a broom to be involved in witchcraft, all you have to do is "allow disobedience" to come into your life, and you are considered a practitioner of witchcraft. In the Old Testament the story is told of a prophet of God by the name of Balaam. One day an enemy of Israel wanted to pay the prophet to come and curse Israel. To shorten the story I'll say that after some arguing with God over whether he should go or not, God finally allowed Balaam to go, but God warned him that he was only to say whatever God put in his mouth to say. And just to let him know that He meant business, God placed an angel with a drawn sword ready to slay Balaam in his path. Now to protect him from the angel, God showed Balaam that he had power over all creation by allowing the donkey that Balaam was riding to see the angel. When the donkey saw that the angel was ready to slay his master, he fell to the ground and hurt Balaam's leg not once but twice. Balaam immediately became infuriated with the behavior of his donkey and proceeded to beat the animal, until God miraculously opened the donkey's mouth and allowed him to speak with human speech. Stunned, Balaam stopped punishing the beast and God finally opened Balaam's eyes and allowed him to see the angel there in his path. This put the "fear of God" in Balaam and he immediately decided against acting against Israel that day - no questions asked. So, when he arrived at where Israel was camped, he went to the top of the hill and began to bless Israel instead of curse them. Thus proving that you can't curse what God has blessed. If you're a born again Christian you have nothing to fear from a witch. They have no power over a born again believer. When they try to cast curses on

Christians, the curse will not rest on a believer's life. The Psalmist David said it this way in Psalm 64:2–4; "Hide me from the secret counsel of the wicked; from the insurrection of the workers of iniquity. Who whet their tongue like a sword, and bend their bows to shoot their arrows, even bitter words." As a matter of fact He promises that the arrows they shoot will come back at them; " . . . but God shall shoot at them with an arrow; suddenly shall they be wounded. So they shall make their own tongue to fall upon themselves: all that see them shall flee." In Psalm 57 David assures us with these words; "They (the wicked) have digged a pit before me, into the midst whereof they have fallen themselves." Let us be sure that we are not found being disobedient to God in anyway.

Daily Verse: "O foolish Galatians, who hath bewitched you, that you should not obey the truth . . ."

Galatians 3:1a

FEAR OF DEPRAVITY

Famous author Samuel Clemens, better know as Mark Twain, once said; "We are all a little like the moon, we have a dark side that we don't want anyone to see." Yes, the Bible affirms that statement when it talks about the heart of man. Jeremiah says in 17:9; "The heart is deceitful above all things, and desperately wicked: who can know it?" A human heart left unchecked will find depravity in all forms of life. The word 'deprave' according to Webster means to "be morally bad, or corrupt." More harmful than the explosive force of an atomic bomb is a human heart left to its own devices. Today depravity walks down the street with us unchecked, in the form of a young lady shamelessly exposing her body; or homosexuals are enjoying top billing on prime time television shows promoting their depraved lifestyle, or as they refer to it, an 'alternate' lifestyle. It is a lifestyle completely in opposition to the one that God created for us. Friend, God created Adam and Eve, not Adam and Steve. Throughout much of the '90's depravity left the closet, and was allowed to parade down our public streets under the guise of "freedom of speech." In today's world, the state that famous author Oscar Wilde found himself in is the same as many people alive today. Listen to what he said about his life as he found it one day; "My gods have given me almost everything my heart desired, But I let myself be lured into long spells of senseless and sensual ease . . . I ceased to be lord of myself. I was no longer the captain of my own soul, and did not know it. I allowed pleasure to dominate me. I ended in horrible disgrace." What a terrible state in which to find yourself. Yet I imagine that many would fit the description if they would only wake up. Satan has lulled the unbeliever into a constant euphoric state where they feel their entire life must revolve around pleasure. Today millions of people will stand in lines for hours for a sixty second thrill at an amusement park. Not that there's anything wrong with the ride, but it's the constant seeking of a thrill that worries me. How far will the human heart lead a person before they no longer reach satisfaction? Today we live with the everyday threat that our children could be taken from us and used to satisfy someone's sexually depravity. Oh, my how far we've fallen. Once a preacher stood on the street corner and cried out against the depravity of his community. A heckler approached him and

Said, "Preacher I just can't swallow all that stuff you just said about the depravity of man." The old seasoned street preacher, without a blink replied back; "That's all right - you don't have to swallow it; you already have it in you anyway." Each of us has the potential to do despicable things to our fellow man if Christ be removed from our hearts. So before you judge some depraved individual, remember what your life was like before Christ entered the scene.

Daily Verse: "Burning lips and a wicked heart are like a pot-sherd covered with silver dross."

Proverbs 26:23

FEAR OF SPIRITUAL BLINDNESS

Did you know that the military have a weapon that is capable of causing a person to go blind from up to two miles away? It's an import from China, that when you point it into your enemy's eyes and turn it on - it sends high-power laser impulses causing temporary blindness and rendering him useless in combat situations. In the same way, Satan, our enemy, has used several of his weapons to blind the eyes of many in God's army. II Corinthians 4:4 states; "In whom the god of this world hath blinded the minds of them which believe not, lest the light of the glorious gospel of Christ, who is the image of God, should shine on them." As you read this today, there are millions of people who belong in God's army, yet don't know it yet. They have allowed the enemy to shine the blinding laser of lust, greed, self, ambition, pride, and many other weapons of the flesh Satan has at his disposal, into their spiritual eyes. Instead of bowing a knee to Christ and joining God's army, they've believed a lie. That lie is the one that purports that we don't have to do anything to be accepted by God. This is one of the biggest secrets used by the enemy today against would be "God-chasers." Even some churches today are preaching that you need to try God, for He has a wonderful plan for your life; as if God is like a new pair of shoes that you can try on for size. Friend, the alternative for not having God in your life is Hell. Don't believe the lies of many who water down the gospel truth for the sake of getting another decision to add to their spiritual belt. The above Scripture claims that the person who is living their life without a meaningful relationship with Christ is blind; without spiritual sight. They wander aimlessly through this life, hoping that everything will turn out good for them someday. The truth is they will die and go to a devils Hell that they probably never believed in, in their natural life. Don't be spiritually blind any longer to the condition of your heart. Do you have a meaningful relationship with the Son of God? If not let this be the day for you; the day you decide to live the rest of your days for Him. I came to Christ when I was 28 years of age. One night a few months later the glory of the Holy Spirit came over me, as I was standing outside gazing up into the sky at all the beautiful stars in the sky. Quickly I remarked at how I had served the devil for the first 28 years of my life, and then tears of remorse began to fill my eyes. The tears ceased when I requested that the Lord give me at least 28 more good years to serve Him. That was over 17 years ago, and he's been true to his Word everyday since then. Each day of serving God is like a new springtime experience as He weaves things in and out of our lives. Please, if you don't understand what I'm saying, you are lost today and in need of a Savior. Ask him to come in and decide that this is going to be the beginning of a great journey together.

Daily Verse: "The Lord opened the eyes of the blind . . ."
Psalm 146: 8a

FEAR OF TRUSTING GOD

So many people think that the blessing of God depends on how hard they work Monday through Friday during the work week. But the truth is that the real blessing of God comes from how you respond on Sunday when the offering plate is passed. According to God's Word, what you put in the offering plate on Sunday determines how well He can bless you the rest of the week. We live in very trying times, yet God's Word never changes. It still says that the first ten percent of everything you own belongs to God. It not only belongs to Him, but according to Leviticus 27:30 it is holy; "And all the tithe of the land, whether of the seed of the land, or of the fruit of the tree, is the Lord's:

it is holy unto the Lord." Many people think that they can separate their secular life from their spiritual life. This just isn't true for a believer, because everything the believer does is ordered by the Lord, so in a sense, the believer doesn't have a secular life. God's Word commands us to get together as a family and worship him. The Christian church has chosen Sunday, the first day of the new week, to do this so let's understand this; how we treat God on Sunday determines how he can treat us the rest of the week. Many unknowing people mistreat God by robbing Him of the tithe on Sunday, and then they wonder why the rest of their week seems not to be blessed. If someone came into your house pretending to be your friend and robbed you, would you welcome them with open arms the next time? The sad fact is that some have become so accustomed to the lack of the Holy Spirit's presence that they don't even recognize that He's gone. Friend, if you're not a faithful tither for some reason or another, before you shut me off, read what God's Word has to say in the New Testament in Romans 2:22, "That thou sayest a man should not commit adultery, dost thou commit adultery? Thou abhor idols, dost thou commit sacrilege?" Now, I must admit, I didn't really understand this verse at first, mainly because I didn't understand what the word 'sacrilege' meant. But once I discovered what the word meant, then the verse came alive to me. The word 'sacrilege' means "to take away from, or rob the temple of God." At once the Holy Spirit brought to my remembrance the Old Testament verse in Malachi where it tells us about the only way a person can rob God. In fact, at the time of the writing the whole nation of Israel was committing 'sacrilege' against God, yet, asking Him to bless them. Read Malachi 3:8; "Will a man rob God? Yet ye have robbed me. But ye say, wherein have we robbed you? In tithes and offerings." God's Word declares if we withhold our tithes and offerings from God's house (church), we become what is known as a sacrilegious person that worships the idol of money. In Luke 16:13 Jesus declares; "No servant can serve two masters: for either he will hate the one, and love the other; or he will hold to the one, and despise the other. Ye cannot serve God and mammon." If we decide to hold to our money then we are telling God that we don't trust Him to provide for us, and that we don't believe His Word when He promises to provide for us. If this is you today, please repent, and make a brand new start, taking God at His Word.

Daily Verse: "Trust in the Lord, and do good; so shall thou dwell in the land, and verily thou shall be fed."

Psalm 37:3

FEAR OF COMPROMISE

If you are working hard for the Master, and Satan can't intimidate you or demoralize you or even discourage you for that matter, then Satan's next strategy will be to try to get you to compromise. Some well meaning, good people who became tired from the fight have given in to compromise. Compromise is a very tricky word. The world as a whole sees compromising as a good thing. It even has the ability to feel good at times. You give a little, and then they give a little, and it seems we can overcome all our differences with a little compromise. A lot of problems and difficulties can be solved with a little compromise to the point where we may be tempted to believe that all compromise is good. But the real truth is it is seldom wrong to compromise in matters of preference, however, it is always wrong to compromise in matters of principle. Just when you feel that you have the battle won, Satan will tempt you to compromise. Remember Paul wrote to the Corinthian church these words; "Let him who thinks he stands take heed lest he fall" (I Cor. 10:12). If we compromise with evil, it goes against everything that we say we believe. It's like we are volunteering to lose. We are willingly yielding to Satan our life that he was unable to gain otherwise by other tactics. Please don't give in to the pressures of the promise of peace. There's no peace in the fight against the enemy. There can never be a truce, because God will not allow it. Satan will offer you the world and many other incentives to get you to compromise what you believe, but be like Jesus, who withstood them all. Remember Satan offered Jesus all the kingdoms of the world, and tried to give him a vision for them by showing them all to him in a moment of time, but the price was too high. Jesus would have to compromise what He believed by bowing down and worshiping Satan.

We can also see the enemy's strategy at work against Nehemiah, the man God commissioned to rebuild the walls around Jerusalem. After repeated attacks from Sanballat who is a type of Satan in this story, listen to what Nehemiah says in Nehemiah 6:2, "That Sanballat and Geshem sent unto me, saying, come, let us meet together in some one of the villages in the plain of Ono." Nehemiah being the wise man that he was, wasn't about to stop his work on the wall to give in to temptation of forming a treaty. Look at what Nehemiah said in the rest of the verse: "But they thought to do me mischief." Good job, Nehemiah–he was very discerning, because they had planned to kill Nehemiah if they got half a chance. Now did Sanballat give up? Think for a moment - does the devil ever give up? Look at verse 4 of the same chapter; "Yet they sent unto me four times after this sort; and I answered them after the same manner." Four times Saballat tried to gain an audience with Nehemiah, but Nehemiah wasn't willing to compromise with his enemy. Why? Because there is no compromise between right and wrong. What fellowship has light with darkness? Friend, don't fear compromise - just don't make it a part of your life, stand strong like Nehemiah did and God will see you through.

Daily Verse: "Commit thy works unto the Lord, and thy thoughts shall be established."

Proverbs 16:3

FEAR OF LACK

Many people are in tight spots today living from paycheck to paycheck, and finding way more month for the money than money for the month. We truly are living in the days that the prophet Haggai of the Old Testament prophesied about, "You have sown much, and bring in little; ye eat, but ye have not enough, ye drink, but ye are not filled with drink; ye clothe you, but there is none warm; and he that earneth wages earneth wages to put in bags with holes" (Haggai 1:6). No matter how much you work or how much overtime you get, the ends don't seem to meet. We try to create a budget, so we can be more responsible, and then the car breaks down, or the washing machine goes on the 'fritz.' Or you get one of those nice letters that tells you that because of the recent natural disaster there has to be an increase in your homeowners insurance. "Oh, did I tell you your automobile insurance is going to increase also, about double of what it has been." Then, of course, there's the credit card companies that drive you crazy with a bombardment of mail trying to get you to use the credit card, and when you finally do use it to pay your $1500 car repair bill, they raise your rate about 8%. It seems that no matter what we do sometimes we have to pinch ever penny that we make. Most of the lack we are experiencing today is coming from America's spiritual disobedience against God. Yes, whether you want to believe it or not, we're under the judgment hand of God. As a nation we have turned our back on God, and if it were not for the church, and many intercessors, God would have already turned us into another Sodom and Gomorrah. Anytime a nation experiences extreme lack it's because God has removed His hand of blessing from it. That's why the scripture says; "Blessed is the nation whose God is the Lord," or shall I say, Jehovah. Today our nation is filled to the brim with false gods, and idols galore. Everywhere you turn there's a new Muslim temple or a Buddhist shrine.

False cults and religions are filling the airwaves with their teachings about eternal life to the point where today the God of the Bible is almost a 'has been' in America. For this reason she shall continue to suffer lack, going month to month depending on her false gods to provide.

Why don't you take a spiritual inventory today, and see if you're trusting God to the fullest? Are you doing what you can for God's church? Are you involved in a ministry for the Master? If not, why don't you pray and ask God for direction now. Then, whatever He says to you - do it. Most of the Christians' financial problems stem from trying to live beyond their means. If we would decide to live on what He provides we wouldn't have any money problems. Today why don't you ask God to help you bring glory to Him with your spending habits now?

Daily Verse: "He that giveth unto the poor shall not lack:"
Proverbs 28:27

FEAR OF PRESSURE

No matter how prepared you are in life, you're bound to see some days of pressure. That's just the way life is. Suddenly the boss will put an overload of work on you to get it done yesterday. Or you'll get so involved in one project that you put off another until you look at your schedule and find out that the put off project is due tomorrow. Finally, you find yourself wishing that you had more hours in a day to work. Or in my case, I've wished I had more energy just to complete what I already started. Most people, who work most of their life away, find that they may have enough money from the overtime, but they don't have any free time to spend it. When they do get spare moments they find themselves using it to do laundry, or the host of other household chores that have been severely neglected by their working all the time. One sure way that you can get everything done that you want to, is to make sure that you invite God into your daily routine. Spend the first part of your day with Him. It doesn't have to be long or boring, but it should be meaningful. Someone once asked me; "How long do you pray?" I always say, "As long as it takes." What I mean by that is, we should remain in prayer long enough to create a memory. Stay until you touch base with God. As soon as He shows up, then you can tackle the challenges of life without fear. One of the churches greatest intercessors of yesteryear,

E. M. Bounds, always said: "I've got so much to do today for God that I can't afford not to spend the first three hours of my day with him." He rose every morning at 3:00 A.M. and prayed until 6:00 A.M., just to get his instructions on what God wanted him to do for the day. Jesus often rose before the morning sun to go off to a solitary place to receive daily instructions from His Father. One interesting thing that I've noticed about Jesus is that He was never moved by the immediate. Or in other words, we never see him pressured by the crisis of the day like most of us. He didn't respond to the day, but instead planned His day. Even when friends came, and asked Him to come and see one of his dying friends, he didn't respond the way most of us would. Most good Christians would jump to their feet, and quickly rush off to see our friend in need. But instead Jesus kept doing what He always did, and then after three days had passed the friend is now dead. Can't you just see the disciples when Jesus says; "Come on guys, it's time to go see Lazarus. Oh, by the way he's dead now." Many said; "No don't go, the Jews are after you." But what they didn't know was that Jesus had been praying, and God had told Him to wait so that His followers could see Him work a miracle in the life of Lazarus. Listen to what Jesus said in the graveyard in John11:41–42, "Father I thank thee that thou hast heard me. And I knew that thou hearest me always: but because of the people which stand by I said it, that they may believe that thou hast sent me." He then went on to call Lazarus back from the dead. How's that for handling the pressures of life? Jesus knew that if He trusted God to smooth out His path, God would make a way to demonstrate His glory. Don't give into the pressures of life but instead set your priorities straight.

Daily Verse: "For we would not, brethren, have you ignorant of our trouble which came to us in Asia, that we were pressed out of measure, above strength, insomuch that we despaired even of life."

II Corinthians 1:8

FEAR OF DETERMINATION

When I read about the achievements of people who were determined to do something remarkable with their lives I am always amazed by the power of the human will. Once a French journalist by the name of Jean-Dominique Bauby suffered a severe stroke which left his body unable to move or speak. With his mind still intact, he developed through human ingenuity, a way to communicate with the only part of his body that was under his control. He could still blink his left eyelid. He trained his therapist to point to the letters of the alphabet for which he would blink twice for "yes" or once for "no." Through this incredible way of communicating he composed an entire book, entitled, "The Diving Suit and the Butterfly" which sold almost 150,000 copies its first week of publication. He was determined to get the book that was in him, out of him, and he was unwilling to let anything keep him from achieving his goals.

If you want to see your goals accomplished in life, you'll have to have the same determination. Oh, you may not have to talk with your eyelid, but you'll have your own set of obstacles to overcome. Most of us are like a wild stallion at approaching life. We run head on into it without any care as to what the outcome of our decisions will be. In the old west one of the ways used to calm a stallion down was to harness it up with a burro. At first the stallion would drag the burro all over the place. For days, maybe even weeks, the two would be gone. Then finally one day, coming in the horizon, you would see the little burro approaching the ranch leading the stallion along like a little calm puppy. The stallion would get exhausted from dragging around the burro, so he would submit to the burro's will. Instead of being known as the "master of the moment," why not decide today to be known as "committed to the cause?" God has uniquely gifted each of us, to work for him in His Kingdom, but so many of us want to make our own way in life. We want to live these dramatic lifestyles of fame and recognition. We want all the rewards, but we'll gladly give Him the credit, if he'll guarantee our success. We must become like Walter Payton, the most successful running back of all time. He accumulated over nine miles of rushing yardage in his lifetime career - getting knocked down about every 4.5 yards. Yes, we may take some falls but we must get back up, and persevere. Many of God's heroes listed in Hebrews 11, "Hall of Faith" got knocked down several times, yet the reason they are memorialized is because they were determined to accomplish God's plan for their lives. Let determination become a way of life for you by expecting the unexpected; then when things happen that surprise you, you are not knocked off balance. If you happen to get knocked off balance, just get back up!

Daily Verse: "For a just man falleth seven times, and riseth up again;"

Proverbs 24:16a

FEAR OF TEENAGERS

I'll be the first to admit that after raising six of them, teenagers are a challenge to live with. If you're a new parent of a teenager, you have entered a whole new world in child rearing. Between the ages of 10 and 16 a child's personality can go from a loving, affectionate, wholesome child to an irresponsible, moody, back-talking teenager in a matter of a couple months. Some of them want to be a child as long as they can, while at the same time they want the car keys to go to the store. It's like they want the best of both worlds–to be a kid, but a kid with adult privileges. To be fair to them, I think it's about as frustrating a time for them as it is to parents.

The problem with being a teen is that it is the age of exploration. They're naturally curious about the things of life, and this is where they get into the most trouble. Instead of applying their curiosity to school-work, and the things that are important to this season of life, they seek after thrills and dangers. This is why they can get involved with religious cults and other activities associated with the workings of the devil. Things like dangerous role playing games, and the mystical arts such as tarot carts, Ouija boards, hypnotism, ESP, black magic, and all kinds of occultism and, even Satanism, are very interesting to them. Most of the teens are lured into the pit by heavy metal rock groups that promote erratic behavior with the lyrics to their songs. Soon to follow are the application of drugs to bring out the best in them. They are taught that they really need these drugs to be able to fully enjoy what the music says. They feel a little pleasure, and are able to escape from the reality of life for awhile. Studies have shown that about 99% of all teens that are involved in "Satanism," began by first taking drugs to become part of the group.

This is where the "fear of teenagers" mostly takes affect. The kids get so high on some type of drug that they can no longer be managed by their parents, so the parents don't know what to do with them. Many just give up, and let the teen raise themselves - having a free run in life. These teens are out in the streets at all hours of the day. Some quit school, and join a gang so they can be a part of a family.

Mom, dad, today I'm holding you accountable, not by my word, but by God's Word. We are obligated by God's word to train our children up in the nurture and admonition of God's teachings. If we fail because of work, pleasure or whatever, it is still on us. If you want to begin being the parent you were supposed to be in the first place, remember that it is never too late, as long as they live in your house, but remember this one phrase. "Rules without relationship brings rebellion." What most lost teens are looking for is loving parents. Not their parent's money, but their parent's hearts. They want you to give them your love, and this is expressed by giving them your time. How do you know if you're spending enough time with your kids? Are they coming and asking you answers to problems or are they seeking answers elsewhere? If they want your opinion, then you have a relationship with them. Don't be blown away by what they tell you either. Just remain calm and keep your cool. Also remember just because the school has several activities - that doesn't mean your teen has to be involved in all of them. Do not allow other people, friends, organizations, activities steal your children from you. Don't allow someone else to make more of an impression on them than you. Don't let it happen.

Daily Verse: "For I know him, that he will command his children and his household after him, and they shall keep the way of the Lord."

Genesis 18:19

THE SPIRIT OF FEAR

Although all negative fears have a spirit behind them, this fear is the "fear of fears." This fear is responsible for creating all the other fears that plague mankind. Heart attacks, nightmares, doubts, and most all the other phobias and anxieties that come against us are caused by the spirit of fear. This strongman of fear is even quite capable of taking the effects of positive fears and turning them against us to magnify our horror. We can always tell that this fear is involved when we see our spiritual vitality being affected. When we begin to have more faith in what the devil tells us in our mind, than what God's Word tells us to accept by faith, then the spirit of fear is involved. This fear directly opposes all of God's laws of the Kingdom. Its first appearance in the Word of God is when the serpent appeared to Eve in the Garden. After the enemy caused the happy couple to sin, we see them hiding from God's presence. They feared that God would find out what they had done. Now don't get me wrong - it's natural for a sinner to fear being in God's presence, but that's not the way God wants it. The spirit of fear seeks to get us into disobedience to God so we become an easy target for temptation. He wants to get us out of perfect love with God, because he knows that "perfect love casts out all fear." Satan knows that if he can get you into fear, then he can get you out of faith. Remember what

Jesus said to the disciples who were tired of fighting the storm all night? They ran to wake Jesus and make Him aware of the situation. Jesus said, "Why are ye fearful, O ye of little faith." He wants to break the hedge, because He knows that after the hedge is broken down the serpent can strike. Remember when Satan approached God about tempting Job, he had legal access into Job's life because Job gave him a doorway through his own fear. Job 3:5 says; "For the thing that I greatly feared is come upon me, and that which I was afraid of is come unto me." Although God restricted his actions, Job's hedge had definitely been broken down by the spirit of fear. Friend, there is no place in the life of a believer to justify any type of negative fear.

Faith is in a marriage with the Word of God; a marriage that allows the Holy Spirit to operate freely in our lives. This produces the things that don't exist in the natural realm, but are in the embryonic state in God's mind. Remember that He is the God that calls "those things that are not as though they are." When the spirit of fear is allowed to operate, it clogs the pipes of God's blessings. So please, don't let the enemy hinder you but, instead focus on God, and His Word, and not on the thing that you may be frightened of. Recognize that this fear has to go and bind it right now with the power of prayer.

Daily Verse: "God hath not given us a spirit of fear; but of power, and of love, and of a sound mind."

II Timothy 1:7

FEAR OF MONEY

Money seems to be the favorite topic of people these days. Even when children are very young they learn that money is what makes the world go round. Money is a very important element of our existence. What amazes me the most about money is how most people handle it. Some treat life like they are playing a game of monopoly. And when it comes to money the sad thing is like the game of monopoly most of them lose. So if you live with the fear of money, either the lack of it, or the proper way to manage it, listen to what I have to say.

Money by itself is neither good nor bad. It is completely neutral and totally dependent on its user for a purpose. Money can be used to help enrich our life with good things, or it can be used to completely destroy our life with addictions, and bondage. Some people have the misconception that money is evil, and they think they have Scripture to support their belief. But the fact is the Bible says in Ecclesiastes 10:19, " . . . money answereth all things." The money I have in my bank account is good money. We use it to provide for our family's needs, and to further God's Kingdom on this earth. It's the love of money that is the root of all evil. I personally believe that God will give you all the money He can trust you with. He knows that the lack of money can lead to all kinds of serious problems in your life. The Psalmist prayed that God would not give so much money that he would forget about him. And he also prayed that God would give him enough money so he wouldn't have to steal to eat, and bring a reproach to God's name. That sounds like a good prayer to me. Luke 12:34 tells us that money only manifests what someone already has in their heart; "For where your treasure is, there will your heart be also." Your heart will always follow your money. When your money is with God, then your heart is in His Kingdom. But if your money is on a boat somewhere out on a lake, then that's where your heart will be. Money is simply a tool that God has given us to use to fulfill his will for our lives. In Matthew 19 Jesus used the topic of money to show the rich young ruler where his heart was. He had come to Jesus all filled with pride for being a devout keeper of the law, and Jesus said that was good, but he lacked in one area of life. He then told the young man to "sell all that he had" and "give it to the poor," then "follow" after Jesus; then he would have heavenly treasures. But we see the sad picture of having the true motive of his heart revealed, for the young man walked away, unwilling to part with his money for the kingdom's sake. Friend, today put your money under the control of the Holy Spirit, and allow Him to direct you into what He wants you to accomplish with it. Use it to keep your heart in line with the Masters Kingdom.

Daily Verse: "For the love of money is the root of all evil. . ."
I Timothy 6:10

FEAR OF CANCER

Researchers say that 36% of all Americans dread cancer. This is interesting since only 23 % fear heart disease, and heart disease takes the lives of 600,000 more lives each year than all the cancers combined. I think the reason for the cancer fear is that they see cancer as a non-preventable evil. Research actually shows that the decision to live a healthy life would prevent 60 to 70% of all cancers. To date, the top three "cancer causers" are tobacco, which is responsible for 87% of all lung cancers; overexposure to the sun which causes 1.3 million cases a year; and, genetic predisposition which attributes to only about 5–10% of all cancers.

Truthfully with all the studies being done on this 21st century plague, we still know very little about it. We do know that cancer develops from an ongoing interaction between genetic and environmental factors. Lifestyle habits, toxic exposure, diets, and improper biochemical imbalances all contribute to cancer. Conquering the fear of cancer can take on a multitude of dimensions. I've always said you don't have to fear the six letter word 'cancer' when you have a relationship with the five letter word 'Jesus.' Let it be known that a positive attitude in the face of this dreaded disease can go a long way in recovery. Once a man was in the doctor's office with his wife. The doctor came in to see him with a fearful look on his face. Not wanting to look the man in the eyes to give him the bad news, the doctor hee-hawed around, but finally got to the point when the patient asked for it straight. The doctor said; "Sir it doesn't look like you're going to make it."

Shocked, the man slumped back in the seat, as the wife jumped to her feet, and got her husband's coat for him. She said, "Come on honey, we have to get out of here now!"

The doctor asked, "Where are you going?"

"As far away from you as we can get," answered the wife, as she led her husband down the hallway of the doctor's office. "We must find a doctor that doesn't confuse diagnosis with verdict," added the loving wife as she shut the car door for her very sick husband.

That act of bravery led to a total recovery for her husband. Let's not allow the curses of this world to dominate our hearts. But let's remember that through Jesus Christ we've been delivered from the curse.

Daily Verse: "Pleasant words are as an honeycomb, sweet to the soul, and health to the bones."

Proverbs 16:23

FEAR OF PREACHERS

God's Word claims that those who "call on the name of the Lord shall be saved." It then goes on to say in the next verse that no one can call on the Lord unless they first hear about Him. Look at Romans 10:14; "How then shall they call on him in whom they have not believed? And how shall they believe in him of whom they have not heard? And how shall they hear without a preacher?" God in His infinite wisdom has declared that people would be saved by the "foolishness of preaching." Most people who fear preachers have had an experience with a preacher that didn't feel so good. Perhaps they were offended by what a preacher preached. Think for a moment about what you experience when you go to the doctor's office for an annual checkup. He pokes and prods at you, asking if this hurts, or that hurts. If you say; "Ouch that hurts," he'll do further examination into the area that seems painful. Pain is a sign that something is wrong. In the same way, when a preacher preaches what God lays on his heart, and it hurts you a little, it's because God wants to heal you of something that maybe wrong in your spiritual life. I've often told people that they don't need to "shoot the messenger." If I say something under the influence of the Holy Spirit, and it brings them under conviction, they need to take it up with God, for He's the one to whom they will answer some day. All I do is preach the Word, which he has clearly written down for everyone to read for themselves. Sometimes the pastor will preach on the financial responsibility of God's people, and some people will get mad and lash out with accusations, "All the pastor wants is our money." It's time to get a reality check with God's people; it takes money to make the world go round. If you'll think nothing of paying the bank a mortgage to live in your house, or paying a utility company for pumping utilities into your house, why should you have any problems with paying your tithes to help the church keep its bills paid? Most preachers demand no more than the required ten percent that God places in His Word.

At the turn of the century many people feared the preacher of God's word for he preached with conviction and power. God was demonstrating his power through many signs and wonders. But today many have resorted to watering down his message to avoid offending their members. Instead we need more preachers like the old nineteenth century preacher Peter Cartwright. He was a circuit riding Methodist preacher, with an uncompromising message. Once as he prepared to preach he was told to calm his message down that day, because President Andrew Jackson would be joining the congregation that morning. As he began to preach he made mention that he was aware the President Jackson was in the audience, he then went on to say that if President Jackson didn't repent he would go to hell when he died. The whole congregation gasped at the comments he made from the sacred desk about the President during his message. But as the President was leaving that day, and he was shaking hands with the preacher, the President commented that if he had a regiment of men like him, he'd be able to whip the world. Don't fear what the man of God says, just make sure it's in the Word of God and by following up by living the Word out in your own life.

Daily Verse: " . . . how beautiful are the feet of them that preach the gospel of peace, and bring glad tidings of good things."
Romans 10:15b

FEAR OF ETERNITY

I believe many people fear dying because they don't know what lies beyond the grave. King Louis the XV of France had such a haunting fear of death that he wouldn't even allow his servants to use the word 'death' in his presence. He had the mistaken notion that if he never heard the word he wouldn't have to face it. His foolish ploy didn't work; he died anyway. James the Bible author gives us some insight about getting too attached to this life; "Whereas ye know not what shall be the morrow. For what is your life? It is even a vapor that appeareth for a little time, and then vanisheth away." If you want to have a better understanding of this verse take an aerosol can, and spray it into the air. Watch the mist fall to the ground, and you'll have an object lesson of what James was talking about. That is all this life is when compared to eternity.

Although I hate to disappoint all the people who worship their physical body these days, God never created this body to last forever in the flesh. He only made your spirit to last eternally. But for the sake of the Kingdom we must endure this life in the flesh, to make it into eternity, for the Bible claims that the natural comes first, and then the spiritual. So when your spirit leaves the body, all you have left is an empty shell. You must realize that you are a spirit that lives in a body that has a soul. When we finally die to this world our spirit leaves our body, and goes somewhere into eternity. Physical death does not end your existence as some falsely informed cults believe. Death simply means you shut the door to the natural life, and open the door to the spiritual life. You walk through a doorway that no man can shut. Many face the death bed with hopes like the famous comedian W C Fields. On his death bed he requested a Bible to read. This was quite unusual since, during his life, he never practiced any type of religious behavior. As he read the Scriptures someone asked him why he was reading the Bible? "I'm looking for loopholes my good man." was his response. The fact remains that according to God's Word there are no loopholes when it comes to eternal life. You shall either conquer the power of death through the blood of Jesus Christ, or you will face the wrath of God and the same punishment that He prepared for Satan and his cohorts. For the Christian, death is like falling asleep in one room and waking up to find that you've been carried to another. Whenever a believer dies in this life they are met in the next one by the Lord Jesus Christ. It's like standing on the shoreline and watching a ship coming into shore. Christ waits on the shoreline of Heaven waiting for all his children's ships to come in. When they finally arrive on the shoreline of Heaven, and the gangplank is lowed, He is standing at the end, waiting happily for their arrival. Look at today's daily verse for what God thinks about the death of His people to this life.

Daily Verse: "Precious in the sight of the Lord is the death of his saints."

Psalm 116:15

FEAR OF CHASTENING

Hebrews 12:5 reads; "My son, do not despise the chastening of the Lord, nor be discouraged when you are rebuked by him." A sure way to grieve the Holy Spirit is despise His chastening. He uses different methods of chastening us to get us on the right track after we veer off the chosen path. If we fear His correction we are sure to not always follow God's perfect will. Listen to what the prophet Isaiah said in Isaiah 8:11. "For the Lord spoke to me with a strong hand, and instructed me that I should not walk in the way of this people." Isaiah was telling us that God sometimes uses a chastening to speak to us. Don't fear the circumstances that he sets up in your life. Each circumstance has an intended purpose. We must see God as a loving father. Scripture instructs us that the Lord only corrects whom He loves. His gentle hand sometimes pushes us along the path of life that we don't understand. Sometimes we cry out to him, "Why, God, why?" We only see in one dimension, while He sees the beginning to the end.

Some people don't understand that God doesn't need drama to speak to us. Most of the time His voice is so practical that we have to wonder if it's Him talking to us or not. Isaiah said that he became so confused about God's voice that God had to use force against him to get His point across. We must understand that the chastening of the Lord is not only for discipline, but also for direction.

When God sees that we are heading in the wrong direction, He sometimes puts a bump in our road of happiness to get our attention. When David was bringing the Ark of the Covenant back to Jerusalem from its twenty year stay at Abinidab's house, God caused the ox to stumble. All of Israel was praising and shouting before the Ark until Uzziah reached out and touched the Ark and the Lord struck him dead on the spot. Scripture says that David was afraid of God that day. But he went and studied and found out that the Ark was not to be carried by an ox, but to be borne on the shoulders of sanctified priests. The ox stood for the strength of man, and God's glory will never be trusted to be carried by man's works. So God used "chastening" to get David on the right track that day. Please "despise not the chastening of the Lord," and use the stumbling blocks that He places in your path to build a ladder to get closer to Him. They can either be stumbling blocks or stepping stones, the choice is up to you.

> *Daily Verse: "Blessed is the man whom thou chastenest, O Lord, and teachest him out of thy law."*
>
> *Psalm 94:12*

FEAR OF A RECESSION

So many people fear the word's–"depression," "inflation," and, of course "recession." This is foolish for these things are not new to the economy of man. In fact, they have been around since the book of Genesis was written. God's Word gives us a clear direction of how to handle things so that our lives won't be disrupted. One thing we can be certain of, as long as we live in an anti-Christ controlled economy, there shall be "lack" in some manner. What the child of God needs to remember is that there's no lack in God's economy as long as they follow God's prescribed plan in his Word. Listen to the words of Genesis 26:1; "And there was a famine in the land, beside the first famine that was in the days of Abraham. . . ." The first thing that you need to remember is that God can only bless obedience. "If ye be willing and obedient, ye shall eat the good of the land"(Isaiah 1:19). Isaac, Abraham's promised son was faced with a crucial decision in his life. The famine was severe, and everyone was packing up, and moving to Egypt to seek food. Egypt was a river city, and was able to sustain life even in some of the worst famines. So Isaac had to decide whether he would take God at His Word or move along with everyone else. He was either to go with the flow, or go against the grain. God instructed him in Genesis 26, "And the Lord appeared unto him, and said, Go not down into Egypt; dwell in the land which I shall tell thee of. Sojourn in this land, and I will bless thee;." So Isaac decided to follow God, and not his friends. While everyone was packing up to move, Isaac was doing the unthinkable. Look at the Lord's instruction to him in the time of famine. "And Isaac sowed in the land . . ." What? Here's a man who is taking the precious only seed he has, with no promise of any more, and using it to sow a crop during a famine. Doesn't he know that crops don't grow without water? Why would he do what must have seemed like a foolish move to so many? Because, God promised to bless him if he stayed. He was only following the direct commands of his God. God always likes to stretch our faith by having us go against the grain. In the same way we must not allow our fears of economic collapse to govern the way we finance the Kingdom of God. Isaac sowed in a famine, and the Scripture says that in that same year he received a hundredfold harvest, because the Lord blessed him. God is able to take our little, and make it enough. Jesus once took the sacrificial gift of a little boy's lunch, and multiplied it to feed probably 25,000 people, with baskets left over for later. We must be more concerned with sowing and not fleeing in times of economic uncertainty. The world doesn't have the answers - that's why the national debt is now so far out of control that it is beyond paying - in the trillions of dollars and increasing by the billions each day with just interest alone. So instead of seeking advice from the world, that doesn't even know how to balance its own budget, follow God's clear instructions, and allow God to bless you when others are panicking.

Daily Verse: "He that observeth the wind shall not sow; and he that regardeth the clouds shall not reap."

Ecclesiastes 11:4

FEAR OF BROKEN FOCUS

It has been stated that the only reason people fail in life is broken focus. There's extreme power in focusing on one thing in life. Most feel that to be a success in life they have to be a master at all things. The truth is that the real masters only do a few things well. When something gets your total focus then you are able to concentrate on doing it, and doing it well. Once a man illustrated the importance focus plays on success by laying a 2x4 board on the floor, and having people walk across it without falling. All who attempted the feat were able to accomplish it with no problem. Then he said that the reason most had no problem was that they were only focused on crossing the board; but, the same board placed between two buildings several stories high would produce a different result. Most would fall before reaching the other side. Why? Because now they were focused on not falling instead of just crossing the board. This fact was proven by the famous Karl Wallenda. His entire family was probably the most famous aerialist's and tightrope walkers to ever perform. He was a meticulous designer, and organizer of props. Everything was always in order. The thought of falling never entered his mind, and most of the time no safety net was used. Then one day while walking the tightrope between two buildings in Puerto Rico he fell to his death. When his wife was asked about the ordeal later she said that for the first time in his career he had become obsessed with falling. He kept checking the ropes, and even personally oversaw the installation of the tightrope, which was something he never did before in his entire career. The simple matter is that he fell because his focus changed. He became obsessed with not falling, instead of just doing the job.

Satan's biggest trick that he tries to put on us is too make us feel like we're missing out on life by not doing everything. God desires that we focus on what he has placed in our heart, and not try to do everyone's dream. Each human being has a specific goal to accomplish in life. God places those goals there when we are very young. We see God calling Sampson, Jeremiah, John the Baptist, Samuel, David, Ester, and several others while they were still in their teens, some while they were still in their mother's womb. Yes all these people found greatness because they found their focus in life, and decided to dedicate their lives to it. If you're not happy about the way your life is then you need to change your focus. Stop looking in the rear-view mirror of life. Have you ever tried to drive your car in forward gear while looking in the rear-view mirror? All you will do is crash into things that you could have easily avoided if you would only been looking forward. Let your focus become like a light beam. When a light is spread out real wide it has very little power. But if you focus the same beam, and add some power, you can burn through inch thick steel. Avoid all forms of broken focus at all costs today.

Daily Verse: "Whereupon, O king Agrippa I was not disobedient unto the heavenly vision."

Acts 26:19

FEAR OF HYPOCRISY

A hypocrite is quite simply explained as someone who wears a mask. Actually it's an old theatrical term. It's giving the appearance that you are more than you actually are. In Jesus' day he radically rejected the Pharisees, calling them, "whitened sepulchers." He said they made the outside of their lives look clean but on the inside they were dead men's bones. In Matthew 23, Jesus pronounced seven "woes" against the Scribes and the Pharisees for their hypocritical behavior. By their actions, they were keeping people from entering into the Kingdom of

Heaven. They prayed real long prayers, were strict in their religious activities like tithing and fasting, yet they omitted more important things from their beliefs - like faith, mercy, and justice. Jesus called them "blind guides trying to lead the blind." Listen to the prayer of the Pharisee who stood and prayed thus, "God; I thank thee, that I am not as other men are, extortioners, unjust, adulterers, or even as this publican. I fast twice in the week; I give tithes of all that I possess." I-I-I-isn't it almost enough to make you sick? The hypocrite sees his behavior as godly when in reality he is a fake. Pharisees are actually deceived people who think that they're right in their religious experience, but really they're dead wrong. Although the actual Pharisees don't exist in our churches anymore, the "spirit" of the Pharisee is prevailing; people who see the sinner as unclean and untouchable. These are self-righteous want-a-be Christians who do all the right things on the outside, but really don't care about Christ's mission on this earth. They want to go to church, and not be bothered the rest of the time. They feel that they've done their Christian duty by attended a Sunday morning service at least twice a month. They are like the cow that owners tried to puff up with air to win the grand prize at the Galveston, County fair back in 1992. The steer named 'Husker' was named as the grand champion for his all around appearance and sold for a hefty $13,500. After being butchered his carcass revealed suspicious findings that caused his title to be revoked. His owner had taken an air pump, and pumped air under his hide making him look like he was full-bodied but in reality he wasn't. He wasn't on the inside what he appeared to be on the outside, and this is what a hypocrite is. Please fight the temptation today to look down upon those who are in the position that you were once in. Remember from where the Lord has brought you.

One of the biggest excuses non-believers give for not going to church is that the church is full of hypocrites. This is true, but they are also there in every other part of your life. The schools are full of them; sports is full of them; and of course the movies you watch; full of them - but that doesn't stop you from participating or going to the other places they can be found. Always remember that if you let a hypocrite stand between you and God that hypocrite is closer to God than you are, and what does that make you?

Daily Verse: "For I say unto you, that except your righteousness shall exceed the righteousness of the scribes and the Pharisees, ye shall in no case enter into the kingdom of heaven."
Matthew 5:20

FEAR OF HEARING THE GOOD NEWS

Can you imagine being a prisoner of war in a German prison camp and hearing that Hitler had been defeated? It's been reported that many of the camps were completely abandoned by the German guards when they found out that the war was over, and the British and the Americans were invading the area. They left the prisoners cheering at the top of their voices, as they heard the good news that the war was over. We too as people, who live on this planet, should cheer with joy as those prisoners did in World War II when we hear the good news that Christ has won and the devil has been defeated. We no longer have to live as prisoners of the flesh. Sin no longer has power over us as it once did. We've been set free by the righteous act of the Son of God if we'll only accept it and live our lives for him. But today sadly, Christ's Kingdom on this earth is not fully achieved. Many of God's would-be soldiers, because of sin, are still held prisoner by the enemy. They are so used to hearing the bad news that they have a fear known as "(eupho-bia" which is the fear of hearing good news. If this is you, and you fear attending a church service because this fear has gripped your heart, fear no more. The Bible is true; it has stood the test of time. It's now docu-mented as historically and scientifically accurate. You don't have to fear making a blind leap into the dark by serving God. He's allowed the knowledge to so increase that even the most skeptical people have to stand up and take notice of the accuracy of the Scriptures. No other one piece of literature can hold a candle to the accuracy of the Bible.

Once a king was burning the pages of the Bible, trying to get rid of it as fast as Jeremiah was writing it. Do you know what Jeremiah did? He wrote it again because he was God-called and not man-called. You can't escape the good news. Many men have given their lives to assure that we would have the Scriptures available to us today. Even the greatest pessimists can't refute the fact that the Word of God is here to stay. Once, several very intelligent scientists set out to refute or prove the Scriptures wrong by using the Scriptures as their point of reference. In conclusion, all the scientists became believers in God and workers in His Kingdom. They said that after studying the Bible with an open mind, they came to the conclusion that only an all-knowing being could have structured the universe as it is. And the Bible could have not been written by a mere human being. Just the incredible fact that the Bible was written over a span of 1600 years by more than 40 authors, all saying the same thing, is an unbelievable feat in itself. Do you know how hard it is to get even two people to agree on something? But the Bible as we have it today is a picture perfect book of pure unity and design. Even the tyrant Napoleon had to admit; "The Bible is no mere book, but a living creature, with a power that conquers all who oppose it." Allow the sheer weight of all the evidence that proves the authenticity of the Bible as the Word of God to be your guide - allow the good news to take effect in you now. Agree with the earnest plea, "Come Lord Jesus, come quickly, come."

> *Daily Verse: "So shall my word be that goeth forth out of my mouth: it shall not return unto me void, but it shall accomplish that which I please, and it shall prosper in the thing whereto I sent it."*
>
> Isaiah 55:11

FEAR OF REPENTANCE

Genuine repentance is a misunderstood quality these days. Some have misunderstood the scripture in II Corinthians 7:10 that reads; "Godly sorrow produces repentance," to mean that human sorrow can also produce genuine repentance. Human sorrow is usually a matter after the fact. Or your sorry because you got caught, and know that punishment is inevitable. The little child who has her hand in the cookie jar when mom comes into the kitchen and gets caught. Immediately she begins to cry, and tells her mother that she's sorry for doing the deed, and she promises to never do it again. Has this little girl truly repented? No, she knows she's in trouble, so she wants to get the least amount of punishment possible. Her tears of sorrow are actually over the pain that she'll soon experience for disobeying one of mom's rules. In reality, the reason for the disobedience is the fact that she doesn't understand the need for the rule. You see mom in her infinite wisdom and experience knows that if Betty eats a cookie before dinner, she'll not want to eat the nutritious foods that are good for her at mealtime. The cookie might taste good to Betty now, but it won't do anything to keep her healthy, and that's all mom cares about is her child's health; thus the reason for the rule. Now if Betty were a little more mature, or open, she might have understood mom's rule, but instead she saw it as her mom keeping something good from her, and wanting all the delicious cookies for herself. Genuine repentance comes when we understand that the things our loving Father withholds from us are for our own good. He will never withhold a good gift that would be good for us. In fact, all good gifts come from above according to the

Scriptures. Now in our story genuine repentance would have taken place if Betty would have gotten away with eating the cookie, then conviction would have eaten her up inside to the point where she would've gone to her mother in deep sorrow, and told her mother what she'd done, asking for her forgiveness. Accompanying the apology would be the promise to do her best not to steal any more cookies before dinner. The desire to change is the first sign that repentance is genuine in a person's life. First you change your mind about something, then you seek to change your behavior. If a person doesn't have repentance in their Christian experience, then they don't have true salvation. You can't be saved and behave any old way you want to. Not that I'm saying that you have to be perfect, you just have to have the desire to be perfect as your heavenly Father is perfect. You must allow the Holy Spirit free access to your will and allow Him to mold you into the person that God intends you to be. Repentance is the first step toward the change that God has in mind for you. If you are still committing the same sins, just as you did before you confessed Christ, then you don't have genuine repentance. Please set yourself up for success today by allowing God's Spirit free access in your life today and REPENT.

Daily Verse: "I tell you Nay; but, except ye repent, ye shall all likewise perish."

Luke 13:3

FEAR OF LOOKING UP

I have to be honest with you - when I first considered this fear, I thought it was a bit absurd. However, I feel that way about many fears in this book, and some that were even too foolish to mention in a devotional. But let's examine what we mean about the fear of "looking up." It is a real fear for some and a sad one. This fear could be defined as a person who is too emotionally immature to look at other people in the eyes when they talk; or it could mean that a person suffers from a deep sense of low self-esteem, and feels unworthy to look at others while communicating. Since I've already discussed these issues elsewhere in this devotional, I want to address this fear from a totally different approach. I want to address it from the standpoint of the enemy, Satan who seeks to stop you from looking for the appearing of the Son of God. Satan seeks to get you in the place that he had the Psalmist David in Psalm 40:12; "For innumerable evils have compassed me about; mine iniquities have taken hold upon me, so that I am not able to look up; they are more than the hairs of mine head; therefore my heart failed me." David said he was so surrounded by sins that he began to look at his own life, and saw how wicked he really was. Faith soon turned into fear, and he saw himself as too far gone to be saved from the multitude of sins that were a part of his life. His says his sins were as the "hairs of his head" in multitude. This in turn led his heart away from God to the point where he couldn't even feel comfortable looking up to the Lord for help. Friend, that's the beautiful thing about the God we serve, He already knows all about you, and still loves you anyway. He knows just how wicked your heart can be without His influence. I'm glad for David's sake, that he soon got this revelation for just five verses later he says; "But I am poor and need yet the Lord thinketh upon me. . . ." Yes, He thinks upon us even in all our sin and darkness. Satan knows that if he can keep you from looking up he can keep you from the Second Coming. Look at what Luke 21:28 has to say; "And when these things begin to come to pass, then look up, and lift up your heads; for your redemption draweth nigh." In verse 26 it says when you see men's hearts failing them for fear, and for looking after those things which are coming on the earth, you know His coming is near. I don't know what you think, but it sort of sounds like modern days to me. God wants us to look up, and not hang our heads in sorrow and fear. He told Israel in the Old Testament to look to the hills for that is where their help would come from. In the same way, lift up your heads and look to the eastern sky for that is where your help will come from. Your help isn't in a bottle or a substance. It's in the looking up to the Lord for all help, and in every time of need. What do you need from him? He is your I AM for whatever help you need.

Daily Verse: " . . . and to them that look for him shall he appear the second time without sin unto salvation."

Hebrews 9:28b

FEAR OF INDEPENDENCE

So many people today seek to be independent. It starts when we are real young, thinking we know more than our parents about what is right for our life. For some reason even with all our twelve years experience at life we think we are so smart. In actuality its because the independent spirit that we inherited from our forefathers in the Garden of Eden is very strong. It's part of the human struggle against the flesh nature that doesn't like to give up without a fight. Don't let this struggle for independence win, for it can be dangerous to your health.

Once there was a man in London England that was so extreme

in his independence that he had to do everything for himself. Even things that he wasn't familiar with, like practicing medicine. Now, he didn't practice on anyone else, for he was an accountant by trade, and not a medical doctor. But one day he noticed extreme pain and reddening in his abdomen, which he self-diagnosed as a need for bladder surgery. So with scalpel in hand, and without the aid of anesthesia he went on to perform the operation. Tragically, the man died from an infection from not having the proper care. As I said before, independence can be hazardous to your self. It always rises up its head saying, "I can do it, or I can handle it by myself." The truth is you can't handle anything by yourself. God never created any human being to be an island. We were manufactured to need help from others, but pride is the powerful force that causes us to be independent, and refuse the aid of others. Some have had a bad experience, and branded all human aid as bad and unnecessary. Please friend, don't allow self-reliance to destroy you as the man who performed surgery on himself. Although most of us wouldn't even think of doing something so foolish on ourselves, isn't living a life all alone, shunning the help and fellowship of others, just as foolish.

God wants you to depend on Him, because dependence is a sign of trust. Trust is a powerful force in this universe we live in. It has the capability of making a person a millionaire overnight, or turning them from a sinner on their way to a devil's hell, to a saint on their way to heaven.

Crucify the independent spirit now and don't be afraid to ask for help.

Daily Verse: "Be not wise in thine own eyes: fear the Lord and depart from evil."

Proverbs 3:7

FEAR OF SELF

As we conclude this study in overcoming our fears, I felt that it would be incomplete without the aid of knowing how to overcome man's biggest foe. That's right friend - You are your own worst enemy. We need to take the advice that was once given to Harry S Truman by his friend Sam Rayburn before he took the office of Presidency after the death of Roosevelt. He said; "Harry, from here on out people are going to surround you and try to get you to only follow their advice; they'll pump you up telling you what a great man you are, but you and I both know they are wrong." Oh yes, the sad fact about all humans is that we aren't really as good as we think we are. Romans 3:23 says: "All have sinned and come short of the glory of God." So the next time you see yourself as high and mighty just know that God sees you as a sinner in need of a Savior. You're filled to the brim with self-righteousness and self-absorption. The self-reliance that exists in you still is what keeps you from experiencing all that God has for you. Some of us look in the mirror, and think we are God's greatest gift to this planet with all our knowledge and good looks. We even secretly think we can do anything without God's help. This is evident by our lacking in prayer time and guidance. Some of us possess an ego the size of Mount Everest, and we mask it under the guise of being very self confident, or having a healthy self-esteem. When in reality we are like scared little kids afraid that everyone won't like us. Friend, don't be self-deceived into thinking you are more than you really are. Only by living out our natural life "on the cross" are we able to be delivered from self. Jesus was our example, although He was without sin, He was still in human flesh. He had to battle the same lusts and desires that attack us everyday of our lives. He willingly faced the cross to show us that victory over self can be achieved by facing our own personal cross daily. Paul put it this way; "I die daily." He understood that the cross is the only instrument to keep the flesh under control. Now take note that crucifixion is always performed by someone else upon the guilty party. You can't crucify yourself can you? Someone else must drive the nails to perform the crucifixion properly. This is our time to depend on the Holy Spirit of God to be our executioner, as Jesus was having the nails pounded into his hands and feet, yes, Roman soldiers were actually performing the feat, but the Spirit of God was the one directing their hands. Every strike with the hammer was God ordained. Jesus said; "I willingly lay down my life and by the Spirit of God I will take it back up again." We must also not resist the Spirit's leading to Calvary. We must let Him direct us to the cross that will crucify everything that stands against our Father. Our only responsibility in the crucifixion is to stretch out our hands, and bravely ask Him to pound the nails that will destroy the flesh nature. We must be willing, like Isaac, to allow our Father to put us to death on an altar of sacrifice so we can be raised in the newness of life. Please destroy the self today and live WITHOUT FEAR!

Daily Verse: "And they that are Christ's have crucified the flesh with the affections and lusts."

Galatians 5:24

FEAR OF STARVING

It is conservatively estimated that approximately forty-thousand people starve to death everyday in our land. More than fifty percent of all our children go to bed hungry at least half the month.

Unlike the man from Buenos Aires, who ate himself to death. The thirty-three year old man weighed 660 pounds, when he was admitted to the intensive care unit for eating an entire pig. The fire department had to be called to take the man to the hospital, for they were the only people who could lift him. Of course we need food to sustain our life, although not as much as we need water, air, and sleep.

Humans can only live a few minutes without air, and a few days without water or sleep. Food on the other hand is a different story. We are built like camels, we have a fat layer that can sustain us in the lean times. It's kind of like our own built in food pantry.

If you have a normal healthy body you can in fact live for quite a few weeks without doing any permanent harm to it. For most people it takes about forty days without food before the body starts to commence into starvation mode. Actually when the body does without food for an extended period of time, it begins to live off body fat. At the same time an internal incinerator begins to burn the waste, and poisons in the body. Only after there is no more waste to burn, does a person begin to starve to death. When the body goes without food for a prolonged time hunger leaves, when it finally does return, that's the sign that the body is beginning to starve.

As you can see most of us are in no danger, of actually starving to death. In fact, according to statistics, most Americans are more than thirty pounds overweight.

Scripture records several Bible characters who went on extended fasts without food. Moses, went on two back to back forty day fasts, and of course our Lord Jesus fasted forty days and "then he hungered." Let us trust God to provide all our needs according to his riches in glory.

Daily Verse: "But my God shall supply all your need according to his riches in glory by Christ Jesus."

Philippians 4:19

FEAR OF BEING UNLOVED

The story is told of a hateful old man who lived in Ephrata,

Pennsylvania around the time of George Washington. His name was Michael Wittman, and he apparently suffered from the fear of being unloved. His hateful demeanor opposed everything that had to do with Christ or the preaching of His Word. He particularly persecuted a preacher by the name of Peter Miller. Reverend Miller was the local Baptist pastor of a church in Ephrata. On several occasions Mr. Wittman had been known to protest Rev. Miller's ministry, and do his best to humiliate him. He opposed everything that pastor Miller attempted to do for Christ. Then one day out of what seemed like providence, Wittman was arrested for treason, and taken more than seventy miles away to stand trial for his crime, for which he was found guilty, and sentenced to die.

Reverend Miller heard of the ordeal, and walked to where Wittman was being held in hopes that he could use his influence as a friend of Washington to help Wittman. Washington then told his friend Miller: "I'm sorry Peter, but I can't grant you the life of your friend."

"(friend?" Rev. Miller exclaimed, "Why this man is my most bitter enemy, who opposes everything I stand for, he's no friend of mine indeed."

Washington was amazed at Miller's diligence for his enemy. "What?" he said, "You traveled over seventy miles by foot to spare the life of your enemy, that sheds a whole new light on the subject. Apparently you see some good in this man, so I will grant you his pardon, effective immediately."

That day Miller went home with his new friend Wittman, who remained a friend from that day forward.

Many people who oppose the cause of good are in similar situations as Mr. Wittman: they have a deep since of feeling unloved. They go through most of their life without seeing the slightest concern from someone else. This causes the fear of being unloved to attach itself to their lives. Hence, they lash out with hateful attitudes to those who try to do good. I say this to the church's shame, for we are supposed to be the body of Christ on earth representing him in this hour of existence. Scripture informs us that while Christ walked the earth he went everywhere doing good, and opposing everything that the devil stood for. Let us not hide our head in the sand any longer, I feel since everyone is coming out of the closet these days, it's time the church came out also, and take her rightful place alongside the faithful saints of the past who gave their very lives for the freedom we now enjoy. Let us do as Christ did and seek out those who are waiting like Wittman, for someone to put their faith in action, and love the unlovable.

Daily Verse: *"But I say unto you, Love your enemies , bless them that curse you ,and do good to them that hate you."*

Matthew 5:44a

Contact Don Nicely
at 330-821-9648
or order more copies of this book at

TATE PUBLISHING, LLC

127 East Trade Center Terrace
Mustang, Oklahoma 73064

(888) 361 - 9473

Tate Publishing, LLC

www.tatepublishing.com